Y0-BCC-818

DEVELOPMENTS IN HUMAN SERVICES VOLUME 1

General Editors

Herbert C. Schulberg, Ph.D.
Frank Baker, Ph.D.
Sheldon R. Roen, Ph.D.

Behavioral Publications
New York
1973

Library of Congress Catalog Card Number 73-6840
Standard Book Number 87705-076-7

BEHAVIOR PUBLICATIONS, 2852 Broadway—Morningside Heights, New York, New York 10025

Printed in the United States of America

Library of Congress Catalog Card Number: 73-6840

Schulberg, Herbert C.; Baker, Frank; Roen, Sheldon R.
Developments in Human Services.
New York Behavioral Publications

June 1973 4-19-73

(Developments in Human Services, Vol. 1)

Contents

The Editors ix
The Contributors x

General Introduction: Human Services: The Challenge of the 1970s

Herbert C. Schulberg, Ph.D.
Frank Baker, Ph.D.
and Sheldon R. Roen, Ph.D.

Developments of the 1960s 4
The Concept of Human Services 7
Operating Human Services Programs 12
Implications of Human Services Programs 18
Summary 28

PART I. TEACHING HEALTH AND HUMAN SERVICES ADMINISTRATION BY THE CASE METHOD

Linda G. Sprague, Alan Sheldon, M.D.
and Curtis P. McLaughlin, D.B.A.

1. The Case Method of Teaching 33
   Sources: Educational Need and Philosophy 35
   What It Is and How It Works 36
2. The Case Method in Health and Human Services Administration 41
   Analytic Opportunities for the Student 42
   Illustration of Concepts 43

Illustration of Issues 43
Institutional Knowledge 44
A Basis for Self-Analysis and Comparison 45
Illustration of Alternatives 46
Insights into the Current Process 46
Illustrative Data for Theories and Hypothesis 47
A Feel for Complexities and Relationships 48
Summary 49
3. A Sample Case with Notes on Its Use 51
Development of the CCMHC 51
Appendix A 83
Appendix B 85
4. Classroom Dynamics: The Heart of the Case Method 91
Preparation for Teaching 91
The Teacher's Role in the Classroom 93
Student Roles 95
Techniques 96
Style 98
A Case Class 101
5. Development of Case Materials 109
Case writing 110
Appendix A 114
Appendix B 115

PART II. THE PLANNING AND ADMINISTRATION OF HUMAN SERVICES

Harold W. Demone, Jr., Ph.D.
and Dwight Harshbarger, Ph.D.

1. Human Needs and Human Services Organizations 143
The Human Services Organization: What Is It? 147
Issues and Problems 151
2. Organizational Issues 157
Organizational Models—Issues and Alternatives 157

Interorganizational Problems 161
Intraorganizational Problems 163
Organizational Change 167
3. Resources and Their Management 171
Government Organizations 172
Voluntary Associations 174
Foundations 178
Policy and Politics 180
4. The Elements of Planning 183
Definitions 183
Nature of Planning 185
Dimensions of Planning 186
5. Developing Operational Plans 197
Health Planning History 198
Health Care Planning 201
Environmental Health Planning 203
Mental Health Planning 205
Facilities Planning 208
Urban Planning and Human Services 209
6. Policies, Accountability, and Social Change 213
The Locus of Policy-Making and Resource Allocations 214
Social Change: Change Agents and Strategies 218
Advocacy, Contest, Conflict, and Militancy 221
7. Planning Constraints 225
Hostility 225
Goals 226
Alternatives 226
Specialization and Professions 227
Interorganizational Constraints 227
Metropolitan Constraints 228
Participation 228
Consumer Participation 229
Consensus 229
Confrontation 230
The Technical Report 230

Money 231
8. The Administrative Process 233
Administration Functions 234
Administrative Strategies and Technologies 238
Budget and Finance 240
Personnel Practices 242
Administrative Role Properties 244
Conclusion 245
9. The Future 247
A Definition of Futurism 247
Why Future Planning? 248
Organization and System Changes 250
Future-Oriented Constraints 257
Conclusion 257

PART III. STRATEGIES IN INNOVATIVE HUMAN SERVICES PROGRAMS

Harry Gottesfeld, Ph.D., Florence Lieberman, D.S.W.
Sheldon R. Roen, Ph.D., and Sol Gordon, Ph.D.

Introduction 267
1. Rationale of Strategies 269
Some Prerequisite Considerations 269
Defining the Problem 271
Theory of Causation 272
Inputs for Solving Problems 273
Mandates and Sanctions 273
Strategies 274
Monitoring and Evaluation 277
Some Strategy Dilemmas 277
2. Upsetting the Apple Cart: The Changing Directions of the Community Service Society of New York City 283
Strategies 285
Problems 289
3. PS Inner City: A Program's Failure, An Educator's Dilemma 292

Sol Gordon, Ph.D.
4. Up from Ashes: Phoenix House 307
Assumptions about Definition of Problem, Causation, and Necessary Inputs 308
Mandates and Constraints 308
Target Population 309
Nature of Services 309
Work Strategy 311
Rewards and Punishments 313
Encounter Groups 313
Educational Seminars 314
Costs and Evaluation 315
Strategy Problems 315
5. When an Agency's Constituency Ages: Kissena Apartments— An Experience in Housing for Older People 317
Changing Strategies 318
Mandates and Sanctions 321
Operational Strategies 322
Evaluation 324
Strategy Problems 325
6. Helping Police Cope with Family Violence: A Training Model in Community Intervention 327
Mandates and Sanctions 329
Preparatory Phase 330
Operational Phase 331
Evaluation 332
Assumptions and Strategies 332
Problems 333
7. A Demonstration Project on a Minimum Budget: The Goals for Girls Project of the Foothill Family Service of Pasadena, California 336
Target Population 336
Problem Definition 337
Assumptions as to Inputs 337
Research Strategy 339

Administrative Strategies and Problems 340
Results 342
8. Conclusion 347

PART IV. DEVELOPMENTS IN HUMAN SERVICES EDUCATION AND MANPOWER

Robert M. Vidaver, M.D.

1. Expanding Parameters of Human Services Responsibility 363
The Widening Appeal of the Human Services 363
The Escalation in Consumer Demand 369
The Search for Identity 375
2. The Changing Dimensions of Professional Intervention 383
The Myth of High Standards of Professional Manpower 383
The Manpower Implications of Community Services 391
3. Opening Up New Manpower Resources 399
Caveats from the Lincoln Hospital New Careers Experiment 399
Human Services Education as a Developmental Process 409
Defining the Professional 419
New Careers Revisited 10 Years After 436
4. Modular Education and the Development of Career Lattices 448
Community Participation 448
The Community-College Mental Health Workers Series 457
Training Goals, Service Responsibilities, and the Associate Degree Workers 468
Baccalaureate and Masters Degree Modules 480
5. Academic Costs, Effectiveness, Evaluation, and the Associate Professional Process 508
The Associate Professional Process 508
Index 525

THE EDITORS

Herbert C. Schulberg, Ph.D., M.S.Hyg. is a clinical psychologist and serves as Associate Executive Director of United Community Services of Metropolitan Boston. He is also Assistant Clinical Professor of Psychology in the Department of Psychiatry, Harvard Medical School, Boston, Massachusetts. Dr. Schulberg's interests and many publications have focused upon mental health and human services program development as well as program evaluation.

Frank Baker, Ph.D., is Head of the Program Research Unit, Laboratory of Community Psychiatry and Assistant Professor of Psychology, in the Department of Psychiatry, at Harvard Medical School. He received his Ph.D. in social psychology from Northwestern University, and before joining the Harvard faculty in 1965, Dr. Baker was an Assistant Professor of Social Psychology at Lehigh University. Dr. Baker has authored numerous journal articles in the fields of community mental health, human services, and organizational systems theory and research.

Sheldon R. Roen, Ph.D., is President of Human Sciences and Editor-in-Chief of Behavioral Publications. Prior to this he was an Associate Professor of Psychology and Education at T.C., Columbia University. He also taught at Harvard, Tufts, and the University of New Hampshire. He was the founding editor of the Community Mental Health Journal and has authored numerous publications on human services and primary prevention.

THE CONTRIBUTORS

Harold W. Demone, Jr., Ph.D.	United Community Services of Metropolitan Boston and Department of Psychiatry Harvard Medical School Boston, Massachusetts
Sol Gordon, Ph.D.	Department of Child & Family Studies Syracuse University Syracuse, N.Y.
Harry Gottesfeld, Ph.D.	New York City Health and Hospitals Corporation New York, N.Y.
Dwight Harshbarger, Ph.D.	Department of Psychology West Virginia University Morgantown, West Virginia
Florence Lieberman, D.S.W.	School of Social Work Hunter College New York, N.Y.
Curtis McLaughlin, D.B.A.	School of Business University of North Carolina Chapel Hill, North Carolina
Sheldon R. Roen, Ph.D.	Human Sciences and Behavioral Publications New York, N.Y.
Alan Sheldon, M.D.	Graduate School of Business Administration Harvard University Boston, Massachusetts
Linda G. Sprague	University of New Hampshire Durham, New Hampshire
Robert Vidaver, M.D.	National Institute of Mental Health Rockville, Maryland

General Introduction

GENERAL INTRODUCTION

HUMAN SERVICES: THE CHALLENGE OF THE 1970s

Herbert C. Schulberg, Ph.D., Frank Baker, Ph.D., and Sheldon R. Roen, Ph.D.

It seems like only a brief time ago that scattered individuals in a variety of professional fields were alerting colleagues to the advent of a new era. These individuals were contending that our comfortable, well-developed roles had become obsolete and that the time had come to reassess traditional services, functions and training programs since the winds of social change would produce drastic impacts for all. The revolutions of community mental health, the War on Poverty, etc., received considerable attention during the past decade for a variety of conceptual, political, and ideological reasons. The results for professionals have ranged from such minor outcomes as euphemistic name changes to such major developments as radically different job roles and avant-garde training programs. The consequences for clients may be discerned in the array of new and exciting, albeit sometimes temporary, social programs as well as in the lingering maladies of a caregiving network that refuses to modify outdated practices.

The editors of this series were among those who disseminated the earlier message about the changing nature of health and mental health services during the 1960s; thus, it is with some trepidation that we once again call attention to impending developments whose impact for the 1970s can be as profound as those of the previous decade.

Although many of us still have not assimilated the intellectual, let alone the functional, implications of community mental health theory and practice, for example, we are already being pushed to expand our conceptual horizons even farther and to consider our professional roles within the still broader context of human services systems and programs. This chapter briefly reviews the current array of forces affecting human services activities, the professional's response to the growth of such programs, and the present efforts to establish human services systems that are conceptually sound, organizationally feasible, fiscally viable, and above all, more effective in meeting people's needs. In view of the incipient nature of the field and with the hope of producing constructive cross-fertilization, the authors of the several chapters in this initial volume have considered the developments from common as well as differing perspectives.

DEVELOPMENTS OF THE 1960s

There can be little doubt in the minds of even ardent skeptics that the rationale for human services and the manner in which they are provided in 1972 differs significantly from the patterns of a decade ago. For example, the psychoanalytic precepts that guided the clinician's definition of problems and his assessment of treatment alternatives continue to be well regarded but no longer serve as the fundamental cornerstone on which a mental health program is built. Social psychiatric concepts that recognize environmental influences as well as the principles of learning theory have become equally relevant for structuring clinical services and guiding personnel utilization. Along with the changes in conceptual rationales we have witnessed related shifts in the professionals' armamentarium; for example, outpatient community care rather than inpatient hospitalization is now the treatment of choice for both acutely as well as chronically disturbed individuals. Furthermore, clinicians have come to accept that they alone cannot resolve all behavioral problems and that the participation of other community care givers, with varying degrees of sophistication, is essential to their mission. One result of this shift is that the practice of consultation is now a legitimate function of human services agencies, and many professionals quite comfortably fill this role. As a concomitant of the clinician's increased community orientation, local citizens have gained increased opportunities to help determine program priorities, and we are coming to respect the value of this previously unfamiliar input. Finally, even traditionally intransigent graduate training programs have been forced to alter their scope and emphasis to at least some degree, although many curricula continue to reflect anachronistic rather than avant-garde perceptions of where and how their students ultimately will function. In general, however, most indices of practice and training point out that considerable change has occurred during the past decade, and it is clear that contemporary social welfare and community mental health concepts and techniques have affected professional caregivers in various significant ways.

It is important to emphasize that it is not only the clinicians who have been subjected to the winds of change during the 1960s; many other professionals have been forced to reassess their functions in the face of mounting societal pressures to alter widespread human plight. For example, the recent monograph *Psychology and the Problems of Society* (Korten, Cook, & Lacey, 1970) is a veritable compendium of potential psychological contributions to such key concerns as the social change process, the resolution of urban problems, the challenge of early learning, the reduction of violence, the gaining of equality for minority groups, and the understanding of campus unrest. Thus, educational, child, and social psychologists are also being challenged to ponder the relevance of their present activities and to determine whether a shift in priorities and tasks is needed for appropriate functioning in the 1970s.

Most professionals concerned with the alleviation of

human distress customarily have attacked the previously mentioned problems from a narrow perspective that generally is founded on a particular theoretic predilection and/or the constraints of an organizational boundary. For example, the activities of child guidance clinic personnel for many decades were shaped by psychoanalytic concepts that defined professional practice along specified lines, encouraging little deviation in clinical technique or experimentation with environmental modes of intervention. In terms of organizational policy these clinics have focused on school-age children and utilized intake practices that excluded teen-agers beyond the age of 16. Thus, the orientation and structure of child guidance clinics, in general, have been such that they most effectively served the children of well-motivated, middle-class families possessing strong internal resources. The children of lower-class families with unstable relationships and meager psychological and material resources fared less well within this narrow treatment system. Furthermore, clinic staffs were relatively ineffective in collaborating with the other community care givers needed to resolve practical as well as psychological problems.

Child guidance clinics are not being singled out for censure since there are numerous other care-giving programs whose operating rules and practices continue to focus on and reward organizational and staff concerns to an equal, if not greater, degree than those of clients. This orientation and value system are so deeply imbued, possibly even revered, that challenges to their continued existence are viewed by staff members as assaults on fundamental and sacred professional prerogatives. Yet despite a profound reluctance to undertake more than marginal change, most professionals are aware that the American society has reached such a state of complexity, perhaps even chaos, that our usual unifaceted or piecemeal attempts to help clients resolve dilemmas are clearly outmoded. We are increasingly willing to acknowledge that the problems of the designated client often are as much rooted in his community's tumultuous social structure and fragmented care-giving system as in his personal psyche. Inevitably, then, our contributions as individual practitioners will always be severely limited if they do not fit into a broader context.

THE CONCEPT OF HUMAN SERVICES

It is the definition of this broader context that we contend is undergoing change. In the past decade our perspective and activities have expanded from the isolated clinic to the more encompassing community mental health program. During the 1970's we will be challenged to evolve our scope even further by designing far-flung human services systems which seek to provide comprehensive and coordinated assistance to clients. March (1968) has described these new caregiving systems as incorporating the following features: comprehensiveness of services; decentralized facilities located in areas of high population density; and integrated program administration that permits continuity of care from one service element to the next with a minimum of wasted time and duplication.

The increasing tendency to designate a community's variety of health and social welfare services as human services organizations reflects not only the desire to provide services more efficiently but also a growing societal as well as professional recognition of the common denominator inherent in the varied problems presented to us by clients. It also indicates an appreciation for the generic quality integral to the helping actions of professional and nonprofessional care-givers despite the multiple technologies utilized by them. The long-adhered-to distinctions between the problems germaine to a psychiatric clinic and an alcoholism clinic, for example, or the traditional distinctions between the functions of different mental health professionals have become increasingly artificial, and many agencies have drastically revised their intake policies and clinical practices accordingly.

Neighboring child guidance clinics and adult psychiatric clinics are being reorganized as combined family-oriented facilities, and agencies that previously excluded alcoholics, drug addicts, and other special problem cases now routinely accept individuals so troubled.

Furthermore, it is clear that genuinely effective, comprehensive services can be rendered only through the forging of systemic linkages that bring together the various care-giving agencies needed to provide a complex array of resources, technologies, and skills. Defenders of the status quo need only follow a few clients through the present system in order to realize that it is poorly designed for meeting the needs of those whom it purports to serve. A working mother may easily obtain psychological consultation for her four-year-old child who is enrolled in a Head Start class but encounter severe difficulties in obtaining such services for her three-year-old who is too young for this special program. Similarly, families with multiple problems often receive help for only one of them because the initial agency to which they turn either does not diagnose the other problems or is unsuccessful in referring the family to relevant resources. The parents of a developmentally disabled child might well have to negotiate individually with the departments of public health, mental health, public welfare, and the rehabilitation commission to ensure that he receives comprehensive services and fiscal assistance.

Despite the bleakness in much of the present situation we are beginning to see examples of concerted, meaningful effort to reorganize program components in such ways that they move beyond the currently fragmented care-giving network. At the heart of these efforts is an implicit, if not explicit, conceptual framework for helping people that recognizes that human services programs operate as a system of organizations whose participants are interdependent and must be appropriately linked (Baker & Schulberg, 1970, pp. 182-206; Holder & Dixon, 1971). Systems concepts increasingly are being applied to the analysis and operation of human services programs, and they are expected to be particularly relevant in defining the problems of management, of changing human services organizations, of interorganizational relations, and of organizational-environmental interaction.

The application of systems concepts to these tasks represents an effort to optimize a rational, planned approach to the development of future care-giving arrangements. Planning has become increasingly sanctioned during the past decade within given categorical fields such as health or social welfare, but with change occurring at an exponential rate the trend of the 1970s must be to broaden the planning base. Systems concepts are of singular value in providing the means to expand our grasp of a person's functioning and problems beyond the limited scope of a single categorical field so as to encompass a greater array of human services. In a related vein Demone and Harshbarger note that the planning trend of the late 1960s has been away from the categorical needs of total populations and instead has been focused on comprehensive multiple-impact efforts geared toward the needs of delimited populations at high risk for numerous human services problems, for example, Model City neighborhoods. Although this focused planning has drawn much praise, its benefits sometimes have been more apparent than real since the programmatic fiscal base is tenuous and much animosity has been engendered in the bypassing of established planning and care-giving structures.

The effectiveness of planning for human services is deemed by Demone and Harshbarger to be dependent on: *(a)* the involvement and cooperation of the target community, *(b)* the participation of established professional groups affected by potential program change, and *(c)* the sagacity of the planners themselves when faced with attractive alternatives in a turbulent environment. The temptation to run off simultaneously in all directions must be resisted. The planner of human services must understand that fundamental conflicts can be created if overly diverse philosophies, services, and human inputs are incorporated within a single enterprise. He must determine whether administrative controls are to be vested in the professional or the community representatives, whether clinical-type services or social action are to be emphasized, and whether cooperative or conflictual strategies are to be utilized. Furthermore, the planner must distinguish between his short- and long-term objectives since they may be antithetical; for example, providing "new career" training to only some of the poor may be of immediate benefit, but it reduces widespread support for the more fundamental and long-range changes needed to alter the poverty cycle. Choice selection is also becoming more complex as legislative actions require that human services develop within the scope of broader urban undertakings; for example, funds for progressive corrections programs and preventive mental health activities are provided in the controversial Safe Streets Act. Demone and Harshbarger suggest the risks and consequences associated with each choice; it is clear that the decisions about a community's human services programs must be determined within the context of its unique environmental and intraorganizational parameters.

A formal process for analyzing the key variables affecting the planning of human services is presented by Gottesfeld et al. They describe in detail the overt and covert processes recognized by Demone and Harshbarger as guiding the actions of planners and administrators. Several key elements reviewed by Gottesfeld et al as relevant to the determination of program strategy follow.

The Problem's Definition.

The characteristics and scope of human problems are generally defined by power groups and their societal agents rather than by affected populations. Although the definitions and optimal program strategies achieved from these differing vantage points may be congruent and lead to cooperative efforts, they may also be disparate and produce strife. For example, the drastic program changes undertaken by the Community Services Society (CSS) of New York stemmed from its board's conclusion that individual casework could only minimally benefit the city's residents since the basic problem is really that of growing social ills afflicting whole neighborhoods rather than individuals alone. The board deemed its new view of the problem to be more congruent with that held by low-income and disadvantaged groups, and the problem redefinition permitted new program strategies to be undertaken.

Theory of Causation

Closely related to the problem's definition is the theory of its causation. Some theories are complex and multifactorial in nature and suggest the need for multiservice programs. Others are reductionistic and emphasize limited but intensive program efforts. For example, the poor achievement of minority groups in most public educational settings may be theorized as *(a)* stemming from insufficient preschool stimulation, *(b)* produced by the teacher's inability to understand children with cultural backgrounds and life styles different from her own, or *(c)* a combination of these and other factors. The first theory would emphasize compensatory preschool education for the children, the second would focus on in-service training for school personnel, while the third would lead to a program strategy incorporating these two services as well as others—perhaps the busing of children to other school districts.

The training and selection of program personnel obviously are related to the underlying assumptions about the problem's definition, causation, and distribution. Problems of a unifaceted nature affecting few people can feasibly be resolved by utilizing highly trained professionals to provide direct services and administer the total effort. When a problem is complex and affects large segments of the population, highly trained but limited numbers of professionals can only be used in selected ways, and difficult choices must be made. New perspectives on these choices are provided by Vidaver in his description of the growing capacities of nonprofessionals to assume tasks formerly restricted to those with advanced training. Gottesfeld et al. concluded, interestingly enough, that when clients are actively involved in determining policy and services, the use of scarce and expensive professional manpower tends to be minimized.

The planning and administration of human services has thus become an undertaking with ever-broadening implications and possibilities that, as Demone and Harshbarger, and Gottesfeld, et al. note, must nevertheless continue coping with any or all of these complexities: *(a)* the lack of a definitive knowledge base; *(b)* alternatives whose feasibility is constricted by statutory or fiscal constraints; *(c)* selected, sometimes even entrenched, perspectives of providers and consumers; *(d)* interorganizational competition for funds, staff, and clients; and *(e)* covert hostility toward selected client groups like alcoholics and drug users. Additionally, the traditional distinctions between the roles and resources of a community's public, voluntary, and private sectors have become increasingly blurred. Decisions and dollars now flow across previously impermeable organizational and governmental boundaries at the community level, as well as between the local, state, and national levels. We can anticipate the increased meshing of public and nonpublic funds and programs through such arrangements as fee-for-service contracts between governmental bodies and private agencies.

OPERATING HUMAN SERVICES PROGRAMS

The characteristics of operating human services programs undoubtedly will assume many novel substantive and administrative features during the coming decade, and as a point of reference for this annual series of reviews on "Developments In Human Services," it is valuable to assess the current state of program development. In those instances in which human services programs are in operation or are being already planned, public health, mental health, and social welfare programs usually are included as key elements. More recently, correctional services are also being considered within this framework because of their heightened public visibility and the increased federal funding available for law-enforcement activities. The NIMH's controversial effort during the past year to establish closer links with the Department of Justice reflects an awareness of both the conceptual relations between the mental health and legal fields as well as the recognition that scarce funds for the expansion of mental health-related activities can be readily obtained through other human services agencies. From the professional's perspective it is ironic to note that most comprehensive human services programs do not include the field of education even though 25% of the mental health professional's man-hours for consultation and education are directed at school personnel (NIMH, 1971). This exclusionary practice has been justified in terms of the unwieldly problems that would be created by including this additional program at the operating level in the community or at the state level of administration, yet the continued separation of education from other human services programs inevitably produces dilemmas as well.

Various examples of evolving human services programs are worth describing, but only a few can be cited here. Formerly isolated physical-rehabilitation facilities are now being designated as integral components of general hospitals, and at the same time they are enlarging their scope of concern to include nonmedical, socially oriented services linked to community-based workshops, vocational training centers, and job-placement agencies. In the psychiatric field the evolving structural pattern and network of liaisons are such that the community mental health center is just one of a variety of community resources that participates in cooperative ways to serve the needs of local citizens. Such a model is particularly evident in rural areas (Kiesler, 1965, pp. 147-157), and in those instances in which mental health programs have assumed a strong social action component (Peck, Roman, & Kaplan, 1967, pp. 103-121). Two-way interaction among agencies becomes routinized, and the use of feedback patterns to adjust program components is institutionalized. The mental health facility and other agencies jointly work with the same troubled family, cooperate in the development of new services, and try to minimize competition with each other.

It can be anticipated that within the framework of the organizational principles specified by Demone and Harshbarger, and Gottesfeld et al., modified or evolving human services programs will develop a variety of structures for providing services to their clients. In his recent review of such developments Demone (in press) was able to identify the following four prominent alternatives that seem to be arising at the community level for ensuring comprehensive human services:

The Information and Referral Center

The information and referral center is based on a simple concept that has been utilized for over 40 years. A small group of generalists receive inquiries regarding any type of problem from the defined community and make appropriate referrals and follow-up based on their knowledge of available local services. More recently, these centers are emerging at the neighborhood level, perhaps in association with decentralized city halls, and thus are in even closer contact with their clients. Most requests for service are referred to those specialty agencies with which the information center is linked, but obviously many problems lend themselves to immediate generic assistance, particularly by those staff members skilled in techniques of crisis intervention.

The Diagnostic Center

The diagnostic center is more medically oriented in conception and design, being based on the premise that a careful analysis of the client's problems will lead to a more accurate intervention and treatment plan geared to his unique needs. In fact, the advocates of this approach urge that all clients be required to enter the community's organized care-giving network through the diagnostic center so that they can be helped in the most comprehensive and efficient manner possible. Although this model offers the benefit of careful problem analysis and subsequent referral to particularly relevant resources, it suffers because most clients dislike being referred after extensive diagnostic work-ups.

The Multiservice Center

Multiservice centers received much of their impetus from federal legislation that provided funds to establish comprehensive programs meeting certain guidelines. These centers reflect the increasingly accepted rationale that human problems are multifaceted in nature and require multiple care-giving responses rather than a single categorical service. Approximately 200 such centers now exist throughout the country, and within them clients can obtain at a single physical location such diverse services as employment counseling, psychiatric consultation, legal assistance, and information on public welfare benefits. Even though these centers have not achieved an optimal level of comprehensiveness because of continuing categorical funding restrictions, they nevertheless have been instrumental in getting professionals to formally cooperate for the first time in providing high-quality services to inner-city residents. For example, a number of urban community mental health centers assume that an individual's psychiatric problems stem from societal and economic factors as well as intrapsychic ones and that effective care must include a broad array of services. Consequently, mental health professionals exhibit far greater concern for program coordination than had been true previously.

Human Services Networks

Human services networks focus on building linkages between existing and planned organizations so as to facilitate client services rather than seeking to incorporate all relevant services within a single agency. This approach recognizes that in most communities it will not be fiscally nor practically feasible for an individual facility to provide by itself all elements of a comprehensive program; in fact, some of the services may already be available elsewhere. The network approach is already evident in meeting the needs of such diverse populations as runaway youths and the elderly. After determining the basic needs of these groups and the essential services for meeting them, a consortium of agencies divides responsibilities according to their particular expertise. The leadership and coordinating tasks are assumed by a single agency, and the others participate in predetermined ways. The comprehensive human services network organized for the elderly residents of the Kissena Apartments by its management stemmed from the premise that the housing development was part of an existing community containing relevant resources. A variety of supporting health, social services, and recreational activities were coordinated for the elderly; perhaps even more important, the elderly were encouraged to volunteer their efforts to operate selected neighborhood projects. Many mental health centers have established comfortable and constructive roles within the framework of a human service network, particularly when their staffs are amenable to nonmedical contributions. The use of "interface teams," which include the staff of several agencies to review specific cases, has been particularly helpful in resolving outstanding problems and in fostering cooperative activities.

It is anticipated that categorical programs and facilities will become less common during the coming years and that comprehensive human services endeavors will expand. For this to occur, however, significant, wide-ranging changes must be made in both organizations and individuals that have traditionally resisted even minimal departures from the tried and comfortable molds of the past. Ironically, the inertia of human services organizations has been reinforced on the one hand by bureaucratized administrative structures, professionalized personnel systems, and relatively independent funding structures, and on the other hand by social values and priorities that change so rapidly and are so overwhelming that they are but tenuously considered.

Demone and Harshbarger outline a variety of change strategies. They stress the need to recognize and respect the antithetical starting points of the human services organization struggling to survive in contrast to the rapid, turbulent environmental forces seeking major changes in the total fabric of our society. Furthermore, human services programs are guided as much by implicit value orientations, ideologies, and professional beliefs as by empirical outcomes, so that potentially forceful and rational arguments are disregarded or avoided. Gordon's description of the painful experiences encountered by white educators in ghetto schools vividly reminds us that value orientations always affect our actions and reactions. Furthermore, rapidly changing ideologies can shift our well-intentioned position from that of helper to intruder. The selection of a change strategy for fostering the growth and integration of human services is thus a complex matter and must be made in relation to particular conditions and constraints. Some choices preclude others, for example, consultation versus advocacy, and the advantages and disadvantages of available options should be weighed carefully.

Of particular contemporary interest as change strategies are the new fiscal policies being designed at the federal and local levels to enhance professional collaboration. There is a growing demand for decreased use of public funds for demonstration projects that are essentially nonreplicable and an increased interest in fiscally rewarding those agencies that facilitate the availability and access of services and ensure the client's continuity of care. Thus, some are espousing that agencies be compensated for referral and follow-up services in the same manner that they are paid for direct treatment services. The federal government's study of strategies for enhancing unified human services is particularly emphasizing a fiscal approach. One proposal would give designated community groups the option of transferring up to 20% of categorical federal funds from one program component to another if local administrators deem this necessary to ensure comprehensive, balanced human services. It would be naïve to contend that human services networks soon will be free of complex interorganizational problems, but revised public policies and funding strategies can potentially have a major impact on their basic function of meeting client needs.

IMPLICATIONS OF HUMAN SERVICES PROGRAMS

A variety of conceptual, political, and administrative forces affect human services programs, seeking to lead them in uncharted directions while simultaneously constraining them from moving too far from established patterns. Although these contradictory pressures create frustrating impasses and tenuous visions of the future, it still is possible to predict that during the coming decade human services programs and their affiliates may well be required to redesign their manpower utilization patterns, their training procedures, their operating practices, and their research foci in some of the following ways:

Manpower Patterns

Planners and administrators are assuming that the demand for additional human services personnel will be maintained during the coming years as society's value system evolves from its anachronistic tradition of solving human problems by custodial welfare measures to a new emphasis on community-based, service-oriented interventions. Although the additional personnel will successfully fulfill certain program purposes, it is unlikely that increasing the numbers of professionals alone will modify the problems created by maldistributed manpower. Vidaver notes that the maldistribution has resulted in inadequate services to the poor, minorities, rural folk, children, and the aged, and he suggests that this situation can be resolved by recruiting new indigenous manpower from these very same groups. Graduate schools have attracted and enrolled only a small portion of the young adult population possessing the potential for success in the human services, and the time has come, according to Vidaver, to concentrate on these other manpower pools as well:

1. Nonprofessionals already working in human services facilities whose advancement has been blocked by antiquated personnel standards.
2. Indigenous community workers with relevant intuitive skills and life styles.
3. Second-careerists seeking new professional roles after having outgrown their initial identities.
4. Related professionals who by the addition of pertinent behavioral skills can more effectively practice their primary tasks.
5. Associate degree and baccalaureate college students who do not aspire to graduate training but who can, nevertheless, adequately perform vital human services tasks.

As training efforts are generated to attract new recruits to the human services field, it will be necessary to monitor and further these developments by emphasizing career growth and guarding against blocked mobility. The manpower challenge, then, is not merely that of generating a new breed of personnel but, more significantly, that of designing an overall training-service system within which individuals of varying ability can productively work toward common goals. The special skills of one group should complement voids in another. Vidaver contends that the crisis encountered by Lincoln Hospital, New York, resulted from its laudable desire to train indigenous new careerists without adequately attempting to integrate them into the program's total structure. New manpower utilization patterns create wide-ranging systemic complications, and a failure to resolve them inevitably produces difficulties. The continuing efforts of the Maryland Department of Mental Hygiene to develop career lattices in conjunction with the colleges are cited by Vidaver as a demonstration that specific services roles can be linked to academic curriculum modules, thus enhancing job mobility and minimizing personal frustration.

Finally, future human services manpower utilization patterns should emphasize that standards of practice are a function of the specific service to be rendered and not of the practitioner's larger identity. When possible, standards should be established so as to encourage controlled experiments in new modes of manpower use. Excessively high standards often are guises for discriminating against minorities, and in addition they are unheeded; for example, the initial Medicare staffing standards for public institutions were never met. Although it may be politically difficult to achieve, Vidaver urges that professional certifications be based on proficiency in clusters of service tasks and not on traditional professional identities. This approach would have the additional benefit of permitting educational curricula to be restructured into congruent career lattices rather than being designed in splendid isolation from the human services fields in which graduates ultimately practice.

Training Programs

It is evident from the preceding analysis of future manpower patterns, as well as from our earlier description of human services trends, that training programs will have to alter their scope and emphasis if they are to be aligned with societal demands and evolving job requirements. The need to proceed immediately with this process is highlighted by the fact that educators face a lag of at least five years between the time of their decision to renovate a curriculum and the appearance of graduates reflecting that change. The urgency of providing contemporary training is made even more critical by considering that the careers of students now being trained for human services will extend into the twenty-first century.

Most university programs have already taken steps in the direction of greater relevance to an era of human services, but it would not be excessively harsh to deem many of these measures as more euphemistic than substantive. In the field of community psychology, for example, Iscoe and Speilberger (1970) have described several innovative graduate programs emphasizing contemporary conceptual frameworks and appropriate technical skills, but these revised curricula are the exception rather than the rule. Jacob's (1971) survey of graduate education in community psychology revealed that only 20% of the sampled departments offered a formal subprogram. The majority of psychology departments offer a single introductory course and perhaps an additional one related to a particular intervention strategy.

In addition to the obvious need for creating more courses substantially relevant to the human services, it is also necessary to consider the more subtle but equally significant problem of how they are to be taught. Sprague, Sheldon, and McLaughlin suggest that the case method refined in university business schools represents a particularly appropriate pedagogic process for meeting our contemporary educational needs. The case is a written description of an organizational situation providing information on the organization, its members, actions, and/or objectives without analysis of those facts and information. The student is thus challenged to develop his own analysis on the basis of the presented material, the educational goal being that of helping the student develop an analytic methodology that can be used throughout his professional career. A specific case may serve any or all of these purposes: Illustrate concepts and issues, provide institutional knowledge, provide a basis for self-analysis and comparison, illustrate alternatives, offer insights into the current process, and provide a feel for complexitics and relationships.

A major impediment to teaching human services by the case method has been the dearth of relevant case materials. As a start toward rectifying this situation, Sprague et al. have compiled an invaluable annotated bibliography describing approximately 60 published cases that can be used for teaching human services program development and administration. Given limited class time and scarce written materials, the case method does not constitute a total educational process. Nevertheless, this pedagogic approach can be successfully integrated into new or existing courses, and its selective use will increase the effectiveness with which human services and concepts and strategies are taught.

Although we are stressing the need for human services training programs to expand their curricular foci so as to encompass a broader array of conceptual and programmatic concerns, we fully recognize the impossibility of producing graduates with in-depth expertise across the full continuum of this burgeoning field. With each addition to the professional's purview the ensuing body of knowledge may coalesce as another subspecialty, or it can stimulate new careers coequal with older professions. The dilemmas that these developments can create for an existing discipline are strikingly evident in Albee's (1970) analysis of the uncertain future of the practicing psychologist. He contends that the problem of growing irrelevance in training and practice has remained largely unresolved and in fact will become more critical with the passage of time so long as solutions are sought primarily within the intramural framework of psychology.

One of the alternatives posed by Albee for the training of psychologists involves the creation of alliances with other professions possessing training facilities, for example, medical schools, schools of social work, and schools of education. This option deserves support since it begins to recognize that human services increasingly will be provided within multidisciplinary settings and that the psychologist cannot effectively be trained within the isolated confines of a university-operated psychological center, the approach that Albee had previously championed. Professionals can expect to face a series of crises in negotiating job roles and work relationships as they enter newly conceived human services programs so that the training of students most logically should occur in multidisciplinary rather than unidisciplinary settings. A broad rather than narrow training orientation is also eminently sensible within the ecological perspective to be described later. The aim should be that of sensitizing students to the fact that much of their effectiveness in meeting client needs depends on the ability to marshal and integrate community resources within a harmonious balance rather than on the individual's interventions alone.

Training for broadened skills must proceed in various ways. Within the university new interdepartmental courses should be designed to demonstrate the relatedness of psychological concepts to economic, sociological, and political principles. Although the specialty of human services personnel is in the realm of human behavior, effective human services programs are the amalgam of several bodies of knowledge, and we should at least be familiar with their fundamental concepts.

Training must also proceed apace within live communities. It is recommended that students be assigned for even brief periods of time to central planning and coordinating bodies like local community councils (Demone & Schulberg, in press). A wide-ranging perspective on human services can be gained from such a vantage point, and the student would rapidly become familiar with his community's power structure, the interorganizational complexities of care-giving systems, the relationship of public and private services, the fiscal and professional constraints on program development, etc. Gluck's (1971) description of consultation to a community council about the merits of an experimental preschool program stresses the pitfalls awaiting the naïve professional undertaking such work, but it also reflects the constructive opportunities available to professionals seeking to influence the community decisions affecting comprehensive human services for their clients.

Another fruitful training experience would be provided students by assigning them to grass-root-type settings rather than restricting their placements to university-based structures. Although social workers have long utilized a variety of community-based facilities, psychiatrists and psychologists have been more wont to restrict their trainees to affiliated teaching hospitals and counseling centers. The developing fields of community psychiatry and psychology are breaking this pattern, however, and experimenting with new training opportunities. Thus, neophyte professionals are being exposed in their training, for example, to the operations of satellite neighborhood service centers that community health and mental health centers increasingly are using for program decentralization. Although the trainee may experience considerable anxiety when assigned such ambiguous and unfamiliar tasks as coordinating his clinical activities with those of a self-help drug group or negotiating program policy with a nonprofessional citizen board, he ultimately will refine the skills and develop the orientation required to work in a setting in which the human services role is determined more by expressed community needs than academic preconceptions.

Finally, particular consideration is urged for the training of research and development (R&D) specialists along the lines suggested by Broskowski (1971). It is clear that we have failed to utilize existing psychological knowledge for the benefit of clients, and although the onus has been placed on the irrelevance of research findings, the problem stems as much from our inability to translate scientific data into specific program details. The industrial and military sectors have long utilized R&D specialists, and human services programs would be equally receptive to personnel who can translate basic scientific findings into practical solutions. Many human services training programs have long been invested in the production of research data, and the time is overdue for teaching our students how to properly utilize these materials so that they may significantly be applied to the field of human services.

Practice

Earlier sections of this chapter have dealt at length with human services program trends, and it suffices at this point to reiterate that their conceptual rationales and organizational structures are in the throes of change, away from categorical restrictedness and toward broader comprehensive concerns. As these developments proceed, a program's need for both generalist and specialist skills will generate incompatible demands on human services personnel. Vidaver suggests that this dilemma can be minimized by establishing teams that in their totality include the full range of requisite skills without requiring that any single individual possess all of these capabilities. Thus, the team possesses a generalist sophistication in broad program areas while individual members contribute unique personal skills toward the comprehensive effort. Teams assigned the responsibility for human services to delineated geographic areas can utilize this functional model of integrated generalists and specialists, and it has met with good success when proper supervisory links are established and maintained.

In addition to the new conceptual principles and technical skills that human services personnel will have to refine for working with unfamiliar client populations, they also will have to develop relationships with previously ignored or unknown colleagues. The description of Bard's work with police officers demonstrates that the staff of the law-enforcement system, generally considered averse to contacts with human services professionals, can indeed collaborate as effective psychological intervention agents when supported by consultation. Human services professionals will also be required to negotiate policy issues and job functions with types of administrators different from the fellow professionals to whom they have customarily related. In many parts of the country the persons assigned responsibility for administering local and state-wide human services programs are management specialists and have not been trained in the social sciences or health fields. Being more often concerned with fiscal and bureaucratic considerations than professional prerogatives, these administrators may well demand a reassessment of previously defined professional roles in their quest for maximal client benefits and minimal personnel costs.

Research

A recent view by Williams (1971) of the Adult Manpower Training Program within the Office of Economic Opportunity led him to conclude that social science research studies seldom are relevant to the major policy decisions of federal human services agencies. Moreover, Williams contends, the social science research community as presently structured is unlikely to produce a consistent flow of studies relevant to social policy-making for the disadvantaged. Only undue optimism or excessive naïveté could lead one to disagree with Williams's conclusion. A perusal of the table of contents in most human services journals has led many to conclude that research reports are of high esoteric interest but limited practical use. The frameworks within which studies are conducted generally lack any relationship to reality since they concentrate on delimited, isolated variables devoid of relevance to the subject's daily existence. The reasons for this state of affairs are diverse, complex, and encrusted by rationales that have long outlived their utility. We would like to suggest some contemporary human services research activities that might constitute small but meaningful contributions to the needs of policy-makers and program directors.

As an alternative to the myriad of methodologically sophisticated but functionally barren studies emerging from research on the individual's psyche, we recommend greater attention to the implications of the ecological model that seeks to understand and predict behavior within the person-environment system (Barker, 1968). From the ecological perspective most behavior represents a transaction in which a person is influenced by the environment, which, in turn, is influenced by the person's response to it. Lehmann (1971) has recently suggested that the conceptual framework for community psychology may well reside in its study of the ecological principles guiding man's complex relationship with his environment. Kelly's (1968, pp. 76-99) study of adaptation within high school environments, for example, illustrates the ways in which ecological analyses, considering both personality variables, like exploration, and environmental variables, like rate of population mobility, can lead to relevant programmatic decisions. The ecological model and its derivative research efforts hold considerable promise and warrant much more of our attention as we grope for recommendations pertinent to the resolution of pressing human problems.

In a somewhat different vein it also is suggested that professionals direct more of their research skills and efforts to the evaluation of human services delivery programs so as to provide administrators with clearer conceptions of which service components are effective and which are ineffective. This basic organizational requirement has been either ignored or handled in an elaborate, ritualized, but irrelevant manner, for example, by assembling common services statistics devoid of evaluative meaning. Demone and Harshbarger, and Gottesfeld, et al. note the difficulty of defining feedback criteria of an either programmatic or economic nature. Although such studies are fraught with conceptual and methodological complexities, they are gaining more attention and sanctions and may yet come to represent a common endeavor for those concerned with the application of research insights to program operation. The descriptions by Schulberg, Sheldon, and Baker (1970) and Caro (1971) of program evaluations in the health and social science fields illustrate many dimensions of this growing area of research activity.

Another significant research endeavor is that of developing biosocial indicators that not only reflect the problem's severity within a given community but also suggest alternative fiscal and organizational strategies for attacking the problem. We can anticipate increasing pressures from funding authorities for data regarding clients served and program budgets, on the basis of which decisions will be made about the nature and extent of fiscal support. Demone and Harshbarger stress the need for organizations to link operational research tasks with those of planning so as to optimize feedback mechanisms that will have an impact on policy decisions, an entirely feasible process when sophisticated client and management information systems are available.

SUMMARY

The finer features of human services programs during the 1970s can only be dimly perceived at present, yet enough of the general outline is evident to recognize that the major characteristics of these programs will include less segmented and more comprehensive approaches to client problems, decentralized facilities closer to population centers, and integrated program administration permitting continuity of care. It is not premature to consider the impact of these developments on participating personnel, and those issues germaine to manpower patterns, training, practice, and research have been highlighted. If we respond appropriately, the human services will remain contemporary and vital; if we do not, our potential successes will inevitably turn to disillusionment and failure.

REFERENCES

Albee, G. The uncertain future of clinical psychology. *American Psychologist,* 1970, **25,** 1071-1080.

Baker, F., & Schulberg, H. Community health caregiving systems. In A. Sheldon, F. Baker, & C. McLaughlin (Eds.), *Systems and medical care,* Cambridge, Mass.: MIT Press, 1970.

Barker, R. *Ecological psychology.* Stanford: Stanford University Press, 1968.

Broskowski, A. Clinical psychology: A research and development model. *Professional Psychology,* 1971, **2,** 235-242.

Caro, F. (Ed.), *Readings in evaluative research.* New York: Russell Sage Foundation, 1971.

Demone, H. Human services at state and local levels and the integration of mental health. In G. Caplan (Ed.), *American handbook of psychiatry.* Volume III, Boston: Little, Brown, in press.

Demone, H., & Schulberg, H. Planning for human services: The role of the community council. In H. Demone & D. Harshbarger (Eds.), *Handbook of human service organizations in context.* New York: Behavioral Publications, in press.

Gluck, M. The psychologist and United Funding: A case study. *Professional Psychology,* 1971, **2,** 330-334.

Holder, H., & Dixon, R. Delivery of mental health services in the city of the future. *American Behavioral Scientist,* 1971, **14,** 893-908.

Iscoe, I., & Spielberger, G. *Community psychology: Perspectives in Training and research.* New York: Appleton-Century-Crofts, 1970.

Jacob, T. A survey of graduate education in community psychology. *American Psychologist,* 1971, **26,** 940-944.

Kelly, J. Towards an ecological conception of preventive interventions. In J. Carter (Ed.), *Research contributions from psychology to community mental health.* New York: Behavioral Publications, 1968.

Kiesler, F. Is this psychiatry? In S. Goldston (Ed.), *Concepts of community psychiatry.* Washington, D.C.: U.S. Government Printing Office, 1965.

Korten, F., Cook, S., & Lacey, J. *Psychology and the problems of soci-*

ety. Washington, D.C.: American Psychological Association, 1970.

Lehmann, S. Community and psychology and community psychology. *American Psychologist,* 1971, **26,** 554-560.

March, M. The neighborhood center concept. *Public Welfare,* 1968, **26,** 97-111.

National Institute of Mental Health. Consultation and education services in community mental health centers—January 1970. Biometry Branch Statistical Note 43, February 1971.

Peck, H., Roman, M., & Kaplan, S. Community action programs and the comprehensive health center. In M. Greenblatt, P. Emery, & B. Gluck (Eds.), *Poverty and mental health.* Washington, D.C.: American Psychiatric Association, 1967.

Schulberg, H., Sheldon, A., & Baker, F. (Eds.), *Program evaluation in the health fields.* New York: Behavioral Publications, 1970.

Williams, W. *Social policy research and analysis.* New York: American Elsevier, 1971.

TEACHING HEALTH AND HUMAN SERVICES ADMINISTRATION BY THE CASE METHOD

by
Linda G. Sprague,
Alan Sheldon, M.D.,
and Curtis P. McLaughlin, D.B.A.

(Part I of Developments in Human Services,
Volume 1,
Edited by
Herbert C. Schulberg, Ph.D.,
Frank Baker, Ph.D., and
Sheldon R. Roen, Ph.D.

Library of Congress Catalog Card Number 73-6873
Standard Book Number 87705-080-5

BEHAVIORAL PUBLICATIONS, 2852 Broadway—Morningside Heights, New York, New York 10025

Printed in the United States of America

Library of Congress Cataloging in Publication Data

Sprague, Linda G
Teaching health and human services administration by the case method.

Also issued in v. 1 of Developments in human services.
1. Social work education. 2. Social case work. 3. Social work administration. I. Sheldon, Alan, 1933- joint author. II. McLaughlin, Curtis P., joint author. III. Title.
[HV11.S67] 361'.007 73-6873

CONTENTS

Preface v

1. **The Case Method of Teaching** 33
   Sources: Educational Need and Philosophy 35
   What It Is and How It Works 36

2. **The Case Method in Health and Human Services Administration** 41
   Analytic Opportunities for the Student 42
   Illustration of Concepts 43
   Illustration of Issues 43
   Institutional Knowledge 44
   A Basis for Self-Analysis and Comparison 45
   Illustration of Alternatives 46
   Insights into the Current Process 46
   Illustrative Data for Theories and Hypothesis 47
   A Feel for Complexities and Relationships 48
   Summary 49

3. **A Sample Case with Notes on Its Use** 51
   Development of the CCMHC 51
   Appendix A 83
   Appendix B 85

4. Classroom Dynamics: The Heart of the Case Method 91
Preparation for Teaching 91
The Teacher's Role in the Classroom 93
Student Roles 95
Techniques 96
Style 98
A Case Class 101

5. Development of Case Materials 109
Case Writing 110
Appendix A 114
Appendix B 115

PREFACE TO THE SEPARATES OF THE "DEVELOPMENTS IN HUMAN SERVICES" SERIES

Widespread inadequacies in the human condition, and concern for the difficulties and complexities of existing social arrangements, have created urgent pressures upon professionals to revise present care-giving mechanisms. Human service programs such as multi-service centers, which incorporate a wide variety of relevant services, are emerging as an alternative framework to the existing pattern of rigid, categorical services for meeting the bio-psycho-social needs of individuals and populations.

The editors of this new encyclopedic series have undertaken to develop materials which can serve as guide posts for those newly entering or already engaged in the field of human services. A flexible approach to the production and distribution of these materials has been devised.

The plan for the series is to publish annually indepth discussions and reviews on the following human service topics:

—Emerging Conceptions of human service such as systems and ecological frameworks
—Administrative and planning tools such as information systems, economic strategies, and legal mechanisms
—Innovative service programs within new organizational models and new communities
—Educational programs for changing professional roles and new manpower requirements

After several years, those who are standing order subscribers will possess an encyclopedic library of human

services in either hardbound volumes or softcover separates.

The first volume contains an introductory overview by the editors, four substantitive sections on different human service topics as enumerated below, and a comprehensive index. Each of the substantitive sections, without introductory overview and index, are available as separates. These are:

Teaching Health and Human Services Administration by the Case Method
Linda G. Sprague, Alan Sheldon, M.D., and Curtis P. McLaughlin, D.B.A.

The Planning and Administration of Human Services
Harold W. Demone, Jr., Ph.D. and Dwight Harshbarger, Ph.D.

Strategies in Innovative Human Service Programs
Harry Gottesfeld, Ph.D., Florence Lieberman, D.S.W., Sheldon R. Roen, Ph.D., and Sol Gordon, Ph.D.

Developments in Human Services Education and Manpower
Robert M. Vidaver, M.D.

The Editors

1 THE CASE METHOD OF TEACHING

> Teaching administration in the classroom is like trying to teach swimming without letting your students go near the water. At Harvard the students are placed in a dense fog and encouraged to wave their arms; at M.I.T. we teach hydrodynamics and make them do pushups.[1]

How *do* you teach administration? What process yields good decision-makers, wise leaders, and effective managers for society's diverse organizations? The above anecdote describes the central problem in the teaching of administration: how to do it when the students can't "go near the water."

The leisurely apprenticeship for administration by which the student learns gradually from observation and slowly increasing practice is simply inadequate for present needs. The nation is becoming insistent that its health and human services needs be effectively met. The institutions and programs for delivering those services are therefore under increasing pressure for effective and efficient administration. Moreover, the trend toward comprehensiveness and integration in the delivery of health and human services serves to intensify the need for wise management at many organizational levels if these challenging goals are to be met.

"How to teach administration," therefore, is not an academic question; rather, it is a critical question for professionals in such diverse fields as public health, medical care, mental health, social work, comprehensive health planning, and education and all of the related governmental agencies. Practitioners in all of these fields find today that administration plays an increasingly important role in their professional lives. How can we teach these professionals about administration? How can we help them become more effective administrators?

As the opening anecdote suggests, there are two approaches in common use at professional schools of administration: (*a*) the "dense fog" of the Harvard Business School's case method and (*b*) the more traditional lecture method implied by the MIT hydrodynamics course. Both pedagogic techniques have the same objective: to teach students to become good administrators. The lecture method of teaching needs no introduction: It is the common pedagogic technique in virtually all disciplines and professions. The case method, however, is not so well known. We present it here not as an alternative to the lecture method but as a powerful supplement to the traditional pedagogic method for teaching administration.

It is well understood that the lecture method of teaching has as many variations as there are lecturers, which is also true of the case method, although there is a surrounding body of orthodoxy. We will describe the philosophical underpinnings of the case method, what it is and how it works, and show the variety of ways in which the case method can be used. Then, using a sample case, we will discuss the teacher's preparation as well as the students'. The same case will serve as a focus for our discussion of the classroom dynamics that are a vital element of the case method.

The case method has had its largest constituency in the professional schools—medicine, law, and administration—and its development is generally associated with Harvard. Since all three authors have had an association with the Harvard Business School, our focus will reflect that institution's.

SOURCES: EDUCATIONAL NEED AND PHILOSOPHY

A professional program must transmit to its students a body of knowledge—a set of basic facts, fundamentals, and techniques. For example, the medical student must know the skeletal and muscular structures of the human body; the administration student must know the accepted principles and conventions of accounting. But factual knowledge is not enough: The graduate of a professional program must be prepared to *use* this body of knowledge to take independent action.

But we cannot talk our students into wise application of a set of facts and techniques; we must help each student develop his own process for making administrative judgments. The lecture method is inadequate to the task of preparing the student to analyze, decide, and act in situations that we cannot predict.

There is an educational philosophy directly related to this need (Gragg, 1954, p. 6):

> It can be said flatly that the mere act of listening to wise statements and sound advice does little for anyone. In the process of learning, the learner's dynamic cooperation is required. Such cooperation from students does not arise automatically, however. It has to be provided for and continually encouraged.

Gaining the student's "dynamic cooperation" is vital if the student is to develop his own process for analysis, decision, and action. Like the medical student on grand rounds, the administration student must learn to observe a set of facts, analyze them, form an opinion, and then defend that opinion. He is expected to improve his performance with practice and to gain the confidence necessary to decisive action.

The case method is a pedagogic process for meeting an educational need—the *application* of facts and techniques. For administration students the case method is also a process for developing "dynamic cooperation" in his education.

WHAT IT IS AND HOW IT WORKS

The case method obviously involves *cases*. Since the term *case* has various meanings, our operational definition may be helpful:

> case: a written description of an organizational situation that provides information on the organization, its members, actions, and/or objectives without analysis of those facts and information.[2]

In a "pure" case-method course, the students receive approximately one case for each class period: There are no textbooks, and there will be no lectures during the course. To an observer accustomed to the lecture method of instruction, it is a curious experience indeed to watch a randomly selected case-method class. Individual styles may vary, but essentially the instructor has little to say: The primary verbalizations of the situation come from the students. The instructor acts as a combination questioner, summarizer, cheerleader, referee, and reference library. The instructor *conducts* his class much the way an orchestra conductor leads his musicians through a symphony.

This appears deceptively simple from the instructor's point of view: Because the students are doing most of the talking, it would appear that they are also doing most of the work, leaving the instructor with virtually nothing to do. As is usually true, appearances *are* deceiving. Cases are *not* an easy out for the instructor. A case-method class depends on careful planning and thorough preparation on the part of the instructor.

The specific objective of a single case discussion may vary widely; some of these objectives will be detailed in the next chapter. Underlying the particular purpose, however, there is a single major theme: to teach the student to glean as much information as possible from a situation and to develop an analysis based on that information so that he may then develop an appropriate plan of action to meet the organization's needs. Our central purpose is always the same: *to teach the student to become an effective administrator.*

This is very different from "teaching administration," which implies simply transmitting theories and facts to the student with the hope that these will prepare him adequately for the administrative problems he will face. We contend that we cannot predict the administrative problems the student will face in sufficient detail to be able to provide him with a "how-to" handbook. We can, however, provide the student with a methodology that will allow him to continue to learn and to improve his administrative skills throughout his professional life. It is much like providing a student not with a list of all the books in the library but with an understanding of the cataloguing system. Two years, even 20 years, from today the student will still be able to effectively use the library to find material that does not now exist.

As with a lecture course, a case course must be built on an organized sequence of educational objectives. In a series of lectures the lecture titles themselves frequently document the course structure. A series of case titles, however, rarely illuminates the underlying structure by which those cases were chosen. Yet the structure must be there.

For example, here is a partial list of the topics in sociology covered in an introductory MBA course in organizational behavior (Hosmer, 1971):

1. Organizational formation.
2. Organizational purpose.
3. Organizational functions.
4. Organizational types.
5. Organizational structure.

This basic structure, with each topic elaborated in some detail, provides the backdrop for the selection of specific cases. Without the underlying purpose and structure the "course" would indeed be little more than a meaningless string of case titles.

What about the reverse? Can the occasional case be

introduced into a lecture course? Obviously, any instructor can hand out a case, but assigning a case is not necessarily using the case method. Using the case method in the classroom means turning the burden of learning over to the student, achieving his "dynamic cooperation." In the context of a lecture course this may be difficult behavior from both instructor and student. However, difficult does not mean impossible. A case discussion within a lecture program can heighten the student's understanding of the material presented in the lecture. It can also provide the student with an opportunity to practice using the concepts and techniques and can prepare him for the material to follow.

A particular feature of business administration training is the *program* nature of that training. This is particularly true of case-method programs in which, for example, an entire year's course schedule is hammered out on a day-to-day basis by the entire teaching faculty. Each case course within the program has a rich but definite structure, and these courses are integrated to form the year's educational program. Such planning and coordination is an absolute necessity if program continuity is to be maintained throughout a year during which the student will work on roughly 800 cases.

However, most professional programs in the health and human services do not center entirely on administration. For example, the course outlined in the Federal Register for nursing home administrators, who are to be licensed under state boards so that their homes will be eligible for certain payments, lists many topics, including problems of aging, technical requirements of home construction, etc. In developing a program in North Carolina to meet this "administrator's" examination, we found that only about 40% of the course time could be devoted to the teaching of administration per se. Yet the course contained only 100 hours of instruction, which may have required more than most active administrators could afford over a six-month period and probably contained more material than they could master within that time span.

This is characteristic of most "administration" programs in the health and human services: Only a small fraction of the total program is allotted to administration courses. Of this fraction only a small subset is generally amenable to case-method instruction. Thus, it is not possible for either the group or the instructor to generate as effective control of the learning process as is possible in business programs.

Thus, the "pure" case method is simply not possible. That does not mean, however, that it must be abandoned as a teaching tool. In the next chapter we will discuss ways of using the case method in such settings. Whether the educational setting is a full course on administration, a short seminar partially devoted to administration, or an in-service training program, we believe that the case method can be an important pedagogic aid.

FOOTNOTES

[1] Attributed to Professor John D. C. Little, MIT, Sloan School of Management.

[2] This definition is consistent with the definition of a case report in Jain, (1968, p. 438).

REFERENCES

Gragg, C. I. Because wisdom can't be told. In M. P. McNair (Ed.), *The Case method at the Harvard Business School.* New York: McGraw-Hill, 1954.

Hosmer, L. T. Academic strategy: A comparison of the plans and objectives of four new schools of administration. Unpublished doctoral dissertation, Harvard University Graduate School of Business Administration, Cambridge, Mass., 1971.

2. THE CASE METHOD IN HEALTH AND HUMAN SERVICES ADMINISTRATION

There are several excellent gospels of the case method (see page 114) that provide a full picture of the Harvard programs, particularly that of the Harvard Business School. But health and human services administration programs differ from business programs in a number of ways. We have already mentioned that "administration" is generally an adjunct to other professional training.

In addition, case material is not available in large quantity. Some of the available cases were developed at business schools to provide those students with the wider relevance of concepts and techniques being covered in their courses. However, material thus focused on issues of interest to business administrators may overlook key issues in the profession from which they are drawn or may represent misperceptions of the professional situation.

Given the limited class time available and the limitations on material, it is therefore unrealistic to think in terms of a total case-method program in the health and human services. We are convinced, however, that the case method of teaching can be successfully integrated into existing courses, thereby increasing the overall effectiveness of the administration segment of those programs.

In order to demonstrate this we will discuss a variety of ways in which the case method can be used within a more traditional educational setting. Obviously, these functions and purposes are not mutually exclusive.

Under the foreshortened conditions of education for health and human services administration, multiple contribution from the cases used is a desirable, if not necessary, outcome.

ANALYTIC OPPORTUNITIES FOR THE STUDENT

A primary focus of the case method is the development of analytic skills in real situations. Thus, a case may be designed to teach the student to:

1. Identify information from a large amount of data.
2. Use technical skills.
3. Use judgmental skills.

Some cases deliberately include large quantities of data, much of which is obviously extraneous. The objective here is to accustom the student to sifting out pertinent information from all the stimuli that the environment provides. The rationale is that the "real world" is accurately simulated by this information overload.

Cases are also used as vehicles for the presentation of problems amenable to analytic solution. In this sense they are "problems"—word problems imbedded in a larger context. The idea here is to provide the student with experience in identifying or modeling a problem in a realistic setting and scope. In a business program with considerable emphasis on mathematical concepts this is an important use of cases: Without it, students would see application of techniques as simple rather than as the complex tasks that they really are. Such cases also serve as exercises in finding existing information and estimating unavailable information necessary for application of a quantitative technique.

Such "analytic case problems" generally require at least two class sessions: the first for identification of the information and method of analysis, the second for solution results and interpretation in light of nonquantitative case data.

Judgmental skills are used at many points in the case

analysis: (*a*) data sorting and selection, (*b*) identification and prioritization of problems, (*c*) selection of analytic procedure, and (*d*) interpretation of analytic results. The instructor can help the student develop his judgmental skills by making explicit those decisions that are being based on judgment and the impact of such judgments on the outcome of the situation.

ILLUSTRATION OF CONCEPTS

Cases are often used to illustrate concepts with which the student is not familiar. For example, the Indian Point Medical Council case (see page 127) describes the statistical impact on bed-utilization rates of multiple hospitals in an area and multiple services within hospitals. The case also displays the responses of community leaders to the findings from the application of this technique. If the concept is somewhat technical in nature, a short lecture or background "technical note" often accompanies the case to provide the authoritative background needed to justify the particular application. Such an approach has the advantage of displaying the usefulness of the technique to the student at the time he is required to master it.

For health services courses, cases drawn from the student's own profession can serve to illustrate the value and relevance of new concepts to that setting. A carefully constructed case and supporting technical note can represent an efficient use of course time. We should note here that this use of a case is actually a substantial departure from the traditional case method.

ILLUSTRATION OF ISSUES

Similarly, cases can be used to illustrate issues in the professional field. In short courses for educators and businessmen we have found that cases are excellent vehicles for getting a class to confront issues that outsiders are not supposed to know about nor enter into. Were we, for instance, to tell a group of hospital administrators that they had little say in the hospital's major decisions, the result would be defensive denial. However, a realistic case showing the decision-making activity in a hospital, with the administrator generally on the periphery, produces immediate recognition of a key problem. As one colleague is fond of saying, "We can bring them to the brink of their own understanding."

Moreover, such a case early in a course (particularly a short course) usually contributes greatly to the classroom process. It allows the group to move relatively quickly to discussion of issues meaningful to them and quickly clears away much of the social and intellectual fencing that characterizes any newly assembled group. In a sense it can open up the process to the point that the case method of teaching can be applied without handing out cases because the students become accustomed to expressing their thoughts in terms of known issues and relationships.

One technique that has had mixed results is the use of cases in which the protagonists are professional groups close to that of the students. Closeness may come in the form of frequent interaction or in terms of professional structures and tasks much like the students', but in an ostensibly different field. Here the instructor hopes that the students will transfer some of their internal hostilities and cultural sets to the situation in the case, then gradually work their way through to seeing their own situation in a less biased way. However, if the students do not see the parallels between their own situation and that of the case, they may quickly lose interest. That is the risk the instructor takes, but the payoffs may be great in a highly conflicted situation.

INSTITUTIONAL KNOWLEDGE

Documents on the case method in business tend not to emphasize that perusal and discussion of a thousand cases can produce a broad understanding of many businesses and their strategies and practices. Since there are no official professional barriers to entering any particular business field, who can say that a tidbit about a steel mill or an insurance agency will not come in handy? Just as the only party certain to benefit from basic research is the huge company that is into every technology, so can the businessman with an eye toward *every* profitable opportunity benefit from a broad spectrum of cases.

While there is not such an advantage to the health and human services professional, he may not be familiar with the full spectrum of administrative roles and responsibilities within his own profession. Cases can be a relatively compact method for introducing the ways in which decisions are made in that profession and the roles of the potential participants in the process of management. The case thus becomes an effective vehicle for illustrating roles and responsibilities in a recognizable context. Such an activity, however, calls for a supply of cases drawn from the professional situations to be studied—something not often available. Yet it is sufficiently important that the instructor should seriously consider writing his own cases to accomplish this indoctrination into management decision-making and behavior in the health and human services.

A BASIS FOR SELF-ANALYSIS AND COMPARISON

When the student has had some administrative experience, cases can provide a basis for evaluation of behavior in similar situations. This is particularly true if the instructor uses role-playing during case discussions. Many students, when assuming a role, are forced to reconsider their own positions on important issues.

As an example, the School of Public Health at Chapel Hill, North Carolina, assigns the extensive Dixon-Tiller studies of the United States Public Health Service to students and has them work for several days to develop an appropriate community health plan. Each student is assigned the role of representative of a community or professional group to which he must remain "loyal" throughout the development task. Such an exercise demands of the student understanding of and sympathy for other points of view. It also shows him the constraints that vested interests place on the behavior of the "rational analyst."

ILLUSTRATION OF ALTERNATIVES

Cases prepared at Harvard typically state that the case was "prepared as a basis for class discussion ... [and was] not designed to present illustrations of either effective or ineffective handling of administrative problems." That is true. But the use of an array of cases does display for the student a lot of administrators—good and bad—in action and can build up in the student a "bag of tricks." It is especially true when the instructor has been associated with the preparation of the case and is willing to tell the students what the real decision-maker actually did in that situation. Although the cases are not always designed to display alternatives, they certainly do so for the complete novice. Since complete novices may be common among professional students, this function should not be overlooked.

INSIGHTS INTO THE CURRENT PROCESS

Even experienced and skilled administrators can gain from case discussions. Case teachers generally feel that they continue to learn through their leadership of case discussions. All of us develop mind sets that are based on experience; in the case of senior executives these sets about operations at a less aggregated level are often years old.

A man may know exactly how things are done in his organization when he did them. (The mixture of tenses is intentional.) A consultant frequently finds that one of his primary functions is to bring management up to date on current thinking about problems and solutions at lower levels in their own organization. Some observers object to this. Townsend (1970) suggests that this is like stealing a man's watch and selling it back to him. Yet the information may have great value whatever the channel of communication. The case discussion can be one such channel.

When used in a setting in which several members of the same organization are present, a case can be a vehicle for the transference of issues and problems to a less threatening level of discussion. Biases and personality conflicts, when they exist, can be discussed in terms of the characters in the case. Under the direction of a skilled case teacher the group can gradually turn toward the needs of the organization itself. If the group begins to stiffen at this turn, the instructor can turn back to the case situation and allow the parallels to sink in more gradually.

ILLUSTRATIVE DATA FOR THEORIES AND HYPOTHESIS

Case studies of administrative situations are grist for the researcher's mill, especially for behaviorally oriented research. (Whether or not they represent evidence is highly debatable. Certainly, hard data is much to be preferred, and in a publish-or-perish situation the case is of little immediate value.) Ideas about the nature and solution of administrative problems must have their origin in a set of clues somewhere: The man who uses and prepares a set of cases is presented with numerous opportunities to draw parallels between situations and to develop a gestalt for approaching and analyzing situations.

A man considered an excellent manager and who was successful as a consultant in his younger days has said that effective consulting is much like case writing and case analysis. The manager has to develop a personal structure of the technological setting, the environment, and the strategy for decision-making. The same preparation can be an effective way of enhancing the research process.

Stanley Davis (1970) of Harvard, in a paper on the subject of comparative management, states:

> Methodologically, case analysis is useful both before and after quantitative data have been amassed. Cases may serve as a prelude to hypothesis-building. They help the researcher to familiarize himself with his unit of analysis, and to capture the pattern of interrelationships. After survey data have been analyzed, cases can help to focus on particular themes. The most common theme is the study of deviant cases.

A FEEL FOR COMPLEXITIES AND RELATIONSHIPS

Sagar Jain (1968) has described the type of case in the mainstream of the current health administration literature: It is at a high level of organizational aggregation and focuses on external forces affecting the environment. As such, it serves the purpose of describing the system in terms of its environment and components. Jain notes that such cases are useful in sensitizing the students of health administration to the importance of the community and its role but suggests that this response may be a way of inferring that most of the problems of health agencies are externally caused and of ignoring the problems of internal organization that are so important to the effective functioning of the health organization.

However, this can be seen in a more positive light. The professional must come to recognize his area as a subsystem of broader systems not fully under his control. Until he does this, he cannot deal with the highly uncertain world in which he must operate on a rational basis. The same needs for a sense of the system exist within the service organization. Cases can help provide a fuller understanding of the interrelationships and complexities of the organization.

SUMMARY

It is a rare case that can be used for only one of these purposes. Most can be used in a number of ways and for a variety of purposes. The Charity Community Mental Health Center (CCMHC) case which appears in the next chapter, can, for example, simultaneously illustrate current issues for the management of community mental health programs, provide institutional background information for novices in the field, and serve as a basis for an analysis of the decision-making process in this environment. If the case is presented to practicing professionals involved in community mental health programs, the instructor can use the case as a vehicle for developing insights into ongoing real processes of which the professionals are a vital part.

The critical element, as we have said, is the instructor's educational objective. It will determine the appropriate focus for a specific case on a specific day.

REFERENCES

Davis, S. M. Case studies of managerial behavior. Paper presented at the Comparative Management Workshop, Graduate School of Business Administration, New York University, Summer 1970.

Jain, S. C. Essay on terminology. In R. Penchansky (Ed.), *Health services administration: policy cases and the case method.* Cambridge, Mass.: Harvard University Press, 1968.

Townsend, R. *Up the organization.* New York: Knopf, 1970.

3. A SAMPLE CASE WITH NOTES ON ITS USE

The CCMHC case that follows is a rich one that can be used in a number of situations: for example, a course on the role of federal regulation and policy; a short seminar on administrative policy and strategy; training programs in human behavior, organizational problems, conflict management, etc. The teaching focus and strategy will necessarily differ in each instance.

We will present the case and, following it, a sample teaching note on the CCMHC developed for a class on strategies for organizational change. We will then discuss preparation for case teaching using the CCMHC as a continuing example. The classroom discussion in Chapter 4 will also be based on the CCMHC case.

CHARITY COMMUNITY MENTAL HEALTH CENTER*

DEVELOPMENT OF THE CCMHC

In December 1967 Dr. Keuning assumed the position of Medical Director of the CCMHC in Lincoln, New York The selection of Dr. Keuning climaxed a lengthy search for a director of the center, for which initial federal fund-

*The case was prepared by G. William Helm, Management Analysis Center, Inc., under supervision of Dr. Roy Penchansky, Associate Professor, Department of Medical Care Organization, School of Public Health, University of Michigan. It is intended for class discussion only and is not intended to represent either effective or ineffective handling of an administrative situation.

ing for both staffing and construction had been received in March 1967. In a letter to the administrator of Charity Hospital in July 1967 the staff psychiatrists of the hospital noted the following reasons for recommending Dr. Keuning's selection:

The esteem with which he is held in academic circles.

His academic record as well as his research and postgraduate education.

His extensive administrative experience.

His age (45).

His open-minded, enthusiastic attitude toward the challenge of developing a community mental health center.

Dr. Keuning had most recently served on the faculty of the University of Westcoast Medical School for seven years, had been director of an inpatient psychiatric unit in a general hospital, and had extensive contact with nonpsychiatric physicians in the hospital. He had contributed significant research and publications in psychiatry and had been head of the American Medical Association Section on Neurology and Psychiatry. While acceptance of the position in Lincoln obviously required commitment to the community mental health center concept, Dr. Keuning was also thought sympathetic to the concerns of private practitioners.

Eight months later, as Sister Catherine became the new administrator of Charity Hospital, some observers claimed that Dr. Keuning was on the verge of being replaced as medical director of the CCMHC. In the interim almost devastating divisions characterized the relations among the principal groups involved in the development of mental health services in Lincoln. Among the most important were the County Mental Health Board, the federal mental health legislation, the Charity Hospital, the pri-

---

The case forms part of a series developed under Contract Number HSM-42-69-41 with the National Institute of Mental Health, Health Services and Mental Health Administration, Department of Health, Education and Welfare.

vate psychiatrists, the University of State, and eventually the Charity Mental Health Center.

County Mental Health Board

In 1963 the state passed an act

> to provide for the establishment of community mental health service programs; to prescribe the powers of counties and certain cities; to prescribe the powers and duties of the state department of mental health; and to provide funds for the operation of local community mental programs.

Inland County, of which Lincoln is the county seat, responded by establishing the mandatory "12-member community mental health services board," the members of which were appointed by the chairman of the elected county board of supervisors.

Several provisions of the act served to invest the board with considerable power and discretion in the area of mental health:

> review the annual plan and budget (of programs) and make recommendations thereon.
>
> all existing child guidance clinics, all multi-purpose psychiatric clinics, all adult psychiatric clinics which are under the administration of the Department of Mental Health and are financed in part by state funds shall be administered by existing local clinic boards and shall be approved for contractual services under contract with the community mental health services board, or administered by the community mental health services board. . . .

The act also provided for the state to provide matching grants "for 75% of the total expenditures for salaries; contract facilities and services; operation, maintenance and service costs; . . . and other expenditures approved." No grants were available for capital expenditures.

In 1968 the county board had among its programs the Inland County Community Mental Health Center in South Lincoln, the Lincoln Mental Health Clinic located near Charity Hospital, an alcoholic unit at another hospital, a school for behavioral change, a special education program in the county schools, a program for retarded children, and a camp for disturbed boys.

Federal Legislation

In 1963 and 1965 the U.S. Congress passed legislation to assist mental health programs. The 1965 act provided for federal staffing grant support for a minimum set of mental health services within a community, including inpatient and outpatient care, partial hospitalization, emergency services, and consultation and education. The act also provided for the expansion of this minimum level of service into a comprehensive program that could include, in addition to diagnostic and rehabilitation services, precare and aftercare services, training of personnel, and research and evaluation.

Staffing grants cover costs of the eligible services on a declining basis—75% of the staffing costs for the first 15 months, 60% for the following year, 45% for the next year, and 30% for the final year. The intent of this type of support is to encourage communities to develop their own financial resources on a continuing basis.

Federal aid was made available through the 1963 legislation for construction, generally to be used to complete the range of psychiatric services in a community. Construction assistance ranges from one-third to two-thirds of a center's cost. A formula based on a state's needs determines the actual percentage of federal aid.

Charity Hospital

The hospital is a 350-bed short-term general hospital operated by the Sisters of Charity. Since 1960 Charity Hospital had provided the only inpatient psychiatric facilities in the Lincoln area, consisting of a 42-bed unit on the fifth floor of the hospital. The unit was divided into two sections, one open and one secured. Rooms were either private or semi-private. Access to the unit was by an elevator from the ground floor that did not stop at the intermediate floors of the hospital. For all intents and purposes the psychiatric unit, like other hospital facilities, served as a "workshop for the private psychiatrists." Prior to the fall of 1968, the hospital was administered by Sister Helen, a figurehead administrator who delegated responsibility for most of the operations of the hospital to an associate administrator and two assistant administrators. The hospital had physicians practicing in all of the major specialities, with the physicians organized into 11 departments.

PRIVATE PSYCHIATRISTS

Nine private psychiatrists dominated the mental health services of the Lincoln area in the 1960s, and by all accounts they enjoyed thriving practices. While holding therapeutic sessions in their private offices, they utilized facilities at Charity Hospital for inpatient care and both inpatient and outpatient shock treatment. The census in the psychiatric unit was usually about 90% of capacity. All inpatient treatment was carried out by the doctors themselves; nurses and attendants performed traditional hospital functions, and no psychologists or psychiatric social workers were on the staff. Chemotherapy and shock therapy dominated treatment. As far as can be discerned, over half the patients were not seen for any care after discharge from the hospital.

The University and Medical School

The University of State, a state-supported educational institution, is located in a community about fifteen miles from Lincoln. The university has, in addition to a large undergraduate program, an extensive array of professional schools, including a school of medicine, a school of social work, and a school of nursing. All of these participate at Charity Hospital in in-service training programs.

The University's Medical School had for a number of years provided the first two years of medical education with students then transferring to a private medical school in the state or going out of state. In 1968 the medical school was actively involved in planning to move to a four-year school for the 1970-71 academic year. Much lobbying was being carried out for increased state funding, clinical departments were being established or expanded, and arrangements for clinical training were being made with local hospitals.

Under the agreement that brought Dr. Keuning to Lincoln, he was both the Director of the Charity Center and the Chairman of the Department of Psychiatry. While it was expected that he would initially divide his time about 90% Charity and 10% University, it was agreed that eventually he would turn over his CCMHC role to someone else and assume a full-time University position. Dr. Keuning's salary was actually paid by the University, with Charity Hospital reimbursing the University. The pattern of staff having faculty appointments and being paid by the University was to be followed for many of the senior staff of the CCMHC.

CCMHC

An active member of the Charity Hospital board of directors saw in the state act and in the federal legislation for community mental health centers an opportunity for the hospital to participate to its advantage in a community mental health program. By splitting responsibility for the five services mandatory for federal funding between the county board's programs and the hospital's psychiatric facilities, the area could qualify for federal funds. The hospital would be responsible for inpatient services, emergency services, and partial hospitalization, including day care. In addition, by expanding the scale of these services, it would be eligible for a federal construction grant to build new facilities, freeing up valuable space in the existing hospital structure. The county board would handle outpatient services and consultation and education services through the existing programs that it now controlled, complete with 75% state funding. After some negotiation this cooperative plan was put into effect in early 1967 under the guidance of county board members, hospital administrators, and private psychiatrists, and federal staffing and construction grants were made to Charity Hospital.

Almost immediately, the lack of specific delegated responsibility for coordination and direction for the overall "center" led to staffing problems, particularly in the nonhospital services. With pressures from the National Institute of Mental Health (NIMH) to justify federal staffing and construction funds being received, it was with unhidden relief that all parties welcomed the arrival of Dr. Keuning.

The steps leading to the selection of Dr. Keuning are not fully recorded, but it seems that Charity Hospital had attempted to recruit a Medical Director for the CCMHC but had been unsuccessful. It then turned to Dr. Leland, who was the Director of the Inland County Community Mental Health Center and, according to some, the *de facto* head of the Lincoln Mental Health Clinic. Leland suggested a psychiatrist who had just finished his residency and had some experience working in a community mental health center. The Charity board apparently decided that this person was not suited to the position. They then turned to the University and asked the Dean of the Medical School to assist them in recruiting.

The Dean decided to recruit for both a Medical Director for the Center and for a Chairman of a Department of Psychiatry at the same time, although it is not clear whether at this point he was thinking of one person to fill both positions or two individuals. It does appear, however, that filling the Medical Director's position was of primary importance, but a problem existed in that some candidates for the department chairmanship did not like the idea of having the Medical School hire a Medical Director for the Center with whom they would later have to work. These individuals apparently thought that they should have the opportunity to select the Medical Director.

During his discussions with the Medical School, Dr. Keuning suggested that he would fill both positions initially, then recruit someone to replace him in the Medical Director's position when he was ready to assume a full-time University position. This alternative also seemed to appeal to the Medical School since it would be starting a Department of Psychiatry about two years ahead of the planned development of such a department.

Dr. Keuning visited the Center in evaluating his interest in the position and found what he later described as a traditional and low-level inpatient unit manned by a not very impressive group of private clinicians. The day-care program was "a very ordinary OT—take them to the zoo-type program. There was obviously no leadership in the psychiatric service."

He presented his ideas for a community program to the associate director of the hospital and the chief of the attending staff, as well as to the private psychiatrists. These included:

The need to have a University service—which would be the mental health center service with its own patient population—and a private service.

The need to have an aftercare program—"there was none as this is not profitable for the private psychiatrists."

The need to start an outpatient program immediately.

The need for home care.

Dr. Keuning says that he pointed out that this program would require a base of administrative authority and control of money and beds. He received assurance that this was what was desired.

Dr. Keuning took the job because he felt that the hospital administration, primarily the associate director, and the attending psychiatrists supported what he planned and because there were three different sources of money—county, federal, and private. "I thought it had a chance to go." Dr. Keuning feels now that he was badly misled and that he did not know enough about the legislation or the agreements that had been reached before taking the job.

He also states that he does not know whether the administrators did not hear or understand him or whether they decided to let him think that he was going to be able to do what he desired. Dr. Keuning strongly feels that he was misled by the associate director of the hospital.

> I don't know whether he was dishonest, ambiguous, or hadn't thought through the implications of what I was saying. It took me six months to figure out that you couldn't believe what he said.
>
> At that time I saw the central problem as getting power from the private psychiatrists—the need to get authority and a base of power in the hospital.

It was only on his second visit, after having accepted the position, that he "learned that the outpatient and consultation services were operated by Dr. Leland and the county and they were not going to give them up."

Catchment Area

The geographic area served by the CCMHC consists of approximately one-half the city of Lincoln, some surrounding county area, and an entire rural county. Within the Lincoln area itself, the population served by the Charity Center (Catchment Area I) numbers about 100,000 and includes a small population of Mexican-Americans and blacks who live in a small ghetto. The rural county is 600 square miles and has a population of about 40,000; it is primarily an agricultural county.

The other half of Lincoln, the remainder of Inland County, and another rural county comprise a catchment area served by the Inland County Community Mental Health Center (Catchment Area II). The center was developed and is administered directly by the Inland County Mental Health Board. The center, which receives financial support from the federal government, is located in the Inland County Medical Center, a 165-bed hospital, which does not have an inpatient psychiatric unit. Dr. Leland is the Director.

Lincoln lies in the middle of a rural area of the state, and farming is a major industry. In Lincoln itself there is considerable heavy manufacturing, and the population is divided among blue-collar factory workers, professionals attached to the large University of State, and persons connected with the usual retail and service elements of a city. The two catchment areas served by the mental health center cover a tri-county area that is considered one marketing and service area.

Facilities

The offices of Dr. Keuning and the general facilities for the administration of the CCMHC are located in a rather large and modern nursing school building connected with the hospital. The nursing school was in its last year of operation in 1968–69, and the three-story building provided adequate facilities for the use of the community mental health center. An underground tunnel provides an inside connection between the hospital building and the community mental health center building.

Initially the non hospital-based services (outpatient and consultation and education activities) were located in the old Lincoln Mental Health Center building in the center of Lincoln, approximately 10 minutes away from the hospital complex. As discussed later, these were moved to the Charity site in July of 1968.

The day-care and partial hospitalization (actually low-intensity care) program is located in the nursing school building, while the inpatient unit is in the main hospital building. The hospital's emergency room is located in the main hospital building near the elevator to the inpatient psychiatric unit. To get from the main hospital to the community mental health center is about a half-block walk through the winding, underground tunnel.

Most of the offices for the staff of the community mental health center were converted dormitory rooms that appear to be completely adequate as far as individual office facilities are concerned. Classrooms were converted for use as conference rooms, and social areas became reception areas. The new building being funded by the NIMH construction grant was begun in 1968. It will be three stories and is located between the main hospital building and the nursing school building. Upon the planned completion in mid-1970 of the new building, it was expected that only the outpatient staff would remain in the nursing school building. The offices of the director and other administrative personnel, as well as facilities for partial care, day care, and emergency services were expected to be located in the new building. Inpatient facilities would take over the upper floors of the new building, with the existing inpatient floor reverting to other medical uses in the hospital. Similarly, it was expected that the hospital would use vacated space in the nursing building for other needs of the hospital.

Program Size

One gauge of the size of the program at Charity is the number of staff people employed. In August 1968, 35 individuals were considered to be CCMHC employees, 26 of whom were nurses. In January 1969, 102 persons were employed (4 psychiatrists, 6 psychologists, 18 social workers, 23 nurses, 21 administrative and clerical personnel, and 30 psychiatric technicians). In June 1969, Charity listed 98 staff members (Table 1).

In June of 1969 no indigenous workers were included in the professional areas, although approximately half a dozen blacks and Mexican-Americans were working as psychiatric technicians. No local neighborhood or rural-area whites were included in any category. In May 1969, however, discussions in staff meetings were suggesting that "there should be a mechanism within the organization to hire people without degrees, but who have traditional background experience," and in January 1970 the first indigenous worker was employed in a therapist role.

In 1969-70 the operating budget of the center exceeded $1.5 million, of which some $600,000 was expected to come from a federal staffing grant. Private insurance payments of almost $600,000 were expected to be the next largest source of funds.

Initial Developments

Dr. F. Steen, a psychologist, joined the staff in March 1968 with an appointment in both the departments of psychology and psychiatry at the University. Like Dr. Keuning, his salary was paid through a contract between Charity and the University, and he had formerly been on the faculty of the University of Westcoast. One of Dr. Steen's chief concerns was with the training of interns in psychology, and he directed the education and training activities of the Center.

From March to June Keuning and Steen worked to develop the programs: Job descriptions were prepared and applicants interviewed. The staff of the Center, in addition to these two, consisted of a half-time psychiatric social worker, a half-time psychiatrist, a full-time psychiatric nurse, and the inpatient nurses, attendants, and the psychiatric attending staff.

TABLE 1
Staff Membership of the CCMHC June 1969

Note—Authorized staffing level also shown

	Full-time	*Part-time*	*Authorized*		*Total*
			NIMH	*County*	
Psychiatrist	3	1	4	1.5	5.5
Psychologist	4	1	5	7	12
Social Worker	12	3	9	10	19
Nurse	20	2	17	0	17
Administrative & Clerical	16	1	11	8	19
Therapist (O.T., R.T.)	4	0	5	0	5
Program Specialists	0	1	2	0	2
Consulting Physicians	0	1	0	3	3
Psychiatric Technicians	0	29	28	0	28
Totals	59	39	81	29.5	110.5

Administrative relationships with the hospital were slow to develop. Sister Helen assigned administrative responsibility for mental health activities to one of the professional assistant administrators, who also had hospital-wide responsibility for dietary and laundry functions. According to subsequent testimony, "He was a tin soldier and did nothing (for mental health)." On one occasion, in mid-1968, Dr. Steen arranged to change the title "psychiatric attendant" to "psychiatric technician," believing the latter implied a higher-level function. At the same time he suggested to the hospital that the pay for these people be raised to reflect the difference between a psychiatric technician and a regular hospital orderly. The attendants employed in the psychiatric unit were said to have qualifications very different from those on the other services. Many of the former were students in psychology at the University who worked on a part-time basis for experience as well as income. Dr. Steen found this difficult to get through the hospital, whose attitude was "why spend money." It appeared to him that primary emphasis was being given to the new building plans.

Dr. Keuning commented later:

> The hospital, primarily the associate director, wouldn't fund any positions and kept us tied up in paperwork. I think this was his strategy: keep us so busy writing long meaningless job descriptions and statements justifying the positions that we couldn't do anything else. We spend days doing this.

Even before the difficulties in working within the hospital became obvious, some animosities seemed to have developed between Dr. Keuning on the one hand and the county board and Dr. Leland on the other. In his second week on the job Dr. Keuning attended a county board meeting and gave a talk about the changes he planned to make. Some of the board members were very annoyed since they felt that much had been accomplished and that they were proud of the board's achievements. Dr. Keuning's remarks were taken as an attack on their activities.

Dr. Leland frequently represented the county board in its relations with Charity, and the board continually turned to him for advice, although there were a number of very active and vocal members. The board was also said to be quite protective of Dr. Leland. His relationship to the Charity Center and Dr. Keuning seems to have been strained because Dr. Leland expected an appointment in the Department of Psychiatry that he did not receive. One observer thinks that the Dean of the Medical School might well have mentioned such a possibility to Dr. Leland before Dr. Keuning's arrival.

According to Dr. Keuning, early in their relationship Dr. Leland suggested to him that the two catchment areas—known as the Tri-County Area—should be run as one program and that Keuning should give him a half-time appointment in the Department of Psychiatry and he would direct both programs. Among Dr. Keuning's reasons for declining the offer was his determination not to get caught in the position, which he felt was common in the mental health field, in which he had as a faculty member the person who was controlling some of the funding sources of the University-run program (i.e., state funds, in this case).

Dr. Keuning went about seeking some well-trained psychiatric nurses. This was in part to supplement the staff and in part because he was dissatisfied with the head nurse who "was scared of the attendings and the hospital administration." In his recruitment activities Dr. Keuning came upon a psychiatric nurse who was a member of the order of the Sisters of Charity but from a different province than Charity Hospital was in. Dr. Keuning thought that it would be very useful to have as the head nurse—and a senior member of the center staff—a member of the order who would live in the convent, which was attached to the hospital.

Dr. Keuning states that he was warned that Sister Elizabeth might cause some difficulties because of her aggressive ways and her stands on "nursing power and authority," but it was worth trading off possible problems to try to strengthen the Center's position in the hospital.

> Had we then had Sister Catherine, our new administrator, I wouldn't have hired her. She precipitated a number of fights that were not desired, and I found myself backing her when I didn't want to. Though on the EST [electroshock therapy] issue [see page 74] she was right, and I was glad to back her. Also, in retrospect, she definitely helped us get to a position to build up an inpatient program.

The Community Mental Health Center senior staff was bolstered in July by the arrival of Dr. I. Walton, a psychiatrist from the University of Westcoast who completed what came to be known as the "Westcoast Mafia." Dr. Walton, 37 years old, who was trained in both pediatrics and psychiatry, relieved Dr. Keuning of a large part of the administrative burden of the Center. Given a more easygoing nature than Dr. Keuning's, he assumed the handling of many of the external relationships with the county board and the community, while Dr. Keuning continued to maintain primary liasion with the hospital and the NIMH. Dr. Walton was also appointed an Associate Professor in the Department of Psychiatry.

Integration of Services

One of Dr. Keuning's early decisions was to move into outpatient care. The reasons for this seem numerous and, at times, conflicting. According to Dr. Keuning, he decided to "atomize" his problems and to place major stress on wresting power from the county board; he planned to pry loose money and positions. His technique was to cut off their manpower, and he decided to develop an outpatient service in part as a means to take manpower from them. As Dr. Walton recollects it, the original movement into outpatient care was for training purposes, particularly for psychology interns and social work students, and this arrangement seems to have been with the approval of the county board. However, it then expanded far beyond the need for training and without approval of the county board.

Dr. Keuning stated that whenever a staff member from the Lincoln Mental Health Clinic approached him about a job, if he was a useful person, he was told that he could not be hired while employed but that should he resign and then apply he would be hired. As another person states:

> Many of the Lincoln staff joined Charity. If not actually recruited by Dr. Keuning, he was certainly glad to have them join, both in terms of strengthening his program and weakening the "opposition."

The therapists at Charity, social workers, psychologists, nurses, and physicians, began to provide some outpatient aftercare treatment "in competition with" the outpatient services of the county board and private practitioners. According to Dr. Walton, they also "recruited patients. Lots of patients began popping up."

One problem with this strategy was that it upset the private psychiatrists, but Dr. Keuning felt that the battle with Dr. Leland and the county board was far more important. The physicians began to boycott the Center; they would not show up for meetings, and one of them would not allow his patients in any of the group activities being run on the inpatient unit.

In July the Lincoln Clinic moved from its location in downtown Lincoln to the CCMHC building. Some observers claim the move was caused by pressure from some of the members of the board of Charity Hospital to bring all services under one roof; this also would mean the renting of unused space in the nursing school building. Another source stated that it was the county board that wanted the Lincoln Clinic housed in the same building: A change in location may have been seen as aiding in staff recruitment. Whatever the reasons, the county board rented space at Charity for the staff of the Lincoln Clinic.

Subsequently, there seemed to be an effort on the part of Dr. Keuning to minimize outpatient services as shown in an announcement he made at a staff meeting in late August 1968:

1. Staff members should not fill up time with outpatients.
2. The county board does not reimburse us for outpatient services. We want them to come to us, with their overflow, and then we can ask them to help reimburse us.
3. We must make the county board come to us for help. That is, we can say we will help you if you will reimburse us. Our main services are inpatient, partial, and day care. We should have outpatients for training purposes and for continuity of care for inpatient discharges. All therapists should start phasing out their outpatients as soon as possible.

The county board was continuing to have trouble filling staff positions, while the Charity Center was attracting many applicants. Reasons for the hiring problems of the county board that were noted include: knowledge in the community of the uncertainty about the future of the Lincoln Clinic, that the Lincoln Clinic was not a particularly attractive place to work, and the county board's seemingly greater interest in the Inland County Community Mental Health Center. The county board was also having trouble finding candidates for the Inland County Center, however. By the summer of 1968, of 21 positions in the Lincoln Clinic only 7 were filled. The county board and Dr. Leland continually sought assistance in recruiting and in obtaining faculty positions at the University to assist in recruiting. Dr. Walton noted that stealing of staff had been a major point of controversy between the Center and the county.

According to Dr. Keuning,

> By the summer of 1968 we had a miniature comprehensive program in operation. We were using the Visiting Nurses Association for home care, we had clinical interns in psychology, we had negotiated with the state hospital, and they were sending over residents who were doing outpatient care. Then we began to pull back our outpatient work—though it was more apparent than real. This was part of a strategy to put pressure on the county to show them that they couldn't do the job but we could.

Dr. Walton noted that the withdrawal of service that was meant to put pressure on the county was the withdrawal of consultation services, coupled with no help in recruiting.

> I told Dr. Gilbert, who at that time was director of the Lincoln Clinic, that I was going to reject any requests for consultation which they needed. This might seem cruel, but in the long run it would mean more and better services. They were dying on the vine.

In planning his approach to gaining control of outpatient services, Dr. Keuning consulted with the regional NIMH staff. They were unhappy with the split in services and expressed the view that it was probably a mistake to have funded the program in the manner that it had been presented. In addition to not providing for continuity, the program was seen as not providing the "essential five" because of problems in providing emergency care and a questionable consultation and education program. "Yet the building was going up."

The NIMH staff agreed to the idea, supposedly presented to them by Dr. Keuning, that it would be useful and appropriate to have the positions budgeted by the county board under center control. They also agreed to apply pressure for greater coordination and continuity and suggested that it would be useful to initiate regular meetings with the county board to discuss integration of services.

According to Dr. Keuning, somewhat about this time he was told that the hospital was losing "a hundred to a hundred and fifty thousand dollars a year because the county wouldn't pay for some of the costs." Dr. Keuning proposed to Dr. Leland that they work together to develop a single integrated program. "I'll help you recruit if you help us with money."

In August of 1968 a steering committee was set up to deal with issues raised by the NIMH of integration of services in the catchment area. Charity was represented by Drs. Keuning, Walton, Steen, and the associate director of Charity Hospital, while the county board was represented by Drs. Leland and Gilbert and the financial officer of the county board. One of the early topics of discussion was recruitment and manpower. Joint recruitment was agreed upon, and Dr. Keuning concurred that persons recruited for the Lincoln or Inland programs could be given appointments at the university.

At the second meeting Dr. Walton proposed that an integrating plan for Catchment Area I be developed first, before dealing with any single component within such a plan. After some discussion there was general agreement that this would be the most logical way to proceed. It was agreed that the components of such a plan should include:

1. Recruitment of new professional personnel for all elements of Catchment Area I.
2. Continuity of service and of therapist and treatment team whether the services to be rendered were inpatient, partial hospitalization, day care, or outpatient, or where indirect services were called for.
3. The joint utilization of space for interviews, conferences, teaching purposes, waiting room, and lounge space.
4. Joint, or combined, record-keeping so that a patient receiving mental health services from any element in Catchment Area I's community mental health program has one clinical record.
5. Removal of administrative duplication so that a given administrative function is carried out by one person for all elements of service in the catchment area wherever possible.
6. Joint funding of personnel.

Dr. Walton remembers the first meeting about integration as dealing with much bitterness, especially on the part of the head of the Lincoln Clinic, Dr. Gilbert, who felt he had been badly treated by the county board. Dr. Walton felt a need to move the focus to common issues, which was attempted in subsequent meetings. Also, in September there was a change in the administration of the hospital, and Dr. Keuning was given considerably more support by the new administrator, which undoubtedly affected the ultimate outcome of the meetings with the county.

After some negotiations an affiliation agreement was reached with the county board whereby the outpatient and consultation and education programs were brought under Charity's control, although specific personnel continued to be paid by the county board and the board continued to control state funding sources for the center's programs. (See the Integration Agreement, page 83.)

As previously noted, the staff of the Lincoln Mental Health Clinic, the result of the combination in 1961 of the Lincoln Child Guidance Clinic and the Lincoln Mental Health Clinic for adults, had physically moved into the Charity complex in July. By January 1969 the integration was completed, but not without the departure of some disenchanted members of the clinic staff who did not like the change from an outpatient clinic in which they specialized in either child or adult therapy to a "homogenized center" in which they had to provide inpatient and outpatient therapy to both children and adults.

The child guidance clinic personnel were particularly distraught. They were accustomed to a team concept whereby a social worker might interview the family and then make a future testing appointment with a psychologist; following this, an appointment would be made with a psychiatrist. Finally, the "team" would meet to discuss a case, and usually after a considerable time had elapsed, the family would be placed on a waiting list for therapy. Very little involvement with the school on these cases took place. As part of the amalgamation agreement, the team approach was discarded, and the therapist had to take responsibility for a case immediately and other specialists could be brought in only for particular questions. Psychologists on the clinic staff were particularly resistant to this change, and several left the staff. One member of the Charity staff expressed the view that there was probably a desire to have some of the Lincoln personnel who joined the staff with the merger not stay on. No efforts seem to have been made to incorporate them into the Center, and as noted, a number did resign.

A Change in Hospital Administration

A major staffing change at the hospital in September 1968 had a significant effect on the center. Sister Helen was replaced as administrator of the hospital by Sister Catherine who was characterized as "highly independent," a "hard driving administrator," "earthy." Within a few months the associate administrator and the two assistant administrators had left, and a new associate administrator, Mr. Lees, was hired.

Some observers assume that, given the difficulties with the private psychiatrists and the county board, Dr. Keuning would have been discharged if there had not been a change in the hospital administration. The state of the relationship between Dr. Keuning and the local practitioners is best symbolized by the fact that, supposedly at the urging of some of the local psychiatrists, he was denied membership in the County Medical Society in late 1968.

From the start, Sister Catherine took the point of view that the community mental health center was an integral department of the hospital with an operating organization that was "compatible with the changing views in this country toward mental health." This point of view was in sharp contrast to that of some of the private psychiatrists who apparently viewed the community mental health center largely as a shell for receiving federal monies and for administering the inpatient unit in its "status quo" method of operations.

Sister Catherine had the mental health center "unit" report directly to her rather than to an assistant administrator, and she had all the functional specialists (i.e., nurses, social workers, and psychiatric technicians) serving in the unit made responsible to the Center Director rather than to the hospital's Directors of Nursing and Social Work. While these changes were strictly administrative in nature, some physicians claimed that many employees in the unit who had been cooperative became uncooperative because their reward system was now related to the mental health center rather than to the hospital. Dr. Walton, however, saw no significant change, and Sister Catherine noted the following explanation for the changes:

> Initially we needed flexibility; therefore, it is organized differently. I have delegated a lot of responsibility to the center staff. Eventually, though, we will have an assistant administrator in the hospital for mental health. The new prenatal intensive-care program will also report to me directly at first, but eventually it will be transferred to nursing.

In defense of her own support of Dr. Keuning's program for the center, Sister Catherine listed in mid-1969 several examples of previous misuse of the hospital by private psychiatrists. These are in good part a list of the focal points of controversies that had taken place with the private psychiatrists since her arrival.

> Frequently the fifth floor was occupied by a large number of relatively routine patients who had been hospitalized primarily for the convenience of the psychiatrist. It was not unusual to have up to a two-week waiting list for beds on the fifth floor even though a number of the routine patients could theoretically have been discharged at any time.
>
> Psychiatrists all too often were in the habit of calling to admit patients at the end of the day when it was inconvenient to process and make arrangements for new patients. At the same time the doctors frequently did not visit the patients until the next day or sometimes two or three days later.
>
> One of the private psychiatrists accounted for a large number of the patients, perhaps two to three hundred in a given year, and at one point his patients accounted for outstanding receivables to the hospital in excess of $175,000. (It is estimated that in 1968 the average charge for one day on the psychiatric ward was $45.)
>
> The average stay of a patient of a private psychiatrist was 20 days, and one patient had been on the ward for an entire year. (The average stay in mid-1969 had been reduced to 12 to 15 days. Table 2 shows inpatient statistics for the period July 1968 to June 1969).
>
> Treatment being given patients on the psychiatric ward was frequently nothing more than "glorified babysitting." This resulted from the lack of therapeutic programs and the relatively infrequent visits by the psychiatrists. Virtually all treatment consisted of shock and chemotherapy.

TABLE 2
CCMHC Inpatient Statistics
July 1-December 31, 1968 and January 1-June 30, 1969

	1968							1969					
	Admissions		*Total patient days*		*Average length of stay*			*Admissions*		*Total patient days*		*Average length of stay*	
Month	*CMH*	*Private*	*CMH*	*Private*	*CMH*	*Private*	*Month*	*CMH*	*Private*	*CMH*	*Private*	*CMH*	*Private*
July	3	55	40	857	13.33	15.58	Jan.	20	52	424	924	21.20	17.7
Aug.	18	67	348	977	19.33	14.58	Feb.	28	38	439	698	15.67	18.3
Sept.	26	51	281	1052	10.80	20.62	March	37	40	419	505	11.32	12.6
Oct.	13	57	230	908	17.69	15.92	April	37	41	607	592	16.40	14.4
Nov.	21	62	229	896	10.90	14.45	May	28	21	272	348	9.71	16.5
Dec.	18	52	231	1024	12.83	19.69	June	38	18	343	114	9.02	6.3
Total	99	344	1359	5714	13.72	16.61	Total	188	210	2504	3181	13.31	15.1

Note—Average length of stay for each month is computed by averaging the lengths of stay for all patients admitted during that month regardless of whether or not they were discharged during the month in question or in some succeeding month. Average loss of stay for period is computed by averaging the lengths of stay for all patients admitted during that period regardless of whether or not they were discharged during that period or some succeeding period.

> The psychiatrists failed to set definite policies on such things as the use of electroshock. In contrast, for example, the coronary unit of the hospital had a complete list of dos and don'ts for special coronary treatment plans, but the psychiatrists were unable or unwilling to devote the time to establishing standard procedures.

Relationship with Private Psychiatrists

Shortly after taking up residence in Lincoln in early 1968, Dr. Keuning invited the private-practice psychiatrists in the area to join him in putting a meaningful program together through service on a planning committee or through individual assumption of various tasks. Each excused himself, however, by suggesting he had "no time." According to Center staff, the psychiatrists continued to envisage the hospital psychiatric staff, now being paid from federal funds, as "residents" to take care of their patients on their order only. At the same time the county board failed to show much interest in Dr. Keuning's program, which they conceived of as administering the hospital-based services. Instead, the board directed its efforts toward the center in South Lincoln and its other programs.

Dr. Walton summarized the issues with the private psychiatrists rather succinctly.

> In the first six months there were no major problems with the private psychiatrists except for the EST issue. Dr. Keuning had called Dr. Lewis, a private psychiatrist who was chairman of the hospital's department of psychiatry, in a few times and "given him hell," but that was about it. Then we changed the role of the social worker and had them stop taking family histories—which a few of the MDs wanted. We told them that the social workers would do this on "consultation," but this was not their usual or only function. This was followed by the emergency-room problem and the admission issue. The final blow was the utilization review letter.

EST Conflict

An early schism between the private MDs and the staff developed around shock therapy. ESTs were being scheduled at any time of the day or night. Sister Elizabeth, the head psychiatric nurse, felt this was bad for both the patients and for administration of the ward, and she set up a schedule limiting the times available for EST. Some of the psychiatrists objected, particularly one who treated primarily outpatients but used inpatient beds for a couple of hours after the treatment even though the beds were also assigned to inpatients. This was usually around dinner time. The nurse and the physician disagreed as to what are nursing decisions and what are medical decisions.

The split was further deepened by the psychiatric technicians' questioning of one physician's treatment that they felt was unethical. When the staff started asking "why," the doctor became verbally abusive of the staff. Supported by Dr. Keuning, many of the staff then refused to assist the doctor in his treatment, and it became necessary to hire special staff to be on hand, further complicating the scheduling issue.

A special investigating committee of the State Medical Society was established to study the treatment from a medical point of view after the psychiatrist brought charges against the Center. According to Dr. Keuning, the report on the EST investigation "did not in any way censure the Center, and it implied that 'elements' of the treatment practice were acceptable though it never dealt with the totality." Whereas some 50% of the inpatients in 1968 received some shock treatment, less than 1% did in mid-1969, although some outpatients continued to receive such treatment, largely from the one physician noted earlier.

Dr. Keuning's position on the staff resistance was that he would back any member of the staff who refused to participate ("tactfully") in a method that he or she did not believe in or feel was right. However, he would not back anyone who did the following:

1. Criticized the doctor to a patient.
2. Told the patient that the doctor was using the wrong treatment method.
3. Tried to persuade the patient to transfer from a private psychiatrist to the Center.

Also, the minutes of a staff meeting in November 1968 included the following:

> Dr. Keuning emphasized that it is important for our staff to behave ethically and responsibly toward all the private psychiatrists and their patients. We must also realize that they have practiced in this community for over 15 years in a specific way, and we cannot expect them to always agree with us. It is our responsibility to protect their right to private practice while demonstrating to them the advantages of the newer uses of the health care team, which is an approach that is being developed in many places in the country at this time. He pointed out that the staff must be patient; that in three or four years the problem will be solved through evolution. Hasty and ill-thought-out angry behavior at this time will only hurt patients and not advance our program.

In the view of some of the Center staff, on the other hand, the private psychiatrists were being unnecessarily abused by a few members of the staff.

Other Conflicts: Emergency Admissions, Student Training, Role of Nonphysicians

Another area of conflict between the private psychiatrists and the hospital and Center focused on emergency admission procedures; a problem was said to exist because of many evening emergency admissions. Prior to 1969 the physician called the supervising nurse on the psychiatric unit, who was responsible to the hospital nursing director, and a patient was admitted unless there were no beds available.

Since January 1969 the physician has had to go through the psychiatric nursing head, who is responsible to the Center's Medical Director instead of the hospital nursing supervisor, and she has had the authority to challenge admissions. Furthermore, every emergency admission must now be seen within 12 hours by the physician, and he must write an explanation of the emergency. While some of the Center's staff have said that it is hard to define administrative and medical policy in psychiatry, Charity has taken the firm stand that admissions belong under administrative policy.

Another flare-up occurred when one of the private psychiatrists refused to allow Dr. Steen to interview his patients in front of students for teaching purposes. Dr. Keuning became quite upset with this "interference," and after some period of struggle through the hospital administration the private physician gave his approval.

Another problem area revolved around the interrelated issues of the therapeutic role of the nonphysician therapy staff, the ability of these therapists to write orders and make notations in the patients records, and the involvement of private patients in the programs of the psychiatric unit such as group therapy. What evolved was that patients would be involved in all program activities unless the physician specifically ordered otherwise.

Emergency Room

One of the more important conflicts arose over the provision of emergency care. Initially, the Center's night time emergency service was a part of the hospital's emergency room, which is run on a contract basis by three private physicians. Daytime emergency coverage for psychiatric walk-in cases was provided by a rotation schedule of CCMHC therapists at the center. In mid-1968, however, the center began to have staff members on call for emergency-room cases so that a trained mental health professional could immediately be involved in psychiatric emergencies. "Being on call meant being available." Nevertheless, this involved calling the therapist at home and apparently did not completely satisfy the NIMH's definition of 24-hour emergency service.

Later, Drs. Keuning and Walton exploited a site visit by claiming that the NIMH was "raising hell" over the emergency service. Psychiatric cases coming into the hospital's emergency room were generally referred to a private psychiatrist for care, and these cases represented a major source of new patients for them. Frequently, these emergency patients were admitted to the psychiatric unit as a patient of one of the psychiatrists without having been seen by the psychiatrist.

"We felt the need to run the emergency service," noted Dr. Walton.

> We were getting those without insurance, and the private psychiatrists were getting those with insurance. Our staff were on call, and they resented taking night calls without pay, but yet we insisted that they see patients.

In addition to the reluctance of some of the private psychiatrists toward the Center's operating the emergency service, the chief of the emergency room also opposed their involvement. The meetings held to attempt to work out a solution to this problem were said to be characterized by open hostility. Dr. Walton indicated:

> Our first wish was to work out of the emergency room, and they agreed because they thought we would get the patients upstairs faster. When our people began taking an hour or two to talk with a patient, things got all clogged up, and it became obvious that it wouldn't work, and we decided that we needed our own emergency room.

After much discussion and disagreement both within the Center and with the hospital over pay, experience requirements, coverage, and funding sources, the Center began in January, 1969, to station a therapist in the Center facility throughout the night and on weekends to receive phone calls and treat walk-in cases. The therapists were selected from among social workers and psychiatrists who volunteered for duty. They were paid $75 for this 12-hour duty; the charge to patients was $25. If a patient goes to the hospital emergency room, the therapist is called and the patient is brought to the Center building either by the therapist or a hospital guard. Signs at the hospital emergency entrance and at the Center's doors also indicate that someone is on duty. From January through June, 1969, the emergency service saw 513 persons; of these, 195 were admitted to the inpatient unit, 184 were referred to the Center's outpatient program, and 28 were referred to private physicians. There were 1,075 telephone calls.

Utilization Review Letter

The final factor in alienating the private psychiatrists from the program was Sister Catherine's sending each one a letter in mid-1969 notifying them that after a patient had been on the inpatient service for 21 days the necessity for further hospitalization would be reviewed by Dr. Walton. It seems that Sister Catherine and Dr. Walton had discussed the problem of long stays, with the former concerned because of the effect of prolonged stays on uncollectable bills and financial factors and Dr. Walton concerned with quality of the program on the unit. According to Dr. Walton, he was not aware that letters were actually sent to the physicians until after the fact. A few of the psychiatrists with whom the Center had not previously had major disagreements took offense at the idea that their judgment in handling patients was to be reviewed.

At a meeting of the executive committee of the medical staff, at a time when things were "pretty quiet," Dr. Lewis got up to give a report for the Department of Psychiatry and announced a "death." Dr. Walton says that he was stunned and told himself, "Oh hell, there has been a death on the unit, and I don't even know about it—here's where I really get it." Then Dr. Lewis went on to talk about the death of private psychiatry at Charity Hospital. The next night at the quarterly medical staff meeting, which is attended by 100 to 125 physicians, one of the psychiatrists called on his colleagues to save his practice. "All of the issues—the place of private psychiatry, the involvement of the federal government, and the role of the Medical School were aired," according to Dr. Walton. This apparently had been precipitated by Sister Catherine's letter to the psychiatrists about reviewing their cases after a 21-day stay.

In talking about these issues in mid-1969, one psychiatrist exhibited his anger by noting he would not be involved with the hospital any longer:

> The center has taken over the services. My concept of the Center was just one person to coordinate existing services in order to get federal grants, particularly for the building. But this thing came out very different from what we anticipated. I don't know what's going on, but I don't think that there is a compatible mix of policy, patients, or staff. Keuning didn't have too much experience in community mental health, either. The center has displaced what private practice was doing in this area and created something new. Obviously, we put too much faith in the hospital administration.

In the same discussion this psychiatrist initially dismissed the thought that there was any attempt on the part of the private psychiatrists to put financial pressure on the hospital by not admitting their patients, although at the time there were only three patients on the ward who had been admitted by the private doctors and one psychiatrist had resigned from the hospital staff. In addition, some of the psychiatrists were rumored to be seeking financial support to start their own private psychiatric hospital. He stated:

> I refer patients to the Center who can't afford care or who are long-term problems. I guess I just have a lower volume of patients now, less desire to admit, and they don't stay as long. We were misled, too. We were told the law says that every patient must be told they do not have to have a private physician. We now know this is not so. They have to be told they have a right to have a physician. But the ratio of Center patients to those we see now must be 100 to 1.

The issue referred to—of the right to a private physician—was related to the emergency-room conflict. What should patients who arrive at the emergency room be told about the available sources of care? Appendix B reproduces the actual statement shown to patients in the center's emergency facility. The minutes of the December 27, 1968, center staff meeting say, "When patients arrive in the emergency service, they should be asked if they have a private doctor or if they want a private psychiatrist."

Reflections

Dr. Keuning feels that had it not been for the fight he had to carry on with the county he could have "saved" some of the private psychiatrists:

> We couldn't do anything with X who, because of his political stand, saw the program as socialized medicine. With Y we had a problem of his own stability and his approaches to therapy. Of course we had real problems with Z. The inpatient unit had been his—every emergency was admitted in his name. Why, he had so many patients he didn't even care if some couldn't pay. Every physician in town knew that if you had a hot psycho on your hands, he would take it over. He was the emergency service in town, and we were directly undermining his practice and couldn't deal with him. Had there been time to spend with them—say to go to their offices and play to them—we could have handled a few. We told them to join us—be on committees—but they wouldn't. I started breakfast meetings, but they didn't show. We let them know that if they didn't join with us, we would starve them out. The odds were overbearing; they couldn't win. They knew that the day of the private psychiatrist was ended. They tried to fight back through attempts to have me censured and through the investigation about EST. But the private psychiatrists were not the big problem—the problems were the hospital and county board. If it had not been for these problems, I would have had time to deal with the physicians to win our battle with the county. But I was willing to make trade-offs to win the key battles.

Somewhat in contrast to Dr. Keuning's overview, Dr. Walton feels that the decisions made were not evaluated in terms of trade-offs. "The thrusts on the various problems which were seen as affecting our ability to establish a meaningful program and training center were not systematic."

With regard to the differences of opinion between the private psychiatrists and the CCMHC staff regarding such things as treatment and staff roles, and the threatened decreases in patient admissions by private psychiatrists, Sister Catherine noted:

> We (the hospital) still retain the right to determine what kinds of services and facilities will be offered. Anyway, if

> the mental health program is taking patients away, where are they? Our census is down to 60 percent, and the number of patients sent from this county to the state hospital has declined nearly 50 percent in 2 years. Is it possible we're handling them in some new areas—outpatient, for example, and preventing admissions?

Reflecting on the conflict surrounding the mental health program, Sister Catherine lists several reasons for the particular difficulties with psychiatrists. First, the psychiatrists do not like the fact that she has delegated so much authority to the CCMHC physician. Second, psychiatrists, because they are psychiatrists,

> can't sit down and air it out. They are too cagey with each other. Attempts to get the psychiatrists to discuss what they want have failed. A committee was set up, but they didn't respond.

Third, the psychiatrists tend to view the CCMHC as separate from the hospital. But it is not. It is the CCMHC. Fourth, too much was "coated over" in the original planning as to what was involved. This still should be a joint effort with the private psychiatrists.

Sister Catherine noted wryly:

> Now they are trying to strangle us financially. But if the census stays where it is, we'll develop an adolescent unit with the excess capacity. I like to view this like a stained-glass window where you get the total structure first and then pull out the individual pieces and develop them, rather than trying to take fully developed pieces and then fit them together. I'm also a politician, and I wouldn't hesitate to go to the legislature for help if necessary. It's not for us or for the building. It's for the patients.

APPENDIX A
INTEGRATION AGREEMENT

Integration of the Lincoln Mental Health Clinic Inland County Community Mental Health Services Board with the Charity Mental Health Center

1. The Charity Mental Health Center and the Lincoln Mental Health Clinic will function as one professional and administrative organization, with no distinction regarding staff in areas of inpatient, partial hospitalization, outpatient, emergency room, and all other services performed at the Center.

2. Advisory Steering Committee[4] will be established consisting of the following members:

The Director, Associate Director, and Chief of Education and Training of the Charity Center;

The Administrator and Finance Officer of Charity Hospital;

The Director, Finance Officer, and two members of the Inland County Community Mental Health Services Board;

The Director of the Regional Consultation Center.[5]

It will serve as a recommending body to the parent organization on policies and procedure within the mental health center.

For example, it will make recommendations to the Personnel Committee of the Inland County Mental Health Board regarding personnel policies and the hiring and discharging of personnel employed by the Inland County Mental Health Board, after initial screening by the appropriate departmental chief.

It will make recommendations to the Inland County Mental Health Board regarding administrative or financial problems that are related to the integration of services.

A committee will be formed to review salary parity, including fringe benefits, to avoid unequal compensation for similar job positions. Membership of the committee would be the finance officers of the two parties, plus the chief of each of the professional areas, when their area is being reviewed. The recommendations of this committee would be forwarded to the Personnel Department of Charity Hospital.

3. The financial responsibility will remain the same as present; that is, inpatient finances will be the responsibility of Charity Hospital, and outpatient finances will be the responsibility of the Inland County Mental Health Board.

4. There will be one telephone number and one front door for the Comprehensive Mental Health Center.

5. A review of this Agreement will take place one year after its effective date.

APPENDIX B

Statement to be made to patients who are to be admitted to inpatient service and who do not have a private physician or psychiatrist:

YOU HAVE A CHOICE BETWEEN HAVING A PRIVATE PSYCHIATRIST OR BEING A PATIENT OF THE MENTAL HEALTH CENTER WITHOUT A PRIVATE DOCTOR. FEES WILL BE CHARGED IN EITHER CASE. IF YOU WISH TO HAVE A PRIVATE PSYCHIATRIST, WE WILL TRY TO CONTACT ONE FOR YOU. IF YOU WISH TO BE A PATIENT OF THE COMMUNITY MENTAL HEALTH CENTER, YOU WILL BE TREATED BY A MENTAL HEALTH PROFESSIONAL. A PSYCHIATRIST WILL BE INVOLVED IN YOUR TREATMENT. YOUR PRIMARY THERAPIST WILL BE A MEMBER OF ANY ONE OF THE MENTAL HEALTH PROFESSIONS. IN ANY CASE, WHETHER YOU CHOOSE TO BE A MENTAL HEALTH CENTER PATIENT OR A PRIVATE PATIENT, YOUR THERAPIST CAN ARRANGE FOR YOUR PARTICIPATION IN ANY OF THE TREATMENT PROGRAMS IN THE CENTER. THE MENTAL HEALTH PROFESSIONALS INCLUDE PSYCHIATRIC SOCIAL WORKERS, PSYCHIATRIC NURSES, PSYCHOLOGISTS OR PSYCHIATRISTS.

CHARITY COMMUNITY MENTAL HEALTH CENTER (CCMHC)

TEACHING NOTE FOR:

STRATEGIES FOR ORGANIZATIONAL CHANGE (SECOND SEMESTER)

Case Summary: historical account of administrative action and reaction over several years.

—establishment of new community mental health program.
—funded under federal and state legislation.
—originated within existing and traditional delivery programs that had previously functioned autonomously.
—integrated, collaborative program developed.
—implications not fully foreseen by participants although intended by the legislation.
—administrative and personal style of program head viewed as a force for change and source of some dissension.
—growing realization of meaning of the federal legislation hitherto perceived as a funding mechanism.

Problem Perceived: Controversial style and actions of Dr. Keuning in establishing CCMHC. What should he do now? What might he have done differently?

Elements of Systems involved initially and in early change:

1. *Legislation*—community mental health act requiring specified programs in specified geographic catchment areas for funding; construction support legislation.

2. *The Boards*—Charity Hospital Board of Direc-

tors and County Community Mental Health Services Board, each controlling some of the services involved (county also ran Lincoln Clinic and Inland County CMHC), requiring collaboration in order to get funding.

Stage 1 Initial Stage

3. *Service Facilities*—Charity Hospital: inpatient, emergency, day care. County: outpatient, consultation, education, contiguous area served by ICCMHC, headed by Dr. Leland.

4. *Individuals*
   a. Nine private psychiatrists controlled care at hospital.
   b. Administrator of hospital delegated control to subordinates; in particular to an assistant administrator.

Stage 2 Early Change

5. *University*— over hospital for training; new CCMHC director also to have faculty position (and departmental chairmanship) and later shift to that job full-time (controversial with other faculty). New psychologist added with joint appointment as Director of Training.

6. *Hospital*—seen as providing bureaucratic resistance.

7. *County Board*—early offense at Keuning's critical remarks. Influential Leland wanted (apparently) faculty position to run both ICCMHC and CCHMC; denied both.

8. *Dr. Keuning*—early strategy to obtain power/autonomy (control over money and manpower) to make program function by focusing on services that would diminish county board efforts. (e.g., outpatient). This threatened private psychiatrists directly;

they reacted by pulling back. Used university affiliation to attract manpower; ICCMHC and County had recruiting problems. Strategy of denial of help to force other groups to come in on his terms. Used NIMH requirements as backup to force integration of services.

Stage 3 Later Changes

9. *New Steering Committee*—three from CCMHC, one from Charity, Leland, head of Lincoln Clinic and county board man. Keuning gives other clinic personnel university affiliation to aid in manpower recruitment. Subsequent new administrator at Charity supports Keuning, who gains administrative control of county's part of the program, although they still control the money.

10. *Services*—new operating philosophy and practices now put into effect, beginning change in treatments orientation and utilization. Produces resistance/dismay and departure of some affected program professionals. Private psychiatrists also affected by philosophy *and* availability of facilities, some of which conflicted with their practices.

11. *Change in hospital administration*—Sister Catherine has vigorous style, philosophy comparable with Keuning's. Changes psychiatric unit's organizational reporting (direct to her). Supports Keuning with utilization review.

Teaching Issues

—Role of federal legislation, through funding, as catalyst for program change.

—Organizational change and resistance; styles and strategies for implementation.

—Systems in interrelation.

Questions

1. Given Keuning's position as new director, what did he want to achieve?

2. What did Keuning actually do in pursuit of his objective?

3. What was the effect of his actions?
4. What data did Keuning use to determine his priorities?
5. How did (specific) other people *feel* about what he did and how he did it?

Developing a Teaching Strategy

The *teaching note* presented here covers four essential aspects of the case:

—Salient facts of the case that need to be brought out.
—Major case problems and issues, particularly those to be emphasized as teaching issues.
—Possible analytic approaches.
—Since the teaching of management focuses on decision-making, action alternatives that can be derived from the analysis.

There is another factor that is not directly addressed by the note but that is vital to its effective use: that is, the educational and pedagogic context in which the case is to be used. The critical backdrop to any teaching note is the overall program of which the case is a part and its place is that program. It is within this framework that the teaching note *for a specific use of a specific case* is developed.

The above note was written for the CCMHC case as it would be used within a full-semester course on strategies for organizational change. This note—as well as all others for this course—presented basic case facts roughly laid out in a systems frame.

The teaching issues raised in this note are by no means the only ones around which a discussion of the CCMHC case can be organized. They reflect the overall structure of the course. We have omitted from this teaching note the handwritten comments around this section referring specifically to previous cases and class discussions, as well as a reference to a case that will follow this one.

An *instructor's note* for CCMHC prepared by Dr. Roy Penchansky at the University of Michigan School of

Public Health identifies many more "theme(s) or framework(s) around which the discussion can be organized." A few of these are:

—Was the function of the Center properly defined, given the professional resources, attitudes, and other constraints and the community needs, resources, attitudes, and other constraints?

—Was it necessary to fight the battles to develop a "meaningful" program?

—Can a "meaningful" program be developed when the Center is tied to a hospital and/or university, or has as a primary function teaching?

The leading questions listed at the end of the note are simply suggestions for lines of questioning that may be useful during the classroom discussion. Some instructors assign questions of this type with the cases to help focus the students' preparation along desired paths.

A question missing from the list is the classic "What should Mr. So and So do?" This is frequently used in case discussions in which a particular objective is the development of an administrative program of action.

The teaching note displays in abbreviated form the confluence of the course's educational objectives and the contribution expected from the particular case. It is a truism that each time an instructor teaches a case, his students add to his knowledge and understanding of it. Thus, the teaching note is also a continuing record of the strengths and weaknesses of the case, central and side issues involved, and fruitful lines of questioning.

FOOTNOTES

[3] The Committee met regularly every two weeks.

[4] A state agency service aftercare patients from several surrounding counties following their discharge from State Hospitals. The Regional Consultation Center rents space in the Charity CMHC building, and negotiations for some form of integration are being pursued.

4. CLASSROOM DYNAMICS: THE HEART OF THE CASE METHOD

In a lecture or seminar presentation, the dynamics of the classroom situation are important but not necessarily critical from minute to minute. They *are* critical and obvious in the case discussion. The student's preparation, which may have included discussion with his colleagues, may be productive by itself, but it remains the teacher's responsibility to ensure that the essential learning occurs during the classroom discussion. The teacher must therefore continuously and consciously juggle process and content.

We will discuss elements of classroom dynamics—preparation for teaching, the teacher's role in the classroom, techniques and style—and then show some of the results with an abbreviated transcript of a classroom discussion of the CCMHC case.

PREPARATION FOR TEACHING

Development of a teaching note is only a part of the case teacher's preparation. And we are assuming that the development of the course objectives and structure have preceded the selection of a specific case. Preparation for a case class, then, involves becoming thoroughly familiar with the facts of the case and the relationships of this case to the overall course objectives. As Professor Robert W. Merry (1954, pp. 134-135) has said:

> The first step in the instructor's preparation of a case is to master the facts. The instructor needs to go over the printed case again and again, making outlines, marginal notes, and written summaries of essential details. If there are figures in the case, he will make many calculations, not only the ones which he himself believes to be correct but also others, which he anticipates that the students may put forward as appropriate and significant. He will scrutinize the apparent issues to make sure that they are the real ones. And if there are important subordinate issues, he will recognize that some questions probably will have to be settled before others. . . . The instructor also needs to view the case itself as a whole, assessing it in terms of the principal areas for exploration and discussion, considering the relation of one to another, and devising key questions to lead into each of them. He may wish to give considerable care to the wording of these questions. By foreseeing the various avenues of connection the instructor can be better prepared to effect transitions from one issue to another, as well as to guide the class into the critical areas for discussion.

Beyond a substantial understanding of the overall educational objectives and of the case at hand, the teacher should also consider his students. Who are they? Young and inexperienced students, practicing professionals, experts on special problems, administrators? What are they like as a group? From roughly similar backgrounds, from a variety of professions, generally comparable skills and experience, wide-ranging variety of skills and experience? Have they ever worked together before? Will they have to again? Are they here by choice, or have they been sent to this course?

Obviously, the longer a case teacher works with a class, the better he comes to know that class. Still, even if the teacher will only meet with the class once, he will find that his classroom work is enhanced by explicit consideration of the students who will work with him.

The apparent "nondirectiveness" of case teaching is but a facade. One of the better "nondirective" teachers we know can write out in advance a schedule of his classes' behavior by five-minute intervals with remarkable accuracy. His predictive capability depends on more than immediate control. He knows his students, their group behavior, their norms, and their biases. He knows the topics with which they are comfortable, their technical skills, cues that he has placed yesterday and the day before. He knows what he wants them to learn and how he wants them to learn it. And he knows how each case fits within the course structure and why it has been placed there. In short, he is always thoroughly prepared.

THE TEACHER'S ROLE IN THE CLASSROOM

Learning to teach by the case method is not unlike learning to ski. At first you observe experienced case teachers, but once in the classroom, all thought of their skills dissipates in the anxiety of facing a class. The neophyte teacher's first priority will be getting the case discussed more or less extensively and systematically. He will be primarily concerned with his own survival and with the development of some respect and liking for him on the part of the class. His emphasis during preparation will be on a complete and thorough understanding of the case.

So it is with skiing: You look at the expert but are more concerned with remaining upright for as much of the time as possible. At some point you discover that you can indeed stand and perform simple actions and that these are no longer conscious efforts. As these become reflexes, you can begin to pay attention to nuances and—more importantly—begin to examine the underlying processes and purposes, much like enjoyment of the rhythm and flow of the downhill swoop. At this stage the new case teacher begins to look at what the case really illustrates and how pursuing specific points within it in discussion will lead to examination of the underlying and more generalizable issues.

However democratic his ideals, the instructor always suggests authority in the classroom. His authority resides in his role as teacher and evaluater, and as an expert in his subject. Teachers obviously differ in the emphasis they choose to place on their authority and the degree to which they are prepared to exert control. Some will demand prompt attendance, will use a call list from which students are requested to initiate the case discussion or respond to it, and will be explicit about the behavior they expect. Others will pay little or no attention to such issues.

Obviously, some balance is desirable. With no guidance as to structure, a formless discussion ensues with little learning. With too much structure, the students merely play the game of outguessing what the instructor wishes. In either instance, learning suffers.

The more *ad hoc* the group being taught, the freer the teacher is to play down his own authority and expertise. With in-service programs and special professional groups, he may in fact *not* be an expert in many areas in which the class members are strongest. Where there is group experience and expertise, the teacher still exerts strong influence in his role as intellectual traffic cop, questioner of logic, and prober of underlying assumptions. In nondegree courses the instructor is generally free of the task of grading; more often than not, therefore, he can act as a catalyst for intellectual risk-taking and open interaction.

In a way the case teacher's role is that of fellow student: He listens and understands and clarifies, but seldom criticizes, for his behavior sets the norms by which the class engages in discussion. His relationship with the students, therefore, is extremely important. Experience has shown that this relationship is best kept relaxed and fairly informal. Essentially, the teacher is concerned with the *value* of the talk that takes place, with broadening judgment and influencing behavior. The teacher must exert some control but still not prevent discovery. If he is successful, there will be productive discourses. If unsuccessful, there will be collective monologue, gaming, irrelevancy, boredom, timidity, and introspection.

The teacher's job is to help, or even to force, the student

to learn to form his own opinions based on a critical and thorough examination of the facts. In this resides a fundamental ambiguity of the case method.

STUDENT ROLES

The student, like the teacher, may play a number of roles and functions in the class discussion. While any student may play a variety of roles, there is a tendency for roles to become crystallized and for the class to set certain individuals into specific roles.

One student may venture the same type of comment about each case that comes up. Obviously, you would like to see this change if the student is to develop in his thinking. Sometimes it is necessary to suggest to such a student that he change his point of view. At other times the teacher may encourage those whose views are predictable to remain silent for a while. By exercising the choice of whom to call on next, the instructor has considerable latitude in the sequencing of predictable viewpoints. He also may ask a student to play the role that he would not normally accept, such as labor leader, patient, nurse, priest, etc.

Students tend to become specialized in the performance of functions for the progress of the classroom discussion. For example:

1. The presentation of facts.
2. The criticism of the facts interpreted by others.
3. The presentation of a framework for analysis and setting case facts into it.
4. The integration of the material presented in the class.
5. The interpretation of the process taking place in the class.
6. The summary of the results of the preceding functions.

Students are more likely to perform the first functions than the latter ones, but again the instructor wants to get a student to do all of these most of the time for himself, if not for the class.

In most classes there is a mixture of experienced and inexperienced students. The experienced student with a strong background in the current topic can be both a resource and a potential irritant. His personal experiences may be useful in illustrating some issues and supplementing technical data in the case, but if he capitalizes on his resources to exert external authority and dominate the discussion, the class often suffers. The instructor must strike a balance between using such a student as a constructive source of information and allowing him to dominate the class.

TECHNIQUES

The teacher has a variety of techniques at his disposal: He can ask questions, restate what has been said, voice his own opinion or knowledge of fact. The case teacher may also encourage his students to use these basic techniques.

Questions are generally aimed at clarification or improved understanding; for an effective case discussion, questions should not be framed as comparisons with the instructor's own prejudices. He may say, "Do you mean that . . .", or "Do you have more to say about that?" Or he may extend a specific statement to its generalizable possibilities. The teacher can then question whether generalization applies to the specific case instance or has broader connotations.

Summarizing and clarifying can be used to provide clues to other students about contributions they can make and to advance the discussion. Asking a student to adopt the role of summarizer is sometimes useful, particularly for that student. For the benefit of the rest of the class, however, it is wise to ask a student at the start of the discussion to provide a summary at the end.

Besides a verbal summary by the teacher or a student, there is the alternative of so ordering the notes on the blackboard that a summary is produced at the end of the discussion. Use of the blackboard would probably be more correctly classified under "style," but there are a few tricks of the trade. Some instructors use the board as an immediate reward system: If the student's remarks are considered worthwhile, some notation goes on the board, which provides a student with rapid feedback. When the instructor feels that the student's comments are repetitious, ill-considered, etc. the teacher says nothing and does nothing. All but the most persistent student will stop and let another student continue the discussion. Or if the student or one of his colleagues believes that the teacher is missing an important point, he can rephrase his comments or ask directly why his comments are not being recorded.

Another handy device is setting up one segment of the board with the heading "If I were there, I'd ask . . ." Cases often do not include pieces of information that a student feels are important; some of this information would be readily available to a person on the scene. When the teacher uses this device, he usually insists that the student consider what difference the answer to that question would make to his analysis and his subsequent decision.

One problem for the instructor is how to deal with that large minority of the class who prefer to remain silent. There are no clear-cut rules. An instructor generally chooses to work toward a climate in which criticism and hostility is played down, making it possible for the more timid students to feel free to join in. He may do this by his own behavior, in which he avoids direct criticism, by cutting off inept comments, or by confronting the students' own predilection for this behavior. A popular technique is to call on the quieter students to begin the case discussion with a presentation of facts in a systematic order. If a student is silent but involved in the classroom process, his facial expressions will mirror this, and the aware teacher may select such clues as a time to call on him. The student who is keyed to respond but does not have his hand up often contributes much more than one who has been semaphoring for five minutes.

The techniques for inducing the quiet student to participate, however, often encourage the talkative ones to monopolize the floor and defeat the initial purpose. Here case teachers have generally taken a position that sanctions imposed on behavior should come first out of the class and out of the instructor only as a last resort. The instructor can certainly make it clear in the abstract that piling up talk is not equivalent to piling up points with him, but he usually tells those who complain about a fellow student to take it into their own hands to silence him.

If there is a problem of lack of preparation on the part of an individual, the teacher does intervene. The norm of hard work and intensive preclass study is one that he does wish to reinforce. This, too, can be handled by having a student open the case discussion and reveal his own ignorance before peer group and authority figure. Further comment is seldom needed from the instructor if the student has to hold forth and obviously is unprepared. In a coordinated program a chronic underachiever may be given this treatment by several instructors within a few days with generally profound impact.

As the class develops skills in case analysis, the instructor can switch his attention to the basic objective of the analysis—commitment to decision-making. The analyses and summaries begin to be judged against their usefulness in supporting action and implementation. If the course is of sufficient length to set norms in these areas of participation, logic, and analysis, the instructor and the students can then "hold each other's feet to the fire" to get a plan of action that the man can live with and carry out with confidence.

STYLE

A teacher's style, like his personality, develops over time. While he will undoubtedly be influenced by others he admires, ultimately he must develop a style congruent with his personality. Therefore, the best case teachers differ widely in style. There are, however, common threads running through such styles.

The best case teachers are genuinely interested in their students as people and for what they have to say. They are interested in results in the classroom and outside it. They are intellectually curious about their subject and communicate their concern for it. While they may value the affection of their students, they do not allow their need for this to control them.

Many students contend that it is important for a teacher to appear not simply as a master of the subject and the facts of the case but as a whole person in the classroom. The case method is a very effective vehicle for this, although teachers will of course differ in the extent to which they are willing and able to share their personal quirks and experiences with their students.

Classes differ, one from another, as much as do teachers. Over time a class will develop its own style as a group—cohesive, warm, and responsive or hostile, disputatious, and competitive. The style that the class develops is a function not only of the particular individuals in it but also their prior experiences and the models that their instructors set for them. This is a particular problem for the case instructor who is teaching a small segment of a course or a program. The case teacher in these circumstances will find it well worthwhile to consider his prospective students' previous experiences with other teachers as part of his own preparation. For instance, an instructor who wants to encourage a full and even argumentative discussion may have an uphill fight if he follows a teacher whose pedagogic approach is highly authoritarian.

This is one of many instances in which the question of directly addressing group-process issues arises. These are ever-present, and it is always possible to pay attention to them. Indeed, some classes may appear to want to spend interminable hours discussing their problems as a group. This may be necessary, but all too often it is a flight from the unpleasant reality of dealing with the subject matter. Most case teachers firmly avoid frequent and extensive process discussions, yet they realize that some attention to the process is essential in all classes.

One useful indicator that such a discussion is warranted is the teacher's awareness of feelings circulating in the class for which he cannot account. Under these circumstances a direct question about what is going on can lead to a productive discussion of the state of mind or of feelings that are impeding the class's learning. Such discussion need not be extensive nor take place during the class meeting; occasionally, a class may prefer to meet longer or for an extra session to discuss processes. Sometimes the discussion will reveal deep feelings about their work, their professional aims, or their concerns with the instructor as a person. Quite often these feelings have to do with the role of the instructor in the classroom as an authority figure, and some discussion of this is often helpful in facilitating the student's development of independent thought and action.

In brief courses with professional groups who have worked together before but to whom the instructor is new, the problem is one of determining whether the activity observed by the instructor is a learning process or the expression of old and constant relationships and anxieties. One way around this is to stop the class and ask whether the discussion represents new ground for the group or is a broken record. However the class responds, the teacher is in a better position to move ahead.

While a class may occasionally erupt with feelings that the teacher finds incomprehensible, he usually is fairly aware of the concerns operating below the surface and keeps in touch with class process through private discussions with other faculty and individual students. He attempts to find out how they are receiving his course objectives and personal style in the classroom. There are dangers to this. He may receive as many varieties of feedback as there are students. It is not unusual that one student is praising the course effusively while another is highly critical of it. Again, there is no easy answer. As with so many other administrative decisions, the first line of defense is a delayed response to the initial feedback. He has to design a respectable sampling process and operate from a confident but flexible view of his strengths and weaknesses.

A CASE CLASS

We have already noted that the case teacher must continuously juggle both process and content. Some of this juggling will be apparent in the abbreviated transcript of a classroom discussion of the CCMHC case that follows.

The class consists of graduate students who are familiar with the case method; they have completed previous courses in organizational behavior and organizational development. Only two brief segments of the two-hour class in organizational change are presented here.

Transcript: Classroom Discussion of CCMHC Course: Strategies for Organizational Change[5]

Professor: Do I have a volunteer to start Charity, or shall I . . . ? Mr. A?

Student A: I'd like to start with a summary of what has happened. I've got an elaborate sort of chart here with groups and dates and events. It would be easier if I put it on the board.

Professor: Do you think we need that?

Student B: I'd like to see it— I'm having trouble figuring out all the maneuvering that's gone on. Mr. C. and I worked out something like that last night; I'd like to compare ours with Mr. A's.

Professor: Yes, but what will we do with it when we've got it?

Student A: Well, I'm trying to trace the relationships between the hospital, the county board, Keuning, the private psychiatrists—all the groups. They changed over time, and I don't think we can understand the current picture without some of that background. And my ideas about what happens next are based on what I think went on there.

Professor: O.K. Why don't you put that on the board, and we'll continue. We'll come back to you when you're ready. Yes, Mr. D?

Student D: We talked about accessibility and quality of care last week, and I think we have to start there. Now I tried to figure out what happened to the patients while all this fancy organizational stuff was going on— it's darn near impossible. The patient is the guy who's missing in this case. That says to me that nobody gives a damn about them; they're all fired up about new departments, unloading a bunch of old-time psychiatrists— The guy who wants some mental help got lost in the shuffle.

Student E: Oh now wait a minute. The place was a mess, and Keuning got in there and cleaned it up.

Professor: What was a mess?

Student E: Here, I'll read it. Keuning said it was ". . . a traditional and low-level inpatient unit manned by a not very impressive group of private clinicians. The day-care program was a very ordinary OT—take them to the zoo-type program. . . . obviously no leadership in the psychiatric service." That sounds like a mess to me.

Student D: Will you tell me what kind of care he's giving now. The patients are just seeing a new kind of disorganization.

Professor: Yes, Mr. B.

Student B: Mr. D may be right. I'm just going over my history of the Center, and the patient just doesn't show up. You start pushing those private psychiatrists around and you know you're pushing their patients around. I could probably argue that the patients were pawns in a power struggle.

Professor: Mr. F, do you agree?

Student F: Yes, but I guess I don't care. What I mean is I think we're seeing an organizational start-up here, and now that it's all over it's time to start worrying about the patients.

Professor: You don't care what happened to the patients during the start-up?

Student F: No, I care. But I'm saying that Keuning couldn't have gotten off the ground if individual patients were his focus. He's trying to build a Center, and now he's got one and can really give a lot of good care to a lot of patients. Now he's got to capitalize on what he's got. Sure he stepped on some toes to get it; it wasn't all that bad.

Professor: Now, Mr. F, we need a little more evidence than that. . . .

Comments. This is an experienced case class; the students are well prepared, and several volunteered to start the discussion. One of the confusing aspects of the case method is apparent within the first five minutes: Several approaches and trains of thought have been produced and are being considered simultaneously. One student is filling the blackboard with an elaborate organizational chronology; another has introduced the issue of quality and accessibility of patient care; another has identified a possible "stage of organizational development"—a concept introduced in a previous class; Student F has jumped ahead with a suggestion as to what Dr. Keuning should do next.

This was a deliberate ploy by the teacher: An objective was to force the class to confront the substantial complexities faced by the people at CCMHC. Calling on Student D was also deliberate: This student has brought up the impact of organizational issues on day-to-day patient care before. He could be counted on to do so here as well.

The discussion that followed had three main thrusts: *(a)* an understanding of what had actually occurred over the previous years (helped substantially by student A's chart); *(b)* an analysis of the Center's organization at "this point in time," including problems, potential problems, and their priorities, and *(c)* the strategies pursued by Keuning with their results. Several students joined Student D in expressions of concern over the impact on patients.

About an hour after the discussion began, the instructor called a five-minute break, then reopened the discussion:

Professor: We've got quite a few issues here; let's sort them out a little. One is obviously the strategy Keuning used in setting up the Center—and Mr. D and Mr. F, you are on opposite sides of the fence in your evaluation of that strategy. Mr. G, you've also raised some questions about the motivations behind Keuning's strategy. Mr. A, Mr. B, Mr. C—your historical summaries are centered on the interactions of the various groups involved, and you've pointed out that the people involved have had to live through all of these maneuverings, so their current views of the situation will be based on their experiences. Many of you are clearly concerned about the impact on day-to-day patient care. Can we now move on to where the Center goes from here—unless we've missed something that we need to consider. . . . Yes, Mr. H.

Student H: The Center has to get rolling. Their funding won't last forever.

Professor: Yes?

Student H: Well their money is from start-up grants on a declining scale. The Center is supposed to become self-sufficient financially.

Professor: That's true. What does that mean in terms of what they do next?

Student H: It means they'd better consolidate their gains. That's not Keuning's kind of work. He'd better leave.

Professor: Mr. J, do you agree?

Student J: I guess so.

Professor: Why?

Student J: The board?

Professor: Mr. C? Perhaps you can help us.

Student C: Yes. Well, Mr. H nailed it—it's time to stop playing games and start running the program. Keuning was great as an entrepreneur, but the Center's now at the point where it really needs an operating manager. Now, he came on with that deal with the Medical School, so he's got an ideal graceful exit all set up. He just turns the Center over to someone else and then goes off to the Medical School and starts crashing heads together over there.

Professor: You all seem to think Keuning should leave the Center, one way or another. Mr. K, you're shaking your head.

Student K: It's nice to talk about his leaving, but realistically I don't see how you can suggest it. There's nothing to suggest he's even considered leaving. Besides, if he doesn't volunteer, just who's going to get him out of there?

Professor: You think any plan of action which involves his leaving the directorship is what? Impractical? Impossible?

Student K: I really do. It just doesn't fit.

Professor: Mr. C? What do you think?

Student C: Well, yes, but it would be a lot simpler if he'd get out of there.

Professor: You painted a fairly rosy picture of what effect his leaving would have. Any second thoughts?

Student C: Well, yes, if his replacement isn't careful, that whole operation could slip and they'd be right back where they started—which would make for some very happy private psychiatrists.

Professor: So what's an alternative? Mr. A?

Student A: Well, I was all enthused about unloading Keuning, too, but that could be disastrous. Look at all those organizational hookups. You take Keuning out and the whole thing could fall apart.

Professor: All right, so what do we do?

Student A: Boy, I don't know. If we keep him, and I guess we have to because *I'm* sure not going to tell him good-by and I don't see anybody else doing it, either, we've got some fence-mending to do. But we've really got to get down to business if the Center is going to do all it's supposed to do.

Professor: Right. Let's be more specific now. Mr. B, Mr. C, can you give us some details?

Comments. The teacher acts as summarizer here; this plus the five-minute class break makes it relatively easy to turn the class in a new direction. The objective here was to move on from analysis to a plan of action—the classic case question: "What should Dr. Keuning do?"

Student H is not a regular contributor to the class discussions; he is always prepared, however, and occasionally makes an abrupt but sensible remark. Student J is not a volunteer and is clearly not prepared. Styles vary, but simply ignoring the student's remarks once his lack of preparation is established is a popular technique. The occasional use of more melodramatic devices—asking the student to leave the discussion, abandoning the class entirely if too many are unprepared, etc.—can sometimes also be useful.

At the end of this transcript segment the teacher is beginning to push the class into development of a realistic, practical plan of action. The class continued for another hour, and by the end of that time two quite different plans of action had been developed. One hinged on persuading Keuning that it was time to devote his attention to the University's Department of Psychiatry while Sister Catherine and Dr. Walton assumed responsibility for the Center;the alternate plan assumed that Keuning would maintain his position at the Center and called for Keuning to invite Leland and Gilbert to work with him, probably offering both University appointments.

The case discussion ended with no conclusion as to which, if either, alternative was "right." The transcript shows a "wrong" approach being headed off early. This is the instructor's judgment at work: While there is rarely a "right answer" to a case, there a generally some "answers" that are unrealistic, unlikely, impractical, etc. There is little sense in pursuing such approaches when more fruitful avenues abound.

Some students become increasingly annoyed at the ambiguities of the case method, particularly an instructor's refusal to "tell which was the right answer" at the end of a discussion. Other students will become highly irritated when the teacher replies, "I don't know," to the inevitable "What did they actually do?" Even when the instructor does know, he will tend to evade the question when he sees his students with pens poised over their notebooks ready to write down the "answer."

A case discussion is not—or should not be—a vehicle for discovering if the students have learned something they have been studying. Nor is it an orderly progression toward a single correct solution by a team. While the method has its roots in a similar method practiced in law and medicine, cases in those areas tend to be much more comprehensive and the process aimed toward helping the student learn the orderly presentation of facts that, if followed and supported by adequate testing and research, lead to inevitable conclusions. Cases in administration frequently appear incomplete, apparently omitting many possibly relevant issues. They simulate the highly imperfect state of information and organizational foresight that exists in reality. The future practitioner is not necessarily supposed to spend whatever it takes to achieve the economic equivalent of health and justice.

Yet the very ambiguity of these cases facilitates the exploration of many avenues and allows a variety of possible conclusions. The case discussion explores the possible alternative arrangements of facts and conclusions leading to actions—with the class discussing and evaluating these alternatives and learning from each other. Experienced case teachers will say that every discussion of a given case is different and that the best case discussions often lead to their own learning. While the case method can be used for teaching basic concepts, programmed learning probably is more effective for that purpose. Cases, however, are extremely effective at eliciting discovery by the students of an ability to apply concepts that they have learned elsewhere to the real-life situations protrayed in the case.

REFERENCES

Merry, R. W. Preparation to teach a case. In M. P. McNair (Ed.), *The case method at the Harvard Business School.* New York: Mc-Graw-Hill, 1954.

FOOTNOTES

[5] We are indebted to Russell Campbell, Robert D. Emrick and Michael Horrigan, graduates of the MBA program, Whittemore School of Business and Economics, University of New Hampshire, for their assistance in preparing this transcript.

5. DEVELOPMENT OF CASE MATERIALS

Since one of the weaknesses of case teaching in human services administration is the low availability of materials, practitioners and teachers should be involved in preparing and disseminating new materials. Appendix B is an annotated bibliography developed for this volume as a first step in the dissemination process.

Most of these available case materials have been developed by business faculty members to provide students with a sense that their administrative concepts, techniques, and skills are more widely relevant. Thus, this material tends to focus on issues perceived as analogous to business decisions. The danger of this approach is in overlooking the key professional issues and factors or, on a few occasions, misperceiving them.

Systematic programs to prepare teaching materials should be mounted by the professional schools involved with health and human services administration, alone or jointly with schools of administration. In several areas, including mental health and family planning, governmental and foundation financial support has been used. The result usually has been a marked improvement in faculty perception of key professional issues.

Except for these occasional grants, course and case development has had an uphill fight in most professional schools. Reward systems offer neither compensation nor security for the preparation of cases, yet such work is hard, time-consuming, and costly. Of course this problem is not peculiar to professional schools in the health and human services. It is a rare institution that fully recognizes teaching skills, let alone course or case development. In business, for example, it is likely that the supply of cases would have dried up if the Harvard Business School were not such a large institution with very strong sanctions on its junior members to prepare cases.

Where, then, will case teaching material come from? The shortrun solution is the second-best materials from business schools plus the slowly growing set being developed in or with other professional schools. Beyond this, the teacher can and should write or supervise the writing of cases in his own field. Cases can be reasonable alternatives to term papers or examinations or can be distilled from field projects. If the teacher works with specialists from other schools, it can prove to be a multipurpose arrangement benefiting both programs. In addition, professional groups should be solicited to subsidize development of case teaching materials specific to their area, usually for use in seminars for their members, just as industrial and government groups have.

CASE WRITING

The *sine qua non* of course development—case or otherwise—rests with purpose, structure, and relevance. Only by putting the cart before the horse can one decide to have a case course and then select the topics. One defines the purposes of the learning experience first, identifies the concepts to be covered, and then seeks appropriate methods and materials for covering these areas.

The need for cases appears as the course is developed. The teacher generates a sequence of topics and experiences to be provided and selects the best available material for each. Inevitably, he or she will recognize weak spots or gaps. For example, he may wish to cover the topic of economic and social measures of performance in the penal system and have nothing that specifically addresses those issues in that context.

At this point he has several alternatives: *(a)* a lecture, *(b)* a penal case with a hint of that issue that he can emphasize, *(c)* substitution of a case with similar issues (one emphasizing the topics of economic and social measures of performance in family planning or Scouting, for instance), or *(d)* he may write a new case to fit like a glove. But how do you go about writing a case, especially if you eschew "arm-chairing" one, that is, making it up?

The professional does not operate in a vacuum. He interacts with clients and practitioners, and like the fledgling insurance salesman, he must exploit his contacts and relatives and even make blind calls. Most institutional and professional contacts can lead to opportunities for case writing. They bring to light situations relevant to the needs of courses under development. The trick is to match these opportunities with existing needs. The case writer must continually make trade-offs between aggressively seeking cooperation at institutions he knows have interesting problems and adapting situations at a more cooperative institution. We have no magic formula for uncovering the appropriate situations or matching them to course needs. That is a matter of professional responsibility, visibility, and judgment. Even when students assist with the contacts and writing as part of their educational process, the teacher serves as an interested and innovative gatekeeper.

How do you go about writing a case, assuming you are not going to fabricate it from literature or prior experiences? The first step beyond identifying a site and a potential topic is to discuss the opportunity with the key leaders of the organization. You should make it clear that your objective is teaching material made possible by their donation of time and information. You *must* state that you are providing neither free consultation nor solutions to current problems. Yet you need not rule out the possibility that the case-collecting process and its output will heighten the organization's understanding of itself through review of the material, discussions with the casewriter, and from student analyses. At Harvard it is a normal courtesy to invite individuals from the organization to sit in at the initial classroom discussion. The promise to give the organization final say over the release of the material prior to classroom use is an essential proviso, as is a willingness to disguise the names of key personnel or even the organization's name and location.

Following agreement on cooperation and confidentiality, the case writer moves as unobtrusively as possible to familiarize himself with the organization, its technology, its history, and the potential case situations and issues. He sets up interviews and requests needed data, generally working on the assumption that too much information is better than too little. He should constantly be refining his outline of the case and how he intends to use it in the classroom.

Most case writers would agree that it is extremely valuable for the writer to leave the organizational setting before beginning the initial drafts. Outside, he begins to define the issues free of the protagonists, to figure out who also has something worthwhile to add, what data the student needs for a solid analysis, what facets should be accentuated or played down, etc. Then he returns to the organization as necessary in search of needed information.

Frequently, the case writer finds that the organization does not have the data he thinks are needed. Obviously, he cannot include it in the final case. Students find such a situation, that is, lack of information in the case that they feel is vital, extremely irritating. Students tend to heap blame on the case writer for such a situation. Yet it is a general rule that if the organization cannot provide it for the case writer, he should not collect it or fabricate it for the students. That such information was lacking is information about the organization, information that is important to the acculturation of students. The student has to realize that in real organizational situations, decisions often are made on less than complete information.

The final step in case writing is securing the organization's permission to use the written case as a teaching instrument. Organizations may insist on changes and often on disguise. Almost always, both can be accomplished without seriously affecting the value of the case. In a few instances, perhaps as much as 20%, the release will not be given, and all the prior effort goes down the drain. Needless to say, careful efforts at identifying early in process those situations in which this is likely to happen are of considerable value. Many organizations find reading an outside observer's description of their activities an extremely valuable—although not necessarily pleasant—experience.

Case teachers often wonder why any organization would allow its experiences to be so publicized. Few performances are all that bad, but a group of students operating with 20-20 hindsight usually end up with a low opinion of the organization. If the student feels that he must contribute something, he will pick everything apart and attempt to find a novel point of criticism. It is the job of the instructor to hold this bias in check, but doing so conflicts with the norm of minimum teacher substitution of his values and opinions into the case analysis, so the organization takes a beating. A sequence of such experiences may account for the high confidence, if not arrogance, of case-trained students.

The teacher can soften the impact, however, by keeping the students aware of the pedagogic reasons for having a specific case at a specific time. If it is evident that the case is there for a stated purpose other than the illustration of good or bad administrative performance, the student is less likely to adopt a judgmental role. This is hardly the primary argument for structure in case-oriented courses, but it buttresses the more obvious ones.

APPENDIX A: SELECTED BIBLIOGRAPHY ON THE CASE METHOD OF TEACHING

Andrews, K. R. (Ed.) *The case method of teaching human relations and administration.* Cambridge, Mass.: Harvard University Press, 1960.

Fraser, C. E. (Ed.) *The case method of instruction.* New York: McGraw-Hill, 1931.

Hamilton, J. A., *Decision making in hospital administration and medical care: A casebook.* Minneapolis: University of Minnesota Press, 1960.

Landman, J. H., *The case method of studying law: A critique.* New York: G. A. Jennings Co., 1930.

McNair, M. P. (Ed.) *The case method at the Harvard Business School.* New York: McGraw-Hill, 1954.

Penchansky, R. (Ed.) *Health services administration: Policy cases and the case method,* Cambridge, Mass. Harvard University Press, 1968.

Sherwood, F. P., & Storm, W. P. (Eds.) *Teaching and research in public administration: Essays on case approach.* Los Angeles: School of Public Administration, University of Southern California, 1960.

Sperle, D. H. *The case method technique in professional training.* New York: Bureau of Publications, Columbia University Teachers College, 1933.

Towl, A. R. *To study administration by cases.* Boston: Harvard University Graduate School of Business Administration, 1969.

Towle, C. *The case method in teaching social work,* New York: National Association of Social Workers, 1959.

APPENDIX B: CASE MATERIAL AVAILABLE FOR USE IN HEALTH AND HUMAN SERVICES ADMINISTRATION

TABLE 3
Sources of Case Material

Note—Cases can be obtained through the agencies and organizations noted in the "Identification" column. Prices, shipping arrangements, policies on inspection copies, etc., vary. Inquiries should be made directly to the appropriate agencies and organizations.

Key to Sources

Identification	*Source*
CPC	Carolina Population Center University of North Carolina Chapel Hill, North Carolina
GPO	Superintendent of Documents Government Printing Office Washington, D.C.
HBS	Harvard Business School: cases available through ICH (see below)
HSA	U.S. Department of Health, Education and Welfare Health Services and Mental Health Administration Rockville, Maryland 20852
HSA (Penchansky)	Penchansky, R. (Ed.), *Health Services* Administration: Policy Cases and the *Case Method,* Cambridge, Massachusetts: Harvard University Press, 1968.
ICH	Intercollegiate Case Clearing House Soldiers Field Post Office Boston, Massachusetts 02163
ICP	Professor Edwin A. Bock, President Inter-University Case Program, Inc. 607 University Avenue Syracuse, New York 13210
PHS	U.S. Department of Health, Education and Welfare Public Health Service Division of Medical Case Administration Arlington, Virginia 22203
University of Michigan School of Public Health	School of Public Health University of Michigan Ann Arbor, Michigan

TABLE 4
Abstracts of Cases for Use in Health and Human Services

Abstract	*Subjects and issues*	*Persons and groups involved*	*Setting*	*Identification*
The Ancker Hospital Site Controversy The case highlights the considerations relevant to the locating of a new public hospital in an urban area. Criteria for site evaluation include city-planning issues, future contingencies of the demand for hospital services, catalyst effects of hospital location in developing a complete medical center, the efficient integration of new hospital and an existing community of hospitals, and the cost/benefit relationships between private and public institutions.	Identifying germane arguments and interest group biases that bear on the choice of a hospital site	Anker Hospital Commission and other public agencies	St. Paul, Minn. 1958-61	ICP # 82
The Artificial Kidney Supply Division Production of an artificial kidney machine to meet a public need poses a difficult policy question for the manufacturer. This is an unprofitable product line; current output levels are low due to the fact that operating costs of the machines are high, thereby suppressing actual demand even though public need is high. Mass-production techniques could reduce per-unit production costs, and product development effort could conceivably reduce the consumer's operating expense. Each of these would require costly changes for the manufacturer. The machine is in danger of becoming obsolete in light of developments of kidney transplant techniques.	Traditional product line decisions where profitability may not be the sole criterion The economics of society-oriented activities; the cost burden and the allocation of the benefits	Sweden Freezer Manufacturing Company Department of Medicine, University of Washington	Seattle, Wash. 1965	HBS TI 55

Blare General Hospital (A) (10G19) *Case commentary (10G19S)* Case focusses on top administrative management of a large 1,100-bed municipal hospital, including municipal officers, board of trustees, hospital superintendent, and immediate subordinates of superintendent. Rising costs, falling employee productivity, poorly defined organizational goals, and an ineffective administrative organization force of board of trustees to examine its method of organization and operations in search for improved means of serving medical needs of community. A new administrative organizational structure is needed.	Administrative organization Administration organization policy Budgetary control Employee productivity Environmental constraints Organizational authority Organizational controls Organizational objectives Organizational relationships	**City mayor** **Board of trustees** **Hospital superintendent and subordinates**	Northeast Hospital $15,000,000 annual operating budget Hospital 1958-59	ICH #s 10G19 and 10G19S 13 and 12 pages Klasson University of Texas
Blare General Hospital Outpatient Dept. (A) (10P11) *Teaching notes (10P11S)* This case is used to illustrate the problems inherent in the utilization of existing plant facilities in the most efficient manner. The case moves the student into a situation where space has been made available due to the movement of a major department to another location. The administrator is faced with the situation of wanting to make an optimum decision within existing organizational and behavioral restraints.	Production problems Hospital administration Plant layout Queuing theory Scheduling	**Deputy administrator**	Northeast Hospital 1,300 OPD patients daily Outpatient hospital 1965	IGH #s 10P11 and 10P11S 24 and 4 pages Robb, Zertuche University of Oklahoma Institut Tech. y de Estudios Superiores de Monterrey
Blare General Hospital *Reference note (10P12)* Reference notes for Blare General Hospital are used as background materials for Blare General Hospital Outpatient Dept. (A)	Production management Hospital history		Northeast Hospital 400,000 patients per year General administration Hospital 1965	ICH #s 10P12 8 pages Raymond, Robb, Boyer Harvard Univ. University of Oklahoma

TABLE 4

Abstracts of Cases for Use in Health and Human Services

Abstract	*Subjects and issues*	*Persons and groups involved*	*Setting*	*Identification*
Blare Hospital Pharmacy (10C14) *Teaching note (10C14S)* The case allows the student to study and to evaluate specific practices and to make general recommendations for the control of inventories and other property. A suggested worksheet permits the student to organize his analysis by *(a)* listing and evaluating each current practice, *(b)* relating factors that influence decisions to change, *(c)* indicating appropriate changes, *(d)* implementing solutions, and *(e)* formulating general recommendations for improving and facilitating controls.	Cost accounting Auditing Inventory control Managerial accounting Systems	Chief pharmacist Auditor Consultant	Metropolitan Hospital Pharmacy	ICH #s 10C14 and 10C14S 14 and 4 pages Hutton University of Tulsa
Case study: induced abortion and background information thereto, April, 1967 The background information for the case broadly describes the extent of the practice of induced abortions in various areas of the world in different legal and institutional settings. The case itself views abortion both as a burden on the public health facilities and a major factor in reducing the population growth rate.	Practical considerations (i.e., exclusive of moral, religious, or philosophical) of public policy on the matter of abortions		San Anon, a lesser developed country in South America	University of Michigan School of Public Health

Changing a community's pattern of medical care The case describes a conflict between a local medical authority that controls hospital staffing and a group medical program to which a majority in the community subscribes.	Monopolistic powers in the practice of medicine and their impact on a patient's freedom of choice The pros and cons of medicine and a prepaid group of practice	Citizens General Hospital Russelton Medical Group	New Kensington, Pennsylvania 1954-64	HSA (Penchansky)
Charity Community Mental Health Center *Part I: development of the center* The case deals with the administrative problems of integrating existing psychiatric services to qualify for federal financial support. Professional autonomy, affiliation with a school of medicine, membership in the local medical association, and administrative prerogatives of a private hospital appear as the major forces contributing to the coordination difficulties.	Administration without a well-defined basis for authority and without recourse to direct sanctions	County Medical Health Board Charity Hospital Univ. of State Charity Mental Health Center Private psychiatrists	The urban center of an agricultural community 1967-70	NIMH, HSA, and MHA
Charity Community Mental Health Center *Part II: structure and decision-making* The participative style of management superimposed on an organizational structure having both a program orientation and a discipline orientation results in extremely complex decision-making procedures and overlapping areas in the divided authority. Administrative stagnation in the hospital appears imminent despite detailed written procedures and job descriptions.	Pros and cons of participative management Unity of command		Charity Community Mental Health Center	NIMH, HSA, and MHA

TABLE 4
Abstracts of Cases for Use in Health and Human Services

Abstract	Subjects and issues	Persons and groups involved	Setting	Identification
Co-Dev family planning service The case describes the design and problems of Southern family planning program. Racial and sociometric considerations are foci of disagreement between the county health department and the Co-Dev clinic administrators. Questions of which segments of the population ought to be emphasized and how best to reach them lead to a breakdown of communications between the two organizations.	Program design in family planning for a nonhomogeneous target population.	Cordice County Development Corp. County Health Dept.	Middle South 1967-68	CPC #s 903 A,B, and C
Cooperative planning for a new school of nursing 1 This case reflects the many different concepts embodied in the nursing function. Differences among the concepts suggest different educational/training requirements. The relative roles of the academic institutions and the medical institution and the demands each places on the student nurse in a training program is cast within the administrative problems of high turnover rates and the increasingly complex skill required in the nursing professions. The case describes the efforts to consolidate the training programs of a number of hospitals under the auspices of an accredited educational institution	The role of a nurse Economies of scale in both cost and quality of training versus relinquishing of control by individual hospitals in their nurse training programs	The major private Boston hospitals and several nearby academic institutions.	Boston 1960s	HSA (Penchansky)

Cooperative planning for a new school of nursing 2 This case, a continuation of *Cooperative Planning for a New School of Nursing 1,* illustrates how one medical institution made the transition from an in-house nurse-training program to an affiliation with a university-based training program. The hospital's handling of the transition treats its faculty and student nurse phase-out procedure and a cost analysis thereof. A band wagon effect on the part of other hospitals joining the consolidated nurse training program as well as presence of an influencial third party, a professional nursing association, appear as complicating factors in the case.	Administering a major change in the training/service function of a hospital	Beth Israel Hospital Northeastern University National League for Nursing	Beth Israel Hospital in Boston Mid-1960's	HSA (Penchansky)
County General Hospital (9G99) *Teaching Notes (9G99S)* This case concerns the difficulties involved with initiating a staff study.	General policy Human relations Organizing Planning	Assistant and personnel directors Chief pharmacist	Southeastern Hospital $485,000 income 500 employees Personnel, nursing, service, pharmacy and general administration	ICH #s 9G99 and 9G99S 22 and 5 pages McCann Louisiana State University
Disease Control Programs (12C7) (A) Describes an analysis of a proposed program to reduce fatalities in motorcycle accidents. The analysis is a cost-benefit study. Students are expected to be critical of assumptions and to determine whether or not the study supports the proposed program. The case includes the issue of valuing a human life.	Planning, Programming and Budget seminar Cost-benefit analysis Cash flow	Analyst	Washington, D.C. Government Public Health Service 1967	ICH #s 12C7 19 pages Christenson, C. J. U.S. Civil Service Commission

TABLE 4
Abstracts of Cases for Use in Health and Human Services

Abstract	Subjects and issues	Persons and groups involved	Setting	Identification
Division of Special Education (A) (14C4) *Instructor's Note (14C4S)* This case presents a discussion between five men representing differing viewpoints on what the purpose of a PPBS is. The context is a state division of special education (education for handicapped children). In addition to general PPBS implementation strategy, the discussants debate questions of program structure design. The case contains extracts from recent Bureau of the Budget PPBS guidelines and extensive notes on program structure design. The student is asked to identify key decisions that must be made before commencing PPBS implementation, to sketch an implementation strategy, and to design a broad program structure for the division.	Planning, Programming, and Budget seminar Program structure	Various	State government Budget and Planning 1969	ICH #s 14C4, 14C4S 29 and 7 pages Taylor, G.M. University of Maryland U.S. Civil Service Commission
Division of Special Education (B) (14C5) *Instructor's Note (14C5S)* This case presents a discussion between five men representing differing viewpoints on what the purpose of a PPBS is. The debate focuses on: *(a)*	Planning, Programming, and Budget seminar Planning	Various	State government Budget and Planning 1969	ICH #s 14C5, 14C5S 17 and 3 pages Taylor, G.M. University of Maryland U.S. Civil Service Commission

different interpretations of planning in a PPBS context, and *(b)* the different types of analysis that are called for by a PPBS—managerial analysis, program analysis, analytic budget back-up, and issue papers. The student is asked to identify planning data required, to identify issues for study, and to establish a set of criteria for selection of priority issues.				
Division of Special Education (C) (14C6) Instructor's Note (14C6S) This case describes an ongoing work-study program to train educable mentally retarded (EMR) children for jobs. The student is asked to design an evaluation study of this program. This requires identification of key program variables and careful selection of appropriate measures of output, effectiveness, and benefit.	Planning, Programming and Budget seminar Output measures Program evaluation	Various	State government Budget and Planning 1969	ICH #s 14C6, 14C6S 5 and 6 pages Taylor, G.M. University of Maryland U.S. Civil Service Commission
Doctors of Medicine and Doctors of Osteopathy in California Describes the evolution of osteopathy as a separate branch of medicine. Problems of standards of practice, educational requirements, and licensing have manifested themselves in terms of the relationship between the osteopathic association and medical association on the state level and between each of these state bodies and its respective national organization. An underlying concern is how best to provide optimum professional medical	Legitimacy and public acceptance of the professions The role of professional associations in maintaining standards of practice; their power as an autonomous monopoly	American Medical Association American Osteopathic Association California Medical Association California Osteopathic Association	California 1959-66	PHS Case Study No. 2

TABLE 4
Abstracts of Cases for Use in Health and Human Services

Abstract	*Subjects and issues*	*Persons and groups involved*	*Setting*	*Identification*
services to the community, focusing on the distinction between doctors of medicine and doctors of osteopathy.				
Drug Cost and Utilization: The Massachusetts Public Assistance Experience The case illustrates the problems of administering a drug-cost reimbursement program. Complexities of the drug industry's pricing schedules, physician's autonomy in writing prescriptions, and pharmacists profit margins lead to legislated regulations which are somewhat vague and unenforceable.	The determinants of drug prices: a further institutionalization of an already peculiar "market"	Massachusetts State Pharmaceutical Assn. Massachusetts Department of Public Welfare	Boston 1948-53	HSA (Penchansky)
Emergency Ambulance Service (A) (13C25) Instructor's Note (13C25S) This case provides a simple, nonnumerical introduction to the principles of systems analysis. The operation of New York City's emergency ambulance service is briefly described. The student is expected to design an analytic framework to evaluate alternative methods of improving the service—definition of subsystems involved, delineation of objectives, choice of effectiveness measures, and formulation of alternatives.	Planning, Programming and Budget seminar Public expenditure analysis Simulation models Systems analysis	Assistant to mayor	New York City government Hospitals 1968	ICH #s 13C25, 13C25S 6 and 13 pages Taylor, G. M.; Gill, R. J. George Washington University

Emergency Ambulance Service (B)(13C26) Instructor's Note (13C26S) This sequel to the (A) case presents the report of an analysis actually performed in New York City, in which dispersion of ambulances was recommended to decrease response time. The instructor's note contains a description of the simulation model employed. The case is intended to provide *(a)* an example of a sound, professional, well-documented analysis and *(b)* an introduction to the technique of simulation modeling.	Planning, Programming, and Budget seminar Public expenditure analysis Simulation models Systems analysis	**Assistant to mayor**	New York City government Hospitals 1968	ICH #s 13C26, 13C26S 34 and 39 pages Taylor, G. M.; Gill, R. J. George Washington University
A Family Planning Fortnight in Sandho District The case describes a family planning fortnight, a periodic intensified family planning effort to evoke mass participation. A verbal sketch of local conditions and people relates the major impact of seemingly unsophisticated methods and minor incidents.	Descriptive: a family planning program in the field	**Field staff of a family planning program**	Sandho District, India	CPC #s 801 A, B, and C.
Family Planning in Tewkesbury County: A Casebook in Community Health This set of cases revolves around organizational coordination and staff motivation issues in a community family planning program. Lack of understanding of technical aspects of contraception is confounded by personal feelings on the part of staff members and the absence of clearly delineated functional responsibilities. Extensive background material and data are given.	Implementing and coordinating a new family planning program within an existing complex of public service organizations	**County Health Department**	Tewkesbury Co. 1960s	CPC

TABLE 4
Abstracts of Cases for Use in Health and Human Services

Abstract	*Subjects and issues*	*Persons and groups involved*	*Setting*	*Identification*
Flame of Hope, Inc. The case deals with a rehabilitation program for the mentally retarded. A candlemaking operation was developed that lent itself to workshop production analogous to the refurbishing of old goods that is currently carried on in rehabilitation workshops across the country. Unique administrative problems are inherent in this candlemaking venture by virtue of the conflicting objectives of rehabilitation of the workers and the need to compete successfully with existing candle manufacturers. Start-up problems of financing are somewhat aleviated by government subsidy grants; but the "new organization" problems of production, product development, and marketing are complicated by the primary organizational and personnel objective: rehabilitating the retarded workers.	Clinical versus "real world" rehabilitation: the controlled transition Balancing conflicting organizational objectives	Flame of Hope, Inc.	New England and other rehabilitation workshops	HBS EA-P454
Golden Age Homes, Inc. (9C24) *Teaching Note (9C24S)* A recently formed company, short of cash for expansion but eager for a public image to strengthen a prospective public offering, tailors its depreciation and deferred expense policies to	Financial accounting Deferred expenses Depreciation Tax accounting	Executive committee Auditor Lawyer	Nursing homes $2,250,000 assets Accounting office 1961	ICH #9C24 and 9C24S 13 and 6 pages McArthur, Sprouse Schulman Harvard University

fit its needs. At the same time the problem of public disclosure of its accounting methods arises. The case opens the sometimes conflicting area of tax accounting versus public reporting and internal accounting. Students are encouraged to discuss the conflicts and take a stand on one side or the other of the legal and ethical considerations.				
Health Services in Chile Chile, being a lesser developed country with a large portion of its population sparsely distributed in rural areas, has faced a difficult problem of providing health services to its people. The case describes the organizational machinery the government established for the administration and implementation of its program and identifies some of the difficulties which resulted.	Planning a national health service program Allocation of resources between preventive and curative functions of a medical program	**Servicio Nacional de Salud**	Chile 194[illegible]-63	HSA (Penchansky)
Improving Patient Care Through Organizational Changes in the Mental Hospital Analysis of the staff of a mental hospital with a sociologist's perspective reveals the *de facto* structure of the organization. Identifying group norms and dissonance suggests how organizational change might be successfully implemented to integrate personnel activities and provide better hospital services.	Adapting the "culture" of an organization to conform to a desired organizational chart; social considerations in management	**Mental Hospital**		The William Alanson White Psychiatric Foundation
Indian Point Medical Council (13G55) Utilization of hospital bed facilities and regional planning; business-community relationships	Production Organization theory Planning	**Physicians** **Industrialists**	U.S. Hospital Large City Planning office 1967	ICH #13G55 5 pages C. McLaughlin Harvard University

TABLE 4
Abstracts of Cases for Use in Health and Human Services

Abstract	*Subjects and issues*	*Persons and groups involved*	*Setting*	*Identification*
Inpatient Psychiatric Services in a General Hospital The case describes a pilot program to increase the scope of medical services rendered to the public by a general hospital. Apprehensions of general medical personnel and public on the effects of breaking with the traditional "treatment in isolation" of the mentally ill are considered. A group-involvement approach both in administration and actual treatment of patients characterizes this case.	Implications of scale of activity on program administration and effectiveness The dependence of program success on type of leadership Distinguishing between an effective medical treatment and an effective medical administrative program	Yale Medical Center	Grace-New Haven Hospital 1958-65	HSA (Penchansky)
Limat The case describes a nonclinical family planning program conducted in a rural setting within a lesser-developed country. Emphasis is placed on selection of program leaders from among the local community and the sociological design of effective communication and contraceptive distribution systems. Program results are presented.	Evaluation of family planning program design and recommendations for program modifications based on preliminary results.		Rootta Block in Limat, a ficticious Indian community. 1959-66	CPC
Loma Vista Hospital (13P7) Case represents an operating control problem in a hospital. Requires scheduling of nurses, relayout and budgeting of resources. Decision-making situation.	Operations management Control Layout Production planning	Manager Nurses' supervisor	California Hospital General administration hospital 1967	ICH #13P7 32 pages J. L. McKenny, N. Baloff, F. Mapel Stanford University

Lutheran Hospital (7P17) The nursing director and her new administrative assistant work toward a division of labor.	Administration Productive activities	Nursing director Administrative assistant	Central Atlantic Services Nursing Hospital, 1961	ICH #7P17 12 pages Thurston, Lortie Harvard University
The Massachusetts Health Protection Clinics The case describes the development of a pilot program of multiphasic screening. The dual nature of the program, research in detecting chronic diseases using multidiagnostic tests simultaneously and administering the tests on a mass basis led to controversies among various interests within the medical profession.	The distinction between a publically administered disease-detection screening program and the practice of diagnostic medicine	Massachusetts Medical Society Massachusetts Department of Health	Boston 1948-53	HSA (Penchansky)
Medical Practice in a Group Setting The Russellton Medical Group was formed to serve the needs of the UMWA medical program in the coal mining communities surrounding New Kensington, Pennsylvania. The case describes the growth of a small multi-office group practice where the participating physicians are denied hospital affiliation.	Developing a new, high-quality group program amid a disapproving local medical community	Russelton Medical Group, Westmoreland County Medical Society	Coal-mining area of Pennsylvania 1952-63	HSA (Penchansky)
Metropolitan Regional (13P76) State Hospital The artificial kidney unit of a large hospital is approaching full capacity, and the efficiency of the schedule becomes a matter of life or death. There are a number of resources to be scheduled, and the case can be used to analyze the scheduling constraints.	Production Equipment Personnel Scheduling	Physician Department head	Central Atlantic hospital 450 beds Renal dialysis unit Hospital 1968	ICH #13P76 10 pages C. P. McLaughlin Harvard University

TABLE 4
Abstracts of Cases for Use in Health and Human Services

Abstract	*Subjects and issues*	*Persons and groups involved*	*Setting*	*Identification*
Nationalized Health Service The case describes the British post-World-War II experience in adopting comprehensive public health service. Popular support has overruled the medical profession's resistance; changes in the role of the physician ensued. Administering control over the medical profession rather than over a medical program has emerged as the continuing problem.	Medicine under governmental control: a trade or a profession	British Medical Association National Health Service Minister of Health	Britain 1946-56	HSA (Penchansky)
Newcomer-Willson Hospital (7G161) *Teaching Notes (7G161S)* Case covers the organization and administrative processes of conducting the activities of a medium-large hospital. It points out the complex nature of hospital administration and focuses attention on the professional administrator and the problems he has in maintaining a healthy organization. It is best used to point out the need for definition of objectives; for example, administrators versus medical staff, and the use of good organizational practices like unity of command, span of control, use of committees, and informal organization.	Business policy Administrative practice Administration Business organization Organization—formal/informal Relationships—interdepartmental line and staff	Administrator (Director)	New England Services 700 employees 235 beds $3,600,000 budget General administration hospital 1962	ICH #s 7G161, 7G161S Wilson Temple University

New England Deaconess Hospital (7G160) *Teaching Note (7G160S)* A major policy decision regarding the possibility of changing the basic form of organization structure. An examination of the reactions of various persons who would be affected by the change. Case is used to show basic principles of organization and personnel reaction to organization change.	Hospital organization Human relations Personnel	Executive director Major department heads	New England Services; very large administration; Hospital 1962	ICH #7G160, 7G160S Field, Hodgetts University of Toledo
The New Training Course This exercise is to formulate a response to a letter soliciting comments on how to conduct a training program for extension educators in the family planning program in India. Couched in this brief case are questions of how to provide useful training and an esprit de corps to personnel required to perform a highly unstructured function.	Designing a training program	Extension educators in a family planning program	India	CPC # 100
The New York City Welfare Department (A) (13H117) Describes the relationship between a union of welfare caseworkers and the City of New York. The union is demanding both changes in working conditions and benefits for welfare clients while the city refuses to admit the negotiability of these demands. In order to dramatize its position the union organizes a work stoppage. The history of collective bargaining for municipal employees and a de-	Welfare administration Union policies Decision-making	Welfare commissioner New York City Mayor Director of Labor Relations, NYC Social Service Employees Union Welfare clients Local 371 of American Federation of State, County and Municipal Employees, AFL-CIO	A welfare department with 7,500 caseworkers and 300,000 cases whose annual expenditures in 1967 were $1.1 billion New York City 1964-67	ICH # 13H117 31 pages M. J. Jedel, T. C. Raymond, M. T. Kennedy Edwin Gould Foundation for Children

TABLE 4
Abstracts of Cases for Use in Health and Human Services

Abstract	*Subjects and issues*	*Persons and groups involved*	*Setting*	*Identification*
scription of the organization of the welfare department are given.				
The New York Welfare Department (B) (13H118) Describes the settlement of the work stoppage organized by the caseworkers' union. A mediator's plan ended the strike after six weeks, with some of the union demands still unmet.	Welfare administration Union policies Decision-making	Director of Labor Relations, NYC Social Service Employees' Union	Welfare department with 7,500 caseworkers and 300,000 cases, whose annual expenditures in 1967 were $1.1 billion New York City	ICH # 13H118 4 pages M. J. Jedel, T. C. Raymond, M. T. Kennedy Edwin Gould Foundation for Children (S)
Noland Hospital (11H101) Hospital administrative and supervisory problems faced by the personnel director	Personnel management Business policy Management development	Personnel director Department heads Supervisors	Southwest Hospital 375 beds Personnel office	ICH # 11H101 4 pages S. Adams Texas Technical College
North Carolina Abortion Law 1967 This monograph focuses on the legislative process and the importance of political skills in enacting legislation in this controversial area. Abortion generally an emotionally-charged subject, reflects a cultural value in which change has been frustrated by institutional constraints.	Moral judgments and the practice of medicine	State representative Arthur H. Jones North Carolina General Assembly	Raleigh, N.C. 1967	CPC monograph
Office of Economic Opportunity (A) (12C50) Comparison of methods for evaluating antipoverty programs. Used in teaching benefit-cost approach to governmental budgeting. Problems of measuring benefits are emphasized.	Planning, Programming, and Budget seminar Benefit-cost analysis Government budgeting		Washington, D.C. Federal government Office 1967	ICH #12C50 33 pages Law, W.; Taylor, G. M. U.S. Civil Service Commission

Office of Economic Opportunity (B) (12C6) After two years of rapid growth this new agency is considering a reorganization of the budget function moving it from the Office of Finance to the Research, Plans, Programs and Evaluation Division. The purported advantage is better integration of planning, programming, and budgeting, but a consultant's report (also included in the case) favors the status quo.	Planning, Programming and Budget seminar		Washington, D.C. Government Office of Economic Opportunity 1966	ICH # 12C6 18 pages Vancil, R. F. U.S. Civil Service Commission
People's Improvement, Inc. The case describes the creation of a family planning activity within a community's economic development organization. Incomplete support of the program among the existing staff results in manning difficulties. The case demonstrates the importance of staff commitment and enthusiasm to the effective operation of a family planning program.	Program staffing Subscribing population data	Peoples' Improvement, Inc.	Four southern counties 1967	CPC # 904 A and B
Physician Response to a Governmental Health Plan The case describes a conflict between the local medical profession and the provincial government over a program of socialized medicine. A monopsony power, the result of the states legislative action, is seen as a threat to his autonomy by the medical practioner. The efficiencies and potential dangers of a compulsory medical program are developed.	The role of the state in the medical care of its people	CCF party's health services survey commission Provincial government college of physicians and surgeons	Saskatchewan 1960s	HSA (Penchansky)

TABLE 4
Abstracts of Cases for Use in Health and Human Services

Abstract	*Subjects and issues*	*Persons and groups involved*	*Setting*	*Identification*
Planning and Implementation of the Community Health Foundation of Cleveland, Ohio Describes the development of a prepaid, group practice, comprehensive, direct service health plan in Cleveland. It traces the plan's history over the course of more than a decade from initial motivations to final reality. Describes actions taken to develop the fiscal structure; to resolve the complex relationships between the plan and the local medical community; to plan and construct a clinic building; and to finally deliver comprehensive health services to a large group of subscribers from all segments of the community.	Health services administration Delivery of medical care Community health facility Descriptive	Foundation administrators Local medical community Labor union officials Community representatives	Cleveland, Ohio 1952-67	GPO PHS publication #1664-3 109 pages A. Yedidia Public Health Service, Department of HEW (S)
A Problem of New Staff Recruitment The case revolves around the filling of family planning training positions. The bureaucratic procedures of the Civil Service Commission's recruiting activities are pitted against the infirmities of the relationships between candidate qualifications and functions in a newly established organization	Institutional process constraints and program administration	The Family Planning Training Center of Danong State Civil Service Commission	Danong, India 1966	CPC # 901
The Reorganization of Pakistan's Family Planning Program The case describes a FP program initiated in 1960 and reports its	Implementing a family planning program Program targets: desired versus expected	Director-General-Health	Pakistan 1960-65	University of Michigan School of Public Health

progress up to 1965. Wide discrepancies between target and actual results are examined in an effort to identify program changes.				
The Reorganization of Philadelphia General Hospital The newly elected reform mayor appointed a lay board of trustees to develop his program for reorganizing the city hospital. The trustees disagreed among themselves on the kind of reorganization desirable: hospital personnel resisted proposed changes and played off one trustee against another; and the hospital's executive director sided with the mayor. The stalemate became a city political battle, fought out in the public press and in the political arena.	Health services administration Role of mayor's office Social planning Citizens' advisory boards	Mayor Hospital board of trustees Hospital personnel Various city agencies	Nation's fourth largest city, with population of 2 million persons Philadelphia, Pennsylvania 1952-53	ICP # 47 34 pages M. Robinson, C. Silverman
The Ross-Loos Medical Group Case focuses on the inception of group medical care. The recognition that economic conditions of lower-income workers were resulting in their receiving inadequate levels of corrective medical care and almost no preventive medical attention led to the creation of group health programs. A group program based on the concept of spreading the cost of medical care over large numbers of people and over time was designed to provide needed care to patients and adequate compensation to physicians. The case focuses on the Ross-Loos Group, a pioneering effort in group medical plans.	The apparent conflict between the professional doctor-patient relationship and the administration of a mass medicine program Institutional obstacles	Los Angeles' All City Employees Association and other public employee groups Ross-Loos Medical Group County Medical Association American Medical Association Judicial Council	Los Angeles 1929-36	PHS Case Study No. 3

TABLE 4
Abstracts of Cases for Use in Health and Human Services

Abstract	*Subjects and issues*	*Persons and groups involved*	*Setting*	*Identification*
A Survey of the Child Welfare Field in the United States (13G345) This survey highlights historical factors that have shaped the present child-welfare policies and structures, reviews the field as it exists today, and explores trends and problems that will be important in the future development of the field. Emphasis is placed on the implications of the changing environment for top administrators in the child-welfare field.	Program for welfare administrators Poverty relief Welfare administration	United States		ICH #13G345 68 pages T. C. Raymond, D. F. Hawkins Edwin Gould Foundation for Children
Teaching Cases in Planning, Programming, Budgeting for State and Local Governments (13C18) This is an introductory paper to a set of 11 cases (ICH 13C19-13C29) in Planning, Programming, and Budgeting for state and local governments. The paper contains a six-page introduction to the case method of instruction, designed to assist the instructor in obtaining maximum usefulness from the cases in the classroom. The paper also contains abstracts of all 11 cases, some specific suggestions for their use, and ranks the cases by topic according to degree of difficulty.	Planning, Programming, and Budget seminar			ICH #13C18 14 pages Taylor, G. M.; Gill, R. J. George Washington University

Three Training Centers The case addresses the question of how long family planning personnel "can afford" to be absent from the field in order to participate in training programs. Training centers for extension educators in a rural district in India are under pressure to shorten their courses despite reservations concerning the associated lessening of the quality of training that could be provided.	Program performance criteria: one of the negative effects Short-term versus long-term perspective of a family planning program	Federal Health Education Center Minister of health	Fabricaland 1968	CPC # 905
Unionization of the Hospitals in New York City The case describes the initial entry of labor unions in the New York City hospitals. The nonprofessional, largely minority-group workers are organized to assure them economic returns commensurate with their contribution to hospital productivity. The hospital's bargaining advantage over the workers as individuals is described as the mechanism by which operating deficits are passed on to hospital employees through a suppressed wage structure.	The workers' right to organize in a "critical industry" (hospitals) The legitimate prerogatives of a union in a public service industry: right to strike The hospital dilemma: a responsibility to provide service to the public in an institutionally constrained economic environment	Local 1199, Drug Employers Union Associated Hospital Service of New York	New York City 1958-6[illegible]	HSA (Penchansky)
The United Mine Workers Welfare and Retirement Fund John L. Lewis's UMWA struggle in the coal-mining industry to secure medical care led to a separate subsequent set of problems: implementing a large-scale medical program in the field. The union's welfare and retirement fund medical program takes the initiative and runs into conflicts with the AMA.	The efficiences of an administered medical program versus the freedoms of the patient and the physician in the practice of medicine Concurrent development of medical facilities and a medical program	UMWA AMA	U.S. Coal Fields 1950s	HSA (Penchansky)

TABLE 4
Abstracts of Cases for Use in Health and Human Services

Abstract	*Subjects and issues*	*Persons and groups involved*	*Setting*	*Identification*
The Urban Planner in Health Planning Describes the present involvement of urban planning agencies in the health problems of their communities. The publication provides an awareness of current health problems and suggests what steps to take toward the solving of them.	Community health facilities Delivery of medical care health services administration	American Society of Planning Officials Local urban planning agencies	U.S. 1969	GPO 90 pages American Society of Planning Officials
The Vasectomy Program in Devi District This case deals with the early experiences with a vasectomy family planning program. Statistical results bring out the shortcomings of the incentive system for both program subscribers and field workers.	Difficulties of restricting the program to a specific target population Program evaluation criteria	State Health Minister Social Security Survey Department of the Rajgot University	Devi District, Vandan, India 1963-66	CPC # 900
The Watts Hospital Describes the demographic and economic evolution of the Watts area, defining the relationship of the ghetto area with the surrounding community. Characteristics peculiar to the area are identified which generally escape consideration in city-wide and county development programs. The many extra-medical administrative problems of a public hospital program are accentuated in a complex racial, political, and economic setting.	Allocation of public services Health services as part of a community	Local planning agencies	Watts section of Los Angeles PHS Case Study No. 5 1963-67 (Riot: Aug. 1965)	PHS Case Study No. 5

THE PLANNING AND ADMINISTRATION OF HUMAN SERVICES

by
Harold W. Demone, Jr., Ph.D.
and Dwight Harshbarger, Ph.D.

(Part II of Developments in Human Services,
Volume 1,
Edited by
Herbert C. Schulberg, Ph.D.,
Frank Baker, Ph.D., and
Sheldon R. Roen, Ph.D.

Library of Congress Catalog Card Number 73-6870
Standard Book Number 87705-077-5

BEHAVIORAL PUBLICATIONS, 2852 Broadway—Morningside Heights, New York, New York 10025

Printed in the United States of America

Library of Congress Cataloging in Publication Data

Demone, Harold W
The planning and administration of human services.

Also issued in v. 1 of Developments in human servi
1. Social service. 2. Social work administrati
I. Harshbarger, Dwight, joint author. II. Title.
[HV40.D45] 361 73-6870

CONTENTS

Preface v

1. **Human Needs and Human Services Organizations** 143
   The Human Services Organization; What Is It? 147
   Issues and Problems 151

2. **Organizational Issues** 157
   Organizational Models—Issues and Alternatives 157
   Interorganizational Problems 161
   Intraorganizational Problems 163
   Organizational Change 167

3. **Resources and Their Management** 171
   Government Organizations 172
   Voluntary Associations 174
   Foundations 178
   Policy and Politics 180

4. **The Elements of Planning** 183
   Definitions 183
   Nature of Planning 185
   Dimensions of Planning 186

5. **Developing Operational Plans** 197
   Health-Planning History 198
   Health Care Planning 201
   Environmental Health Planning 203
   Mental Health Planning 205
   Facilities Planning 208
   Urban Planning and Human Services 209

6. Policies, Accountability, and Social Change 213

The Locus of Policy-Making and Resource Allocations 214

Social Change: Change Agents and Strategies 218

Advocacy, Contest, Conflict, and Militancy 221

7. Planning Constraints 225

Hostility 225

Goals 226

Alternatives 226

Specialization and Professions 227

Interorganizational Constraints 227

Metropolitan Constraints 228

Participation 228

Consumer Participation 229

Consensus 229

Confrontation 230

The Technical Report 230

Money 231

8. The Administrative Process 233

Administration Functions 234

Administrative Strategies and Technologies 238

Budget and Finance 240

Personnel Practice 242

Administrative Role Properites 244

Conclusion 245

9. The Future 247

A Definition of Futurism 247

Why Future Planning? 248

Organization and System Changes 250

Future-Oriented Constraints 257

Conclusion 257

PREFACE TO THE SEPARATES OF THE "DEVELOPMENTS IN HUMAN SERVICES" SERIES

Widespread inadequacies in the human condition, and concern for the difficulties and complexities of existing social arrangements, have created urgent pressures upon professionals to revise present care-giving mechanisms. Human service programs such as multi-service centers, which incorporate a wide variety of relevant services, are emerging as an alternative framework to the existing pattern of rigid, categorical services for meeting the bio-psycho-social needs of individuals and populations.

The editors of this new encyclopedic series have undertaken to develop materials which can serve as guide posts for those newly entering or already engaged in the field of human services. A flexible approach to the production and distribution of these materials has been devised.

The plan for the series is to publish annually indepth discussions and reviews on the following human service topics:

—Emerging Conceptions of human service such as systems and ecological frameworks

—Administrative and planning tools such as information systems, economic strategies, and legal mechanisms

—Innovative service programs within new organizational models and new communities

—Educational programs for changing professional roles and new manpower requirements

After several years, those who are standing order subscribers will possess an encyclopedic library of human

services in either hardbound volumes or softcover separates.

The first volume contains an introductory overview by the editors, four substantitive sections on different human service topics as enumerated below, and a comprehensive index. Each of the substantitive sections, without introductory overview and index, are available as separates. These are:

Teaching Health and Human Services Administration by the Case Method
Linda G. Sprague, Alan Sheldon, M.D., and Curtis P. McLaughlin, D.B.A.

The Planning and Administration of Human Services
Harold W. Demone, Jr., Ph.D. and Dwight Harshbarger, Ph.D.

Strategies in Innovative Human Service Programs
Harry Gottesfeld, Ph.D., Florence Lieberman, D.S.W., Sheldon R. Roen, Ph.D., and Sol Gordon, Ph.D.

Developments in Human Services Education and Manpower
Robert M. Vidaver, M.D.

The Editors

1. HUMAN NEEDS AND HUMAN SERVICES ORGANIZATIONS

The next decade will severely test the fabric of American society. A number of important current questions will be answered differently during this period, and the outcomes will hold major significance for the direction and stability of America. We should become more certain of the conditions under which it might be possible for cities to support meaningful, productive life styles, or whether they will become burnt-out shells—depressing monuments to societal indecision, error, and poor planning. We should be better able to determine the extent to which public schools might become sources of excitement and meaningful learning or whether those that remain will provide prototypic social paradigms for uncritical conformity and limited intellectual vision. We will become more and more painfully aware of the serious limitations of our inadequate and overburdened health delivery systems. Whether or not new models of health delivery systems will emerge, survive, and actually deliver health services without discriminating on the basis of ethnicity and income should become evident during these years.

These represent only a few of the extremely serious questions confronting American society. Racism and more subtle but equally devastating forms of ethnic prejudice continue to plague our social and economic relationships. Generations of Americans in inner cities and regions such as Appalachia are being socialized into life styles that have at their core a dependency on outdated, dysfunctional, and demeaning systems of welfare. And vast numbers of middle-class citizens, on entering mental health settings, are asking why affluence does not produce feelings of "the good life."

The abuses of alcohol and, more recently, drugs continue annually to inhibit large numbers of persons from engaging in meaningful lives. Correctional institutions appear to be little more than a significant bench mark in the life of a criminal, a kind of alma mater to which he returns periodically for continuing education. Mental hospitals, despite often dramatic changes during the 1960s, continue to place a very disabling stigma on former patients. Whether or not community mental health centers will, nationally, become more than a subsidy for middle-class therapists' office space or alternatively small state hospitals is still an open question. And after almost a decade of community mental health most state mental health departments still spend 90% of their budgets on institutions and despite decreasing censuses continue to act as if the state hospital remains their principal form of intervention.

The common thread running through all of these problems is that they are being dealt with by what might be described as human services organizations, that is, by organizations in the public or voluntary sector that have as their mandate primary, secondary, and tertiary prevention of biosocial problems. Moreover, they carry the implicit mandate that their combined efforts should contribute to the improvement of the general social welfare and the development of proadaptive or active, rather than passive, ecological behaviors among a population.

Within the broad framework of comprehensive health and welfare services these organizations have been given substantial responsibilities for *(a)* the prevention or lowering of incidences of certain problems, *(b)* the reduction of the duration of occurring problems, and *(c)* the rehabilitation of persons who have experienced selected problems in living.

Using a comprehensive definition of human services, one that might include such apparently diverse socializing organizations as prisons, mental hospitals, rehabilitative services, and public schools, these organizations are expected to produce behavior repertoires among people that lead to their dealing with their personal environments in such a way that they can gain some control over their own destinies and exercise some freedom of choice in their lives.

All industrialized societies have found it necessary to create some system of health, educational, and welfare services. Some have become more complex and elaborate than others (e.g., the United States is the only industrialized country in the world that does not have a system of national health insurance), and there are differences in both the efficiency and effectiveness in the operations of these organizations. However, they are omnipresent in all industrialized countries.

These organizations, with few exceptions, have been funded and operated by varying combinations of federal, state, local, and voluntary funds. Their origins and growth patterns have generally coincided with the development and/or recognition of human problems in industrial society. Welfare systems arose around the themes of children, the aged, and poverty and were principally oriented toward providing some means of support for poor and orphaned children. It should be noted that an orphaned child probably would not have found himself without human resources in an earlier, preindustrialized society. Rather, some subunit of his family, in the extended family structure of that period, would have taken him into their home. Formal societal intervention would not have been necessary. However, industrialization created mobility patterns that severely hampered the classic extended family. Thus, if social intervention was to occur, it became increasingly necessary for this function to be taken on by formally organized nonfamilial complex organizations. (In a sense it is a bit surprising that the rudiments of a human service system emerged at all, given the Protestant ethic of individualized competition and achievement and the ideology of social Darwinism that prevailed at the turn of the century. Perhaps the key variable, after all, was the spirit of humanitarianism.)

The pattern is to identify a biosocial problem, followed by public and professional concern and concluding with the development of a categorical delivery system. As industrialization and the complexity of work, residential, and mobility patterns increased, larger amounts of national resources have been allocated to organized attempts at problem remediation. Over the last few years the average annual growth of the health industry has been 11%.

In order for a human services organization to arise, it is, and has been, necessary for legislative or other bodies formally representing communities to appropriate monies for support. (Free-standing, categorical fund-raising efforts soliciting funds directly from the public have seldom had a major impact on problems, even though substantial amounts of money have been raised collectively.) In turn, funds have been most likely appropriated in those problem areas that could be empirically verified and that held the potential for solidifying a base of political support—most evident during the depression and the years of the Roosevelt administration, a time of both unprecedented expansion of human services in the welfare sector and a vast expansion in the numbers of people who identified with and voted for, the Democratic party.

Such a remedial, reactive orientation toward social problems and the need to maintain a consumer constituency have been major factors in the development of human service systems. The debates about welfare and national health insurance also illustrate these principles. Such factors have played powerful roles in continuing the tendency to react to problems by developing organizations to remediate rather than generating thrusts in the direction of altering molar patterns of human ecology that might reduce the prevalence of such problems.

The history of human services organizations in America has not been particularly distinguished. Attempts to deal with complex and vexing social problems have been generally reactive and consistently underfinanced, understaffed, and lacking access to avenues of power in the private sector that might bring about significant partnerships for change in social systems. But however myopic our vision might have been, it has not been lost. Substantial amounts of resources are currently being channeled into human service organizations. Approximately one-third of our over $700 billion gross national product (GNP) is being spent in the human services. (Whatever the values of such statistics, some absurdities are built into the data. For example, we include in the GNP both the wages paid to a coal miner and expenditures by former miners to delay and make as painless as possible their deaths from "black lung.") Massive and sometimes powerful human service organizations do exist. The potential for biosocial intervention and change is present. It may be that an adequate proportion of the GNP is presently invested, but this will never be known with our present dysfunctional delivery system.

THE HUMAN SERVICES ORGANIZATION: WHAT IS IT?

In beginning the study of human service organizations, it is important to realize that they are both similar and different from other complex organizations. They share problems of differentiation-integration (e.g., Lawrence & Lorsch, 1967), resource acquisition (e.g., Rice, 1958), and role strain and role conflict (Biddle & Thomas, 1966). They also differ along important dimensions, which in turn give human service organizations a highly unique character. There are complex organizations, and there are complex organizations.

One of the most important characteristics of an organization is the development and use of criteria that provide information feedback to that organization and serve as indicators that shape organizational policy decisions. They have assumed two primary forms: *(a)* economic indices, usually assuming the form of profits or some relative comparisons of organizational income to payments; and *(b)* programmatic outcome indices that show the impact of an organization on its target environment, such as changes in the number of products sold to or consumed by a given population, changes in recidivism rates, changes in academic achievement test scores, etc.

Although these criteria are relatively easily developed in, say, business organizations, they are quite problematic for most human service organizations. Some proprietary (profit-making) institutions do exist in the human service industry. Proprietary hospitals are a classic example, although nursing homes may be the largest single class. Most recently day-care and homemaker services have been offered by major profit-making organizations. Generally, however, human services organizations are supported out of public and voluntary resources and do not expect to make a profit. Neither can they tally indicators of their effectiveness as easily as a sales manager charts the sales of new cars. What kinds of feedback might indicate to a welfare agency that it is having a desired impact on a community? Case load? Changes in case loads? Migratory patterns among welfare recipients? Similarly, how might a community mental health center examine its roles and impact in community life? By the number of persons requiring hospitalization? Patients remaining in treatment? Changes in rates of alcoholism and drug addiction? Crime rates? Church attendance? Divorce rates? What are the indicators of meaningful, productive community lives?

Whatever the political dimensions underlying human service organizations, their origins seem to lie in social values. Health, education, and welfare organizations generally express societal concern. And although the concerns and values operate to provide a general base of public support, operationalizing these values in such a way that the impact of an organization can be reliably and validly assessed is a major problem for virtually all human service organizations.

To a large extent these problems have been largely ignored by human service organizations. (Who has seriously questioned our system of public education?) We have not, until recently, begun to conscientiously deal with the problems of program outcomes, community social indicators, and a level of analysis of organizational impact that goes beyond simple health indicators, welfare case loads, and educational test scores. Instead, we have developed elaborate and often ritualized professional organizations, identities, and behaviors (see, e.g., Goffman, 1961; Harshbarger, 1970a) among the actors in human services organizations. These, in turn, have often taken on a life of their own and have become the criteria by which an organization is judged by those who must make resource allocation decisions.

These underlying factors create some important and unique taxonomic dimensions in human services organizations. The following comparisons between private (profit) sector, production-oriented organizations, and public-private (nonprofit) sector, human services organizations indicate some of these organizational differences (Harshbarger, 1970b).

Collectively, these dimensions lead to nonprofit, public, and voluntary organizations that have a nature and character that generally differentiate them from profit-making organizations. Their actors perform their roles within professional-organizational sanctions and safeguards that protect them from the viscissitudes and vagaries of political pressures that might be brought to bear on actors in other types of organizations. Physicians, teachers, social workers, nurses, psychologists, and many other professionalized employee groups account to each other via their professional organizations and to their organization's funding sources in terms of criteria that have typically been professionally developed, sanctioned, and legitimized. They control the crea-

TABLE 1

Private, profit sector, production organizations	*Public-voluntary, non-profit sector, human services organizations*
The organization is structured and organized in accordance with production cycles-systems.	The organization is structured and organized in accordance with professional values and membership subgroupings.
Organizationally defined tasks provide the primary bases of social segregation and interaction.	Professional membership groups provide the primary basis of social segregation and interaction. Task definition is usually developed by these groups.
Social hierarchies and social power are based in the formal organizational distribution of power.	Social hierarchies and social power are based in professional hierarchies and their relative possession of power.
Intraorganizational norms and behaviors are largely based in production standards of desired efficiency (in both formal and informal organizational subsystems).	Intraorganizational norms and behaviors are largely based in the values of professional and organizational membership groups.
The first allegiance of an individual is to his organizational membership group.	The first allegiance of an individual is to his professional membership group.
The allegiance of the individual to the organization is assumed and is not an area of major conflict.	The allegiance of the individual to the organization is problematical and may be an area of major conflict.
No (or very limited) use of job tenure.	Widespread use of job tenure.
Organizational and role performance of the individual is assessed by a profit criterion.	Organizational performance of the individual is assessed by criteria based in professional value judgments.
The consumption of materials is end-product oriented.	The consumption of materials is means or process oriented.
Relatively clear definition of the end product(s).	Relatively unclear definition of the end product(s).
Cost-effectiveness indices are relatively easily developed.	Cost-effectiveness indices are difficult or impossible to develop; the major problem is the measure of effectiveness.
The overall mission or purpose of the organization is established by a small group (e.g., board of	The overall mission or purpose of the organization is established by a relatively large group (e.g.,

directors) that acts in the best interests of the organization and its ownership.	legislators) that acts in the best interests of the public and that often has conflicting interests.
The primary criterion for the development of new purposes for the organization is that of organizational survival.	The primary criterion for the development of new purposes for the organization is public interest. It is assumed that meeting public needs will give certainty to organizational survival.

tion of, and access to, data that are indicative of organizational performance. In short, these organizations and their resident professionals have, through the design and control of information-feedback systems, far greater control over the social construction of organizational reality than is exercised by actors in other kinds of organizations. The major exception is the research-consultation-oriented profit-making organization whose professional employees manifest the same role strains and whose management must accommodate to the process of dual identification.

ISSUES AND PROBLEMS

The Dilemma of Stability and Change

With a few notable exceptions, effective civil service regulations and organized professional groups have acted as stabilizing influences in most federal, state, and local human services organizations. Political patronage has been reduced to a point that, in most states, a change in state or local government elected officialdom does not appreciably affect the community programs of a human service organization. Simultaneously, there has been an increase in the degree to which these organizations have become staffed by persons labeled as professionals.

Although these factors have created intraorganizational stability and integrity, the environment surrounding human services organizations has undergone major and radical changes in recent years. Emery and Trist (1965) have described these changes in environmental texture as increases in environmental turbulence.

At a broad community level, we face the very difficult problem of meaningfully joining communities that seem to have lost their sense of direction in the midst of a storm and community human service organizations that are capable of navigating only in relatively untroubled waters.

One major issue of the present and the foreseeable future is whether or not human services organizations can move out of their often traditional molds and develop strategies for a very rapidly changing society. The difficulties involved in this process are multiple. Representative problems include the development of change mechanisms that will be effective in what are often highly insular organizations such as schools and hospitals; that do not alienate organizational constituencies; that do not eliminate the best of organizational programs in order to eliminate the worst; and that promise reasonable stability during the change process and do not make life so uncomfortable for organizational actors that, through a combination of attrition and anxiety, the organization is rendered ineffective. Those same mechanisms that have reduced political influence in human services organizations have contributed to a system that has become more responsive to its own needs than to those of the consumer. For example, the public human service administrator is faced with multiple constituencies; first are the employees, next are federal peers, then are his elected officials, fourth are the clients, and last are the taxpayers. Inevitable conflict of interest is the result.

The Problems of Resource Acquisition and Allocation

The first job of every administrator is to continually monitor the external environment of the organization to maintain the flow of resources into the organization. Any decrease in either the level or reliability of resources will have real consequences in terms of positions and programs in his organization.

During the past decade the level of funding for the human services has expanded considerably. U.S. health expenditures alone increased from approximately $23 billion in 1960 to over $60 billion in 1970. Yet in 1970 in the United States a 10-year-old boy had a shorter life expectancy than in 21 other countries in the world; 12 countries had lower rates of infant mortality; one-sixth of all admissions to Cook County Hospital in Chicago died; and there was a purported national shortage of 50,000 physicians and 200,000 nurses as the system was organized. The entire structure of our health-care system is open to question.

The stagnation of the inner city and the decline of rural populations have jointly brought into question major issues in mobility, residential patterns, and adequate schools while financially exhausting our welfare systems.

Although resources have increased, the frequency, intensity, and complexity of the problems that face us have increased at a much more rapid rate. Even a three- or fourfold increase in human service funding patterns over 10 years may be inadequate in view of the exponential increases in the biosocial community problems facing human service organizations.

It may be that increases in funding simply cannot keep pace with increases in problems. If that is the case, administrators of problem-focused human services organizations will have to seriously re-examine that organization's operating and survival strategies. What will be the organizational and community consequences of maintaining present patterns of community resource allocations? What are the implications in continuing existing organizations and their respective approaches to community problems? Is it likely that multiple agencies will continue to compete for funds under conditions of relative scarcity, or might they work out, through new program designs, mutually compatible patterns of sharing resources? Might they work out such patterns if the consequences involve the demise of one of those organizations? Is it possible to generate new models of human services organizations under these conditions?

Which Organizations Shall Survive?

It would seem obvious at this point in time that we are desperately in need of a substantial reorganization in the human services. In many areas this is beginning to occur and hopefully will maximize the effective use of human services resources. However, the problem is how decisions are to be made regarding what specifically is to be reorganized and how that is to be accomplished. What are our criteria? How can we assess the impact of human services organizations in communities?

Gathering the appropriate data to make decisions regarding these problems has been problematic. The secrecy of many agencies regarding data on their activities in communities is understandable, given the potential consequences of openness; that is, they might find this data used as evidence for some other agency's effectiveness and their own relative ineffectiveness. It is probable that funding authorities (e.g., legislatures, United Funds) will have to force a level of organizational disclosure that is unprecedented.

Simultaneously, there will need to be developed more effective indicators and criteria that can put available data to use in assessing both community needs and problems, as well as organizational impact on those problems. Presently, we do not have sufficiently valid biosocial indicators to suggest much more than problem severity. We are unable to look at new models of organizations and programs and make reasonable probability statements about the impact and effectiveness of proposed models.

Such indicators are a must. They are a vital but missing element in the maturation of potentially valuable systems-analytic models or organizations and communities. The beginnings have been made. (See, e.g., Baker & Schulberg, pp. 182-206, 1970; Baker, 1970.) Much more is needed, and it is needed rapidly. For cautions see Noble, (1971).

Planning

In designing the structure and functions of human service organizations, the last unit that is usually added is one relating to planning. (Operational research has a slightly higher priority.) When and if operating funds are reduced in the future, it is likely that this will be the first unit to feel the impact of these restrictions. To the business-oriented executive, planning is equated with product development, an overhead item to be vigorously controlled. As is the case with many minority groups, planners are the last to be hired and the first to be fired.

Yet planning is a vital element in program development. It is even more critical during periods of budgetary limitations and major social change, such as the present, when the soundest thinking should be going into the development of medium-range goals and programs. It is somewhat paradoxical that budgetary restrictions are likely to lower the priorities on planning and the number of staff members involved in planning at the very time when planning effective strategies of survival is most critical to the organization.

In rearranging organizational priorities having to do with planning, it would seem adaptively functional to combine in one unit those positions having to do with both operational research and planning. In effect, this would place in one administrative structure the organizational functions of information feedback and the organizational guidance system. Although one often finds this to be the case, research and planning offices are as likely to be found in separate, often relatively noncommunicating parts of an organization. This makes about as much sense as designing in a rocket environmental monitoring information feedback systems that operate independently from the guidance system. Yet it is precisely this kind of functional independence that characterizes relationships between program researchers and planners in many human services organizations.

In an era in which environmental turbulence is making it extremely difficult, if not impossible, to develop long-range plans, it would seem important that short- and middle-range plans be the best that they can be. Perhaps it is only a question of whether organizational growth will assume the form of maximal or minimal "disjointed incrementalism" (Braybrooke & Lindbloom, 1963). If that is the case, then it becomes even more essential that resources, which seem to be rapidly diminishing relative to the immensity of problem increases, be used in the most rational manner possible.

2. ORGANIZATIONAL ISSUES

As indicated earlier, the human services organization exists and operates within parameters that give this organization a unique character. The human service organization is seldom required to make a profit. Nor are the results of its efforts customarily clearcut and tangible. Often it must survive in an environment of social-political pressures; of conflicting constituencies; of sit-ins; of high-level executive appointments and summary dismissals; of middle-level civil service rules and tenure; and of professional standards. Not surprisingly, the organizational problems that it must face, although in some ways similar to other forms of organizations, have a uniqueness that reflects the nature and character of this form of organization.

ORGANIZATIONAL MODELS—ISSUES AND ALTERNATIVES

As with other forms of social organization, the human service agency must be structured to fulfill certain functions. It must be able to deal with change, anticipated and unanticipated, in the external interorganizational environment. If the organization is designed to be responsive, changes in the surrounding political system should not disrupt it severely. Less flexible structures may suffer severe organizational strains.

At the same time, internal organizational stability must be developed and maintained. There must be a relatively reliable and internally consistent division of labor and differentiation of roles. Predictability and flexibility are required simultaneously.

These two factors, internal and external organizational reliability, are paramount in the development of an effective model of a human services organization. If there is no reliability, then an organization cannot be expected to fulfill even the simplest of missions. Neither people nor organizations will perform rationally and consistently under conditions of environmental uncertainty or unreliability.

Yet decisions regarding the real or potential predictability of these functions cannot be limited exclusively to intraorganizational issues. No organization exists in isolation. An organizational chart, complete with accurate diagrams of functional pathways of communication and decision-making, cannot by itself yield valid information on which predictions about an organization's performance can be based. The first, and most important, consideration is one concerned with the environment in which the organization must survive. Given the external demands generated by survival itself, how should an organization be structured? What kind of internal structure is necessary to withstand the buffeting of the outer environment? What kind of internal structure will best glean available resources from the outer environment?

Decisions that create new organizational structures, whether as reorganizations of or additions to existing organizations, or as new organizations, are filled with risk. And although these decisions are of tremendous import, they tend to be made in relative haste. Too often, environmental pressures and internal structural strains have been neglected, only to return to haunt the organization's inhabitants.

Every organization will, within rather wide limits, take whatever steps are necessary to maintain itself. It will, if necessary, expend inordinate resources to continue its existence. And the larger the proportion of resources that are required for organizational maintenance, the smaller the proportion of resources that are available for goal attainment. The consequences of decisions about organizational structure and real and lasting in their effects.

There is abundant information that would suggest that many past models of human services organizations have not been particularly effective in meeting their organizational and sociocultural goals; for example, the poor are receiving medical care that does not begin to approach minimal acceptable levels; the cost escalation is making medical services a luxury even for the middle class; although mental institutions consume over 90% of most state mental health budgets, few provide services other than institutionalization; educational systems are outdated and antiquated; and welfare reform has become a major national effort.

In each of these cases we are, in the 1970s, dealing with organizational models in which the basic form was usually designed prior to the turn of the century. (Welfare, the most contemporary model, was last fashioned in the 1930s.) They have become organizational dinosaurs, consuming quantities of resources that are vastly disproportional to their social utility.

Only one state, California, in 1970, has passed legislation that may, through the use of medical paraprofessionals, broaden the base of its medical care. Only one state, North Dakota, in 1968, has begun a serious effort to reorganize its educational system. National health insurance and welfare reform still await action by Congress.

At local and regional levels decision-making processes regarding new and modified organizational structures have lacked maps and compasses that might serve as effective guides to the decision-making process. Too often there has been no framework within which there might be a concerting of decisions in the public interest. Rather, well-intentioned decisions have been made in quarters far removed from third parties, such as consumers and other human services organizations, who will be directly affected by these decisions.

It would seem appropriate that decisions regarding human service organizational structures, particularly in the development of new organizations, should be made within some kind of general systems framework, one that attempts to define, integrate, and interdigitate available resources, target populations, present delivery systems and capabilities, felt consumer needs, and organizational needs. It makes little sense for communities to attempt to add additional physicians to an already overburdened and inadequate model of service delivery; it makes little sense to expand a welfare system that has outcomes that rarely go beyond maintaining sustenance among its clients; it also makes little sense to add another school to an educational system that is based on a nineteenth-century philosophy of education.

Specifically, the following considerations should be included in decisions regarding the structuring of new, or the restructuring of old, human services organizations:

1. Can the target population be defined? Are there patterns, such as age or career, that help define any movement in or out of this target population and might serve as points of maximally effective intervention?

2. What is the target system? What are the sources of its funds? Where are decisions of resource allocation made? What are subdivisions of the system? How are the units related? What kinds of exchanges are transacted?

3. What are the system goals? What are specific goals of subunits within the target system? Can these goals be organized in a manner that is consistent with the needs of the target population? How much redundancy is there? What elements within the target population are actually affected by these goals?

4. What are the external system relationships? What functions outside of services themselves must be maintained in order to ensure the survival of the target system?

5. What are some outcomes of services that might be agreed on by all parties involved with the new or restructured organization?

In short, what is the context in which a new or modified organization must survive? What are the systemic community and interorganizational properties of that environment?

If most of these questions cannot be answered satisfactorily, then it makes as little sense to develop a new neighborhood storefront or multi-service center as it does to add one more unit to a highly bureaucratized and centralized organization.

INTERORGANIZATIONAL PROBLEMS

Slowly, over the past 10 years, there has begun to emerge a language that may ultimately permit the articulation of interorganizational relationships. This language, partially based on general systems and social systems theories is aimed at developing multilevel conceptions of interorganizational relationships, dependencies, and resource exchanges. Conceptual papers by Levine and White (1961), Litwak and Hylton (1962), Evan (1966), Gross (1967), Warren (1967), and Baker and Schulberg (1970, pp. 182-206) are representative of these developments.

At a community and interorganizational level the problems faced by human service organizations are different, depending on the kinds of interorganizational relationships that have been worked out in the past. Following Warren's (1967) treatment of the ways in which interorganizational units interact in the decision-making process, we might find four types of decision-making contexts: *(a)* a unitary context, for example, a city health authority in which the units are organized for the achievement of inclusive goals; *(b)* a federative context, for example, a council of social agencies in which each unity has its own goals but that share some formal organization for the accomplishment of inclusive goals; *(c)* a coalitional context, for example, a health planning committee in which participating units cooperate to attain some desired objective, but informally and on an *ad hoc* basis; and *(d)* a social-choice context in which organizations may relate around a certain issue, although they do not necessarily share any inclusive goals and in which authority rests at the unit level.

Each of these contexts defines a kind of interorganizational environment, a set of relationships that carries certain assets and liabilities and places certain kinds of parameters on the participating organizations.

These interorganizational relationships are likely to take place in differing kinds of community environments. Emery and Trist (1965) described four types of environmental causal textures or areas of interdependencies that are characteristic of the environment itself: *(a)* a placid, randomized environment in which there are few disturbances and resources are distributed randomly; *(b)* a placid, clustered environment in which there are few disturbances but in which resources are distributed nonrandomly; *(c)* a disturbed-reactive environment in which similar units, or organizations, compete for available resources; *(d)* a turbulent field in which there is both a competition for resources and, simultaneously, a number of changes in the environmental field itself.

Terreberry (1968) has suggested that organizations are experiencing increasingly turbulent environments. Human services organizations in urban areas are finding themselves having to compete for limited resources and at the same time deal with the dynamic properties of a rapidly changing social environment.

Human services organizations, within these multilevel community and interorganizational contexts, find themselves entering into relationships and decisions that are aimed at multilevel outcomes. Such outcomes might be approached in terms of their relevance to community needs, interorganizational relationships, and intraorganizational needs. In approaching these problems and in entering into decisions about meeting community needs, each human services organization hopes to enhance its resources through interorganizational decisions and resource exchanges.

These transactions, or exchanges, Levine and White (1961) have noted, assume three primary forms: *(a)* clients, *(b)* labor services, and *(c)* resources other than labor services. Although the first two can be documented and empirically demonstrated relatively easily, it is the latter category that is probably the most intangible, yet the most important, in the life of an organization. The components of exchange in this category will differ, depending on the nature of the human services organization, but will include vitally important exchanges such as those relating to political support, as well as other exchanges having to do with exchanges of information about clients, other organizations, etc.

In a community an organization ordinarily directs its principal efforts at survival and growth. For human services organizations one method will be to attempt to increase resources by directly meeting community needs (e.g., fees for service, increased United Fund support); in part, these efforts will be aimed at negotiating productive, profitable trade-offs of organizational resources. A partly qualifying trend just beginning to surface is the refusal of some organizations to grow on "soft" money (having already suffered cash flow problems or funds dried up in policy shifts) or on funds that require major intraorganizational changes or long-range commitments.

INTRAORGANIZATIONAL PROBLEMS

As the external requirements, or parameters, that operate on and around an organization assume some structure or form, internal organizational positions, roles, and norms begin to emerge. Over time the tasks people perform and the ways in which they relate to each other become sufficiently routinized to allow for necessary levels of predictability in everyday organizational life. Imbedded in these developmental processes are both the elements that are required for long-term organizational stability, goal-setting, and growth, as well as the potential for excessive routinization, bureaucratic red tape, boredom, and organizational dry rot (Gardner, 1965). It is this dilemma that confronts all organizations, large and small.

Every organization is at some time engaged in the difficult process of making decisions about its centralization or decentralization, formal or informal organizational demands, performances of old tasks or searches for new ones, maintaining organizational sanctions or changing these sanctions, and maintaining patterns of authority and decision-making or changing those patterns. These are but a few of the issues that center around maintaining internal organizational reliability in an interorganizational environment that is changing and placing new demands on its component organizations.

Terreberry (1968) has suggested that most major internal organizational change is induced through changes in the organization's external environment. Recent experiences in the field of mental health would support her position. Through the development of effective and decentralized community mental health programs in such places as the Canadian Province of Saskatchewan and the states of California and Minnesota and the advent of new chemotherapies, mental hospitals have found themselves with dwindling rates of patient input and increasing rates of patient output. In Saskatchewan the result has been the closing of some hospitals and a radical reorganization of others to accommodate a different patient population. Minnesota and California have experienced a similar phenomenon.

Most human services organizations, however, are neither quite as antiquated nor as likely to be as drastically affected by environmental changes as the traditional mental hospital structure. Most human services organizations, for example, rehabilitation services and welfare systems, are sufficiently in touch with their interorganizational, socio-politico-economic environments to be somewhat responsive to changing demands but sufficiently bounded by protective mechanisms and constituencies to prevent the generation of major internal organizational changes.

Within most human services organizations two kinds of internal regulatory devices operate to place limits and sanctions on intraorganizational behavior: *(a)* a bureaucratized organizational structure and *(b)* professionalization of staff members. In examining the problem of social regulation in organizations, Hall (1967) has indicated that in an organization's effort to maintain some level of intraorganizational reliability and /or social control, an organization will rely on professional norms and standards if possible; if this is not possible, then hierarchical, bureaucratized systems will emerge. The greater the degree of professionalization the lesser the bureaucratic hierarchy; conversely, the lesser the degree of professionalization, the greater the degree of bureaucratization.

By definition, an organization is a regulated system of behaviors and exchanges. In a human services organization the key is to both use that social regulation to move toward productive ends and to generate internal change processes that shift and guide behaviors toward these ends.

Every new member of a relatively bureaucratized human services organization (i.e., an organization possessing the characteristics of specialization, a hierarchy of authority, a system of rules, and impersonality; Blau, 1956) is immediately confronted with the organizational demands and limits on his behavior. The strategies of his own behavior that will ultimately lead to career advancement become clear in a very short period of time. Such strategies have typically involved a redirection of one's own interests to those of the organization (Merton, 1957, pp. 207-244; Kornhauser, 1962; Daniels, 1969). Too often the results have been the dulling of interests and the blunting of potential organizational change processes.

Instant solutions to these problems are not immediately available. Even the more obvious suggestions are filled with difficulties. One of the more prevalent strategies to deal with bureaucratized human services organizations, and one that has achieved some notoriety, is that of decentralizing large and very complex human services organizations. However, few, if any, workable means of decentralizing have been achieved. The most visible recent attempt to decentralize a human service organization has been in the administration of the New York City school system. Not only is there some question whether the decentralized districts (each of which contains a pupil population about the size of the Boston school system) reflect a meaningful decentralization, but as Kristol (1968) suggests, there also are serious questions surrounding a real decentralizing of decision-making power that is commensurate with organizational restructuring. If human service organizations are to be meaningfully decentralized, stronger local authority is necessary. Effective decentralization, Kristol indicates, does not diffuse authority.

Functional strategies of organizational change have not come easily to the human services. The factors of tradition, bureaucracy, and professionalism have combined to render change extremely difficult and problematic. For an assessment of this problem in one area of the human services, the mental hospital, the reader is referred to Goffman (1961) for an overview of the problem and to Hirschowitz (1967; 1969) and Harshbarger (1967) for a view of change strategies and outcomes in single mental hospitals.

New models of human services organizations have, slowly begun to emerge to meet needs created and intensified by rapid population shifts in both urban and rural areas. One of the more popular emergent organizational models in urban areas has been the neighborhood service center, an organization that is made up of interdisciplinary staff members, both professionals and nonprofessionals. But as O'Donnell and Sullivan (1969, p. 10) and Demone (1972), in a review of the literature on neighborhood service centers, have indicated, unless such organizations resolve some very basic problems, numerous organizational malfunctions result. For example, a neighborhood service center must deal with such issues as either emphasizing *(a)* professional direction and administration *or* resident participation and neighborhood control; *(b)* the provision of services *or* social action; *(c)* professional service *or* nonprofessional services; *(d)* information and referral *or* client advocacy and follow-up; *(e)* collaborative and cooperative methods *or* contest and conflict tactics.

The foregoing do not represent all of the issues that confront the neighborhood services center as an organization, and there is no right or wrong way to decide these issues. There are risks and particular constellations of consequences for moving in either direction on any given issue. The point is that role choices must be made by all organizations. They cannot be all things to all people. Moreover, the choices have to be made with a continual view toward the external consequences of these intraorganizational decisions.

ORGANIZATIONAL CHANGE

In large and small ways every organization must attempt to regulate and incorporate into its life the changes in both its external and internal environments. Sometimes this takes the form of building protective barriers in and around an organization so that it is not significantly affected by external changes; at other times, structuring internal organizational relationships so that they continue as they have operated in the past.

As a general rule organizations are more susceptible to change the greater the number of pluralistic interests that directly affect their welfare. A school system, for example, with its single authority, a school board, and a single major source of revenue, local property taxes, is likely to be less open to organizational change than a local mental health organization that survives through a mixture of local, state, and federal funds. Parenthetically, it is worth noting that progress toward desegregation has seemed to have developed a greater impetus in those school districts that have come to rely on federal funds, and hence developed a more pluralistic base of support, than in districts that maintain independent funding sources.

A language of organizational change structure and processes has begun to develop, albeit slowly, and with the softest of data to serve as guides to effective and productive change. Bennis and Slater (1968); and Bennis and Harris (1970) have suggested, at various times, organizational units that are task oriented and temporary in their life and structure. Bennis and Harris (1970) described "organic populism," a form of organizational structure that arises around a problem and a group of concerned, competent persons and that has a relatively temporary organizational life. People in this organization would be differentiated by competence and training, not rank, and leaders would serve primarily linking-pin functions.

Other students of complex organizations, particularly persons who have maintained some long-term association with National Training Laboratories and the T-group movement, such as Bennis, Benne, and Chin, in *The Planning of Change* (1969) and Blake and Mouton (1961) in *The Managerial Grid,* have attempted to articulate strategies of organizational change. Generally, such models of changes as these have involved the adoption of a T-group-oriented model of the change process and integrating it into critical segments of the target organization. In the application of this approach there has been a tendency to focus on the change process per se and a tendency to neglect the long-term consequences of these strategies. As yet it is unclear under what conditions and toward what ends this change strategy is likely to be maximally effective. However, there is virtually universal agreement that it is a powerful change strategy, one that has the potential for generating not only positive organizational changes but also long-term and negative reactive forces within an organization. The latter might be particularly true in human services organizations in which ideologies and professional beliefs are often substituted for empirical outcomes, rendering any evidence of positive organizational changes rather difficult to come by.

A parallel development over the past 15 years has been the growth of the field of systems theory and research as a conceptual framework within which to examine organizational relationships and changes. The field is growing and developing conceptual models but as yet lacks the data base and skills necessary to transpose data across organizations. For an examination of the uses of general system theory in health systems the reader is referred to Sheldon, Baker, and McLaughlin's *Systems and Medical Care* (1970). Von Bertalanffy's (1956) is a more basic text.

It is likely that major, long-term structural changes in organizations and the models that planners envision in designing new organizations will lie in a system's theoretical conception of structural relationships and outcomes. The technologies of change and organizational maintenance will probably lie in approaches reflecting system diagnosis and using those clusters of change tactics best designed to achieve chosen results, controlled by whether goals are short-or long-range and whether the organization views itself as *ad hoc* or permanent. Critical to effective change is an awareness that organizations are made up of people and that their needs must be reflected in the change process.

3. RESOURCES AND THEIR MANAGEMENT

The roles, relationships, and problematic issues that link government, foundations, and voluntary health and welfare agencies are highly complex and in constant flux. Howard (1965, pp. 649-654) describes the latter as follows:

> Questions at issue range from the highly pragmatic—how to secure—*now*—care urgently needed by one group or another—to those involving fundamental philosophies. Among the latter are the nature of the "good society," pluralism, private enterprise, optimal rates of social change and progress, government, bureaucracies (private, whether sectarian or non-sectarian, and governmental), the societal roles of justice, philanthropy and charity, and church-state relationships.

In addition, the historical stereotypes and myths about roles and interorganizational relationships seldom represent contemporary reality.

Some general issues have been decided. Only the government has the financial capacity to raise the level of financial and medical care for larger numbers of low-income people. Which is not to suggest that selected individuals cannot be helped by private enterprise, for veteran, religious, and private social welfare organizations have often given assistance to their members or selected families and individuals at risk; the latter, however, have been the exceptions.

Beyond these fundamental pragmatic issues, organizational functions and roles are becoming increasingly blurred. At best organizations can now be classified as public, quasi public, quasi private, and private. Consider the following:

1. Religious organizations, theoretically separated from the state by constitutional provisions, own tax-deductible property, are the recipients of tax-deductible gifts, and receive government support for specific functions; also, certain of their selected social welfare activities are subsidized by the United Fund.

2. Federal, state, and local governments, in establishing new statutory programs, increasingly suggest that the newly developed organizations secure nonprofit charters.

3. Long-established voluntary organizations, (e.g., the Visiting Nurse Association, receive more than 50% of their operating budgets from Medicare and Medicaid and from contracts with local school and health departments.

The following discussions, entitled Government Organizations, Voluntary Associations, Foundations, and Policy and Politics, are separated in part by sanctions and functions and in part for convenience. Shibboleths notwithstanding, a lack of clarity in making these distinctions is the rule.

GOVERNMENT ORGANIZATIONS

Perhaps most at tension within government is the unclear relation among its various levels; federal, state, county, and local. Issues of philosophy (subsidiarity, centralization and decentralization, and control of various taxing mechanisms) and political power compound the problem. But sheer size, inertia, and the general ineffectiveness of the federal government in delivering direct personal services to people (Veterans' Administration hospitals may be a partial exception) have now led many politicians, public administrators, and political scientists to advocate various forms of federal, non-categorical subsidization of state and local governments. It is reasoned that sheer logistics make it advisable to develop local management and control of programs designed to meet individual, neighborhood, and community needs. As this debate continues and experimentation occurs, new-old struggles between the various levels of government and between local groups wanting community control have developed and intensified.

A side issue, but also a critical one, is the continuing debate between the advocates of categorical and block grants. The revenue-sharing proposals of Presidents Johnson and Nixon represent one position. On the face of it they make considerable sense, but the vigor and heat generated by the opponents suggests that the issues are not simple. Categorical grants can be used to stimulate national priorities and subsidize programs dealing with problems lacking local appeal (e.g., alcoholism). Also, powerful constituencies are usually reflected by each category. A balanced perspective would suggest that both options are needed and that flexibility and timing are the key variables.

Some relevant problems: Large-city mayors want direct access to federal largess, bypassing the traditional federal to state to local formula; the one-man, one-vote Supreme Court ruling is slowly freeing urban areas from the domination of rural areas; town, city, county, and even state boundaries are frequently meaningless as problem-solving areas for human service organizations; efforts to regionalize government flounder even though the failure to develop new and more rational catchment and service areas may make the government increasingly unresponsive to the needs of its citizens; as both the white and black middle class flee the core city for the suburbs, the qualitative differences between central city and suburban schools, and other socializing institutions, are accentuated even further; of the major social institutions, only health, social welfare, and cultural activities are still superior in the urban environment, with the latter primarily serving an affluent user population.

As grants-in-aid and contracting mechanisms have become increasingly common, the issues of quality control and accountability have become even more important. Again the question of role functions is at issue. Shall the federal government do this centrally or via its regional office? Or should this function be delegated to an even lower level of government; and if so, which level?

As information systems become more sophisticated and fully exploit computer technology, it is clear that the vendor will be in a much better position to guarantee high standards if the vendor can organize to do the job.

One important management control in governmental human service organizations is in planning and budgeting. With isolated exceptions state and local governments have fallen far behind the federal government in budgeting technology. Most state and local governments continue to rely exclusively on object-item budgeting, and their emphasis is primarily on fiscal control. Budget bureaus are inadequately staffed, and program planning is seldom legitimized at either the operating department or budget department level.

It is true that reform efforts, grants from federal agencies, and even some local appropriations are breathing new life into antiquated managerial mechanisms, but considering the pressures on state and local government and the inadequacies of their responses, time may be running out as alternative structural procedures are sought.

VOLUNTARY ASSOCIATIONS

Voluntary human services organizations are big business. Billions of dollars are donated every year for operating and capital purposes. Additional billions are received as fees, grants, and contracts from individuals, third-party organizations, government, and foundations.

Standards developed by the National Information Bureau (1968) for philanthropic operations stress responsibility and public trusteeship and suggest specific operational procedures:

1. Board—an active and responsible governing body

serving without compensation, holding regular meetings, and with effective administrative control.

2. Purpose—a legitimate purpose with no avoidable duplication of the work of other sound organizations.

3. Program—reasonable efficiency in program management and reasonable adequacy of resources, both material and personnel.

4. Cooperation—evidence of consultation and cooperation with established agencies in the same or related fields.

5. Ethical promotion. Ethical methods of publicity, promotion, and solicitation of funds.

6. Fund-raising practice—*(a)* No payment of commissions for fund-raising. *(b)* No mailing of unordered tickets or merchandise with a request for money in return. *(c)* No general telephone solicitation of the public.

7. Audit—annual audit, preferably employing the Uniform Accounting Standards and prepared by an independent certified public accountant, showing all support/revenue and expenditures in reasonable detail. New organizations should provide an independent certified public accountant's statement that a proper financial system has been installed.

8. Budget—detailed annual budget, translating program plans into financial terms.

The critical ingredients that differentiate governmental from voluntary organizations are the sponsorship and the trusteeship responsibilities. Typically, the voluntary association offers the individual citizen a greater opportunity to participate in its operation. Citizens are not advisers, but serve policy-making functions in the organization. They, rather than elected and appointed officials, possess the ultimate authority.

At a somewhat less visible level voluntary organizations are not constrained by the increasingly inflexible civil service system, which hampers many governmental organizations. They are potentially much more flexible, although many voluntary associations have failed to capitalize on this difference.

To be effectively differentiated from their governmental peer agencies, a voluntary system must maximize its citizen participation and flexibility. Currently, at a time when individuals are becoming increasingly disenchanted with formal, large, complex, governmental organizations that are seen as distant and inflexible, these are rare opportunities for citizen participation in making voluntary organizations responsive to real needs.

In referring to the health industry, but with equal application to the entire voluntary human service system, the National Commission on Community Health Services (1967, p. 22) commented:

> While the role of the voluntary health agency may appear to have grown less distinct and increasingly difficult to separate from the totality of the health system of the community, this does not mean that its importance has in any way diminished. On the contrary the obligation of the voluntary health agency to the community is even more urgent and compelling than it was in previous years to perform effectively both in its own right and as a genuine partner of the governmental agency. Each has an obligation to be of maximum help to the other in fulfilling their complementary, respective, and joint functions.

It may be that the National Commission has understated the case. Since the 1930s the United States has been dominated by a theory of public administration emanating from the writings and practices of Harry Hopkins. The theory was clean and simple: If an activity was to be a continuing one, the government should operate it. Goods and selected temporary services could be purchased. After almost 40 years of experience this model is now being questioned. Direct human services to people as a function of government have worked well only within certain limited parameters and have seemed unable to deal effectively with the radical changes of post-World War II America. Unfortunately existing services have changed slowly, if at all. Broad-based constituencies and political forces have essentially stalemated the possibility of substantial change. The public administrator is faced with complex and essentially existential conflicts of interests.

Consequently, with increasing frequency consideration is being given to the purchase of services. In this model the government determines priorities, sets standards, and monitors activities conducted for it by service delivery organizations operating on a grant-in-aid, contract, or fee-for-service basis. At this point in time it would appear that organizational flexibility is enhanced and priority change is possible. No longer is the public administrator responsible both to his employees and to the consumers. Role conflict is reduced.

As with any large-scale change in the human services, certain losses may occur. If voluntary agencies do agree to participate in major contract and grant-in-aid arrangements, they abrogate certain freedoms. By definition they must be willing to accept all individuals covered by the agreement. Discrimination is not permitted. Although the latter may not be a problem for many agencies, it may present difficulties for sectarian organizations or agencies established to deal with specific nationality or racial groups.

An additional issue, one which is often debated but seldom resolved, is the proportion of an agency's budget that may be secured from third parties and still not adversely dominate the agency. It is common knowledge in the rehabilitation field that many rehabilitation agencies are unwilling to criticize the state agency, even though it may need such criticisms, and that the specialized agencies are potentially the most appropriate informed bodies. Ecologically, the organization has become over-dependent on a limited resource base. In sometimes not so subtle ways the locus of policy has, via an ecological process, moved outside of the organization.

The voluntary sector has also created an additional form of ecological dependence. That is, through the development of professional overspecialization it has become fragmented, conservative, and increasingly dependent on the value systems of professional organizations.

FOUNDATIONS

According to the Foundation Library Center (1968, p. 55):

> In its purest form a foundation may be defined as a non-governmental, non-profit corporation or trust, deriving its income from its own endowment managed by its own trustees or directors, and established to make grants for the support of social, educational, charitable, religious, cultural or other activities serving the common welfare. Though not fully meeting specifications of this definition, two other types of organizations are generally recognized by professionals in a broader sense: (1) grant-making organizations; either company-sponsored or family foundations, deriving their funds largely from annual appropriations rather than from endowment; and (2) endowed organizations, called operating foundations, which use most or all of their income to support research or other activities conducted under their own auspices.

Definitional complications are many. Many foundations do not include that term in their title; some others that do use the term are not generally considered foundations. Although in 1970 there were probably more than 10,000 "foundations" in the United States, the bulk of the assets are concentrated in a small group of foundations. Thus, a relatively small number of full-time employees and active board members make policy and allocate the bulk of funds.

These organizations are now divided by law into two types, the private foundation and the public foundation. The private foundation has secured most of its funds from a single individual (e.g., the Ford Foundation) and the public foundation from many individuals (e.g., community foundations). Until the 1969 tax amendments the private foundations were potentially the most creative of all public or private funding organizations. Their constituency was limited to the original supporters (and their families). The philanthropists were limited only by their own inventiveness and the rather limited and unclear law administered by the U.S. Internal Revenue Service. Not in the market for additional donors, they were not required to concern themselves with the attitudes of potential supporters. On the assumption that the broader the base of support the more constrained the organization, the private foundation could be much more flexible than its public counterpart. A fear of Congress (which eventually did act to control their activities), their internal bureaucratic problems, and staff and board differences of opinion have made these organizations much less innovative than possible.

No current discussion of American foundations can take place without mention of Congress's Tax Reform Act of 1969, which contained a section taxing foundations and further regulating their activities.

To agency executives planning to go the foundation route in securing program support, the net result of this law, requiring *(a)* an excise tax on investment income and *(b)* a minimum distribution of income for charitable purposes, may be to create a short-run increase in available funds but a long-run diminution of resources.

Perhaps an even more important consequence of this law is the threat of negative sanctions on foundations, should they exert political influence directly or indirectly. (Financial transactions that might benefit donors or selected other people are also proscribed).

Generally, an immediate result within foundations has been an increase in their tendency to react conservatively to proposals that might have public policy implications. Since most foundations have traditionally been cautious, we can expect to see a further drying up of certain types of venture capital.

Another possibility is suggested by Walsh (1970), who indicates that the foundation staff will now play an increasingly larger role in defining and sometimes generating projects that are to be supported by certain foundations. For smaller foundations that cannot justify full-time well-trained professional managers, joint clearinghouses are being developed to give advice and to act as brokers between worthy applicants and foundations.

POLICY AND POLITICS

Webster defines politics as "the science and art of government; the science dealing with the organization, regulation and administration of a state . . . ;" and "in a bad sense, artful or dishonest management to secure the success of political candidates or parties." For the purposes of this section we are concerned with developing a focus on political roles enacted in human services, organizations, both in and out of those organizations, whether public or private, profit or nonprofit. An administrator, by definition, finds himself in conflict situations or in interactions where he needs the resources and support of persons within and outside of his organization. A majority of administrators' many contacts have political overtones, and administrative favors are given and received. Credits are accumulated and selectively expended.

Mattison (1965) suggests that in understanding this process we start from the perspective of the politician. What are his needs? What would be his model program?

1. The proposed program should be positive, visible, and perceived favorably by the constituents of the politician.
2. The programs should not contain negative components or lead to a tax increase or public disagreement by significant authorities.
3. Favorable effects should be credited, in part at least, to the politician or to his party. Defects, if any, should be the responsibility of the opposition.
4. Programs should be immediately responsive to his constituents. They should be sexy. Drama is preferable. Odds on success should be high.

From the point of view of the elected official, who is subject to re-election every two, four, or six years, such constraints are reasonable. Operating on a limited time-achievement span, subject to the vagaries of voters demanding instant solutions, and responsible to conflicting interests, his preference may be to choose no solution rather than one that may cost money, create dissension, and contain uncertain results. Similar constraints are found in all large organizations that are subject to diverse and pluralistic constituencies. For example, a United Fund with an annual fund-raising campaign operates within these tight constraints. Lacking an ability to compel payment, such as taxes, they can be rejected annually by their givers if their programs are too unpopular or controversial.

Broad-based constituencies are not ordinarily conducive to risk-taking, with low organizational risks being sanctioned, often through silent resistence, not only by those individuals receiving direct services but also by those thousands or millions of people (or their representatives) who subsidize a program. A lack of organizational action and improved service delivery systems that disturb the status quo often has its roots in this broadly defined supportive constituency.

The innovative and creative agency administrator constantly confronts such constraints, tests their limits, and extends or changes them. At the same time he has to be constantly aware of the political realities faced by his major funding sources. A constant source of tension, these fundamental discrepancies, if openly faced and acknowledged, might be reconciled. However, what appears to be an unreasonable demand by an administrator or an unreasonable rejection by the funding source may be justifiable and rational, depending on one's vantage point. Viewing politics as the art of the possible, compromises may be negotiated, but only to the degree that the opposition is understood. Mattison reminds the human services administrator that he, too, is a politician.

Most private and public health and welfare officials formally reject and deny their political roles. An acknowledgement of a political role has been seen as in fundamental conflict with their professional status, although they might ordinarily acknowledge that effective administration requires certain intra- and interorganizational political skills.

Schaefer's study (1962) of public health officers found them denying a political role yet expressing concern over local political pressure or domination. They seemed to yearn for a utopia with public health in but not of government whose determinants would be science and professionalism.

Since public health officers viewed their motives as "right and pure" (compared to politicians), they saw themselves as in key decision-making roles unfettered by political influence. Further, since "the motivations of those with whom he (the public health officer) is dealing were regarded as venal or base, effective negotiation and adjustment may have been impossible." (Schaefer, 1962, p. 326)

What seems so missing, and so necessary, is a view of instrumental political behaviors as both essential and legitimate in the roles of those persons administering or delivering services in human service organizations. Professional ideologies, with their clear and present views of the past, must undergo change. The sense of appropriate reality confrontation and sense of what is legitimate needs a radical updating.

4. THE ELEMENTS OF PLANNING

Effective community and human services planning in the United States has been an exception not a rule. Our cities have burgeoned, and our rural areas have been drained of their populations. The distribution of our social resources has been unplanned, largely undirected, and lacking in systematic area or regional attempts to create selectively manageable, humane, and productive environments.

In this chapter we begin to delineate some of the basic elements in the planning process, a process that is as complex as it is relevant to the survival of all of us. Although these elements are probably neither unfamiliar nor surprising to most readers, it is important that some consensual base be developed if we are to begin moving toward the use of action-oriented planning to achieve livable communities.

DEFINITIONS

The World Health Organization (1958) defined planning as containing five steps:

1. The collection of information essential for planning.
2. The establishment of objectives.
3. The assessment of barriers and planning for their removal.
4. The appraisal of the apparent and potential resources, funds, personnel, and determination of their interrelationship.
5. The development of a detailed plan of operation, in-

cluding a definite mechanism for continuous evaluation.

Feingold (1969, p. 864) suggests that "Planning . . . is concerned with change, or, in the legislative language, with interference."

Mott (1969, p. 797) describes planning as "an effort on the part of some group or organization to alter the behavior and conditions of other people."

Schools of social work have focused on the teaching of community organization rather than planning, although the definitions overlap. Rothman (1964, p. 24), for example, describes "community organization as geared to the attainment of some social welfare or to the solution of some social welfare problem." The strengthening or rationalizing of existing services, establishing new ones, or changing some negative aspect of an existing community structure, all may be legitimate community organization and planning goals.

To others community organization should not be equated with planning but viewed as one of many methods available to planners. Schools of social work are thus criticized for an overemphasis on a single procedure. Complementing this criticism is the suggestion that process instead of goals are highlighted. For example, Ross (1955, p. 51), a leading scholar of community organization, focuses on "community integration . . . community morale . . . and a spiritual community." The possibility that communities as a heritage of our rural past may not be a meaningful contemporary urban territorial base and that a focus on means, not ends, may divert important energies and thus be counterproductive underscores the weakness of the overemphasis on community organization. The counterargument has been explicated by Pray (1947) who suggests that it is an improper usurpation of role for the social welfare professions to give professional leadership to substantive goals.

Operationally, what is being suggested is that man should have some control over his fate, that he has a right to participate in goal formulation and decision-making regarding the means to ends. The current view focuses on the integration of planning and implementation.

That all too often in human service organizations planners have been the last to be hired and the first to be fired is symptomatic of more serious problems in developing and rationally using resources. Historically, we have not taken planning seriously. As Slater (1970) has suggested, we have tended to be a nation of highly mobile people, a country in which the accepted solution to undesirable living conditions has been to move on. Until recently we had not begun to view ourselves as living in a relatively closed ecological system, one in which there were real limitations to "moving West." We have tended to plan neither our cities nor our human services systems. People have been left to fend for themselves, while those who were able moved to greener pastures, pastures that are now in limited supply and anything but green. In the United States, Slater suggests, everybody thinks that he is the only person in America. That is a hard and harsh reality for a planner; Slater suggests everybody must ultimately realize that he must live with everybody else.

NATURE OF PLANNING

Since change is inevitable and apparently exponential, the wise man usually tries to reduce the elements of luck and chance. Planning implies looking ahead and is based on the premise that events are often related and do not occur singly. It assumes certain cause and effect relations. In the following section we will discuss some of the difficulties in applying the principles of informed planning, for many of the variables are difficult to identify, and people do not always act in their own self interest. Nevertheless, events do occur in some relationship to each other; more than luck, magic, and chance are at work.

In the human services field organized planning occurs

categorically and generically; it can be found in public and private, profit and nonprofit organizations. Categorical planning can be as all encompassing as in the entire field of mental health or as specific as planning for late-adolescent female depressions. It can include the entire medical care system or focus on kidney dialysis and transplantation. Broadly or narrowly conceived, all of these topics would be considered categorical planning, for they do not include other fundamental institutional roles inseparably related to man's good and ill health—his condition as a social animal, his economic and employment status, his housing and education. Only voluntary community health and welfare councils have attempted to view the entire human services network, and even those organizations have usually excluded formal education.

DIMENSIONS OF PLANNING

General and High Impact

A distinction should be made between planning for the general population and especially targeted groups of a high-risk or high-incidence nature. Ordinarily, public bodies are committed to serving an entire eligible population on a case basis, although programs may never actually reach universality. Usually, such delivery arrangements are state supported, sometimes partially subsidized by the federal government. The one major exception is the public health field, which traditionally has concerned itself with primary prevention and high-risk groups.

More recently a new trend, federal to local government, bypassing state government, has stimulated a variety of new programs designed to serve special populations, for example, Model Cities, neighborhood service programs, and Head Start.

Either choice, generic or high impact, has its

advantages and disadvantages. To illustrate, we might briefly note some of the consequences of the more recent federal to local government high-impact programs: New agencies are developed; new actors come into their own; new organizational relationships are established; although the ostensible goal is to reduce duplication and overlapping, the result is usually opposite. Old linkages are violated or ignored; politicians and bureaucrats are often threatened.

Attractive at first, these new arrangements often contain the seeds of their own destruction. As Newman and Demone (1969) have noted, the influence necessary to effectively bypass state governments would have to be amassed by larger and more formidable coalitions than presently exist in the health and welfare system. Each choice is constrained, and an understanding of the alternatives and their implications is a necessary input to effective planning.

Organizational Behaviors

Since it is likely that specific organizations will be asked to alter their programs, success will be enhanced to the degree that the planners are knowledgeable about target organizations. If the goal is to persuade family service agencies to treat more alcoholics or to convince them that they need in-service training in order to deal more effectively with those alcoholics and their families already being seen, a strong familiarity with these organizations is desirable. Further, some sort of reward or inducement mechanism is usually necessary. It could be public recognition, additional funds or staff, and even threats of negative sanctions. It could be as simple as demonstrating to them that they are already treating a number of alcoholics and their families and that they have not been maximally exploiting modern intervention techniques. Whatever suasion is chosen, it should have relevance to the concerned organizations.

Systems Analysis

That systems analysis is no panacea but useful as a tool for dealing with some civil problems is the conclusion of the Denver Research Institute (Gilmore, Ryan & Gould, 1967, p. 1028). Conditional success is dependent on the removal of the numerous obstacles. The Denver Research Institute concludes that while the application of systems theories to community problems (environmental problems, poverty, crime, health, etc.) by defense industries is "... unlikely to absorb any great share of total defense resources, ... its greatest promise is in improving the quality of government administration."

When analyzed, these "new" tools turn out to be those presently used by planners and long evident in planning literature. They have evolved from three different sources: *(a)* the defense systems developed by engineers after World War II, principally as a consequence of the new weapons technology, *(b)* biology, and *(c)* social system theories.

Robert Colbourne (1968), an engineer, then with Mitre Corporation, developed a dozen rules for good systems analysis in a one-page house document:

1. Formulate the problem—it is reasonable to apply 50% of the effort to thinking about the problem. "It's more important to find the 'right' objective than the perfect analytical procedure."
2. Systems analysis should be systems oriented. Although component studies are important. . . . "emphasis should be placed on the simultaneous consideration of all the relevant factors, even if this requires the use of unaided judgment."
3. Alternatives should not be excluded arbitrarily or without analysis.
4. Set forth hypotheses early.
5. The question, not the phenomenae alone, determines the model.
6. The "question" should be kept in mind at all times. The selected model is only a tool, the goal should be foremost.
7. Mathematics and computers although helpful are limited.
8. The enemy is not inert. The opposition must be identi-

fied and its systems, operations and strategies must also be studied and analyzed.

9. The analysis should include uncertainties.
10. Detailed treatment should come late in the study. A rough treatment of many models is better than a careful and detailed treatment of a single model.
11. Suboptimization is necessary or models may become excessively large.
12. Partial analysis is better than no analysis. Inquiry can never be complete.

One concern often ignored by contemporary systems analysts is the frequent need for historical and developmental information. A clearer understanding of the reasons underlying present policy may reveal sources of pressure and key actors not previously identified and reduce error repetition. Since this type of information is seldom available in documents and may even be difficult to obtain by sophisticated interviewers, it may be necessary to immerse oneself in the working of target organizations (Fogelson and Demone, 1969).

Friendship in the Consultative Process

Second in importance to an intimate knowedge of the subject and system is an extended friendship with the many key actors. An open and honest relationship permits a frank exchange on issues, and to the extent that knowedge is shared, major mistakes are less likely to be made. Of course, these same friendships may serve to inhibit change efforts, for the desire to solve problems may be contraindicated by the desire to sustain and enhance personal relationships—a major dilemma in the development of effective human service consultation.

Coordination

One does not easily "bring into common action" (i.e., coordinate) even similar programs. And when the agencies have disparate aims, objectives, skills, and beliefs, the process is compounded. Yet both public and voluntary organizations are increasingly claiming for themselves a coordinative, collaborative, and linkage role.

Whatever the circumstances and time, acknowledgement of a coordinative function stems from two factors: *(a)* pluralism and *(b)* the absence of a formal central administrative authority.

Faced with the extraordinarily complex array of interests and organizations, especially in newly developed fields of interest (e.g., drug programs in the early 1970s), the customary choice among intervention strategies will be coordination. The assumption is that if agencies meet and talk together about common interests, they will be both less parochial and more likely to cooperate, possibly even to collaborate. Although coordination is useful, even vital at times, it is important that planning not stop with coordination. It is a beginning, a means, not an end in itself.

Involvement

A powerful technique is involvement. Even resistant individuals committed to the status quo may sometimes be persuaded to consider alternatives when they are consulted and participate as a major force in the process. A more cynical view would describe involvement as co-optation.

Consumer Participation

Belief in consumer participation, an essential ingredient of a democracy via the ballot box, and occasionally through public advisory committees, and integral to the voluntary association through policy-making boards of trustees, has now become an act of faith widely advocated and built into most contemporary federal and state statutes. As with all panaceas it will fail to bring about the desired ends, frustrating the true believers but likely producing some lesser but still important results. If we are to assume that all large complex organizations have a tendency to close in on themselves and to prefer the reactive to the proactive, any institutional mechanisms that will help to counteract these tendencies are beneficial in allowing for another countervailing force to technocracy.

Planners, too, will have their consumer participants and the same exaggerated promises and resistances. If consumers are involved as "representatives" of the population of users, they will surely fail to live up to expectations. They have not been chosen randomly, they are not "representative." At best, they represent themselves. If a representative sample of opinion is wanted, an appropriately designed household survey is better. If consumer representation is selected to broaden the base of participants, to challenge the status quo, and to contribute case material, then this method will be productive. Most importantly, it is eventually the consumer who makes the final judgment about what kinds of services are desired, how they are to be delivered, their form, and the setting (Hochbaum, 1969).

Coalitions

Two complementary principles are at work in the current emphasis on coalition planning. First is the acknowledgement that the pluralistic nature of our society usually requires the cooperation of a wide variety of organizations and individuals if planning is to succeed. An equally important point is that coalitions and alliances formed at various stages in the planning process are necessarily flexible and subject to change. As the nature of the suggested changes becomes more specific, allies tend to become more discriminating in their support (Fogelson & Demone, 1969).

Leadership

In addition to formally ascribed leaders, in most complex environments informal leaders also develop. The latter may not possess the influence or power to bring about major change against opposition, but they often possess veto power in issues related to their spheres of interest.

Further, informally achieved leadership is not highly stable but is constantly shifting, depending on the issue under consideration, with the internal system dynamics being critical variables. Nevertheless, identification of issue leaders is critical if change is to be successful.

Politics: Power and Influence

Despite a current mythology that posits power among individuals and organizations, it seldom exists in the simplistic terms expounded by its critics. Power implies the capacity to determine outcome, a capacity seldom found in our pluralistic society.

Many individuals and groups have influence, especially the capacity to veto undesired recommendations. We do not suggest that power and influence are not important. In fact, identification, recognition, and working with such individuals and groups is vital for success. We merely deplore many current simplistic explanations. Most groups and individuals with influence or power use their capacity sparingly. Further, such sanction capacity varies by issue and time. For the most part such strength is used to defend or promote private interests, not for the public good. Exceptions from the "sparing-use criteria" are those groups whose functions include the formal use of influence. Included would be political parties, organized labor, chambers of commerce, taxpayers' associations, and the League of Women Voters. This does not imply that these and similar groups use their strength indiscriminately but that their interests are broad and they are expected to speak out on a variety of issues.

The world of real power relationships requires extraordinary political sophistication on the part of planners

> Knowledge of the political dynamics of planners would (also) contribute to development of more realistic theory to

> guide practice, and to theory that reconciles the rational elements of the current models with relevant political factors (Mott, 1969, p. 802).

Reinforcing this premise, Mott (1969, p. 802) goes even further:

> It is difficult to see how planning can be made more effective, regardless of improvements in planning technologies, data collection, and analysis, without explicit recognition of the functions of power, and thus of politics, in making decisions that involve conflicting values and interests.

Incremental Planning

It is usually necessary to accept incremental planning to achieve goals over a period of time. Both administrator and planner must avoid rigidity as to the amount and form of these incremental changes. An historical perspective is particularly useful to their egos, for change is a continuing process often occurring in modest steps. Such a perspective may also help community groups develop an historical sense of gains.

Estimating Costs

The determination of costs is a critical component of effective planning. This type of question will be uppermost in the minds of most sanctioning bodies. In a two-page statement developed for the Massachusetts Vocational Rehabilitation Planning Project in 1967, Newman suggested that of the four options:— *(a)* ignore; *(b)* consciously reject as a planning responsibility; *(c)* treat as a staff responsibility after all the basic work has been done; and *(d)* integrate cost issues throughout the planning process—the latter is the most effective. He also suggests that if you cannot or do not cost out a proposal, then it is not a recommendation but a statement of principle or philosophy and that if you cannot cost the recommendation, do not expect implementation.

Future Planning

By definition, all planning is future oriented. But a special future view has developed in recent years. Almost faddish now, dozens of groups are involved in futurism. A World Future Society has been established, international meetings are held, and a journal exists. The United Nations now includes a future planning unit.

Kopkind (1967) cities some comments on the subject: A *Fortune* editor—"the greatest advance in the art of government (in) nearly a hundred years." Daniel Patrick Moynihan—"It is an idea whose time is coming." Michael Harrington—"one of the most radical suggestions put forth by a responsible body in our recent history." To Tom Hayden, it is "a new barbarism." At the moment opinions are not polarized according to any identifiable ideology, although strong opinions are common.

For the purposes of this section we shall focus on certain implications for planners. The final chapter of this monograph will examine some of the more general substantive issues.

Because the art is so new, agreed-upon definitions are not yet available, but some tentative efforts at clarification are possible.

> . . . it is a collection of vaguely related, political and intellectual happenings that have to do with new ways to analyze, anticipate and control the social environment. Involved are elements of old-fashioned central planning and new-fangled futurism; but the participants are more than planners and less than utopians. . . . They dream of using social science instead of presure politics to solve the nation's problems. (Kopkind, 1967, p. 19)

One point is clear: The maximum use of modern and future technology is included in future planning—soft ware and hardware. Donald Michael (1967) lists a number of existing social engineering technologies already available: systems analysis, planning-program-budgeting systems; economic control mechanisms; the human engineering of weapon systems; the application of new managerial theories, and the use of behavioral science research in urban design. Additional technologies include new research on the relation between human behavior and physical structure; the growing application of operational-evaluation research; games theories; model building; and simulation. Raymond Bauer and Bertram Gross have been working intensively on social goals and social indicators. The latter would parallel the economic indicators now used so successfully by all industrialized nations.

Underlying many of these advances is the latest generation of computers. The computer allows the future planners to store large amounts of data, extrapolate, build models, simulate experiments, and test hypotheses. For the first time complex models, which more nearly resemble what goes on in real life, are possible.

The key question, as yet unanswered by the future planners, is: Who poses the questions to be answered?

5. DEVELOPING OPERATIONAL PLANS

To the administrator or planner, developing operational plans means confronting the social, political, and economic facts of life. It means developing a conceptual framework in which the planner or planning group can assess its efforts and propose directions in the light of regarding what is salient and what is feasible must be made. Alternatives have to be examined in terms of short- and long-term gains and costs.

In the development of operational plans a planner or a planning group must continually remind themselves of the sometimes overlooked fact that they may influence the lives of many people if their plans are implemented. Through the establishment of policies, priorities, and resource allocations they are placing limits on the possible. Conditions are being created within which some behaviors and not others can and will occur. Shall such specific programs as drug abuse and alcoholism be given priority over more general programs such as those of community mental health in the relative allocation of resources? Shall a community sell bonds for the purpose of constructing low-cost housing or for the purpose of a more adequate human service agency or hospital facility?

Developing operational plans means engaging in the operations that actively place limits on some kinds of human interactions and facilitate other kinds of interaction and community development. Hopefully, what is facilitated moves in directions that best meet the salient needs of a community.

Operational plans do not come easily. As noted in the previous chapter, many mixed, varied, and often conflicting interests must be taken into account. Planners must work with both fantasy and reality. Their idealism may spur them on, but their knowledge of practical politics will make them successful.

HEALTH PLANNING HISTORY

The capacity to learn from previous generations and to improve the quality of planning helps to distinguish *homo sapiens* from animals. Thus Man has always planned. To suggest the evolution of form and structure, we will highlight the American health planning field in the twentieth century.

Health planning as a discrete entity can essentially be traced through three separate but overlapping subsystems. One theme reflects the 50-year history of voluntary health and welfare planning councils, with emphasis on coordination and community organization. Next, perhaps, was the emphasis on hospital beds and construction beginning in the 1930s. Last was the physical. City planners in the last decade or so began to emphasize the individual in his environment. Structurally, four steps, not necessarily sequential, can be identified. Health divisions or councils were formed as integral components of voluntary health and welfare councils. Subsequently, sometimes as a spin-off and sometimes independently, hospital councils were established. At first they were envisaged as broad-based hospital facility-planning organizations, but for the most part they became federated trade associations representing hospital administrators and some trustees. Next, stimulated by the federal Hill-Burton Construction Act new hospital councils were developed as quasi-public facility-planning organizations.

During the 1960s a series of experiments in *ad hoc* state planning occurred in mental health, retardation, and rehabilitation. Essentially fully supported by the federal government, grants-in-aid were made to state-designated authorities. On the whole these intensive short-term efforts (usually two years) were surprisingly productive, expecially mental health and retardation. The latter two were closely tied to federal construction and staffing grants and essentially offered rewards for selected efforts. The rehabilitation planning effort (as with comprehensive health planning, to be discussed next), more process oriented than goal oriented, have yet to be as productive.

And finally, the late 1960's saw the passage by Congress of the Partnership for Health Act and the Regional Medical Program. As a consequence new quasi-public comprehensive health planning agencies have generally replaced the facility planning organizations.

In some areas all forms of "health planning" still exist, although in an unclear and stressful relation. The 1970s should shake down roles more clearly.

Despite the long-standing form and structure, until recently financial support and sanctions were very limited.

The principal financial base had been the United Way movement and its predecessor organization, although in the 1960s the hospital councils began to be self-supporting. State and local governments, as has been their wont, generally disdained planning and offered neither financial nor moral support, although some health officers and their aides participated as individuals. (In a few states the Hill-Burton Construction Act was used by state health departments to stimulate some rationality in hospital construction.)

At the point that federal funds became available and some teeth were put into the planning effort, new, independent, free-standing organizations were developed on the premise that the previously undermanned, underfinanced, and limited-sanctioned agencies had not been successful. It has been suggested that the use of the existing health-planning apparatus that had developed strong community links and support related to the larger social welfare system would threaten the complete dependence on the federal counterpart organization. It was safer for the bureaucracy to establish a new system.

At this point certain trends are obvious. State government is nominally involved via 314A Comprehensive Health Planning agencies, but they have been assigned limited powers and limited budgets. If the states wish to assume a more significant role, they will find it necessary to appropriate larger sums directly from their own budgets, expand the A agencies' influence by statutory and regulatory charges, and remove it from the control of state-operating agencies.

Except on paper, and with some singular exceptions, local governments have been effectively bypassed.

The regional 314B agencies, although statutorily comprehensive, have been principally concerned with facilities, primarily hospitals. It is likely that this interest will expand to include health services, although human services, broadly conceived, and environmental planning will probably continue to receive short shrift. Trends already evident also suggest that state governments will assign certain statutory review responsibilities to the 314B agencies, thus confounding further their confused voluntary-public status. It is reasonable to expect that increased state control over the B agencies will follow the latter's increased responsibility. At the moment, the private sector, especially general hospitals, still dominates the B agencies. Consumers are principally represented by the business, financial, and legal interests and the "professional poor."

A separate effort directed principally to heart, cancer, stroke, and kidney disease—the Regional Medical Program (RMP),—is an effort to regionalize facilities and providers to offer improved services. Essentially controlled by the nation's medical schools, RMP has concentrated on continuing education of health professionals, formalizing linkages between teaching and community hospitals and individual physicians, and the support of some new services. It suffers the same tensions and strains as comprehensive health planning, although its more limited charge makes it currently more viable.

Certainly, these models are temporary, although comprehensive health planning in any form is unlikely in the near future. We know too little, and it is too threatening. Pluralism, marketplace decisions, and incrementalism will undoubtedly remain with us, and at this point in time such an arrangement is probably advisable.

An interesting and important side effect is that large state departments (especially Public Health, Mental Health, Welfare and Rehabilitation) are for the first time in most states developing a planning competence of their own, if only to defend their own interests. At the state level this may be the most significant development of the 1970s.

HEALTH CARE PLANNING

In developing operational plans for health care, the planner must deal with established community interest groups that are equal in their power and complexity to those groups encountered in comprehensive urban planning. It does the planner little good to rail against the medical establishment; it is equally dysfunctional for him to behave as if that establishment did not exist or that it cannot be changed.

As noted in our historical analysis, comprehensive health care planning has not been an integral part of the American medical scene, although there has been some limited health care planning. Historically, the planning that has occurred has usually been based on assumptions suggesting the long-term continuation of the individual practitioner, fee-based medical delivery system. Only recently has there been a realization of the very serious limitations on both the services that can be provided and the target populations that can be reached through the use of this model. Daniel Schorr's *Don't Get Sick in America* (1969) provides a very thorough descriptive analysis of these problems.

For the planner concerned with comprehensive health care, the preceding should mean an increase in the power of his position. National Health Insurance may be only a few years away; comprehensive health planning is already legislatively enacted and beginning to test its political muscles. The planning of health services is being seen increasingly as a community problem, not a problem that is the exclusive province of a select group of medical practitioners or hospital administrators.

An effective health care planner must combine in his talents the long-range views of a sophisticated theoretical-conceptual orientation and an accurate short-term perception of present political reality; too often in the past offices of planning have been characteristically one of these or the other. That is, either they operated a "wishful thinking" model of planning, one that was relatively conceptually advanced but detached from political reality, or they operated in a "political reality" model, one that was effective in short-term gains but lacked long-term concepts and direction.

Presently, there exists a greater impetus for change in health care delivery systems than at any time in the recent past. The inadequacies of traditional models of service delivery have generated forces for change both inside and outside professional health organizations. It is in everyone's best interest that health care systems change and begin to truly serve the needs of a total population. However, whether the plans that are developed focus on more and larger medical schools and on an attempt to meet the current health crisis through simply producing more physicians or whether these plans realize the critical need to develop alternative models of service delivery will probably be the major issue confronting the health planner at the outset of his operational efforts. Although it can be statistically demonstrated that producing more physicians who will practice in existing solo practitioner models of service delivery will place us farther and farther behind in meeting critical health needs, planning and developing alternative models of health care will be anything but easy.

The classic planning model, (Aronson, 1964) includes the following steps to strengthen the health care planner's position: *(a)* developing an advisory planning group that represents political power in a community; a group that is politically sensitive to community needs; *(b)* developing some instrument of survey research that puts together an overview of existing facilities and resources with an overview of community needs; *(c)* the development and assessment of new models of health delivery, with these designed to move the existing system in the direction of greater comprehensiveness; also included would be the placing of priorities for resource allocation regarding new facilities and program development, thus providing an opportunity to reward potentially more effective delivery systems; and *(d)* developing plans for action. It cannot be assumed that a community will rationally contemplate alternative models and act in its own best interest. Unfortunately, communities that are in greatest need of more effective health delivery systems are likely to be those communities that are most disorganized and anomic. Consequently, the planning group must include in their design a variety of means of political action that will help to ensure a follow-through on their efforts. Not to make this latter step a critical part of the planning group's actions would be to risk inaction, atrophy, and the creation of just one more interesting idea that is collecting dust on a shelf.

Also, unfortunately, if a health care or any other planning group is unsuccessful, it most likely will be due to the lack of effective implementation strategy and capacity. It is this oversight that all planning groups are most likely to commit; it is also the oversight that is most difficult to avoid.

ENVIRONMENTAL HEALTH PLANNING

Architect Erro Sarrinen often suggested that if any element of design or architecture was to be understood, it had to be seen in the context of the next larger unit. That is, an article of furniture could only be understood in the context of the room; a room only understood in the context of other rooms and their joining corridors; a house or building, in turn, had to be viewed in relationship to the larger surrounding factors in the environment, such as terrain and topography, other buildings, etc.

Using the language of systems analysis, similar approaches are being applied to areas of planning. For example, effective antitoxin delivery systems to combat mercury and lead poisoning make little sense if steps are not taken to curb the frequency and probability of these forms of poisoning. Ultimately, major environmental variables must be brought under control if we are to plan for a relatively healthy society.

Some historians have suggested that the decline of the Roman Empire was not due to such socioeconomic factors as affluence, taxation, increased leisure time, and changed child-rearing practices. Rather, the upper classes of Roman society literally poisoned themselves to death through their routine use of lead drinking containers. Similarly, one might argue that through a variety of means, generally much more complex and imaginative than those used by the Romans, we are committing chemical suicide.

Compounding these ecological problems is that across the United States local and county public health offices have tended to lack the political power and clout that might have lead to some effective environmental controls. Ecologically, such a condition has probably been in the best economic interests of special interest groups, such as the chemicals and housing industries, as well as the fee-based medical practitioner. Through what is an unintentional and unorganized coalition of public and private interests, public health departments have been able to render little more than advice and relatively innocuous programs, and then only after protracted political warfare.

Further compounding the problems of environmental health is the systematic nature of environmental problems. The American Public Health Association (1968,

p. 358) has pointed this out in their suggestion that:

> if it is decided to reduce air pollution by prohibiting apartment house incineration, the storage of the wastes pending their collection may create problems of rodent and insect infestation, while collection services must be increased over and above those formerly required for the incinerator residue. Disposal will also create additional problems. . . .

At this point in time the Federal Environmental Protection Agency is only beginning to test its strength. National and local concerned citizens' groups are beginning to develop programs for environmental ecological controls but as yet have not significantly reduced the release of potentially harmful pollutants. Only a few industries have begun to generate even minor self-regulating procedures. Whether or not these efforts can be coordinated and effectively brought to bear on the significant environmental health problems facing the United States *before* these problems reach crisis proportions is open to question. It is a major task that confronts the health planner concerned with environmental planning.

MENTAL HEALTH PLANNING

For over a decade various segments of the mental health professions have been actively struggling to free themselves from their historical orientations and major concerns with individual pathology and treatment. Since the report of the Joint Commission on Mental Health (Gurin, Veroff, & Feld, 1961), these efforts have gradually and continually increased.

The passage of the 1963 Community Mental Health Centers Act made available modest amounts of federal resources to facilitate this effort. Basically, it was an enactment of the joint commission's recommendations that intervention in mental health problems occur early and as close as possible to the patient's home community. With the development and deployment of these resources, strategies were generated to facilitate mental health programs that focused on intervention at the level of the community rather than at the more traditional level of the individual patient. Disease models of mental illness began to share with biosocial models of family and community problems.

Among those mental health professionals who have vacated their one-to-one therapy and mental hospital orientations, a considerable amount of first-hand knowledge has been generated regarding how operational mental health plans might be effectively developed and implemented. Demone, Spivack, and McGrath (1966), Fogelson and Demone (1969), Freed, Schroder, and Baker (1970), and Freed and Miller (1971) have provided case studies of many of the political-professional problems that are generated when mental healthers engage in community action.

Such case studies as these suggest three primary sources of problems that are likely to confront the mental health planner. First is the resistance of the target community. Mental health or any other kind of human service programs cannot be delivered as a *fait accompli.* No matter how good the programs, the probability of their being unsuccessful, even rejected outright by the community, are increased to the extent that community members have not played an active role in the development of the program. While this may seem an overly simplistic observation, and certainly nothing new after the turmoil of the late 1960s, it remains a serious problem for some mental health professionals and planners. They continue to assault and insult communities through a lack of genuine regard for community needs and, most importantly, a willingness to share influence with their communities. Many good words and thoughts have been expressed about this problem; it is something that mental health professionals "know." Yet communities continue to have to fight for a voice in mental health planning and programming.

The formula $e = f(q)(a)$ symbolically expresses this

problem. In this formula *e* refers to effectiveness of programs, *f* to a mathematical function, *q* to program quality, and *a* to community acceptance of these programs. Thus, if the program is of poor quality but highly accepted, or if the program is of high quality but is not accepted, the effectiveness is roughly the same. The equation has been reduced to an outcome of zero through the inclusion of a zero as a multiplier. The program will not function effectively.

A second major problem area is the resistance of established mental health groups in communities in which new community mental health programs are being proposed. Combinations of medical-psychiatric, welfare, and other interests may actively resist the development of these programs and facilities. Although the issues tend to become abstract and philosophical; (e.g., socialized medicine, the uses of nonprofessionals, etc.) at the core of the problem usually lies a displacement of political-economic interests. And, realistically, it is probable that individual psychiatrists in a community *are* likely to find that their political positions have been diminished by the development of a community mental health center. (Their practice may be enlarged as their individual influence decreases.) However, it is also possible that a community mental health center will act in their, as well as the community's, best interests. The two are not necessarily mutually exclusive.

In part the problem is also conceptual. If the disciples of community mental health advocate a monopolistic or oligopolistic model, they are both denying the realities of our pluralistic society and actively inviting major resistance. Community mental health does not require the building of another complex bureaucracy.

Finally, a third set of problems confront the mental health planner from inside the community mental health professions themselves. As Roland Warren (1969) has so perceptively described it, mental health professionals, having made a commitment to a community approach to mental health problems, do not really know what to do with themselves. Warren likens urban communities and some of their resident human service professionals to the old Broadway hit *Hellzapoppin,* a play filled with spontaniety, involvement, and wit that exploded beyond the confines of the stage into the audience. However, Warren suggests that the mental health professionals seem to bear more of a resemblance to Hamlet rather than the characters in *Hellzapoppin,* and, like Hamlet, having found themselves in the midst of *Hellzapoppin's* communities' change and conflict, wonder whether "To be, or not to be . . ."

FACILITIES PLANNING

In the final analysis the development of a human services program will often lead to some form of facilities planning either through the development of new facilities or the modification of existing ones. For better or worse we tend to link our programs to bricks and mortar. Such an approach has had the obvious asset of providing a new territorial base from which programs can be developed and protected but has also carried the liabilities of potential isolation, inflexibility, and great expense.

To the planner of facilities for the human services, facilities planning should be seen as an outcome of program development not the structure within which major programs will be generated. The questions of what facilities will be needed, where, and at what cost should be feasible resultants of program design and innovation. Unfortunately, in the past we have too often reversed this relationship. We have found ourselves with already constructed facilities that place enormously restrictive parameters on the nature of the programming that is possible within their confines.

The core issues in facilities planning are those of programs and priorities. For purposes of the present discussion it might be assumed that these have been worked through, although as the reader may know only too well, it can never be safely assumed that these are closed issues.

In developing plans for facilities, Spivack and Demone (1970) provided the following model; a model with areas of concern that should be coordinated and supervised by the planner in the order listed:

I. Comprehensive and long-range planning.
   1. Budgetary planning.
   2. Legislative involvement.

II. Project planning.
   1. Communications and community organization.
   2. Statewide site location studies.
   3. Site selection.
   4. Complete administration of architect selection procedures.
   5. Architectural contract administration, management. Consultation to and free dialogue with architects and their local clients (staff of future facility) during all phases of architectural work.
   6. Architectural programming research.
   7. Site planning studies.
   8. Schematic drawings.
   9. Preliminary design studies.
   10. Final design drawings.
   11. Working drawings.
   12. Review and release of construction contracts and schedules.
   13. Construction and on-site design modifications.
   14. Establishment of maintenance standards, schedules and procedures, and their supervision.

III. Evaluative research review and feedback.
   1. Continued research.
   2. Review and feedback.

The use of this model will not ensure effective facilities planning; however, it will prevent some of the more serious errors and provide a set of guidelines and bench marks against which the facilities-planning process can be monitored.

URBAN PLANNING AND HUMAN SERVICES

Historically, human services organizations have been only peripherally involved, if at all, in the processes of urban (city) planning. An exception to this would be our schools, a form of human services that has usually been given a site location in the early development of communities. Even this inclusion has been limited. Schools, conceptually, have rarely been seen in terms of their full potential in a community. Rather, they have been regarded as a physical facility, one in which a known, constricted, and predictable socialization process is expected to take place. The full potential of schools as a major community resource and the multiple uses of school facilities have rarely been taken into account in physical planning.

Conceptually, the plans for urban areas have been narrow, limited, and only marginally successful. However, as Logue indicates in his forthright and occasionally humorous "The power of negative thinking," (1969) the planning and execution of effective community and human services development is a realistic, practical possibility, but it demands more than we have given it up to now.

Perhaps as indicative of the limited views of human services is that human services organizations have tended to emerge *after* the development of urban problems rather than in a preventive framework. Community models for human services development seem to have paralleled the use of the fire department from which firemen are called to extinguish a blaze. Too often human services organizations have been developed and activated after the fact, when the best that might be done is to minimize damage.

Ardell (1969) has noted that a number of recent legislative acts may operate to change this situation. The Comprehensive Health Planning and Public Health Service Amendments of 1966 asked for health planning that included both long- and short-range comprehensive health plans and service delivery systems. Similarly, model cities, model neighborhood development legislation, and the Safe Streets Act place the human services in a somewhat better position to influence urban planning.

These legislative acts theoretically provided human service organizations with resources to be allocated;

hence, contingencies can be placed on the allocation of resources in such a way that effective multilevel planning must occur before resources will be allocated. Thus, in order for there to be urban, core-city redevelopment, there must be certain networks of human services that are planned. Without these plans the physical changes in a community's bricks and mortar cannot occur. Similarly, before new hospitals are to be built in suburban areas, existing and planned comprehensive networks of inpatient treatment facilities must be examined for that geographic area. It may be that other facilities, such as outpatient clinics, would more effectively meet community needs.

The preceding represent simple questions with very complex answers and assume implementation of legislative intent. They have to do with expenditures of billions of dollars. Until recently, the human service professional or the human services planner found himself excluded from the urban planning process. There was no effective way for him to intervene in plans for the inner city, the suburbs, or whatever. Aside from his skills he lacked resources with which he could effectively barter. Recent legislation suggests that changes might be under way. How effective planners are in the bargaining process and how well they might use these resources is still an open question.

Rand (1969) makes the simple but powerful observation that the new towns of tomorrow are being designed today. The constraints under which we may live are being developed now. Tomorrow will be too late to question today's assumptions.

6. POLICIES, ACCOUNTABILITY, AND SOCIAL CHANGE

A number of factors combine to render human services organizations less open to changes in policies and resource allocations than might be true in equal-size profit-making business organizations. For one, most human service organizations have become relatively bureaucratized, with various organizational pressures operating to continue, largely unchanged, intraorganizational routines. Another factor has been the tendency for these organizations to become professionalized through the selective hiring and retention of employees who meet certain criteria in their training and experience. Generally, these criteria have been developed and maintained by various professions, such as associations of social workers, physicians, psychologists, rehabilitation counsellors, etc., independently of the concerns of any particular human services organization or community.

A third factor giving rise to long-term organizational inertia has been the relative independence of human services organizations in their patterns of funding. Public schools, hospitals, social welfare organizations, and state mental hospitals have not been constrained by profit-making responsibilities. Criteria other than profit are applied to determine success, such as caseload, number of patients, and number of persons receiving particular kinds of training. These outcomes have typically been assessed in terms of their social utility by respective funding organizations, such as legislatures, city councils, or United Funds. Barring major and obvious discrepancies between the cost of a human services organization and its assessed social utility, that organization will continue to operate with only minor changes in its internal roles and external relationships.

These factors have, historically, equipped human services organizations to survive and grow remarkably well in environments that have been relatively stable and predictable. And as long as the environment remained relatively low in its turbulent qualities, the cost of these organizations were generally commensurate with their social utility.

However, it would be inaccurate to describe the environments in which human service organizations must survive in the United States today as stable and predictable. Rather, as noted earlier, these environments, particularly in urbanized areas, might be more accurately described as high in environmental turbulence (Emery & Trist, 1965). High levels of stress are being placed on the adaptive abilities and resources of human services organizations, organizations that have too often in the past behaved like Procrustus, requiring that their clientele design their problems to suit the organization's capabilities.

The present chapter is concerned with adaptation and change in human service organizations. Its focus will be on the locus of policy-making and resource allocation, models of social change and change agents, and the nature of the change strategy. The purpose of this chapter is to provide an overview of strategies that are likely both to increase a human services organization's responsiveness to client or environmental needs and to maximize the effectiveness of their interventions.

THE LOCUS OF POLICY-MAKING AND RESOURCE ALLOCATIONS

Virtually every human services organization is directly accountable to some form of superordinate organization known as a board of trustees or directors, a council, or some similar title (ultimately the executive and legislative branches in government.) The formal function of these superordinate bodies is twofold: *(a)* to monitor, however nominally, the routine activities of the organization and *(b)* to establish major organizational policies and approve the allocation of the organization's resources.

In order to successfully perform these two formal functions, however, other perhaps more important informal functions must be effectively carried out. For example, in formally monitoring the activities of an organization, little can be gleaned from formal accounting procedures regarding where staff spend their work days, although this information may be valuable in developing some overall view of how and where resources are being expended. A more important informal activity for a board member is his interaction with staff members, often during off-duty hours.

Another major informal activity is the degree to which a board serves to link both the community's power structure and that organization's client community. The lines of communication must run in both of these directions if the organization is both to survive and maintain its relevence to community problems.

Board members who are members of what might be loosely termed a community power structure are potentially invaluable in negotiating on behalf of an organization vis-à-vis superordinate bodies (e.g., city councils, state legislatures, federal review boards, United Way budget committees) that control major resources. An organization that lacks board members who can and will perform this vital ecological function is likely to find itself deficient in survival resources, beginning to atrophy, and ultimately dying.

Although this adaptive strategy has a number of functional properties in terms of an organization's political and economic growth and survival, it has often resulted in human services organizations becoming more responsive to funding agencies than to client communities. It has become almost commonplace to hear of human services organizations charged with having grown away from, or being irrelevant to, the needs of their client communities.

Although there have been many attempts to deal with this problem through developing better community relationships, conducting relatively accurate surveys of needs, etc., in the final analysis the problem has become one of the degree to which communities are to share in establishing policy and allocating resources in these organizations. The local organizations that have emerged through Office of Economic Opportunity funds have been leaders in this effort, although their attempts to develop "maximum feasible participation" among the poor in their programs and organizational development have become controversial and problematic, at the very least.

Two major issues have emerged from the above: *(a)* Shall community representatives share in the development of policies and programs? *(b)* If so, at what level shall the sharing of power occur? In the confusion resulting from these issues, client power in policy-making has been seen as a means of legitimizing influence in the execution of policy. Board members often become agents of interference in the daily activities of the organization or at best have begun to monitor daily organizational activities with considerable diligence, persistence, and not so subtle hints that their observations are likely to influence their decisions as board members.

In other situations, such as the subject of a case study by Gilbert (1969), in which citizens and professionals clashed in Pittsburgh's community action program, citizens' groups have been primarily influential in dealing with nonbasic issues confronting the organization.

Beck (1969) has suggested that "community control" is a distraction not an answer to the problem of making agencies responsive to their client communities. Citing Etzioni's use of "inauthenticity," Beck suggests that human service organizations that respond to confrontations with poor or minority groups by placing some of these persons on policy-making boards may be giving a false response to a real need. The major problem is that of the distribution of wealth; a minor and perhaps related problem is the immediate one of service delivery.

Although having representative members of the client community in policy-making bodies may be a worthwhile end, it should be seen realistically for what it is—an attempt to improve the service delivery system, a system that may already be operating under conditions of inadequate staffing and financing. Placing community members on the policy board may simply raise expectations in the community and not lead to meaningful changes in community life.

A policy-making and resource allocating board should represent both the community it serves and the community from which it receives resources. Very often these are two mutually exclusive groups. Human services organizations in urban ghetto or Appalachian communities receive finances and legitimizing political sanctions from those parts of society that have wealth and political power to give. By and large these are not the organization's clients. In turn, a human services organization must be relevant to the needs of the community it serves. Through the use of what Saul Alinsky terms "native leadership" (1945) or indigenous community leadership, organizations that truly serve "the people" can be shaped.

In short, that is what the board of a human services organization is about. Political representatives from resource providers and persons in need form a group that must compose and orchestrate a score known as organizational policies. To do this effectively, they must be highly integrated and in touch with each other, as well as with the groups that they represent. A primary task of the human services organization's leadership is to facilitate this integration. And it is in their best interest to do so; ultimately, they must play the composition and face the critics.

SOCIAL CHANGE: CHANGE AGENTS AND STRATEGIES

Social change has become a major and pervasive contemporary problem. People are finding themselves both deeply involved in it and overwhelmed by it. Human services organizations are being called on to deal with many of the dysfunctional, often crisis-ridden outcomes of social and technological change, as well as to intervene in the change process itself. Very often staff in these organizations have found themselves simultaneously trying to deal not only with change processes and their outcomes but also attempting to generate models of the change process that might give them a means of intellectually grasping and exercising some control over the flow of events.

An immediate problem that any human services organization must face in developing policies and programs aimed at social change is that of *why* they are about *what* they are about. That is, what is the purposive nature of their proposals? Where should it take both the organization and the client community? As Rein and Miller (1966) have asked, what are the potential assets, liabilities, targets, and yardsticks of success?

Moreover, what is the framework in which the change program is being developed? Moynihan (1966) has suggested that powerful differences arise in programs depending on whether they are conceptualized within a "bureau of the budget concept," with efficiency the guiding principle; an "Alinsky concept," with conflict the guiding principle; a "Peace Corps concept," with provision of services of major importance; or a "Task force concept," in which the primary concern is that of political effectiveness.

Freidmann (1969) has pointed to an additional problem in conceptualizing social change programs, which, if unresolved, tends to create a basic ambivalence in the host organization, (i.e., whether the emerging programs are seen by the host organization as system maintaining or system transforming.) Too often, in efforts to avoid this fundamental policy conflict, programs that are actually system maintaining are marketed as system transforming to client groups. Conversely, there is a tendency to market system-transforming programs to resource-providing groups as programs of system maintenance. Finally, there is a tendency for organizations not to really attack this problem in their internal relationships. As might be expected, the outcome is one of increased levels of confusion and conflict both within the organization and in relationships with outside groups.

In his research on purposive social change Roland Warren (1965) has suggested that three basic types of social change strategies are available. They are:

Collaborative Strategies

Collaborative strategies are appropriate when there is agreement on the issues among affected parties. The primary role of the change agent is that of enabler or catalyst, and his main concern is ensuring that decision-makers have all the necessary information. Even though the successful use of this strategy is limited to those issues on which there is agreement, there is a tendency to attempt to apply this model to a larger range of issues, including those that are disputed. Such attempts are likely to increase the level and intensity of disagreement and conflict. Warren suggests that welfare councils have historically tended to operate in this model.

Campaign Strategies

Campaign strategies are appropriate to situations in which there are issue differences or disputes about whether or not an issue exists or how an issue should be resolved. The primary role of the change agent is that of persuader, and his task is to create a higher salience of the values and interests people have regarding a particular problem, for example, through the use of "educational" campaigns. He may also try to bring pressures to bear on significant persons to make them realize that certain decisions on this problem are in their best interests.

Contest strategies

Contest strategies are appropriate to situations in which there is issue dissensus, a basic disagreement regarding the issues and values involved; the primary role of the change agent is that of contestant in which he competes for power and resources that will affect the direction of decisions about a given problem or issue.

Warren further suggests that contest strategies might be seen as consisting of four types: *(a)* behavior within accepted social norms, for example, legislative debates; *(b)* processes aimed at changing the distribution of power in a community, for example, voter registration and/or political campaigns aimed at unseating certain incumbents; *(c)* behavior that violates community norms, for example, social action or protest activities, such as sit-ins, rent strikes, etc.; *(d)* behavior that might be termed conflict in the stricter sense of the word, for example, harassment of public officials or physical violence.

In a practical sense a number of change strategies are available to the practitioner. Within the framework of the many factors that affect the design of the social change process, the following represent only a sampling of available models:

1. Ombudsman (The American Assembly, 1967).
2. Strategies of coordination (Demone and Newman, 1970; Torrens, 1969).
3. Strategies of community organization (Rothman, 1964; Murphy, 1960).
4. Strategies of community development (Sanders, 1958; Dunham, 1960).
5. Forums, conferences, and seminars (Carter, 1967, pp. 489-498).

6. Bargaining (Brager and Jorrin, 1969).
7. Consensus (Scheff, in press).
8. Consultation (Caplan, 1964; Downs, 1965; Sussman, 1966).
9. Legal strategies (Curran, 1965).
10. Contest (Alinsky, 1945).
11. Self-study and evaluation (Mann, 1957).

ADVOCACY, CONTEST, CONFLICT, AND MILITANCY

Historically, human services organizations have tended to be seen as agents of intervention that stabilized social systems. The settlement house or the mental health clinic, for example, provided a means of stabilizing relationships between persons and their social environment. The concern within these kinds of organizations was that of facilitating an adjustment between a person and his milieu. The cumulative effect of these efforts has generally been to stabilize, not transform, social systems.

Which is probably less true today than earlier in recent history, although the number of human services organizations as agents of system-transformation is still relatively few. However, human services organizations are increasingly becoming involved in advocacy, contest, and conflict; sometimes their style is one of militancy. While it would be inappropriate to end this section without examining some of the problems generated by this change in organizational postures, it is difficult to do more than briefly focus on some of the risks, liabilities and assets, and complexities of these organizational behaviors.

Advocacy might be viewed as assuming a number of forms, with these varying along a continuum of means. A human services organization, or certain of its staff members, might assume the role of advocacy planner, as Peattie (1968) has described it; the role of advocacy litigant, along the lines of Nader's Raiders; the role of advocate militant, such as in the civil rights or rent strikes movements; or the role of violent advocate, such as that referred to by Hofstadter (1970). Or contrariwise, the organization may use moral suasion. Admittedly, these are oversimplified roles or types, but their purpose is to define possible points on a continuum of low to high degrees of intensity or extremism in acting out an advocacy position.

When the intensity of this role increases, it should be noted that a number of other differential properties of the social change process are generated. For example, the extent to which the advocate will be able to exert control over outcomes will be reduced as his role intensity increases. Similarly, the degree of risk to both the advocate, or the advocacy organization, and the group for whom advocacy is being enacted is substantially increased. As intensity of advocacy increases, they may all find themselves and their causes, however worthwhile, in serious jeopardy.

These relationships are hypothetically reflected in Figures 1 and 2:

Whether or not a human service organization should or should not be engaged in an advocacy position is a major issue in itself. Obviously, it will be decided differently under different environmental conditions and constellations and political power. Our feeling is that the role is both a legitimate and viable one, but one that brings with it certain risks and by definition excludes other means of social change. Consequently, an organization should be fully aware of what it is doing and not assume an advocacy posture inadvertently or because of political pressures or support that might vanish under the stress of conflict. After all, organizations are made up of people. They will not work harmoniously with organizations that are attacking them.

It is unfortunate but accurate to say in many instances that if a human services organization does not assume an advocacy position for its client population, no one will. And organizations that have adopted this position

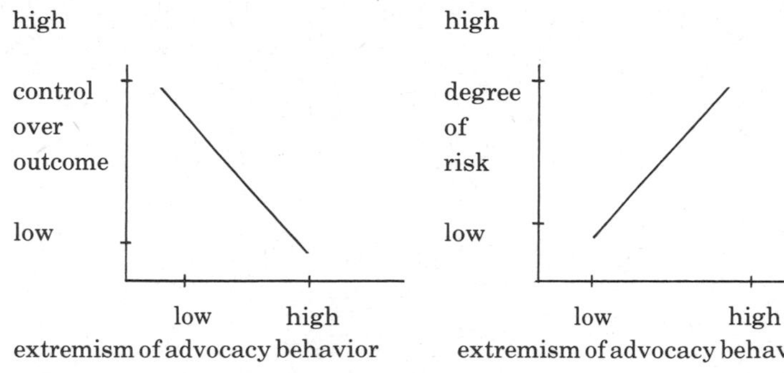

Fig. 1. The relationship between extremism of advocacy behavior and control over outcome.

Fig. 2. The relationship between extremism of advocacy behavior and the degree of risk to advocates and constituents.

have been a distinct minority. By and large they have deserved the hostility and charges of irrelevance that have been aimed at them.

It is also unfortunate but accurate to say that in assuming an advocacy position, a human services organization is likely to be seen, and perhaps to become, as Peattie (1968) described it, dangerously similar to other manipulators of the poor's interests. Further, it is easier to attack one's friends. They may be more understanding of political constituencies. Perlman and Jones (1967), who studied 20 neighborhood service centers, report that "social action has shown a disconcerting tendency to direct its strongest fire at the allies and benevolent neutrals, close at hand, rather than at the more distant enemy." And this makes sense, for according to one Spanish-speaking American leader, your friends will understand why it is necessary to sit in on them rather than those who are hostile or who lack understanding of the genuineness of their cause.

The poor need advocates, and human services organizations can become advocates. But if they do, as we feel they should, it should be through reason and reality, not rhetoric.

7. PLANNING CONSTRAINTS

Because planning customarily implies individual or organizational change, it is not surprising that resistance often develops. Influence, power, politics, accommodation, and compromise are key intervening variables. Since it is unlikely that American planners will ever be given sufficient power to guarantee implementation of their recommendations, some accommodation is therefore likely. In fact, the American marketplace mechanism not only assures contest but permits the design of alternative countervailing planning organizations. Recently, this has been identified as advocacy planning, but even without a specific identification it has historically been a part of the American scene.

Often at issue in the politics of planning and change is organizational autonomy and possibly even survival. Simon, Smithburg, and Thompson (1961, p. 453) remind us that the "existing pattern of organizational behavior has qualities of persistence; it is valuable in some way or it would not be maintained."

The following dimensions represent commonly encountered constraints in human services planning:

HOSTILITY

In their analysis of alcoholism planning Demone and Newman (1970) described a series of obstacles. Most important was the hostility toward alcoholics among the various human services professionals. Such a negative set is not directed exclusively to alcoholics, for many groups, including the delinquent, the drug dependent, the criminal, and even the chronically ill and the aged, may face similar attitudes at the hands of the so-called care givers. Other obstacles noted ranged from apathy to personality variations among key actors.

GOALS

The more general, theoretical, and abstract the goals, the more likely it is that agreement can be achieved. It is the selection of subgoals or operating goals and means to be used in achieving them that stimulates controversy. Intraorganizationally, it may require reallocation of resources and roles, while interorganizationally it may imply impingement on the territory of another organization.

Banfield (1962, p. 78), in his analysis of governmental agencies, suggests that the formulation of ends be left vague. "Serious reflection on the ends of the organization, and especially any attempt to state ends in precise and realistic terms, is likely to be destructive of that organization." He believes that the obvious confusion, overlapping, and inconsistency found in public organizations is not accidental but a reflection of the role of public organizations in a democratic society. Required to accommodate to conflicting interests, consistency is seldom possible.

ALTERNATIVES

The ideal-type planning model promotes the identification of alternatives. To what extent do we really have a range of feasible alternatives? The existentialists note the frequency of situations in which man is faced with impossible choices. There is often no clear option between good and evil, no way of avoiding some unpleasantness. Can planners committed to implementation realistically conceptualize the total range of alternatives? In developing state plans for mental health in the early 1960s, the administrators and planners were working within severe boundaries. The states were spending over 90% of their funds in institutions, and the community mental health model, although only one of many options, had already been enacted by Congress, reinforced by NIMH guidelines, and supported by precedents in many states.

When feasibility is included as a criterion, alternatives must always be examined within a context. What do the laws say? What are the system maintenance requirements? What kind of consensus can be identified? What are the chances of success? (Demone, 1965)

SPECIALIZATION AND PROFESSIONS

A major obstacle to social change is specialization. The increasing categorization, proliferation, and specialization of the human services network has produced people whose perspective stems from their professions and categorical areas. In turn these specialists relate to special interest groups. Peer-oriented prestige values dominate. As they rethink their domains and boundaries and especially as they aim for comprehensiveness and relevancy, they find themselves in conflict with other specialists. Psychiatrists are surprised to learn that pediatricians, psychologists, special educators, and vocational rehabilitation counselors also lay claim to competence in retardation. One can predict that such domain and territorial confrontations will become increasingly common, especially as the movement toward human needs and services expands. The "whole man" does not fit the arbitrary boundaries established by the various special interest groups (Newman & Demone, 1969).

Advice to the administrators and planners entering this thicket: Keep your guard up, or be prepared for major changes.

INTERORGANIZATIONAL CONSTRAINTS

Given the various levels of government—federal, state, county, city, and town—and the many governmental organizations that do not reflect these five boundaries but regionalize on an interstate or substate basis, when combined with the various possible types of voluntary agencies—federated, corporate, and independent—whose geographic coverage may in turn be unique, it is clear that maximizing interagency cooperation and planning is confronted with complex territorial barriers.

When these impediments are combined with variable agency goals and objectives that also may be conflicting or overlapping, the problem is further compounded.

In addition, domains may be discrepant. Agency objectives are established intraorganizationally and may be different from those created by other agencies. Competition for funds, sanctions, leadership, staff, and clients are all part of the community scene. (Levine, 1966)

METROPOLITAN CONSTRAINTS

Banfield (1965) describes four basic obstacles to comprehensive metropolitan planning that are inherent in all comprehensive planning, although their specifics may differ.

First he reminds us of the rapidity of change, with much of it unanticipated. Second, he notes that a metropolitan area (or a city) has no objectives. Public purposes are not delimited or operationalized. Agreement occurs on such a generalized level that it begs the question that must be answered. The transition to the third obstacle is obvious: With respect to major policy issues, major differences of opinion exist. (Should low-income housing be supplied in the suburbs? Which should be sacrificed, rapid transit or the automobile?) Finally, Banfield claims that even if we were to agree on goals, we do not have the know-how to achieve them. (How do we educate slum children, eliminate poverty, prevent the growth of ghettos, or build a beautiful city?)

PARTICIPATION

As noted earlier, one of the common strategies to enhance the likelihood of implementation of recommendations is to involve the key actors and organizations in the study and planning process. Although this is a useful and important tactic, it has counterproductive effects as well. Mott (1969, p. 749) notes that those who have a vital stake in the outcome "are likely to influence the questions to be considered, how they are to be approached, the alternative solutions to be considered and the causes of action to be selected."

True it is process, and true it is democratic, but the result of participation is almost always a series of watered-down recommendations reflecting the possible more than the desired. Nevertheless, it is incremental movement and usually positive.

CONSUMER PARTICIPATION

We have already suggested some of the advantages and some of the limits in the current emphasis on participation. The involvement of consumers is a special subcase. Consumers are likely to stress accessibility of services. The provider has the responsibility to include issues of quality. The consumer may demand neighborhood-based specialized services that can only be supplied adequately on a regional level. Hochbaum (1969), in discussing health services, suggests that the fundamental differences are ideological. The health professionals are usually concerned with medical-care considerations, the consumer with social, political, and racial aspects of services.

CONSENSUS

Overlapping with the participation model is one that aims for consensus not only among the planning participants but among all affected organizations. Feasible recommendations with a high potential for implementation are significant components of the consensual model. Its problems are three: *(a)* Some problems are irreconcilable where fundamental differences exist; *(b)* it assumes that all interested parties can be identified and involved prior to the decision-making process; and *(c)* if successful in achieving the first two steps, the agreement usually is composed of a variety of trade-offs that might be acceptable to the participating organizations but may bring about little real change.

The primary problem with the consensual model is that it cannot be used effectively with conflicting issues. When values are divergent or when fundamental organizational patterns are threatened, agreement will never be achieved by consensus, only by coercion or substantial exchange.

CONFRONTATION

An old tactic revived in the mid 1960s—confrontation—has become currently popular as an intervention method. It is also laden with pitfalls and constraints. When individuals and organizations are pushed, they tend not only to push back but to resent the threats and accusations that are necessary to the confrontation model. Further, once confrontation is used, it tends to exclude the use of other social planning and change techniques, for example, collaboration, cooperation, coordination, participation, etc. Following sit-ins, bomb scares, threatening telephone calls, and angry accusations in the press, the organization employing these tactics should not be surprised if the attacked agency fails to cooperate not only with respect to the matter in question but in other issues, also. Later losses may significantly offset immediate gains.

THE TECHNICAL REPORT

Another common planning model is the writing of technical reports. An expert or small group of experts is sanctioned by some organization to study a predetermined problem and to recommend solutions; on paper at least, this resembles the rational-man model. Data are gathered and analyzed, goals determined, alternatives selected, and means to achieve the goals may be included.

That such a report may gather dust is obvious, although if written on a politically "hot" subject, it may gather press if properly handled. Information may be influential, given proper circumstances.

The possible failing of such a model is its naïve assumption that the scientist-planners can be objective and neutral. Mott (1969) notes several sources of bias that are often present. Planners seldom choose the subjects to be studied. Furthermore, once the subject is determined, their professional bias may enter into the criteria that govern the evaluation and selection of courses of action. Prevention or treatment may be emphasized. Causes may be perceived as genetic, environmental, social, or economic.

Since planners are seldom self-employed, at some point they must report back to their organization, one that probably employs an executive and may have a board or elected officials to whom the executive in turn reports. They have colleagues and probably a family.

And to repeat, the problem of implementation is not likely to be organizationally assigned its proper political priority.

MONEY

Unlike the social service system, the health industry until recently has been relatively immune to public attack. As long as low-income people received large amounts of public funds—beginning in the 1930s—especially in periods of relative affluence and high employment, the recipients were subject to widespread criticism. Debtors prisons have a long and proud tradition among Anglo-Saxons, and people can still be imprisoned for nonpayment of debt in some jurisdictions.

As the nation's second largest industry, and as the government picks up one-third of the health bill, the immunity of the health industry from large-scale public criticism is rapidly dissolving. Medicare and Medicaid have heightened public attention. Hospital bills of well over

$100 a day and an industry whose costs are inflating without concommitant increases in either quantity or quality of services are particularly vulnerable to criticism. With health no longer considered a privilege but a right, the public now demands the right to establish policy and insists on accountability.

Wealth and popularity often bring problems, as the health industry is now learning.

8. THE ADMINISTRATIVE PROCESS

Central to the functioning of every organization is the administrative process. No organization can afford to be without both administrative talent, ideas, and technologies, for their absence places an organization's resources in jeopardy and minimizes the effective and creative use of those resources (MacKenzie, 1969). Unfortunately, the full and productive use of administrative talent, ideas, and technologies seems to be the exception rather than the rule in the human service organization.

Cynics have suggested that the "Peter Principle" (Peter and Hull, 1969) has found its most effective application in those organizations that comprise the human services. Historically, many of these organizations have tended to award highest prestige to their most effective practitioners, that is, those professionals who are most competent in their discipline. However, administrative positions have often been assigned to those professionals who are less interested or less able to become highly skilled practitioners. This custom is particularly evident in medicine. Consequently, there has been a tendency for persons who are professionally less competent and subsequently less valued by their peers to rise to the upper strata of human service organizations. Or if they meet all criteria, they are faced with nearly insurmountable negative stereotypes. What is needed is full status and sanctioning for human service professionals and nonprofessionals who have administrative talent and who might choose to carve out administrative careers for themselves. It will occur only when we realize that effective administration requires different skills from effective practice, but ones that are equally complex.

The material in this chapter is designed to shed some light on administrative functions, roles, strategies, and technologies. Although it by no means encompasses all of the highly complex organizational behavior in which administrators engage, hopefully it will give some structure to a neglected, often denigrated, but vitally important element of the human service organization.

ADMINISTRATIVE FUNCTIONS

The functions of persons in administrative or managerial positions have been the subject of numerous writers and researchers. A representative sampling of this work over the past 50 years might include that by such persons as Taylor (1923), Barnard (1938), Roethlisberger (1941), and Likert (1961, 1967), as well as others too numerous to mention in this short space. Summarizing and attempting to extract those factors that seem common to the many and varied approaches to the study and practice of administration and, further, attempting to view these factors in terms of human services organizations, the following would seem to be important and consensually validated administrative functions:

Data Input Monitoring

What are the sources of data that the organization uses in examining its performance? How are the data used? How reliable and how valid are these data? Effective administration requires that the monitoring of organizational data input be performed in such a way as to prevent the organization from developing faulty bases for its internal decision-making, hence risking its resources through erroneous problem-solving strategies stemming from these decisions.

Problem Conceptualizing

Although no one administrator can be expected to be

the problem conceptualizer for his organization, it is incumbent upon him to ensure that this function is being performed in the organization. An effective division of labor and a matching of the skills and interests of individual employees with their actual organizational assignments are strategies that are likely to make it easier to carry out this function.

Unfortunately, dysfunctional organizational and/or professional norms in human service organizations, anachronistic merit systems, or personal insecurities and inadequacies often lead to a funneling of problem conceptualizing into limited administrative offices and channels.

Problem Analysis

What are the relevant variables both within a problem and surrounding that problem that need to be brought to bear on effective problem analysis? The issue here, as in problem conceptualizing, is to stimulate the appropriate persons and establish the necessary conditions. The more open the communication channels, the more likely there will be multiple information input leading to a relatively accurate consensual validation of problem analysis.

Organizational Decisions and Action

Where and how are decisions made in organizations? What mechanisms are there to generate action on those decisions? Some recent research (Harshbarger, 1971) has indicated that small groups are far more accurate in solving problems if they make decisions through consensus rather than through an autocratic decision-making process, even though, under both conditions, there was a free and open transmission of communication. Further, and most importantly, the research suggested that persons would be likely, if given the choice, to choose a centralized or relatively autocratic, rather than a consensual, decision-making structure. Thus, what we might desire in the way of decision-making structures and what is most likely to be the most accurate kind of decision-making structure may often be contradictory.

Going beyond how decisions are made, an effective administrator must deal with the problems of generating feasible outcomes and actions to implement these decisions. Given the emphasis that human services organizations place on group and organizational process, there is a tendency to substitute process for outcome in organizational decision-making. That is, human services professionals are so accustomed to "feeling good" during and after meaningful group experiences that they tend to transfer a point of view that is appropriate to the therapeutic process to the organizational decision-making process.

Effective organizational decision-making and implementation have never been the long suits of human services organizations. A much more critical examination of these organizational functions has been long needed.

Purposive Follow-Through

Effective involvement, decisions, and action are not enough. There must be the kind of follow-through that ensures that the job will be done or further decisions rendered to add the necessary resources to complete the task. Clarification of the task, a work program, and a time schedule are all useful management tasks. Otherwise, the best laid plans . . .

Feedback

Every organization must operate with multilevel feedback designed to alter or sustain decisions throughout the organization. Unfortunately, human services organizations, with their professional biases and ideologies permeating the everyday work process, have tended to substitute professionally appropriate value judgments for relatively hard data on outcomes of decisions. Although we give lip service to relatively scientific and empirical bases of feedback, the kinds of information to which we are responsive and the kinds of information that we are likely to manufacture and transmit are replete with our professional ideologies that, by definition, are slanted and one-sided.

Beyond this problem there are the problems of what, among relatively hard data, shall constitute feedback and what information-transmitting structures will lead to reliable information transmission. Outcome rather than process information needs sanctioning. Moreover, will the information be received and assimilated by persons who need to know? And finally managers need to be trained to integrate data into decision-making.

Generating Organizational Change

No environment is static, although we sometimes seem to act as if this were the case. An effective administrator must both monitor changes in the external and internal environments of the organization as well as think through the realistic possibilities and strategies for change in the organization. As Bennis et al. (1969) have indicated, this is by no means a simple problem, rather one that demands that the agent of change have a credible, workable plan for organizational change as well as a fairly accurate view of the consequences of those changes.

Human Relations and Communication

Intimately tied to the many other functions that have been mentioned, the problems of human relations and communication that arise in a human services organization are myriad and infinitely complex. They demand, to a greater or lesser degree, virtually constant monitoring of group and interpersonal processes in the organization. Given the very human focus of the activities of most human services organizations, one might expect there to be an abundance of resident experts in these problems. Unfortunately, the pressures and problems of the human services organization often have the same divisive and communication-inhibiting effects that one finds in many other kinds of organizations. It is incumbent upon the administrator to keep the social machinery oiled and functioning. (For a humorous and perceptive account of this process, the reader might read parts of Jim Bouton's *Ball Four* in which he describes social interventions by the manager of the Seattle Pilot baseball team, interventions designed to ease tension and open up communication among often hostile teammates.)

ADMINISTRATIVE STRATEGIES AND TECHNOLOGIES

Democratic Management

One of the most currently popular sociotechnical means of reaching decisions, democratic management, as described by Bennis (1965), injects a note of pluralism into organizational decision-making practices that have too often been relatively autocratic. As Gomberg (1966) has noted in a critical commentary, this management strategy has become one of the more modish, avant-garde philosophies of students and leading academic figures in prestigious business schools, as well as in many complex organizations.

Slater and Bennis (1964) describe democratic management as containing maximum communication independent of organizational status; consensual decision-making; organizational influence of the individual based on knowledge and competence; an organizational atmosphere permitting free expression and open communication networks; and a focus on human needs and concerns, one that accepts the inevitability of confrontation between the individual and the organization.

The issues involved in the uses of democratic management strategies in reaching organizational decisions are multiple. Gomberg (1966) suggests that it may be more of a value framework than a management strategy; that is, it may be a guiding philosophy but practical only under certain, as yet unknown, specifiable conditions. Bennis (1970), in a later view of the strategy, reaches similar conclusions. When Bennis the scholar turns to Bennis the actor, even more complexities are noted. (See his article, "Searching for the 'Perfect' University President," in the April 1971 *Atlantic*.) As an academic vice-president and a candidate for a college presidency, he presents a witty and penetrating analysis of leadership in complex organizations. At the core of the problem is where, when, and under what conditions these management practices are likely to lead to more effective organizational adaptation. Can this model, which was originally designed as a function of the experiences of certain large, task-force-centered consulting firms, be appropriately extended to the human services?

In addition, it might be helpful to consider the model as twofold, one that is aimed at both the communication processes and networks in organizations, as well as with the specific decision-making practices of that organization. In terms of the former, the model would seem to hold promise for human service organizations, that is, greater openness of communication networks across intra- and interorganizational boundaries would seem desirable. In terms of the latter, and specifically the uses of consensual decision-making, the model as yet lacks enough application to specify its potential for long-range versus short-range decisions, consumer versus professional decisions, community versus intraorganizational decisions, and a host of other yet untested dimensions.

Critical Path Method

Among the newer technologies for reaching organizational decisions is the critical path method. Basically, it refers to a set of activities, following an adequate and consensually validated definition of the current problem, to determine the necessary activities to move toward problem solution, the sequence of those activities and the requirements in terms of activity time and other organizational resources.

Originating in engineering, the critical path method forces a relatively graphic description of the job to be done, the time necessary to accomplish it, and the sequence of events. In addition, it facilitates a relatively accurate estimate of the organizational costs involved, leading to further budgetary and personnel planning.

BUDGET AND FINANCE

Planning, programming, budgeting systems (PPBS), a concept that swept the federal government during the late 1960s, is currently being adopted by organizations throughout the human services. Early forerunners of PPBS date back prior to World War I; early applications were tried in the Department of Agriculture and the Tennessee Valley Authority. The Hoover Commission Report of 1949 highlighted the performance budget (Taubenhaus, Hamlin, & Wood, 1957). Put simply, general organizational objectives are validated, and organizational activities that contribute toward the achievement of these objectives are identified, separated, and classified. Costs are then identified, and a functional program budget is developed that specifies the relative costs of each program and its components. Following these activities, it is then possible to make some decisions regarding the attained benefits, in terms of improvement, say, of service delivery systems, when these benefits are contrasted with their respective costs. In short, it is a means of arriving at estimates of cost-effectiveness, or cost-benefits ratios.

The evolutionary components and processes involved in the development of PPBS have included such technologies as performance budgets, program budgets, functional budgets, and cost-benefit analysis. In less than two decades accountants and systems analysts have provided the human services with increasingly complex and sophisticated procedures for examining their activities, but the adoption of these technologies has been slow, problematic, and hesitant.

Two problems are paramount in the uses of PPBS. One is the process of social change that leads to the adoption of PPBS as a sociotechnical system. How can this come about? What is necessary in related organizational changes (e.g., the existing decision-making structures) to implement effectively such a technology? What are the organizational change problems, strategies, programs, and outcomes that must be taken into account? What will be required in the way of talented change agents?

The other problem has to do with PPBS itself. Not only do human service organizations often lack the relatively "hard" data that other kinds of organizations might have; there is contained in the suggestion that PPBS is a better decision-making system the implicit notion that its use will permit accurate, effective decisions. Unfortunately, nothing could be farther from the truth. In the human services ultimate decisions regarding the uses of organizational resources are based on relative, not absolute, differences and on moral-laden value judgments. Is it "better" to rehabilitate a client with an appendectomy, an AFDC mother, an adult male alcoholic, an amputee, or a youthful drug-dependent person? (And what about programs for the aged or chroncially ill?) What criteria are to be used? Who asks the questions? Whose opinion is to be final? Can accurate cost figures be established? What is the basis for the prognosis? The translation into quantitative data may be illusory. As difficult as client-oriented objectives may be, they are relatively simple compared to efforts at objectifying prevention or efforts to change systems, subsystems, and organizations.

PERSONNEL PRACTICES

In human service organizations it has been the public agencies that have led the way in designing merit systems and organizing fringe benefits. Developed not as a positive step forward but as a means to control the spoils system, they have created problems of their own, particularly in rigid job descriptions and classifications. However, in recent years in the federal government, many states and some large and middle-sized cities, have attempted to move from various forms of negative controls to progressive personnel management systems.

As with most management functions personnel administration has become a function of both personnel specialists and line officials in operating agencies, with its basic objective, as Stahl (1962) has noted, that of maintaining effective human resources and human relations in the organization. It is one of the fundamental procedures necessary to get a job done. As a specialized function, it is concerned with such problems as developing and carrying out employee relations policy, handling problems as they arise, working with organized labor, developing methods of recruiting new employees and of evaluating employee performance, organizing and maintaining communication links between employees and management, and maximizing employee potential and maintaining personnel policies.

As specialized departments in large organizations few personnel departments fulfill all these functions equally well, even though the professionalization of the personnel field has lifted its sights and standards. In smaller organizations not justifying separate specialized staff, such roles are usually enacted by one of the professional staff and the office manager. In fact, such assignments are strongly advisable, for adequate procedures are more likely to be developed if a clear role assignment is made.

Stahl (1962) describes the following broad duties as typical of personnel practices: (*a*) developing policies and instructions; *(b)* job analysis and evaluation (in collaboration with supervisors); *(c)* recruiting, interviewing, processing, and evaluating; *(d)* salary and wage administration; *(e)* advising on employee relations; *(f)* developing and assisting in performance standards and evaluation; *(g)* staff training and development; *(h)* advising and participating in staff separation from service; *(i)* informing employees of their rights and obligations; *(j)* maintaining employee records; *(k)* personnel research; *(l)* and public relations (of nonspecialized nature).

Widely recommended as a critical management ingredient is a formal employee performance appraisal mechanism that is carefully linked to salary increments. Unfortunately, in the human services these evaluation and feedback systems have often become dysfunctional through the interference of professional ideologies that have contaminated decisions regarding what behaviors are relevant and appropriate to the positions and roles being evaluated.

Ideally, the goals of such a system are: *(a)* to motivate employees; *(b)* to discriminate between employees with high and low potential; *(c)* to improve management's capacity to make decisions about salary increases, promotions, and transfers; *(d)* to develop an objective rating system for use by supervisors; and *(e)* to inform employees how they are viewed by the organization in order to estimate future opportunities.

The basic models are two: *(a)* a system in which employees are rated against each other and *(b)* one in which the individual's performance is measured against preestablished objectives and/or contrasted with his own previous experience.

Thompson and Dalton (1970) suggest that an objective-focused approach may be a functional alternative that: *(a)* permits improved capacity by one employee without automatically requiring that another employee receive a lower rating; *(b)* does not require the manager to play "God"; *(c)* reduces the focus on personality traits; *(d)* is future oriented, anticipating rewards that motivate; *(e)* allows most or even all employees in an organization to feel a sense of accomplishment and movement if this is deserved; *(f)* is flexible for both the supervisor and the employee; *(g)* and permits open rather than closed systems accommodating variations in the increasing number of complex multiorganizations.

Ford (1969, p. 35), writing from the perspective of the Bell System, came to a similar conclusion. He noted that job turnover increased despite better two-way communication, improved salary and benefit plans, supervision, industrial relations, and management policies. In addition, better employees left at a faster rate than less valued employees.

In conclusion, it is not that money, benefits, human relations, and organizations are unimportant, but most important is the job itself. Is it meaningful? Is it responsible? Is it stimulating? Ford recommends that we focus on improving the nature of the job. Too often we have treated a job as though "a job is a job is a job." He concludes (1969, p. 35): "Use me well. Let my life mean something."

ADMINISTRATIVE ROLE PROPERTIES

Various writers have pointed to the many role properties of effective administrators, for example, the administrator as actor (Batten, in Sonthoff, 1964); as organizational catalyst (Hower and Orth, in Sonthoff); as guardian of organizational resources (Ewing, in Sonthoff); as friend and counselor (Moment and Zaleznik, in Sonthoff); and as a technician in human relationships (Sayles, in Sonthoff). It is possible that such a list could be extended *ad infinitum.*

With so many alternative and legitimate roles, it is clear that the first consideration must be the capacity to be able to shift roles comfortably, frequently, accurately, and effectively. In the complex and kaleidoscopic demands of human service organizations, perhaps the most definable characteristic of the administrative role is not what it is but that it is constantly in flux. An inability to perform this behavioral shift with comfort will take its psychological and physiological toll in the human outcomes created by high levels of stress. The result is too often seen in both lowered tenure of position occupancy and in the lowered reliability of performance of role incumbents.

CONCLUSION

In his provocative book *Up the Organization* (1970), Robert Townsend reminds us to take both our technologies and our organizations with a grain of salt. Very often, Townsend suggests, the success of complex organizations is not because of the way they operate but in spite of it.

9. THE FUTURE

A DEFINITION OF FUTURISM

Eldredge (1968, p. 382) offers a preliminary operational definition of futurism:

> ... first, the long-range projection of sociocultural change; second, the search for independent and semi-independent variables responsible for this change; and, third, the attempt to manipulate these variables toward long-range goals in a feedback planning process.

By the application of scientific or disciplined means it is presumed that society can make better use of its limited resources. It can serve to identify potential future trouble spots. It can help to extend future options (Eldredge, 1968).

Traditionally, futurists have focused on economic concerns, although recently the interests of physical and social planners have extended its functions to larger socio-political-demographic-ecologic-economic-ethical issues.

Myrdal (1968) in his analysis of Asian poverty illustrates the interrelation of ethical issues. What is required to reduce poverty, according to Myrdal, is a new set of political-economic values, for no government can effectively operate in contradistinction to societal norms that sanction sloth, laziness, superstition, mismanagement, and corruption.

Structural changes will be impotent against such overwhelming counterproductive standards.

WHY FUTURE PLANNING?

Although there is no qualitative measure of social change, the number of patents taken out annually at the U.S. Census Office may give some indication of a change rate. Since 1850 it can be roughly plotted as an exponential curve, one that is highly accelerative. Clearly, cumulative technology is exponential, for if inventions are new combinations of existing elements, then the broader the base the easier it is to invent.

Presumably, social inventions are similarly knowledge based and, certainly, social change is strongly related to changes in technology. Alvin Toffler (1970, p. 89) in writing on "future shock," posits a picture of geometric change:

> Milleniums of change will be compressed into the next 30 or 40 years, as a wholly novel civilization—superindustrialism—explodes into being in our midst. "This new society will embody values radically different from today's with the drive for material success subordinated to bizarre new aesthetic, religious, moral and social goals. It will be crammed with new forms of antibureaucratic organization—rapidly shifting, kinetic, ad-hocracies. It will offer a dazzling variety of choice with respect to products, culture, jobs and life styles. Yet the single most important feature of this new society will be its pace.

Donald N. Michael (1967, p. 888) generally concurs, concluding that the results will ". . . alter the very core of our way of life, values, beliefs, and aspirations over a 50-year perspective." His may be a conservative estimate.

More specific is Platt (1969, p. 115) who describes the rate of change as an "S curve."

> In the last century, we have increased our speed of communication by a factor of 10^7; our speed of travel by 10^2; our speeds of data handling by 10^6; our energy resources by 10^3; our power of weapons by 10^6; our ability to control diseases by something like 10^2; and our rate of population growth to 10^3 times what it was a few thousand years ago.

Extrapolation would lead one to expect even greater changes in the future.

Nuclear war, famine, poverty, overpopulation, and pollution are but a few of the immediate major threats to our survival. Thus the capacity of our formal organizations to respond to crisis and to change becomes even more vital. In New York City in 1968 school racial conflict and teacher, garbage, police, and longshoreman's strikes all occurred within a few days of each other. Perhaps our administrative crises share the same "S curve" of technological change. Unfortunately, our organizations are rarely, if ever, prepared to cope with simultaneous multiple crises.

As organizations need stability, so does man. They both need predictability, some sense of control over their own destiny. Anarchy has always been quickly repressed even if retrogression and loss of individual freedom is the result. An assumption of the mental health field is that if man does not learn to cope with the individual crisis as it occurs, anxiety, bewilderment, and irritability are likely to develop. If the crises pile up on each other in an endless exponential cycle, then breakdown and mental illness are possible results. Alternative coping mechanisms—drugs, alcohol, dropping out, and communes—are variously adaptive and maladaptive.

Bell (1967) describes four principal bases of change in our society: *(a)* technological development; *(b)* the diffusion of goods and privileges throughout our society; *(c)* structural changes, particularly the centralization of the political system and the husbanding of human capital, and *(d)* the relation of the United States to the remainder of the world.

Future predictions range along a continuum of a world with justice, dignity, humanity, and autonomy to one that is filled with injustice, overpopulated, polluted, and surviving on a subsistence diet in an all-encompassing state. Automation is seen as a boon to problem-solving as well as a means of depriving us of our privacy and self. Improved management skills are touted both as freeing man from drudgery and as depriving him of the right to democratic participation.

ORGANIZATION AND SYSTEM CHANGES

Ideology and Service Delivery Systems

Fundamental to the changing order of the human service system are the ideological changes going on in American society. They are variously described as changes in the moral order from integrity and wholeness to honesty and antihypocrisy (Dixon, 1968), from absolutism to relativism, and from pragmatism and simplicity to existentialism.

These values, these folkways and mores, find themselves imbedded in public policy not necessarily as a result of any conscious effort but in the way key decisionmakers respond to issues. The attack on scientism and professionalism, if continued, will certainly undermine professionally developed health and welfare programs. Dixon (1968, p. 259) states:

> The feeling is that an orderly establishment creates a premature closure on authority—that it necessarily thwarts the individual. Progress must be antiauthoritarian; responsibility must be exercised in role, not in rule.

Now, the professional is told, local availability of services and community control are more important than quality. Task analysis and differentiation of function permit the development of new paraprofessionals or technicians. But this development conflicts with the increasing hostility toward specialization, for paraprofessionals are by definition limited specialized extensions of their professional surrogates. Quality control, a logical extension of the roles of government and professions, is undermined by expressions of the morality of equality of opportunity and the effort to compensate for centuries of discrimination of selected minority groups.

Health in the 1970s

Hilleboe (1968) has ventured some predictions about

the nature of the American health industry in the 1970s. *(a)* The bulk of expenditures will remain in the acute and surgical illnesses requiring hospitalization; improvement in vaccines, increased transplantation, and an increasing blurring between public preventive and private clinical medicine are also likely. *(b)* The fields of rehabilitation and biomedical engineering offer considerable promise, and the proportion of the health dollar expended in chronic illness is expected to increase steadily. *(c)* In mental illness, addictive disorders, and retardation, increased attention will be paid to social causation and treatment, although slow but steady understanding of biomedical factors will also take place. The program focus will continue to shift from the institution to the community. Mental health and generic care-giving programs will be increasingly linked. *(d)* Increasing attention to maternal and child health, nutrition and family planning, can be expected. More concern with the prenatal period and the first few years of life is likely in response to recent research about the importance of these years. *(e)* Acute communicable diseases are still serious problems in economically depressed urban and rural areas. A massive attack would allow for substantial return on investment. *(f)* Accidental and occupational hazards, injuries, and deaths will continue to grow. Primary prevention by manipulation of the agent and environment is very hopeful.

The public concern with environmental issues, which began in the late 1960s, is likely to level off in the early 1970s, although the problems themselves will continue to increase. The essential issue of the 1970s will be to retain sufficient public interest to force the necessary changes and controls. One major recent step, broadening the base of concern beyond a small cult of conservationalists, promises some modest breakthroughs.

Changing Organizational Models

Dixon (1968, p. 263) suggests that "it may be pure

fantasy to think of today's hospital as having the capacity to be a community health center."

Two principal options seem to be possible. One is to extend the general hospital into the community. The other is to develop community health centers that extend back into the hospital. Lacking a comparable systematic facility base (as general hospitals), the social welfare system has moved toward a multiservice, neighborhood service, or comprehensive service model roughly organized along catchment lines. Despite the continued emphasis on all of these models there is reason to believe that each contains major structural defects and that the 1970s will see a new focus on availability, guarantee of equal access to, and continuity of service via an extended linkage and referral system that may not deliver major services on its own. Such a network model implies an acceptance of the pluralistic nature of our society and attempts to maximize the assets and control the deficits of this system. Another element of the pluralistic model will be alternative models accommodating to various regional idiosyncracies and encouraging flexibility.

Multiorganization Complexes

Thompson (1967, p. 157) states that social purposes in modern societies increasingly exceed the capacities of complex organizations, and call instead for action by multiorganization complexes.

Space exploration, hydroelectric dams, and multistate port authorities are examples of the combining of resources from a variety of sources to achieve a goal beyond the capacity of any given organization. These alliances may be *ad hoc* or may reflect mergers bringing about multiorganizations. What should be clear is that multiorganizations need not be large nor the result of advances in technology and hardware. For an example on the smallest scale, voluntary community-planning councils with multiple functions are multiorganizations. The complexity of the human services field is certain to bring about new, more complex, and probably larger organizations. That this will conflict with the goals of community control is also clear.

Postbureaucracy

Classical structure implies clearly delimited rules and regulations governing goals, functions, and responsibilities in order to maximize efficiency. The chain of command, best exemplified by the military, goes from top to bottom. Unfortunately, this model, effective in many ways, is contrary to many cherished beliefs, such as democracy and participation, among others. Ever-increasing technology and specialization requiring open management responsive to new ideas is in part antithetical to the traditional bureaucratic structure.

These combined forces are gradually transforming the classic arrangement into a more open, modified version. The "maple tree," partially collegial model of organizations permits a freer interchange and communication (up and down), less individual supervision, and a greater team orientation.

Bennis (1969, pp. 44-45) has hypothesized a breakdown of contemporary management (i.e., bureaucracy) for four major reasons:

> (1) rapid and unexpected change; (2) growth in size beyond what is necessary for the work being done (e.g., inflation caused by bureaucratic overhead and tight controls, impersonality caused by sprawls, outmoded rules, and organizational rigidities); (3) complexity of modern technology, in which integration between activities of very diverse, highly specialized competence is required; (4) a change in managerial values toward more humanistic democratic practices.

The new leadership concept, according to Bennis (1969, pp. 51, 61), contains four kinds of competencies:

> (1) Knowledge of large, complex human systems;
> (2) practical theories of intervening and guiding these

> systems, theories that encompass methods for seeding, nurturing, and integrating individuals and groups;
> (3) interpersonal competence, particularly the sensitivity to understand the effects of one's own behavior on others and how one's own personality shapes his particular leadership style and value system;
> (4) a set of values and competencies which enables one to know when to confront and attack if necessary and when to support and provide the psychological safety so necessary for growth.

Shick (1970, p. 18) suggests that as we move into the postindustrial state the role and structure of government will shift to a focus on "concerting the polity and the economy to achieve public objectives. As a result, the government changes from a *doer* of public activities to a distributor of public benefits." The welfare bureaucracy will be dismantled. Instead of thousands of governmental units and social worker-bureaucrats investigating recipients and requiring "casework," the system will be centralized and automated. Based on some form of guaranteed annual income adjusted to the cost of living, modeled organizationally after the Internal Revenue Service, including its programmed and sampling monitoring procedures, the indignities of investigation will be severely limited. A similar move can be seen in discussions about national health insurance and in education. It requires an increasing transfer of controls from the legislative to the executive branches, and while subject to resistance on the part of the legislative branch, the transfer is inevitable as the individual forms of control continue to break down, accompanied by a rapid cost escalation.

The Contract and Grant-in-Aid Mechanism

Another significant change, as implied above, will be the alteration of the government's direct personal service role. It will subsidize grant-in-aid and contract direct services, giving the government better management controls and enhancing its capacity to alter priorities. The increasing blurring of public and private functions and the further development of quasi-private and quasi-public organizations will continue. A new form of human service marketplace will be the result (Shick, 1970).

In turn, government will need fewer and better trained personnel with professional and technical competence. Establishing guidelines, writing contracts, and monitoring standards, they will be working closely with senior contractee personnel, and as such they will have to be paid comparably.

Cost Control Budgets

Whatever the form, it is clear that budget control mechanisms will be an accepted administrative arrangement in human services organizations. Attempts to objectify budgetary analysis will continue, albeit with enormous difficulty. Combined with sophisticated information systems, management tools are likely to be substantially enhanced.

Industry and Social Welfare

Profit-making in the human services represents a significant future development. As the health industry approaches 10% of the GNP, and the production, distribution, and consumption of knowledge 30% of the GNP, it is clear that health and education will no longer be the principal domain of do-gooders, academicians, or physicians. Such an enormous economic potential is ripe for the "social-industrial complex." Although proprietary hospitals have not gained a substantial foothold in the health industry, nor profit-making institutions in the educational field, in recent years the nursing home, homemaker, and day-care center have recently invited considerable for-profit investment. The Job Corps program similarly excited some brief interest, as did the Peace Corps. The growth of the pharmaceutical industry is well known, and the knowledge industry now contains many of our corporate giants.

The underlying issue rests on control. Who establishes the goals, sets the priorities, and monitors the system? Michael Harrington (1967, pp. 58, 60) suggests:

> What is at stake is nothing less than how the Americans of the twenty-first century are going to think and live. . . . For when business methods are sincerely and honestly applied to urban problems, with very good intentions, they still inevitably lead to anti-social results. It is exactly when cross concerns are not paramount that the real problem—the inapplicability of business methods and priorities to the crisis of the cities—emerges most clearly.

Harrington may be overreacting, but certain trends are clearly evident: The human services complex is a growth industry, and the profit-making sector is moving into this enlarging arena. Substantial changes are ensured—as are the social-developmental risks.

New Technologies for Management

Although most discussion of technology focuses on the physical or hardware side, as noted earlier, there are a number of social or soft-ware developments with equally significant implications. The focus on new result-oriented budgeting systems, operational research, simulation, systems analysis, social and economic planning, the linkage of function to structure, new forms of organizational analysis, games theory, and programmed learning are illustrative of these developments.

Necessary to many of these tools is the modern complex computer that permits the aggregation and analysis of large amounts of data. The major factor limiting its use is the lack of skilled personnel to exploit these developing technologies in relation to the human condition. It is already quite clear that many of our most cherished social institutions and values are under attack and likely will be increasingly so in the next generation. Michael Harrington (1967, p. 890) states:

> Such concepts as private investment, the nation, state, privacy, Federal, state and local prerogatives, free enterprise, freedom of science, these and other terms which carry with them a variety of deep beliefs and needs may be so transformed as to be unrecognizable or disappear altogether.

As a consequence, Michael Harrington (p. 891) predicts the development of regional-size educational systems and the dissolution of local school districts; a conflict between information systems and privacy; and priority setting conflicting with private and business freedom.

FUTURE-ORIENTED CONSTRAINTS

That Soviet Russia has had a future-oriented approach to the solution of major social ills has served to constrain comparable American development. Particularly antithetical to American values were the post-World War II Russian five-year plans that were perceived as mechanisms of social control.

Eldredge (1968) suggests that the major Western effort most resembling macro-future planning was that found in the quasi-democratic Fifth French Republic. It was designed to improve France's economic status by influencing the development of private industry. This regionally focused "indicative planning" demonstrated a future-oriented capability not found elsewhere in the Western world. Its sector-oriented industrial base may account for its general acceptance.

CONCLUSION

The service maze is living up to its psychological analogy. As it becomes increasingly difficult to negotiate, specialists become increasingly remote, and depersonalization accelerates, more money is expended, and both service gaps and overlap are more obvious; we have both a present and future problem.

Equally important, increasing population, urbanization, congestion, mobility, sharpening of class and social differences, and continued ethnic tensions are helping to create a feeling of alienation from the decision-making and increasingly technically oriented care-giving systems (Newman & Demone, 1969).

The increasing interest in modern management and planning technologies suggested earlier in this monograph reflect some current answers to the need to humanize, rationalize, and economize. It is clear the task will not be an easy one and will probably become exponentially more difficult as each year passes without a major solution.

Newman and Demone (1969) recommended four steps that, taken together, would be of some help: *(a)* The full exploitation of technology; *(b)* the development of strong, competent government; *(c)* citizen participation at the policy level; and *(d)* program management procedures that focus on the consumer not the provider.

As noted earlier, we have substantially increased our ability to manage large numbers of variables via the computer. Data analysis, simulation, and fiscal management are all enhanced.

But this escalation of technology is correlated with further estrangement between the technocrat and the citizen, and complex organizations and their consumers. The separation of policy-making from implementation and the design of methods to involve the citizen in the major decisions are critical issues.

But authority cannot be shared if it does not exist, and executives cannot open up their organizations if their activities are stifled with detail and their authority unclear and ambiguous. Agencies and institutions cannot share that which they do not possess. McGeorge Bundy (1968) suggests that the executive branch of government must be strengthened if it is to fulfill effectively its responsibilities. Lacking clearly concentrated authority and responsibility, constrained by laws laden with detail and restricting flexibility, hampered by tables of organization that make subordinates essentially independent, the governmental executive must be strengthened if government is to work.

People and their problems are not categorical despite their proliferated organizations.

REFERENCES

Alinsky, S. *Reveille for radicals.* Chicago: University of Chicago Press, 1945.

Ardell, D. B. Urban-planning/health-planning relationships. *American Journal of Public Health,* 1969, **59,** 2051-2055.

Aronson, J. B. Planning for community health services. *Public Health Reports,* 1964, **79,** 1101-1106.

Baker, F. General systems theory research, and medical care. In A. Sheldon, F. Baker, & C. McLaughlin (Eds.), *Systems and medical care.* Cambridge, Mass.: MIT Press, 1970.

Baker, F., & Schulberg, H. C. Community health caregiving systems: Integration of interorganizational networks. In A. Sheldon, F. Baker, & C. McLaughlin (Eds.), *Systems and medical care.* Cambridge, Mass.: MIT Press, 1970.

Banfield, E. C. Ends and means in planning. In Maileck, S., & Van Ness, E. H. (Eds.), *Concepts and issues in administrative behavior.* Englewood Cliffs, N.J.: Prentice-Hall, 1962.

Banfield, E. C. The uses and limitations of metropolitan planning in Massachusetts. In *Issues and problems of Boston metropolitan area development.* Boston, Mass.: Metropolitan area planning council, 1965.

Barnard, C. *The functions of the executive.* Cambridge; Harvard University Press, 1938.

Beck, B. M. Community control: A distraction, not an answer. *Social Work,* 1969, **14,** (4), 14-20.

Bell, D. The year 2000—Trajectory of an idea. *Daedalus: Proceedings of the American Academy of Arts and Sciences,* 1967, **96,** 639-651.

Bennis, W. Beyond bureaucracy. *Trans-Action,* 1965, **2,** 31-35.

Bennis, W. G. & Slater, P. E. *The temporary society.* New York: Harper, 1968.

Bennis, W. G., & Harris, T. G. Organic populism. *Psychology Today,* February, 1970. **3** (9), 48-54, 68-70.

Bennis, W. G., Benne, K. D., & Chin, R. (Eds.) *The planning of change.* New York: Holt, Rinehart, 1969.

Bennis, W. G. Post-bureaucratic leadership. *Trans-Action,* 1969, **6** (9), 44-61.

Bennis, W. A funny thing happened on the way to the future. *American Psychologist,* 1970, **25,** 595-608.

Biddle, F. J., & Thomas, E. J. *Role theory: concepts and research.* New York: Wiley, 1966.

Blake, R. R., & Mouton, J. S. *The managerial grid.* Houston: Gulf Publishing Co., 1961.

Blau, P. M. *Bureaucracy in modern society.* New York: Random House, 1956.

Brager, G. A., and Jorrin, V. Bargaining: A method in community change. *Social Work,* 1969, **14,** (4), 73-83.

Braybrooke, D., & Lindbloom, C. *A strategy of decision.* New York: Free Press, 1963.

Bulletin of the Foundation Library Center, 1968, **9** (3), 55-56.

Bundy, M. Godkin Lectures, Harvard University, 1968.

Caplan, G. *Principles of preventive Psychiatry.* New York: Basic Books, 1964.

Carter, L. F. The traveling seminar and conference for the implementation of educational innovation. In *Social Research in Federal Domestic Programs.* Committee on Government Operations, House of Representatives. Washington, D.C.: U.S. Government Printing Office, 1967.

Committee on Environment of the American Public Health Association. Environmental factors in health planning. *American Journal of Public Health,* 1963, **50,** 358-360.

Curran, W. J. Progress in mental health legislation. Address given at Seventeenth Annual Mental Hospital Institute, San Francisco, September 1965.

Daniels, A. H. The captive professional: Bureaucratic limitations in the practice of military psychiatry. *Journal of Health and Social Behavior,* 1969, **10,** 255-265.

Demone, H. W., Jr. The Limits of rationality in planning. *Community Mental Health Journal,* 1965, **1,** 375-381.

Demone, H. W., Jr., Spivack, M., & McGrath, M. Decision-making issues in the development of community mental health centers. Paper presented at the New England Psychological Association, Boston, November 1966.

Demone, H. W., Jr., & Newman, E. Mental health planning and coordination: Can it really be accomplished? In H. Gruenbaum (Ed.), *The Practice of Community Mental Health:* Boston: Little, Brown, 1970.

Demone, H. W., Jr. Human services at state and local levels and the integration of mental health. In G. Caplan (Ed.), *American handbook of psychiatry.* Vol. 2, New York: Basic Books, 1973.

Dixon, J. D. The health agenda for the future. *Milbank Memorial Fund Quarterly,* 1968, **46,** (259-264,Pt. 2).

Downs, A. Some thoughts on giving people economic advice. *The American Behavioral Scientist,* 1965.

Dunham, A. Community development. *Social Work Yearbook,* 1960, **14,** 178-186.

Eldredge, H. W. Futurism in planning for developing countries. *American Institute of Planners Journal,* 1968, **34,** 382-384.

Emery, F. E., & Trist, E. L. The causal texture of organizational environments. *Human Relations,* 1965, **18,** 1-10, 21-32.

Evan, W. M. The organizational set: Toward a theory of interorganizational relationships. In J. D. Thompson (Ed.), *Approaches to organizational design.* Pittsburgh: University of Pittsburgh Press, 1966.

Feingold, E. The changing political character of health planning. *American Journal of Public Health,* 1969, **59,** No. 5, 803-808.

Fogelson, F., and Demone, H. W., Jr. Program change through mental health planning. *Community Mental Health Journal,* 1969, **5,** 3-13.
Ford, R. M. The obstinate employee. *Psychology Today,* 1969, **3** (6), 32-35.
Freed, H. M., & Miller, L. Planning a community mental health program: A case history. *Community Mental Health Journal,* 1971, in press.
Freed, H. M., Schroder, D., & Baker, B. The west side story. Unpublished manuscript, Illinois State Psychiatric Institute, 1970.
Friedmann, J. Notes on societal action. *American Institute of Planners Journal,* 1969. **35,** 311-318.
Gardner, J. W. How to prevent organizational dry rot. *Harper's,* 1965, **231** (1385), 20-26.
Gilbert, N. Maximum feasible participation? A Pittsburgh encounter. *Social Work,* 1969, **14,** (3), 84-92.
Gilmore, J. S., Ryan, J. D., & Gould, W. S. Defense systems resources in the civil seeker. Washington, D.C.: U.S. Government Printing Office, 20402, cited by Boffey, P. M. systems analysis: No panacea for nation's domestic problems. *Science,* 1967, **158,** 1028-1030.
Goffman, E. *Asylums.* Garden City, N.J.: Doubleday, 1961.
Gomberg, W. The trouble with democratic management. *Trans-Action,* 1966, **3,** (5), 30-35.
Gross, G. M. The coming general systems models of social systems. *Human Relations,* 1967, **20,** 357-374.
Gurin, G., Veroff, J., & Feld, S. *Americans view their mental health.* New York: Basic Books, 1960.
Hall, R. H. Some organizational considerations in the professional-organizational relationship. *Administrative Science Quarterly,* 1967, **12,** 461-478.
Harrington, M. The social-industrial complex. *Harper's,* 1967, **235** (1410), 55-60.
Harshbarger, D. From chronic wards to therapeutic communities: II. The struggle for survival. *Hospital and Community Psychiatry,* 1967, **18,** 310-314.
Harshbarger, D. High priests in hospitaldom. *Hospital and Community Psychiatry,* 1970, **21,** 156-159. (a)
Harshbarger, D. The human service organization. Unpublished manuscript, Department of Psychology, West Virginia University, 1970. (b)
Harshbarger, D. An investigation of a structural model of small group problem solving. *Human Relations,* 1971, in press.
Hilleboe, H. E. Public health in the United States in the 1970's. *American Journal of Public Health,* 1968, **58,** 1588-1610.
Hirschowitz, R. G. Changing behavior in the state hospital organization. *Psychiatric Quarterly,* 1969, **43,** 591-611.
Hirschowitz, R. G. From chronic wards to therapeutic communities: I. Preparing and developing staff. *Hospital and Community Psychiatry,* 1967, **18,** 304-309.
Hochbaum, G. W. Consumer participation in health planning: Toward conceptual clarification. *Journal of the American Public Health Association,* 1969, **59,** 1698-1705.

Hofstadter, R. The future of American violence. *Harper's,* 1970, **240,** (1439), 47-53.

Howard, D. S. Relationships between governmental and voluntary agencies. *Encyclopedia of Social Work,* New York: National Association of Social Workers, 1965.

Kopkind, A. The future planners. *New Republic,* 1967, **156,** (8), 19-23.

Kornhauser, W. *Scientists in industry: Conflicts and accommodation.* Berkeley: University of California Press, 1962.

Kristol, I. Decentralization for what? *The Public Interest,* 1968, **II,** 17-25.

Lawrence, P. R., & Lorsch, J. W. Differentiation and integration in complex organizations. *Administrative Science Quarterly,* 1967, **12,** 1-47.

Levine, S., & White, P. E. Exchange as a conceptual framework for the study of interorganizational relationships. *Administrative Science Quarterly,* 1961, **5.**

Levine, S. Organizational and professional barriers to interagency planning. In Planning responsibilities of state departments of public welfare. Proceedings of a conference at Brandeis University, 1966.

Likert, R. *New patterns of management.* New York: McGraw-Hill, 1961.

Likert, R. *The human organization.* New York: McGraw-Hill, 1967.

Litwak, E., & Hylton, L. F. Interorganizational analysis: A hypothesis on coordinating agencies. *Administrative Science Quarterly,* 1962, **6,** 395-426.

Logue, E. J. The power of negative thinking. *Boston,* 1969, **61,** (2), 36-38, 57-61.

Mackenzie, R. A. The management process in 3-D. *Harvard Business Review,* 1969, **47** (6).

Mann, F. C. Studying and creating change: A means to understanding social organization. *Research in Industrial Human Relations,* Industrial Relations Research Association, 1957.

Mattison, B. Political implications in good public health administration. *American Journal of Public Health,* 1965, **55,** (2), 183-189.

Merton, R. K. Role of the intellectual in public bureaucracy. *Social theory and social structure,* Glencoe, Ill.: Free Press, 1957.

Michael, D. N. Social engineering and the future environment. *American Psychologist,* 1967, **22,** 888-892.

Mott, B. J. F. The myth of planning without politics. *American Journal of Public Health,* 1969, **59,** 797-803.

Moynihan, D. P. What is community action? *The Public Interest,* 1966, **5,** 3-8.

Murphy, C. G. Community organization for social welfare. *Social Work Yearbook,* 1960, **14,** 186-190.

Myrdal, G. *Asian drama: An inquiry into the poverty of nations.* New York: Twentieth Century Fund, 1968. 3 vols.

National Commission on Community Health Services. *Health administration and organizations in the decade ahead.* Washington, D.C.: Public Affairs Press, 1967.

National Information Bureau. *The volunteer board member in philanthropy.* New York: 1968.

Newman, E., & Demone, H. W., Jr. Policy paper—A new look at public planning for human services. *Journal of Health and Social Behavior,* 1969, **10**, 142-149.

Noble, J. H., Jr. Protecting the public's privacy in computerized health and welfare information systems. *Social Work,* 1971, **21** (1), 35-41.

O'Donnell, E., & Sullivan, M. Service delivery and social action through the neighborhood center: A review of research. *Welfare In Review,* 1969, **7,** 1-12.

Peattie, L. Reflections on advocacy planning. *American Institute of Planners Journal,* 1968, **34,** 80-88.

Perlman, R., & Jones, D. *Neighborhood Service Centers.* Washington, D.C.: Office of Juvenile Delinquency, Department of Health, Education and Welfare, 1967.

Peter, L., and Hull, R. *The Peter principle.* New York: Morrow, 1969.

Platt, J. What we must do. *Science,* 1969, **166,** 1115-1121.

Pray, K. L. M. When is community organization social work practice? In D.S. Howard (Ed), *Community organization: Its nature and settings.* New York: American Association of Social Workers, 1947.

Rand, G. What psychology asks of urban planning. *American Psychologist,* 1969, **24,** 929-935.

Rein, M., & Miller, S. M. Social action on the installment plan. *Trans-Action,* 1966, **3** (2), 31-32.

Rice, A. K. *The enterprise and its environment.* London: Tavistock Publications, 1958.

Roethlisberger, F. J. *Management and morale.* Cambridge: Harvard University Press, 1941.

Ross, M. G. *Community organization: Theory and principles.* New York: Harper, 1955.

Rothman, J. An analysis of goals and roles in community organization practice. *Social Work,* 1964, **9** (2), 24-31.

Sanders, I. T. Theories of community development. *Rural Sociology,* 1958, **23.**

Schaefer, M. Politics and public health. Unpublished doctoral dissertation in Public Administration, Syracuse University, 1962.

Scheff, T. J. Toward a sociological model of consensus. *American Sociological Review,* in press.

Schorr, D. *Don't get sick in America.* Nashville, Tenn.: Aurora Publishers, 1970.

Shick, A. The cybernetic state. *Trans-Action,* 1970, **7** (4), 15-26.

Sheldon, A., Baker, F., & McLaughlin, C. P. (Eds.) *Systems and medical care,* Cambridge, Mass.: MIT Press, 1970.

Simon, H., Smithburg, D. W., & Thompson, V. A. *Public administration.* New York: Knopf, 1961.

Slater, P., & Bennis, W. Democracy is inevitable. *Harvard Business Review,* 1964, **42** (2), 51-59.

Slater, P. *The pursuit of loneliness; American culture at the breaking point.* Boston: Beacon Press, 1970.

Sonthoff, H. What is the manager? *Harvard Business Review,* 1964, **42** (6), 24-36.

Spivack, M., & Demone, H. W., Jr. Mental health facilities: A model for physical planning. *Social Science and Medicine,* 1970, **3,** 513-528.

Stahl, O. G. *Public personnel administration.* New York: Harper, 1962.

Sussman, M. B. The sociologist as tool of social action. In A. Shostok (Ed.), *Sociology in Action.* Homewood, Ill. Dorsey Press, 1966.

Taubenhaus, L. J., Hamlin, R. H., & Wood, R. C. Performance reporting and program budgeting: Tools for program evaluation. *American Journal of Public Health,* 1957, **47,** 423-438.

Taylor, F. W. *The principles of scientific management.* New York: Harper, 1923.

Terreberry, S. The evolution of organizational environments. *Administrative Science Quarterly,* 1968, **12,** 590-613.

The American Assembly. The ombudsman. Meeting at Columbia University, October, 1967.

Thompson, J. D. *Organizations in action.* New York: McGraw-Hill, 1967.

Thompson, P. H., & Dalton, G. W. Performance appraisal: Managers beware. *Harvard Business Review,* 1970, **48** (1), 149-157.

Toffler, A. Coping with future shock. *Playboy,* 1970, **17** (3), 88-99 ff.

Torrens, P. R. A pilot program in coordination of care between an urban teaching hospital and the community's general practitioners. *American Journal of Public Health,* 1969, **59,** 60-64.

Townsend, R. *Up the organization.* New York: Knopf, 1970.

Von Bertalanffy, L. General systems theory. *General systems.* Yearbook of the society for the advancement of general systems theory, 1956, **1,** 1-10.

Walsh, J. Foundations: Taking stock after the Tax Reform Bill. *Science,* 1970, **167,** 1598-1599.

Warren, R. L. Types of social change at the community level. *Papers in Social Welfare,* 1965, No. 11. Waltham, Mass., Brandeis University.

Warren, R. The interorganizational field as a focus for investigation. *Administrative Science Quarterly,* 1967, **12,** 396-419.

Warren, R. L. The mental health drama: Hamlet or Hellzapoppin? Paper presented at National Institute of Mental Health Regional Office Staff Meeting, Dallas, October 1969.

World Health Organization. Suggested outline for use by countries in discussing health education of the public. *A 12/Technical discussion/I,* March 31, 1958.

STRATEGIES IN INNOVATIVE HUMAN SERVICES PROGRAMS

by
Harry Gottesfeld, Ph.D.,
Florence Lieberman, D.S.W.,
Sheldon R. Roen, Ph.D.,
and Sol Gordon, Ph.D.

(Part III of Developments in Human Services,
Volume 1,
Edited by
Herbert C. Schulberg, Ph.D.,
Frank Baker, Ph.D., and
Sheldon R. Roen, Ph.D.

Library of Congress Catalog Card Number 73-6871
Standard Book Number 87705-078-3

BEHAVIORAL PUBLICATIONS, 2852 Broadway—Morningside Heights, New York, New York 10025

Printed in the United States of America

Library of Congress Cataloging in Publication Data

Main entry under title.

Strategies in innovative human services programs.

Also issued in v. 1 of Developments in human servic
1. Social service--United States--Case studies.
I. Gottesfeld, Harry.
[HV91.S74] 361'.973 73-6871

CONTENTS

Preface v
Introduction 267

1. **Rationale of Strategies** 269
   Some Prerequisite Considerations 269
   Defining the Problem 271
   Theory of Causation 272
   Inputs for Solving Problems 273
   Mandates and Sanctions 273
   Strategies 274
   Monitoring and Evaluation 277
   Some Strategy Dilemmas 277

2. **Upsetting the Apple Cart: The Changing Directions of the Community Service Society of New York City** 283
   Strategies 285
   Problems 289

3. **PS Inner City: A Program's Failure, An Educator's Dilemma** 292
   Sol Gordon

4. **Up from Ashes: Phoenix House** 307
   Assumptions about Definition of Problem, Causation, and Necessary Inputs 308
   Mandates and Constraints 308
   Target Population 309
   Nature of Services 309
   Work Strategy 311
   Rewards and Punishments 313

Encounter Groups 313
Educational Seminars 314
Costs and Evaluation 315
Strategy Problems 315

5. When an Agency's Constituency Ages: Kissena Apartments—An Experience in Housing for Older People 317
Changing Strategies 318
Mandates and Sanctions 321
Operational Strategies 322
Evaluation 324
Strategy Problems 325

6. Helping Police Cope with Family Violence: A Training Model in Community Intervention 327
Mandates and Sanctions 329
Preparatory Phase 330
Operational Phase 331
Evaluation 332
Assumptions and Strategies 332
Problems 333

7. A Demonstration Project on a Minimum Budget: The Goals for Girls Project of the Foothill Family Service of Pasadena California 336
Target Population 336
Problem Definition 337
Assumptions as to Inputs 337
Research Strategy 339
Administrative Strategies and Problems 340
Results 342

8. Conclusion 347

PREFACE TO THE SEPARATES OF THE "DEVELOPMENTS IN HUMAN SERVICES" SERIES

Widespread inadequacies in the human condition, and concern for the difficulties and complexities of existing social arrangements, have created urgent pressures upon professionals to revise present care-giving mechanisms. Human service programs such as multi-service centers, which incorporate a wide variety of relevant services, are emerging as an alternative framework to the existing pattern of rigid, categorical services for meeting the bio-psycho-social needs of individuals and populations.

The editors of this new encyclopedic series have undertaken to develop materials which can serve as guide posts for those newly entering or already engaged in the field of human services. A flexible approach to the production and distribution of these materials has been devised.

The plan for the series is to publish annually indepth discussions and reviews on the following human service topics:

—Emerging Conceptions of human service such as systems and ecological frameworks

—Administrative and planning tools such as information systems, economic strategies, and legal mechanisms

—Innovative service programs within new organizational models and new communities

—Educational programs for changing professional roles and new manpower requirements

After several years, those who are standing order subscribers will possess an encyclopedic library of human

services in either hardbound volumes or softcover separates.

The first volume contains an introductory overview by the editors, four substantitive sections on different human service topics as enumerated below, and a comprehensive index. Each of the substantitive sections, without introductory overview and index, are available as separates. These are:

Teaching Health and Human Services Administration by the Case Method
Linda G. Sprague, Alan Sheldon, M.D., and Curtis P. McLaughlin, D.B.A.

The Planning and Administration of Human Services
Harold W. Demone, Jr., Ph.D. and Dwight Harshbarger, Ph.D.

Strategies in Innovative Human Service Programs
Harry Gottesfeld, Ph.D., Florence Lieberman, D.S.W., Sheldon R. Roen, Ph.D., and Sol Gordon, Ph.D.

Developments in Human Services Education and Manpower
Robert M. Vidaver, M.D.

The Editors

INTRODUCTION

This monograph is primarily aimed at those who are involved in the planning or administration of human services programs. Every planner, administrator, or consultant of these programs constantly makes assumptions about the nature of the problem with which he is dealing and what kinds of inputs will make an impact on the problem. He faces a variety of constraints from funding, agency and community sources, employs program strategies in the light of his assumptions and the constraints placed on him, and finds that employing the strategies bring forth their own problems. Program planners and administrators are generally only vaguely aware of most elements of this process; the elements become more visible when a program crisis is reached. The authors of the monograph believe that if a planner or administrator is aware beforehand of the kind of assumptions he is making, the nature of his strategies, and the kind of problems the strategies may entail, he will be clearer about his program and able to plan better and to anticipate and deal more effectively with the problems that inevitably arise.

The first chapter deals with the theoretical rationale of the nature of strategies in human services. In the chapters that follow the authors chose a variety of programs from the fields of community mental health, social work, and education, each of which was innovative and had achieved recognition as an outstanding program of its kind. By way of contrast one of the authors chose a program of his own that he felt was a failure and describes in personal terms what happened. In each instance administrators of these programs were interviewed and the programs were discussed from the point of view of the assumptions, constraints, strategies, and strategy problems. The chapters are written on the basis of the interviews and literature relating to the programs. The final chapter presents the authors' thoughts and conclusions about the implications of the strategies of these programs and how the authors' theoretical rationale was supported, modified, or changed as a result of what they learned about these programs.

The choice of programs from the fields of education, social work, and community mental health was only for the purpose of presenting a variety of fields and programs. The authors believe that the strategy principles cut across the human services fields and probably would apply equally well to other fields, for example, comprehensive health. The description of programs from different fields should be helpful to a program planner or administrator in a given field in that it may suggest strategies that have had few applications as yet in his own field; there has been little cross-fertilization at the program level in the social sciences. It may also serve the purpose of removing the heavy emotional investment one has in his own specialty; looking at programs in other fields may allow for more objective considerations.

1. RATIONALE OF STRATEGIES

It seems appropriate to think in terms of strategies in discussing human services. The term was originally used in describing the projection and direction of large military movements and has a secondary dictionary definition of a careful plan, method, or clever scheme for gaining an end. Strategies suggest broad-sweeping concerns. In a general sense community mental health, social work, and education have all attempted strategic campaigns to better the human condition by developing programs that involve organized service delivery systems to targeted populations. Tactics are smaller-scale actions designed to implement the strategies but with more limited or immediate ends. It is sometimes difficult to determine where strategies leave off and tactics begin, and although this chapter focuses on more general plans and methods—strategies—it does not attempt to differentiate in its discussions between strategies and tactics.

SOME PREREQUISITE CONSIDERATIONS

Before particular services delivery strategies can be seriously considered, certain prior issues need to be faced. Every strategist founds his strategy on a series of assumptions that may or may not have any reality base. Among these assumptions are his definition of the problem, the reasons he believes the problem exists, and what he thinks it requires to solve the problem. In addition to his assumptions he is faced by the mandates and sanctions of his agency, funding sources, etc. Program strategies typically evolve from the assumptions of the program planner and the mandates and sanctions that may encourage, set limits, or modify the planner's assumptions.

Assumptions are rarely made explicit. Often they contain many unconscious factors. In addition it is sometimes difficult to discover the base on which many programs and much planning is done. Schorr (1968, pp. 7, 8) discusses this difficulty in his analysis of several government programs involving social policy and services to people. He noted that "unstated objectives could not be assumed . . . and of the technical accounterments of the social sciences that their sophistication and the sheer volume of their data easily hide from sight the assumptions at their core." Morris and Rein (1967, p. 34) in studying poverty and community action in the United States, also found that the

> constant interaction of means and ends makes the goals and assumptions of the projects hard to define. Statements from different sources, or at different times offer varying explanations of intent.

Similarly, Kahn (1969) in discussing the practice of social planning accepts that choice and assumptions affect the totality of activities involved in planning.

All of the processes discussed in this monograph involve both knowledge and assumptions, the latter particularly necessary because of the less than adequate knowledge in the field of human services. However, even if knowledge were more exact, assumptions would be necessary for assumptions are in reality the theory, hypotheses, and questions that evolve from the interrelatedness of the multiple factors involved in human lives. What is involved in planning is making these hypotheses operational.

The question of assumptions applies in the assessment of a program so that there is usually confusion between a program's impact and how it is conducted. Freeman and Sherwood (1970, p. 4) state:

> It is often believed, by those who rely on the quality of the service rendered, that if a program is run properly it can also be assumed that the desired changes are taking place and that these changes are due to the program.

It is suggested that the assumptions themselves are often not made explicit. But at a deeper level and underlying many of the assumptions are value orientations. The role of values and preferences is discussed in detail by Kahn (1969, pp. 96-129) who notes that at all stages of planning facts need to be confronted with values and values with facts.

DEFINING THE PROBLEM

The act of defining a problem is not a neutral, intellectual exercise. People define a problem because it bothers them, their reference group, or their society in some way, and the definition implies a need to change the situation. For example, in our culture individuals who are addicted to drugs are perceived as a problem by most other people who would like to change the drug addict. However, in the subculture of the drug addict as well as some other cultures it may not be seen as a problem. In some primitive societies the person under the influence of drugs may even be revered.

Which leads to a consideration of the definers. Who are they? Since defining is an act of power, it is usually the power groups and their agents of the society who do the defining. The definers are almost always those without "the problem." Thus, the problem of "illiteracy" is defined by literate people, the problem of "poverty" by people who are not poor, the problem of "illegitimacy" by people who have children through wedlock. The social stratification between those who define "the problem" and those whom "the problem" fits are probably related to the qualities of strategies adopted in social work, education, and community mental health.

How the problem is defined is of considerable importance. If in a war or revolution the enemy is defined as the leaders and their immediate supporters, certain kinds of strategy relating to defeating the political leaders are called for; but if the enemy is defined as an entire population, other strategies relating to conquering and subjugating the people are required. In mental health, if the problem is seen as the recognition and treatment of neurotic and psychotic symptomatology, certain strategies related to the efficient delivery of conventional mental health services seem appropriate; but if the definition of mental health is the social competency of individuals or the relief of community strife and tension, a whole new set of strategies may be necessary.

THEORY OF CAUSATION

Closely aligned with the definition of the problem is one's theory of the etiology of the problem. A major problem that has been identified in education is the poor achievement of blacks, Puerto Ricans, Mexican-Americans, and American Indians. One theory of causation is that the minority child from the moment he enters school is so poorly prepared to produce what is required that failure is almost inevitable. At home the child receives poor training in verbal skills and auditory and visual discrimination and little intellectual stimulation. An educator who subscribes to this theory may be inclined to compensatory education programs in which the minority child receives extra training in utilizing verbal skills and in sensory discrimination.

Another theory of the etiology of this problem is that most teachers are white and middle class and do not understand the culture of the minority child, are frequently intolerant of his way of life, and have difficulty communicating with him. A believer of this theory is likely to emphasize programs that train minority people for school positions or train existing school personnel to understand better the cultures of minority groups and the culture of poverty.

INPUTS FOR SOLVING PROBLEMS

Two program planners may have similar definitions of a problem and its etiology, but each may have different assumptions as to what may solve the problem. For example, poverty may be defined similarly and may be seen as arising from a combination of factors such as poor education, poor skills, discrimination, large, unplanned families, poor health, etc. However, one planner may believe that the necessary input to solve the problem is sufficient professional help—help in developing work and educational skills of the poor; health care; counseling; advocacy. Another planner may believe the necessary input to solve the problem is, regardless of skills and educational lacks, to give the poor responsible, well-paying jobs.

Which of these various assumptions are based on reality? Overall there has been relatively little research to test any of these assumptions. This is equally true in the fields of education, social work, and community mental health. A good example of an exception in education is the research by Coleman, Campbell, Hobson, McPartland, Modd, Weinfield, & York (1966), which indicates that the input of compensatory programs for minority children is likely to have little effect on their educational achievement. For the most part program planners will have to proceed dangerously on a small body of knowledge on which to base their assumptions. The road to hell is paved with untested assumptions.

MANDATES AND SANCTIONS

Whatever strategies a program planner might like to adopt, he will be bound by the mandates of the institution, the sources of funding, and the community. For example, governmental funding of community mental health programs requires that a certain population be served by the center and specific kinds of services be provided. Control is exercised by licensure, contract terms, and accountability through statistical reporting systems as to what monies were expended and what services were given. Of course, the mandates themselves may be the strategies of the higher-order funding agencies, but they do put limitations on what a local organization or system might prefer to do. Similarly, the local community may desire a particular mode of operation or program which the "establishment" has little interest in developing.

STRATEGIES

The Population

Based on a program planner's assumptions and mandates, he will select a population to which he addresses his service program. Typically, a mental health program that defines the problem in mental health as those people who have neurotic or psychotic symptomatology and has the mandate of serving a given community opens its doors and serves anyone from the community who asks help from the program with his neurotic or psychotic symptoms. However, another mental health program, which operates under the assumption that adult neurotic and psychotic symptoms develop in early childhood and only intervention at that time is likely to have any impact, may choose as its population parents of young children for educational, training, or psychotherapy programs. A mental health programmer who operates under the assumptions that the definition of mental health is a community in which the people live together harmoniously may choose as his population those elements in the population that have manifested strife. Strategies are frequently directed to specific elements of the population because it is believed that the effects of changing a certain age group, a group causing social disruption, a leadership group, etc., will have special leverage in solving the problem. For example, many poverty programs have been directed toward manpower training programs for young adults on the assumption that by obtaining a well-paying job the youth could obtain for himself and his family the goods and services that would move them out of poverty. Contributing to the choice of youth as the targeted population is that youth are considered to be of an age most trainable. They are also the age group most likely to be troublemakers if they are unemployed.

Equally important to the strategy of the population chosen is the strategy regarding the role in services the target population plays. Will the client population play as active a role in giving as receiving services? The role of the population depends on one's assumptions about the population and the nature of the problem. If one believes that the problem is of great complexity and severity, and people caught in the problem are helpless, then the role of client is likely to be perceived as passive. If one assumes great potential strength in the client population in coping with the problem, then the population will be seen as playing a more active role. A good example of the latter is an organization known as Recovery, which has group meetings for formerly hospitalized psychotic patients, utilizes no professional help, and believes that by following certain principles of behavior emotionally disturbed people will be able to manage their own lives successfully.

Services

A number of strategies apply to the delivery of services. First, what services and how many? Those who believe that many services are needed to deal with the many facets of the problem are likely to favor multiservice programs. In addition to strategies regarding what services are to be provided, there are strategies relating to how to deliver these services. Plans must be made as to where to locate the services so they are most likely to be utilized, how to inform the population to be served that the services are available, and how to administer and coordinate these services in an efficient manner.

Community mental health programs are multiservice programs aimed at making services more accessible to people of all ages, socioeconomic levels, and types of psychological problems. Further, the treatment program attempts to meet the requirements of patients at all stages of their emotional disturbance: incipient, acute, chronic, or in remission. The strategies adopted for achieving these ends include:

1. Coordination of a variety of different kinds of mental health services through good management practices to suit patients' needs.
2. Location of some services in the community in which they are most likely to be utilized.
3. Educating the public as to the nature of mental health, emotional problems, and where services can be obtained through workshops, lectures, consultation programs, etc.

Closely aligned with the nature of services is the nature of staff. What type of staff is needed? Highly skilled, partly skilled, or unskilled; paid or volunteer; many or few; service or administrative? Some of these determinations have been already made by prior considerations that were discussed. If the problem is seen as difficult and complex, requiring multiservices, and it is believed that the client population should play a passive role as recipients of service, the staff that is required is likely to be skilled, paid, many, and involved in both service and administrative functions. On the other hand, when the problem is perceived as being able to be solved by the self-help of people who are directly involved in the problem, staff may be few and serve administrative and coordinating functions. Community action programs aimed at mobilizing local citizens tend to use few professionals and these mainly for training and administrative purposes.

Since staff is frequently a key element of programs, there are administrative strategies aimed at increasing staff morale, staff development, and making efficient use of staff. Management practice, systems analysis, and cost effectiveness are some of the administrative approaches to reaching these strategy objectives.

MONITORING AND EVALUATION

Many program administrators are so convinced of the assumptions of their programs and so invested in the programs themselves that it is difficult for them to look objectively on how the program is going, on whether it seems to be effective and reaching its goals. Nevertheless, evaluating and monitoring programs is an important strategy. It enables program administrators to determine to what degree goals are being realized. While the social sciences have often been vague and unclear about what their overall programs have been aimed at (terminology difficult to make operational is often used, such as "self actualization" and "positive interpersonal relationships"), and it has been difficult to determine the overall impact of programs through research procedures, more limited goals can be defined and the program assessed in those terms ("the number of children who can read at a fifth-grade level" or "the number of people who have been working six months or more"). The operations of the program itself can be assessed ("the amount of time the average client has to wait for an appointment"), the degree of progress the program has made can be monitored, and the rapid feedback of these kinds of information can lead to better implementation while the program is still ongoing.

SOME STRATEGY DILEMMAS

Despite careful planning and the adoption of well-thought-out strategies, complexities, problems, and program dilemmas inevitably follow, which results because the problem the program tackles is complicated and usually has roots and ramifications throughout all forms of institutions within our culture. Programs are limited by funds, time, staff, mandates; vested interests battle against the program; and knowledge about program implications is inadequate. Some of these strategy dilemmas are outlined below:

I. Social problems are complex and interrelated and any program will necessarily be limited.

Researchers in the social sciences have indicated that social pathology indices are often highly related to each other. For example, deteriorated housing rates, percentage of population unemployed, percentage of population on welfare, percentage of population not voting, juvenile delinquency rates, infant mortality rates, and percentage of high school dropouts are usually highly correlated with each other. These indices are part of a "poverty" cluster and suggest that in poverty areas low income, poor housing, poor education, crime, poor health, etc., are highly interrelated. It also suggests that a program in education, health, political action, etc., by itself is unlikely to have much effect on a given sphere of social pathology. In specific terms, a program giving remedial help to high school dropouts in an effort to have them return to high school is also contending with such problems as youths' need to contribute to the support of their poor families. Economic conditions may make jobs more important to youths than schooling, crowded and poor living conditions at home may make it difficult for them to study at home, poor health may interfere with their school work, and the existence of racial and ethnic prejudices may make them less hopeful about the values of obtaining a high school diploma and consequently less motivated. These problems may be so massive that they override the positive values of the remedial program.

Job-training programs for low-income youth often fail

to consider other complex factors that are vitally related, such as the general economic conditions of the country and the employment opportunities that are available. A youth who completes a training program that gives him some minimal skills may find that there are not enough jobs available for semiskilled workers. Or he may find that he obtains a job and in a recession is among the first to be fired. Or he obtains a job and soon finds that the job is being automated out of existence.

II. Innovative programs will threaten vested interests.

Many people profit from the status quo. Other people feel more comfortable with the status quo than having to adapt to new conditions, even if the status quo seems miserable. Whenever a new program enters into a community, it will be actively or passively resisted by these groups. The Anti-Poverty Program in offering new jobs to local citizens quickly threatened the local politicians who held power in large part through their ability to dispense patronage. Local politicians were also threatened by the social action programs aimed at local government of which they were a part. In many instances local politicians were active foes of the antipoverty programs and were often successful in their opposition. On the other hand, many poor people in the community who stood to benefit from the program reacted apathetically and failed to support it.

III. Coordination of agencies or programs can impede freedom.

It is nice to be the agency that coordinates but often frustrating to be coordinated. Larger agencies and institutions tend to be in the dominating role and under the banner of coordination tend to constrain smaller agencies that often differ in philosophies and mandates. What well-funded community mental health centers attempted to accomplish with less affluent local agencies in their catchment areas is now being attempted by larger conglomerate efforts such as Model Cities. Who is to be the coordinator and who is to be coordinated has led to internecine power struggles and widespread frustration and anger. Also contributing to the frustration of the smaller agencies is that they frequently have had little to say in what is to be the nature of the coordination.

IV. A knowledge base is absent for the planning of programs.

Many social sciences are still in an incipient stage of development. There has been little generally acceptable theory as to what is effective. Often programs are developed from different sets of philosophical viewpoints. Program evaluation is relatively scarce and has made little impact on the kinds of programs that are being developed. Basic research on the nature of the problems to which programs address themselves is even scarcer and thus far has given program planners little knowledge on which to develop their plans. Program planners are forced to undertake programs on the basis of their personal experiences, hunches, and intuitive feelings.

V. Implementation of programs may depend on qualities and number of staff that may not be available.

When programs fail, the planners and administrators are likely to blame the implementation. It is true that budgets for programs are commonly cut back, often eliminating or reducing key staff. At other times key staff positions go unfilled; manpower with special types of skills may be difficult to attract. High turnover of some positions result in discontinuities of program operations. When programs succeed, the planners and administrators are likely to see their planning, policy, and administration as crucial elements. However, it may well be that the staff personnel who were able to execute the plans and policies were the essential elements of success.

VI. Differing strategies used in a program may tend to negate each other.

A program employing various strategies may find that one strategy may cancel out another. For example, placing services out in the community may fulfill a strategy of making services more accessible but may make it difficult to fulfill efficient, coordinating strategies involving other services located within the institution. A strategy that succeeds in winning the support of a powerful community group may also gain the enmity of other groups that are opposed to this community group.

VII. Mandates and sanctions may severely limit the program.

Mental health programs are often dependent on federal, state, and local aid to support their programs. Frequently, this aid is determined by monitoring the program through recording services as "number of patient visits." Institutions having a larger number of "patient visits" will receive a larger proportion of funds. However, if the institution conceives of its role as "consultative" or "social action," for example, it may find these efforts are not reimbursable and may be forced by economic pressures to offer more conventional, direct services.

VIII. Changes resulting from a program may set in motion forces creating new problems.

A successful program strategy sometimes results in bringing forth a new community problem. For example, a small, successful program for addicts may result in many new referrals to the agency. The large influx of addicts seeking help may stir neighborhood resentment about their presence and even arouse community pressure to remove the program from the neighborhood.

2. UPSETTING THE APPLE CART: THE CHANGING DIRECTIONS OF THE COMMUNITY SERVICE SOCIETY OF NEW YORK CITY

On January 29, 1971, social workers and others involved in various aspects of social work and social welfare discovered that a social work agency had made the front page of the *New York Times*. The implication of the news was that the Community Service Society (CSS) of New York City was ending all casework with families and individuals because casework has not helped the poor. The reactions of individuals and organizations to this report varied according to the degree of investment in casework as a method or profession, the kind of assumptions held about what this service could or could not do, and opinions about what should be done, anyway. Letters to the editor and editorial comments in the profession's periodicals, discussions both formal and informal in a variety of agencies attested to one thing: CSS, as the society is affectionately and alphabetically known, has upset the apple cart, and rolling around, helter-skelter, are history, tradition, and the future of casework.

The history of the CSS is the history of the development of social work, particularly in the area of social casework within the United States. The predecessor of the CSS was the New York Charity Organization Society and the New York Association for

Improving the Conditions of the Poor, both these organizations merging in 1939 to form the CSS, which became the largest private family agency in the United States. The board of trustees of the society has been representative of Who's Who in New York, its endownment large. To quote from editorial comment in the Social Service Review (1971):

> Some critics have wondered to what extent the change has been influenced by financial considerations. Will the new program be more or less costly? Will the "shared power" notion extend to the investment policy of the agency and the allocation of income on its endowment, the book value of which is sometimes the subject of conjecture?

The changes that are being suggested for the CSS and its new directions resulted from concern that the organization's existing programs were not attaining the desired goals. As formulated by the board of trustees, the agency's goal is the delivery of services to the socially disadvantaged in New York City.

The history of the CSS and the Charity Organization Society has demonstrated concern with the poor, though emphases have varied with the times. The original CSS spokesmen have been characterized according to above (1965, p. 5) as

> missionaries, in the most literal sense, of a new benevolent gospel. They viewed themselves as exponents of a holy cause, priests lighting a path to secular salvation. Charity organization was a crusade to save the city from itself and from the evils of pauperism and class antagonism.

The CSS has provided leadership and innovation from its beginnings not only in practice but also in the training and education of social workers. In 1898 the New York Charity Organization launched a pioneer course by its six-week summer school in Philanthropy, which by 1904 became a full year's course and today is Columbia University School of Social Work. Other cities followed the lead set by the New York Society.

Though the CSS has traditionally been associated with the development and growth of casework, it has always been concerned with service needs. From the beginning, the Charity Organization Society centralized information about the charities in the city, studied gaps in service, developed new charities, extended old organizations, and influenced legislation. Early history shows efforts in many diverse areas of social action—housing, health, child labor, and sanitation.

What is different today? What does the change really signify? How much of a change is there? What does it all mean?

These questions and many others were raised in an interview with Dr. Edward Mullen, director of the CSS's Institute of Welfare Research, under whose aegis a study of New York and its problems and a review of interventive strategies was completed (Stimson & Stimson, 1970; Young, 1970).

The studies began out of a growing conviction on the part of the board of trustees in conjunction with the research staff and administration that the agency was not reaching its goals through its existing program. It was felt necessary to review the resources, commitments, and finances of the agency and to consider the most effective use of these resources. There was finally a personal sense of crisis in cities today and in New York in particular.

STRATEGIES

A primary assumption was that a social systems model is needed to perceive the problems of a city like New York because problems occur in interaction with multiple causation and it would not be feasible to isolate the problems of individuals. The strategy flowing from this for the most viable intervention would be on a multi-system level.

In preparation for the CSS planning for the 1970s, its Institute of Welfare Research undertook in the fall of

1969 a survey of New York City's major social problems and the approaches that have been used to prevent and resolve urban social problems. It has also surveyed the opinions of the trustees, committee members, and staff about the city's major problems and recommendations for the future program of the CSS.

The basic conclusion reached was that New York City is in a state of increasing deterioration (Stimson & Stimson, 1970).

> The situation in New York City is not only a matter of persons with problems, but rather one of whole areas afflicted with social ills. Most of these ills (for example, concentration of drug addiction, of poverty, of separated women, and high proportions of births out-of-wedlock) arc not recent in origin. From our data we can determine that such afflicted areas have existed for at least twenty years; from the work of others we learn that many of the areas have been badly afflicted for a far longer time.

The continued existence and growth of these undesirable social situations and the continued existence of a large number of socially disadvantaged people indicate that existing programs of intervention are not realizing their goals.

It is believed that the problems of individuals stem from the problems of the system. In addition the disadvantaged groups have relatively little influence on the system. It is assumed that this has occurred because there has been a breakdown in the democratic process, the findings of the study showing a relationship between lack of political participation and participation in the larger society. Over time the social system has formed itself to operate to the advantage of those in power and to the disadvantage of those out of power. Because human beings tend to internalize social arrangements, those in power (or the advantaged) tend to feel powerful and those out of power (or the disadvantaged) feel powerless.

The question of those who have power and those who do not is explicitely dealt with in the study. It suggests that the powerful bring to bear empirical knowledge of the consequences of social conditions and the solutions and then see which of these fits with what the people want and are willing to accept.

Part IV of Supplement II of the research report recommends strategies for intervention, which were arrived at after an analysis and survey of major interventions in social problem areas. The strategies that are recommended are as follows:

1. Social policy and planning services—would include analysis of major task force reports and planning, reporting recommendations, criticism, monitoring, and involvement of the groups that would be most immediately affected by the changes. An inventory of data on social problems and listing of services would assist planning of services.
2. Professional and technical assistance to neighborhood groups and institutions.
3. Project development and evaluation activities.
4. Comprehensive community data collection and dissemination services.

Such strategies are related to planning to remove special disadvantage of groups, which in effect means helping groups to obtain social influence and power. The agency will provide three basic services. The disadvantaged groups will be identified through its data bank. It will attempt to make contact with these groups, partly by opening its system to make the agency accessible to them. Work with the community groups will involve strategic ways of their utilizing that influence for self-development such as education for skills. Thus, the activities of the agency would become primarily consultation, mediation, training, locating of funds, development of programs of utilization of power groups, and coordination of a variety of institutions and community groups together in a meaningful way, which contrasts to the previous service pattern that emphasized individual and family counseling, shifting the emphasis on the one-to-one or individual focus to the group or community. Such a shift is necessary because the causation lies within the system rather than within the individual and only system inputs will effect outcome.

The revised program will focus on certain areas of the city, an area being defined as geographic, situational, or subject. When a geographic area is chosen, the society will select specific areas in which there are fundamental and interrelated problems, on the basis of local and CSS resources and the capability of success. A local policy committee will be formed of interested, representative groups in each neighborhood, and the chairman, a person of recognized stature, will become a member of the society's proposed departmental committee on program operations. Each area will decide and plan for the type of service that is needed or desired.

Major administrative changes and structural reorganization are being planned both for efficiency, facilitation of the new planning, and to change the focus of the system from service delivery to delivery of services. The reorganization will integrate program planning at the general director's level. A staff of planning consultants, including an economist, a home economist, four therapeutic treatment specialists, a group process specialist, and two lawyers will be related to the general director's office. There will be four program departments: a department of program operations; a department of public affairs; a department of volunteers, instruction, and personnel; and a department of research and evaluation. The members of the general director's office, the directors of the program departments, the department secretaries, the assistant director of public affairs and the directors of fund raising and public relations are to work with a standing committee of the board on planning.

The size of the board of trustees will be reduced, and to facilitate its becoming more representative of the city as a whole, it will include a meaningful diversity of minority, ethnic, socioeconomic, sex, and age groups.

A research dimension will be built into every activity.

In addition collaborative and independent studies and research development activities will be undertaken to add to an understanding of the city's social problems as well as to ways of preventing or resolving these problems. An ongoing urban-social-problem computerized information service to provide current data on New York City's urban social problems, its population, and program evaluations will be available for CSS planning and activities and as a resource to public and private groups throughout the city for their planning.

The implications of these changes in relation to staff are considerable. With different services, different skills are needed. Thus, on the upper level of organization planning consultants are being incorporated into the structure. Greater emphasis will be given to an interdisciplinary approach. Greater use of indigenous workers is being planned, and in the long run a smaller basic staff will be used.

PROBLEMS

Changes of this nature must be threatening to staff. Dr. Mullen believes that the major problems are of an internal nature. The reactions to the changes have been of an emotional nature, people feeling threatened and angry. Basically, the strategic changes have been from the top "despite the bottom." It is hoped that the 18-month transition period that has been provided will enable staff to experience and understand the necessary shift in orientation so that they can contribute and assist in the goal achievement of the agency. There is a danger of sabotage, even unconsciously, if there is resistance to the plan.

Staff attitudes and skills are of the utmost importance, but what skills and how to develop these skills are still problem areas.

There will also be changes in the physical plant, the eventual plan being to move out of existing offices,

TABLE 1
Outline of Assumptions, Strategies, and Strategy Problems of CSS Changing Program

Problem definition
- The continued existence and growth of undesirable social situations and large numbers of socially disadvantaged people

Causation
- Breakdown in democratic process
- System operates to advantage of those in power
- The disadvantaged have no influence
- The disadvantaged feel powerless

Necessary inputs
- Changes in nature and delivery of professional services
- Opening of service delivery system to the disadvantaged

Mandates and sanctions
- Board of trustees report
- Agency purpose and goal
- Time limit for changes
- Financial limit—revenues of agency

Strategies
- Target population
  - NYC's socially disadvantaged population—active role but dependent on agency
- Service programs
  - Identification of population through agency's data bank
  - Opening of system to above group
  - Services to groups and communities—consultation, mediation, training, fund-raising
  - Administrative reorganization
  - Personnel changes and staff training
- Monitoring and evaluation
  - Formalized: linkage of program with evaluation, research, and forecasting

Strategy problems
- Staff morale
- Staff development
- Lack of knowledge about new skills—what and how

though several local units will be kept, some in particular areas.

Financing is also of concern. It is mandated that the annual cost of the basic program and basic staff shall not exceed forecast revenues beginning October 1, 1972, when the plan is to start, which does not preclude the board of trustees from providing additional amounts of the society's funds for special projects or from securing outside funding.

In essence the changes in the report are set up on a broad base. Many policies still have to be developed and will continue to be developed and changed. However, there is a basic framework. Dr. Mullen says that the report is the Bible.

3. P S INNER CITY: A PROGRAM'S FAILURE AN EDUCATOR'S DILEMMA

Sol Gordon

I suppose I have many of the attributes and attitudes that mitigate against success in directing an inner-city educational project. I am white, Jewish, a university professor of education who has taught only one year in the public schools and a would-be "New Lefter,"—if it were not for the New Left's opposition of Zionism. Three years ago, as a civil rights activist, I was in trouble in Mississippi because I did not think illiterate adults, even if they were black adults, should teach illiterate children.

I started out earning my living as a clinical psychologist. As chief psychologist of one of the nation's leading child guidance clinics, I discovered that mental health services were primarily for the middle class. (The poor were eligible but were considered to be "unmotivated for treatment.") When I suggested that "lack of motivation" might be a symptom that could be dealt with, my colleagues did not understand me. Later, when I found that the "community mental health" movement was not much different, I left the mental health field to enter the hallowed halls of the university to teach and, hopefully, to influence students, teachers, and mental health professionals who worked in the "inner city." As a practicing clinical psychologist I thought I had both the practical and theoretical experience to work successfully in the urban ghetto. I taught idealistically, but it did not take long for my credibility gaps to show. I worked with black community groups, but it did not take long for my "whiteness" to show. I worked with the United Federation of Teachers, but it did not take long for my political naïveté to show. I worked hard to secure a laboratory public school so I could find out how things really were. I wanted to help university students become better-prepared professionals, and I wanted to prove that black children in an all-black school in a deteriorated black neighborhood could at least learn to compute, read, and write in keeping with "national norms."

Sometimes I *do* wonder if it is not too late for people like myself to have a role in the black inner city. How does one respond to a lead article in the African-American Teachers' Forum* that begins with the following three sentences?

> We are witnessing today in New York City a phenomenon that spells death for the minds and souls of our Black children. It is the systematic coming of age of the Jews who dominate and control the educational bureaucracy of the New York City Public School system and their power-starved imitators, the Black Anglo-Saxons. It is . . .this coalition or collusion [that] . . . is one of the fundamental reasons why our Black children are being educationally castrated, individually and socially devastated to the extent that they are incapable of participating in, and carrying through to a reasonable conclusion, any meaningful educational experience.

In fact, just being white complicates role definition. For instance, I was invited by a neighboring university to teach a course to experienced teachers who were in training to become supervisors in the ghetto schools. At the end of the semester the class seemed to consist of nine angry black teachers and nine angry white teachers, who apparently identified with the blacks, and

*The African-American Teachers Association, which consists of several hundred militant black teachers in the NYC public school system. They are much more influential than their small membership would suggest.

one frustrated professor. I remember the first class meeting. I have a reputation for being an effective and popular lecturer; but after about 20 minutes I was interrupted by one of the students who said, "I'm not interested in your lily-white thoughts. You are talking about *me,* and *I* should be teaching this course. Why don't you sit down and *listen?*" Somewhat defensively I refused to abdicate my role, but I did not teach very much that semester; nor did I learn much. Later in the course I did listen. But by then it was too late. When I said that virtually every index of pathology correlates positively with poverty, I was called a racist. A violent opponent of the war in Vietnam, I was the recipient of invectives like: "Don't talk to us about pathology. What about *your* war in Vietnam?"

I do have some assets. One of my heroes was Martin Luther King (all my heroes are dead), and I believe in "black power." Of course, this does not protect me in a riot, nor does it make me feel safer on a Harlem street at night. I remember walking with a black minister in still-tense Watts not long after the riots, that is the revolt; and as it approached evening, the black minister abruptly left for another appointment, and I felt as though I had lost my insurance policy.

As I think about it, I am not always sure I know what "black power" means anymore. I used to think that in a place like Bedford-Stuyvesant it meant that black people would be the power structure. I did not think "hate whitey" had anything to do with it. I still think that people who cannot live where they would like should at least control the institutions and own the homes and stores where they do live.

I was director of Yeshiva University's short-lived Project Beacon. Unimpressed by training programs for teachers, psychologists, and guidance counselors for the public schools, several of us university professors began to re-think our roles and goals. We were not sure how to go about it, but we were certain of one thing. The internship phase of the training must be in the ghetto schools; and the university professors themselves must become involved in the "politics" of schools.

Project Beacon was invited by the district superintendent of schools in April 1967 to develop several programs at P S "Inner City" (a code name for a real elementary school) to improve its educational level. Eight new teachers fresh from Project Beacon training, 15 graduate students, and several university consultants accepted the challenge with me.

Certainly, I was aware before the project began of many traps waiting for me. At the time we were introducing our program another university had failed ignominously in the same district with an educational plan that I had thought was excellent.

We began by trying not to make the usual mistakes. The university would be "voted in" by the Teachers Union and the Parents' Association, so that they would be involved in the program. Our work was reviewed at the monthly meeting of a governing board consisting of myself, the district superintendent of schools, the principal, two parent and two teacher union representatives, the chairman of the local school board and a community representative, and an influential local minister who warned me that if we did not succeed we would be "the last white people that will ever be given a chance in this community." The five black and four white members seemed to be a workable and representative group.

The school was to be the model for a forthcoming decentralization of all the schools in the district and would be permitted a large degree of autonomy. We began inauspiciously by being awarded one-fifth of the requested amount of Title One federal funds. (And if it had not been for a Ford Foundation planning award, we would not have been able to get going at all.) P S Inner City was suggested for the "project" because it had the reputation of being one of the worst schools in Bedford-Stuyvesant. It is an old, wretched building without adequate anything in the heart of one of the most deteriorated areas of Brooklyn. To its credit, P S Inner City tries hard to educate its 1,300 black children who are all poor, most of them on welfare. But you can not buy education with a credit card.

I will never forget my first visit to the school. The halls and stairwells were littered with dirt. Cracked plaster, broken windows, and torn shades seemed natural in that setting. The smell of urine extended far beyond the bathrooms. But worse than anything I could imagine was the lunchroom. The noises, the disorder, and the masses of children in a tiny, ugly basement room seemed to express the tone of the school. My first impulse was to flee. I thought that nobody could succeed here.

And, of course, the neighborhood complemented the school. Even the one little vest-pocket park was, and still is, useless because of filth and neglect.

When it came time to commit myself, I made the mistake of over doing it. I did what we psychologists refer to as the unconscious process of over compensating due to guilt (as a consequence of my impulse to flee). The faculty welcomed the involvement of the university; but I must have stimulated, without conscious intent, too many rescue fantasies. At a faculty meeting several disappointing months after our project began, one teacher shouted at me. "We thought you knew everything!" Another accused me of making false promises. "You said that you would bring in experienced teachers." I had never promised anything of the kind.

The September 1967 teachers' strike found the black teachers teaching and the white teachers on the picket line. I supported the union. At an emotionally charged meeting toward the end of the strike, a black teacher pleaded for a reconciliation that, in fact, did occur: "The union did what it had to do, and we did what we had to do. Now let us return together and teach."

A black administrator was hired full-time as project coordinator. He was strict and quickly antagonized some of the teachers. But the tone of the school and a lot of other things improved because of him. I never thought I would support an authoritarian approach to a disorderly school, but I soon discovered that the children themselves had total disrespect for lack of discipline and anyone who tolerated it.

It was hardly four months after we had begun that we began to lose the support of many of the teachers. As an active, public defender of the United Federation of Teachers, the loss of teacher support was a bitter pill to swallow. The opposition stemmed from substantive issues, however much I may have felt at times that the "issues" were based on irrational fears. A few months later, and with a shift in focus to early-childhood projects, we secured the support of most of the teachers; but other problems developed, including the residual opposition of a small, militant, angry group of teachers.

I would have preferred to report that the district superintendent was a rat, the principal was hostile, and the local school board was made up of "Uncle Toms." The facts are that the district superintendent was cooperative, the principal (both the old and new one) was my most ardent supporter, and the local school board was "dominated" (chairman and vice-chairman) by two exceptionally capable, militant black women who supported our program. It did turn out that the "governing board" did not, in effect, have much power. It soon became clear that it was more an advisory board. Virtually all important decisions were still being made by the Central New York City Board of Education. (In the same way, the other New York City "decentralization" projects such as I S 201, Two Bridges, and Ocean Hill should not be considered valid tests of decentralization unless they acquire real control with real money to spend.)

Which was perhaps the most serious of our organizational (should we say, disorganizational) problems. But we had other problems, too.

As a psychologist, I know that teachers, like everybody else, become defensive when they feel they are being attacked. They are on the front line, and outsiders are suspect. They are frustrated enough, and we compound it. But it does not help much to understand this.

Our own Beacon teachers, concentrated in the fourth grade, complained that we had not prepared them adequately for teaching at a school like P S Inner City. They were right, but now at least we can profit from this experience by introducing changes in our current university training program. Yet despite objections from many teachers, our six classes in the fourth-grade saturation program involving heterogeneous grouping, with one exception, did well.* The non-Beacon teachers objected to heterogeneous grouping and the "noise" from fourth-grade classes; a few said they were tired of white educators "experimenting" with black kids. One teacher tried to explain the low achievement level of the black children of P S Inner City by suggesting that many white teachers do not like black kids. I personally have not noticed that black teachers, in general, are more effective in teaching black children than white teachers.

We developed a learning center for 23 illiterate fifth graders outside the school in rented quarters—a crash program to teach them to read. The pupils who were selected for the program were at least two years retarded in reading. These children were taught intensively in small classes of five to seven students. A wide range of curricula materials were available, and a contingency management system was instituted to increase motivation. All teachers were new teachers, former Project Beacon students who worked under the direction of a coordinator.

"Well," said some of the regular class teachers, "give me six or seven kids and I'll also teach them to read." "Yes," I said, "but children like these have had

*I am convinced that homogeneous grouping is an educational disaster for most of the black and Spanish children in ghetto schools. The catastrophe in the ghetto schools is compounded by the fact that invariably the least experienced and often the least able teacher is assigned to the lowest tracts.

individual remedial reading without success." You'd think that our reducing the class size considerably in the fifth grade would make teachers happy—but it did not. When I suggested that perhaps some of the children in the first and second grades were actually not being taught to read, I was sharply criticized. It *did* seem to me that a significant number of the children were memorizing their basal readers and that when it came to independent reading in the third grade, they could not manage it.

A few of the teachers were personally angry at me. "Before you came," one teacher said, "teacher morale was high." My (resented) answer: "What good is high teacher morale in a school with low pupil achievement?"

Our difficulties were compounded by lack of comprehension and misunderstanding in every sphere. For example, there was the great idea of holding "coping sessions" for the bright but uneducated fifth graders who would have to return to P S Inner City after four months of special training. We would, in guidance sessions, prepare them for their return to the main building and talk about problems relevant to them. Being a well-trained psychologist with a good deal of experience, I took on this role myself. The children flatly refused to consider the possibility that they would have to return. "We like it at the Learning Center, and we are going to stay here." The notion that they were "poor" was completely foreign to them. When I tried to talk about white and black issues, they resented it. At the end of this phase of our program we ran into problems when the parents of the children from the Learning Center did not want their children to return to P S Inner City. We had problems when some of our own staff got fed up and quit. We had problems when I made the mistake of allowing a *Washington Post* reporter to do "a story" about our work. He gave a fairly accurate picture of the program's progress. As a result the community was so angry that we could not recover; our program was terminated barely seven months after its beginning.

Maybe we all expected too much. Thirteen hundred is too many children in one building, with a dungeon lunchroom comfortably seating 300, with no gymnasium, and with no place for a retreat if a child is upset. Thirteen hundred is too many children for one nurse twice a week, a doctor twice a month, and no mental health services.

What does a teacher do with no one to help with the disturbed, difficult child? What does she do when her educational aids are stolen and will not be replaced for a year or more, if at all? What does she do when her classes, too large already, are often disrupted by the need for absorbing other children when a regular teacher is absent? (There is always a shortage of substitute teachers at P S Inner City.) What does she do if she does not know how to teach reading to children who have not learned to read in the first and second grades? What happens to the educational process when the children move in and out of school all through the school year? What do I say to a guidance counselor who says to me, "You're lucky the four children we suspended last year never came back"? What happens in a school when in one-fourth of the classrooms much of the day is spent in trying to maintain order? What does a principal do when it takes six months to fill a vacancy for an assistant principal because none of more than 100 educators on a "merit system" list wanted to come to P S Inner City? What does a school do in the face of daily invasions by truants from the neighborhood junior high school who steal and who harass the younger children? What does a school do when it cannot wrest control of its own playground from the neighborhood hoodlums? It calls the police almost daily, but that is as far as it goes.

I must confess to being incredibly naïve to think that I could "operate" an innovative experimental program in an overcrowded school that was in a reasonably constant state of anarchy. Apart from the conditions I have already described, $15,000 worth of equipment was stolen from the school in a recent two-year period. P S

Inner City itself is slated for replacement. As there is no telling when this will come about, community pressure forced through a budget for some immediate repairs. When it came to making the repairs, the teachers, the principal, and the local school board were not consulted. Many of the repairs actually completed were either irrelevant (including cleaning the outside brick of the building) or done at times that interfered with the educational process. (Our protests went unheeded.)

My first impression of P S Inner City was dominated by the broken glass that littered the school yard. I had the fantasy that eventually the school would be buried beneath tons of glass, and I communicated this fear to some of my co-workers. I playfully suggested a slogan for our war against broken glass: *Broken Glass Cuts Black Feet.*

One morning this slogan appeared in big, white, painted letters on the school's outer walls. One of my co-workers had taken me literally and had prematurely initiated his own campaign.

Hell broke loose. The incident provoked teachers, administrators, and parents to an anger that far surpassed any previous protest about the school. That children were not learning very much or that obscenities were scrawled on the walls seemed not to have attracted a comparable reaction.

Pressure was exerted on me to fire the culprit, but I refused. I pointed out that we must be allowed some mistakes. When the fuss died down, a black administrator confided: "Look, if a black man wrote it, it wouldn't have made much difference. A white man cannot do a thing like that anymore in a black community." I discovered that there are a lot of things a white man cannot do anymore.

White people cannot expect to move in and out of black communities with impunity anymore. Even civil rights activists like myself must expect to be disappointed and unappreciated in our relationship with the black community leadership. We are past the time for easy understanding. The only thing that will matter to the black community now will be power. Hopefully, they will use it more wisely than we have.

If we look at the total picture of education in the ghetto, we do find a few schools in which children are being educated even when classes are large. This seems to occur only in schools that have exceptional administrators who, in turn, attract an exceptionally talented staff. Such schools have no difficulty in staffing. By contrast, schools like P S Inner City have inappropriately trained personnel at all levels. One factor is that, like all professions, education has in its ranks only a limited number of talented and creative individuals.

But all in all, I feel that our work in P S Inner City was important even if all we did was contribute to the education of 36 children out of 1,300. It is important because 36 children matter. But the irony is that we were thrown out even before we helped 36 children much.

In my view, a fair-minded educator, observing the results of "P S Inner City" after seven months of actual operation, would declare the program very promising and encourage its continuation. In my judgment, that it was overwhelmingly rejected by teachers (most of whom were not involved in Beacon programs)* is no credit to those teachers. Likewise, that the initially cooperative leadership of the district superintendent's office and the local school board backed down when "the crunch" came is no credit to that leadership.

Considering that all the parents of children in both learning centers reported that their children, for the first time, liked school and attended regularly, how do we justify the early termination of the program?

How do these reports compare with charges that children were somehow being harmed in the "disorderly" classes conducted by Beacon teachers (especially considering that almost total chaos reigned during the previous school year)?

*The few teachers supporting us were Beacon participants.

It is true that the new principal taught us the importance of discipline and order. But Beacon's "disorderly" classes did not cause the program's failure. And our experience also taught us the importance of comprehensive courses in teaching of reading and math in our training department. But even so, Beacon children *did* make significant progress in these subjects in a school in which some 90% of the children graduate to a junior high school unprepared to meet its minimal standards.*

In the end almost everyone turned against us. There is no doubt: We failed. But not because we were white, Jewish, insensitive, or inadequate. Obviously, that we were unable to involve more teachers because of lack of money was a serious fault. But our failure was due to a number of interlocking reasons that, as yet, we do not completely understand.

I left P S Inner City more convinced than ever that black children, even in an all-black school in the worst neighborhoods and even *without* parental cooperation, can at least learn to read and write and do arithmetic at acceptable levels of grade achievements. (Beyond this minimum education perhaps parental support is needed, but I do not know.) I do not accept that lack of parental support means that chiidren cannot learn. I do accept that overcrowded classes, lack of special services, and terrible school conditions, as well as the lack of training received by most teachers, are contributing factors in the noneducation of children. I *do not* accept the contention made by some that the average teacher in the ghetto is a racist or does not want to teach. Most are teaching under intolerable conditions, and to compound problems, they do not, for example, know how to teach reading to children who have not learned it in the first grade.

Be that as it may, I am convinced that we must: (a) offer a formal reading readiness program to preschool

*And their chances of dropping out of high school or getting a general diploma are 92%. (The figure is 97% for their Puerto Rican peers.)

and kindergarten classes and (b) devote all in-service teacher training for the next several years to the diagnosis and remediation of reading programs.

Several of our subprojects were kept. They include the reading readiness programs in the kindergarten, which will be extended in the fall to prekindergarten, the McGraw-Hill science, the first-grade bridge class and others; but I would be less than honest not to predict a rapid decline and deterioration of P S Inner City. Despite a very capable and dynamic principal and the few ongoing projects, no school in the ghetto survives educationally without special attention or projects like the More Effective Schools. (Perhaps if the community school is built, a new impetus will envelop P S Inner City.)

For the sake of the children of P S Inner City—at the present rate perhaps 5% will go on to college—I pray that I am wrong in my prediction.

Certainly we made mistakes, but why did our mistakes arouse much more negative and hostile reactions than the more pervasive mistakes of boards of education? I partly know the answer. It is in the question of why we have riots now that the general status of the black has improved. We have to accept that people like myself have spoiled our opportunities to be effective decision-makers for public schools. It does not mean that those of us who continue "the struggle" must do so without dignity. White people can only harm the "black power" movement by supporting the racist elements in it. With all my fears and uncertainties it is hard not to be inspired by a response made by Reverend Milton Galamison to one of my white students—a teacher in training for the ghetto schools. "Why should we teach in schools where we are not wanted?" His reply was, "As one who has been unwanted all my life, I can say to you that we must do what we think is right regardless of how people feel about us."

For me this was a sober experience. The district superintendent playfully torments me with the aside,

"We'll make a bureaucrat out of you yet." Toward the end my colleagues described me as being either in a constant state of shock or depression (not one of them felt that we had a snowball's chance in hell of operating a successful project in P S Inner City—New York City). No, the experience has not changed my position regarding "black power," nor has it dampened my admiration for Martin Luther King. I still believe that black children can be taught successfully in an all-black school. However, the experience has forced me into a realization that I personally have no power base, that I personally will have a relatively minor (or no) role in whatever happens in the inner city. At the university only a few were interested and excited—more were worried and frightened; most were indifferent. Perhaps nothing has happened except that I am now a much better teacher, and I have more "credibility." But that is the way things are.

TABLE 2
Outline of Assumptions, Strategies, and Strategy Problems of PS Inner City

Problem definition
- Low achievement level of public school pupils

Causation
- Overcrowded, chaotic school lacking staff, facilities, and services
- Teachers poorly prepared to teach
- Poverty conditions and crime rampant in neighborhood

Necessary inputs
- Program has broad support and involvement of local community, teaching staff, and educational officials
- Teachers need training in how to teach basic skills
- School is run in an orderly way

Mandates and sanctions
- Community and teacher expectations
- Board of education regulations
- Teachers' union rules

Strategies
- Target population
  - Pupils (passive role in services)
  - Teachers (active and passive role in services)
- Service programs
  - Saturation program in one grade

- Heterogeneous grouping
- Learning center for illiterate fifth graders
- Teacher training program
- Developing a community and teacher governing board

Monitoring or evaluation

- Mostly informal monitoring (reports)

Strategy problems

- Governing board of community and teachers lacked power
- Only small portion of expected funds forthcoming and thus many teachers and pupils in school had only limited contact with program
- Distrust of white program administrator in black community
- Children did not want to return to school from the Learning Center
- Program caught in community-teachers' union struggle

4. UP FROM ASHES: PHOENIX HOUSE*

Drug abuse has reached epidemic proportions. In New York State alone more than one million people currently smoke marijuana/hashish, more than 200,000 are current LSD abusers, over 100,000 are cocaine abusers, and there are 64,000 heroin users (Chambers, 1971, pp. 157-159). Addiction is the greatest cause of death for people aged 15 to 35.

On May 2, 1967, five men moved into a few furnished rooms on the top floor of a tenement on the west side of Manhattan. They had just left a hospital ward, free—for the moment—from physical addiction to heroin. They pooled their welfare checks to pay the rent and "hustled" food. They saw the life on the floors below them—alcoholics, drug addicts, the police cars, ambulances, and vans from the morgue that pulled up outside. They were five frightened men, terrified by the possibility of returning to the life downstairs, for each had vowed he would not. Out of a need to cut themselves off from the lives they had led as heroin addicts, they had banded together. To that miserable floor where they lived they gave a name that summed up their hopes: Phoenix House, after the mythological bird that rises from its own ashes (Phoenix House, 1970, p. 5). Other addicts joined them. They soon expanded from one floor to the entire building. From this small beginning

* The material presented was obtained through an interview with Mrs. Pauline Kaufmann, director of Phoenix House Institute, and by published and unpublished literature on Phoenix House made available by Mrs. Kaufmann.

Phoenix House has become one of the nation's best-known residential treatment facilities and now has 15 houses and more than 1,000 residents.

ASSUMPTIONS ABOUT DEFINITION OF PROBLEM, CAUSATION, AND NECESSARY INPUTS

Phoenix House operates on the assumption that the drug addict is an emotional infant who has had faulty training in interpersonal relationships in his own family. His parents never taught him to assume responsibilities. Typically, he was pampered and/or ignored. Taking drugs fits this life style in that it is a form of childish gratification and a means of avoiding life's responsibilities. Until the drug addict matures into an adult who can assume responsibility for himself, he is not likely to give up drugs.

What is needed is a relearning within the family situation. An environment must be provided in which family life is again presented to the addict but in a new form—a form in which concern, warmth, and interest are shown in him but in which the addict is not coddled or pampered. This family situation must allow and encourage him to gradually assume responsibilities. It is not to permit him the use of drugs and to show him the destructive implications of drug usage. Role models are to be provided by those who have successfully kicked the drug habit and have learned to assume mature responsibilities.

MANDATES AND CONSTRAINTS

Funding for Phoenix House is both private and public. The sources of funding have not put constraints on the kind and nature of services. However, the public funding requires that staff positions follow civil service regulations, that is, staff must be eligible under civil service regulations and must pass tests.

Phoenix House has had a long, arduous fight to make former addicts fit addiction specialist lines under civil service regulations. Also, since there are funds from city welfare, all welfare regulations apply. In order to give flexibility to the fiscal arrangements the Phoenix House Board of Directors have frequently bought or rented facilities and funded innovative programs from their own monies.

The middle-class community initially is often against having a residence for drug addicts in their area, but generally the community usually overcomes their fears and with time may actually welcome a treatment center. There have been no difficulties in establishing treatment residences in ghetto areas.

TARGET POPULATION

The population served is anyone of any age who expresses the need to give up the use of drugs. These include drug addicts as well as drug experimenters and may involve any type or frequency of drug usage from occasional use of marijuana to daily injections of heroin. The assumption here is that the drug user may easily move from experimentation to addiction and from milder to more serious drug usage.

NATURE OF SERVICES

The heart of the Phoenix House program is the Phoenix House itself, which serves as a functioning therapeutic community and "family" of up to 100 residents. Every house has a form of induction center to which anyone can come and ask for help. The program is explained to the person seeking help, and he is invited to attend meetings during the day in which he can talk to addicts. There is no pressure on him to join; on the contrary, the potential Phoenix House resident has to convince others that he really wants to become a resident of Phoenix House.

The tactics here are to increase the addict's motivation for help. Also, the tactics behind having him meet other addicts is to give him a preliminary run-through of what he will be facing in Phoenix House: the confrontation sessions, the role of addicts at the house. He quickly learns that his peers will not allow him to lie as he did at home or on the streets. The induction period may last between six weeks and several months. The amount of time depends on the space available in the house and the addict's demonstrated motivation in remaining drug-free and participating in the activities at the center.

The initial interview serves as an initiation into a new society and is the beginning of an effort to shatter the addict's defensive street image of himself as an independent, sophisticated, strong person. Such an image-shattering process involves sharply confronting the prospect with the childishness and meaninglessness of the addict's behavior and destructiveness. The interviewers can spot his ruses and rationalizations. The interview is in sharp distinction with the conventional institutional treatment of addicts in which the addict finds himself forced to accept treatment.

When the prospect is finally accepted into the "family" as a new sibling, he usually gives up his own clothes, which are associated with his street image, and wears those provided by the community. He may later earn the privilege of wearing his own clothes when it is felt that they will not cause him to revert to his street image. His physical dependence on the community for food, clothing, and shelter are all symbolic of his emotional dependence for growth and maturity. The new resident is viewed by the other residents as an emotional infant. He is unable to make decisions because his mind is controlled by whim instead of mature reasoning. The only decision he can still make on his own is to leave.

During the first 90 days the new resident receives no mail, phone calls, or visits from his former friends and family. This is to eliminate external pressures that they might put on him and to avoid his use of friends or family to "cop out" on the stresses of the new situation. Later, the staff decides when he is ready to handle these and other privileges. Governing Phoenix Houses are two cardinal rules: no violence and no drugs. Life in the therapeutic community includes family activities, encounter group sessions, and seminars. People learn through these activities what their original patterns of behavior were within a family and begin to develop new, more adaptive patterns of behavior within a family structure. Former addicts who have made it provide role models.

The purpose of the new family structure is to help the resident learn to relate, share, and feel responsible for other people. Trust, affection, concern, and emotional honesty become the established modes. The family situation includes job functions and a reward-punishment system, as well as recreational activities.

WORK STRATEGY

Since a common failing of addicts is their inability to make productive use of their time, work and the responsibility of a job are important first steps. The job functions are tasks necessary to the functioning and maintenance of the community. Each job is viewed as important both to the community and to the resident.

The progression of job functions represents an increasing degree of stress to which the resident is subjected as part of the maturation process. A usual first-job assignment is the service crew, which is considered probably the most menial job. The service crew cleans toilet bowls, empties garbage, and does other "dirty jobs." Before the resident leaves the service crew, he must learn to accept authority and follow directions.

Following this job is the kitchen crew, which is responsible for preparing and serving the meals. Here the resident is subjected to additional stresses: Meals must be prepared and served on time to as many as 100 persons.

He may then become a member of the maintenance crew, which is responsible for periodic painting and repairs in the house. Each crew is under the direction of a supervisor who is responsible for seeing that everything is done properly. Here the resident begins to assume slightly more responsibility.

From the maintenance crew the resident may go into the office where he is exposed to clerical and administrative work. Here work is to be completed by a deadline. The resident is expected to budget his time and set priorities. In his business interactions he also learns how to deal with people.

When the resident progresses to the job of expediter, he encounters his first strenuous stress situation. He is responsible for knowing and reporting the activities of every resident in the house. The task of knowing everything that goes on with everyone in the house at all times is of course impossible. He is expected to work with the other expediters as part of a team. The expediter's job is structured so that the resident will learn to experience failure and not interpret it as personal. If a resident has not been demoted from a job function prior to this time, he usually gets demoted as an expediter.

By the time a resident reaches the expediter job function, he usually sees himself as one whom newer residents can emulate. For many residents the next job, that of coordinator, represents the assumption of mature responsibility and independent behavior.

Each department of the house has a coordinator; some coordinators are responsible for more than one department. There may be both staff and resident coordinators in a community. The staff coordinators (coordinator trainees) are directly responsible for running the house. The coordinators determine how group sessions will be run and what aspect of behavior or attitude they will work on with an individual. The coordinators are largely responsible for gauging other resident's emotional growth. In this job the resident learns to assume major responsibilities.

REWARDS AND PUNISHMENTS

The other important component of the family structure is the family's reward-punishment system. The rewards are promotion in job function and privileges. The punishment system includes "haircuts" (verbal reprimands), shaved heads, and the wearing of signs, as well as demotion and loss of privileges. For more serious offenses, or for continuous repetition of the same offense, a male resident may be scheduled to have his head shaved. Female residents do not have their heads shaved but they are required to wear a stocking over their hair for a certain period. In addition to a head shave the resident may be required to wear a sign with his offense printed on it. Residents say that although the shaved head and the sign seem to be cruel to outside observers, the purpose is not just to humiliate. It serves as a constant reminder to the resident not to repeat his behavior, and it singles him out as one who needs a great deal of help from other residents.

ENCOUNTER GROUPS

In addition to family situations the treatment program focuses on encounter group sessions. Encounter is, in fact, often described as "the core of the therapy." Regularly scheduled group meetings usually occur about three times a week.

An encounter group is problem-behavior and emotionally or attitude oriented and usually includes different people each time it meets. The cardinal rule in an encounter group in a community is "to confront the person with something he can change." If a resident wishes to confront another resident with his behavior, he requests to be placed in the same encounter group. Before encounter sessions resident coordinators go through the encounter request box to decide the composition and focus of the encounter groups. If several residents have their names in the encounter box to "get" another resident, the coordinators may or may not decide to put them all in the same group, depending on the changes they feel the resident can handle and should be exposed to. Occasionally, the coordinators may decide that a resident needs to be "wolf packed," that is, confronted by the entire group, or they may decide that after being confronted, they will not allow the group to support him. Usually, however, an encounter group is structured to confront a person with his behavior and then "to patch him up" (support him) and give him positive alternatives to his behavior. Such sessions usually last about two hours. At times, because of hostility generated, an encounter session may go into an extended group session lasting as long as 8 to 12 hours, but these are rare.

EDUCATIONAL SEMINARS

In addition to family situations and encounter sessions, the residents participate in daily one-hour seminars. Seminars provide a reminder of the outside community to which the resident will return and teach him how to interact socially without drugs. For example, in mock speaking seminars the residents learn how to speak in front of a group. The social graces seminar includes social-situation role-playing. Educational seminars are part lecture and part discussion or debate on anything from abstract concepts to personal experiences.

All of these structured learning situations are directed toward helping the resident learn nonaddict behavior and attitudes. When a resident actively starts to re-enter the outside world and once again is faced with the fears and anxieties of a change in environment, he begins to question if he really knows who he is and if he can separate from the structured community without resorting to his acting-out behavior. He wonders if he will be able to lead a drug-free life and how he will be able to tolerate leisure time when it is no longer structured for him. At present a large number of graduates remain in the therapeutic community as psychiatric aides, school counselors, street workers, etc. They keep in touch with their Phoenix family and share in many Phoenix functions.

COSTS AND EVALUATION

About 1,200 people have been treated through Phoenix House. The average cost of treating an addict is about $3,800 a year, a fraction of the cost of a residential treatment center.

Evaluation of the program is primarily through records that are kept of the progress of residents while they are at Phoenix House and follow-up as to what happens to them when they leave Phoenix House: Statistical reports are issued by the program's Information Control Center. The overall dropout rate is 40% (Phoenix House, 1970, p. 18).

STRATEGY PROBLEMS

Strategy problems that have emerged include the following:

1. Drug addicts who are poorly motivated will not undergo the rigors of the program. Therefore, the program is not reaching this group of addicts.

2. Women addicts have been found to be more difficult to motivate and effect changes in than male addicts. It is believed that this is because the female addict suffers from a more self-derogatory attitude.

3. Residents are not permitted to bring their children into Phoenix House. The need for their children, especially by the women, is a pull away from Phoenix House.

4. It is sometimes difficult to wean people away from Phoenix House. It has become a second home to them, and some people are reluctant to leave and take their place in the community.

TABLE 3
Outline of Assumptions, Strategies, and Strategy Problems of Phoenix House

- Problem definition
  - Drug addiction
- Causation
  - Emotional immaturity due to faulty familial experiences
- Necessary inputs
  - Structured residence in which addict can relive a new, therapeutic family experience
- Mandates and sanctions
  - Community fears of addicts
  - City regulations regarding staffing and expenditures of monies
- Strategies
  - Targeted population
    - Drug addicts or experimenters who are motivated to change (move from passive to active role in services)
  - Service programs
    - Residential structured environment
    - Therapeutic work program
    - Encounter groups
    - Educational program
  - Monitoring or evaluation
    - Records of progress of residents; statistical reports
- Strategy problems
  - Separation from their families brings hardships to some residents at Phoenix House (particularly women with children)
  - Difficulty of ex-addict leaving Phoenix House
  - Only small fraction of addicts can be helped by Phoenix House under present funding arrangements

5. WHEN AN AGENCY'S CONSTITUENCY AGES: KISSENA APARTMENTS—AN EXPERIENCE IN HOUSING FOR OLDER PEOPLE*

It has been and will remain a common phenomenon for an organization to be founded and funded to meet a particular and critical need for a specialized population. What happens when, in time, the needs and the characteristics of this group changes? Does the agency disband? Does it use its resources for a new cause? Or does it attempt to understand and to meet the needs of the same population with its new problems and changing needs? The latter alternative is the one that will be discussed here.

In 1936 a small group of refugees from Nazi persecution founded Selfhelp to help fellow refugees begin a new life in America. Many of these people came from Nazi Germany; they were predominantly Jewish. All were uprooted from their homes. Many had been inmates of concentration camps; most had lost sisters, brothers, parents, even children. Too many had witnessed the death of these close relatives.

Selfhelp began with a small group of volunteer workers. It assisted in finding housing, jobs, health care, and a new way of life. Some of the refugees rented larger

* From an interview with Dr. Kurt Hertz, executive director of Selfhelp and United Help, Inc.

apartments and maintained themselves by taking as boarders newer refugees, providing foster homes until the newcomers became oriented to the new life. Thus self-help and help to others became one. With increasing numbers of refugees and problems, Selfhelp began to need and use a professional and salaried staff, but it has continued to have a large and active group of volunteers who donate time and energy to assist the agency's programs.

In 1955, United Help Inc. was founded as a national agency to distribute money that was received when there were no heirs for retribution funds obtained from Nazi Germany. The money was mandated for use for the welfare of former victims of Nazi persecution. United Help has funded sheltered workshops, homes for the aged, Selfhelp (which then became United Help's service arm), and a housing development, Kissena Housing.

CHANGING STRATEGIES

As United Help's target population became elderly, the agency defined its foremost need to be decent housing. Over time, the neighborhoods in which they had originally settled had changed, both because neighbors and friends moved or died. The new neighbors tended to be of different ethnicity and age, and there was less opportunity for meaningful social interaction. Children were moving to the suburbs of New York. Loneliness was a serious problem.

Many of the apartments in which they lived were too large, particularly for those who had earlier acted as foster-home parents to new immigrants. Too many of the apartments were in buildings without elevators and in a state of progressive deterioration. Thus, an important new strategy for United Help became the development and building of a housing project (Hertz, 1970, 1971).

Several assumptions were the impetus for this development. It was felt that one's home assumes increasing importance as the place with which to identify, particularly for those who live alone and with aging and retirement are losing status, income, and purposefulness. It was assumed that having one's own apartment was a symbol of independence and of one's worth as a member of society.

Once the strategy of developing housing for the elderly was established, other criteria had to be formulated. Where should it be located and what kind of housing should it be?

It is a commonly voiced opinion that segregated housing for the elderly results in isolation because it removes the aged from the mainstream of life. On the other hand, United Help came to the opinion based on research in this area (Carp & Carp, 1966; Rosow, 1962, 1964) that normal neighborhoods tend to isolate the aged; attempts to create friendly and neighborly attitudes between the young and the old by intentionally placing them in the same apartment building were doomed to failure. It was assumed that people establish friendship selectively, within age groups, and that age peers provide role models for patterning. For the older people acceptance of their age peers as a new reference group and as a source of standards for themselves offers chances of developing clear, acceptable new roles to which they can make satisfactory adjustments. In addition, this might obviate the need to cling to youthful standards that have become dysfunctional for their present time of life.

Though the strategy of developing a housing project exclusively for the elderly was chosen, it was assumed that other inputs were necessary to provide opportunities for participation in heterogeneous life and the larger community. With this in mind it was necessary to pick an area in which people of various ages lived and one that offered the amenities of a normal community, such as transportation, shopping, theaters, and houses of worship. Such an area would provide a milieu in which the tenants could live in accustomed ways and not have to discard their daily routines. It was assumed that the maintenance of useful life patterns would contribute to a feeling of self-esteem, particularly if the aged retained complete control of their own activities and lives. Moreover, it was necessary that each individual have freedom of choice in terms of his activities, just as he would in any normal healthy living arrangement.

In addition to these critera for consideration of the location of the housing was a conviction that it was necessary to facilitate contact with children and other relatives. It was assumed that an extended kinship system existed for the population they were serving and that a give and take existed between the generations as well as an accepted system of mutual aid despite their living apart and despite the geographic distance of the living quarters. Thus, the project was located in an area to facilitate such contact.

The basic philosophy under which this project was begun emphasized the positive aspects of life in older age and the belief that continued self-maintenance and independence contribute to both physical and mental health. Of course, there was an understanding that as people age, health and physical management become of increasing concern. Therefore, it was seen that planning needed to include other inputs: the facilitation of many medical, financial, and supportive services. With this in mind it was considered necessary to plan apartments that would be physically manageable both in size and facilities. These needed to have adequate cooking facilities. To offer an opportunity to participate in a planned way with diversified age groups, it was felt that easy availability of an older adult center could be necessary, which suggested the strategy of cooperation with and inclusion of an on-site community center—The YM&YWHA of Greater Flushing.

When the plans were formulated, a program evolved that integrated the housing with an older adult center and a family service agency. The older adult center was built adjacent to the apartment house for the elderly and partly extending into it and is operated by the Y whose youth center was constructed on the same grounds and shares its entrance lobby with the older adult center. Thus, the overall design offered tenants a choice of activities either programmed exclusively for the aged or of general interest to adults of all ages. In operation, 80% of all tenants are members of the Y. Though some complain about the noise of the children and youngsters, many participate in the activities open to all age groups. In addition, the larger community is brought naturally into the community of the aged.

MANDATES AND SANCTIONS

Housing projects are expensive propositions, and planning had to take into account the resources of the agency as well as the limited financial resources of an aging population. Financing was arranged under New York State's Limited Profit Housing law and a 90% mortgage provided to enable construction. This law mandates that the annual income of a tenant can not exceed his rent by more than six times as much and that a tenant must be a resident of New York State for at least one year prior to entrance into the housing. In addition, it was planned to give preference to low-income applicants, and with this in mind an arrangement with the department of social services has ensured a rent allowance equivalent to the rent for recipients of old-age assistance. When tenants have small fixed incomes that would necessitate their applying for public assistance to meet the rent differential between their old and their new apartments, United Help has provided rent subsidies. To maintain this as a facility for the aging, a minimum age of 60 years was established, except for couples where one partner may be younger.

By sponsoring an apartment building, the agency assumed the role of landlord, that is, it entered into a legal contract with independent tenants who would have the same rights and obligations as tenants elsewhere. But when a social agency is the landlord, it provides services exceeding those normally provided in this role. Thus, United Help saw itself as concerned with the well-being of each individual living in the buildings and as needed to consider other inputs for the health and welfare of the tenants. They had to be available when desired; in addition, the agency might have to take the initiative if intervention was considered indicated in the interest of an individual incapable of coping with his problems. Therefore, the agency offered a comprehensive service system. For the aged in particular this engenders feelings of security about the future. Such services are offered by Selfhelp.

OPERATIONAL STRATEGIES

The first tenants moved in on June 17, 1964. Monthly rents ranged from $68 to $78 for efficiencies and from $95.20 to $105.20 for one-bedroom apartments for couples and 44 nonbedroom apartments for single persons, all equipped with full kitchen facilities, bathrooms, and ample closet space. A second building has been constructed, a 19-story structure with 288 apartments, 72 for couples and 216 for single persons, within walking distance of the original Kissena Apartments and the senior center.

Self-government by the tenants has been encouraged and resides with a democratically elected tenant council that represents them in dealings with the administration of the project and the agency. Under the aegis of this council each floor within the development elects a floor captain who facilitates access to members. At night each tenant puts a sign on his door before he retires and then removes it in the morning. At that time the floor captain looks out to see if all signs are taken in, and if not, he ascertains what difficulty exists and obtains whatever service might be indicated for his neighbor. To further the concept of mutual aid, tenants have formed a committee that looks after the sick whether they are in their apartment or in the hospital. Thus, an unusual degree of mutual aid has developed among the tenants, coupled with a strong feeling of independence and self-reliance. There is a great pride in the actual buildings and the gardens. Many tenants have folding chairs that are kept in designated sitting areas for their pleasure. Social life thrives in such an atmosphere.

The maintenance of the buildings and its operation is done professionally. A managing agent is employed part-time; he employs maintenance staff, and obtains estimates and contracts for purchases. The maintenance people tend to be more permanent than is customary in many housing developments and are in their manner and involvement part of the total milieu. Tenant problems relating to operation of the building and its vacancies are dealt with by a full-time manager.

United Help operates a cafeteria that serves two meals a day—one meal during the summer months—and coffee and cake in the afternoon. A very small percentage of the tenants are regular users. Originally, it had been assumed that users of the Y would patronize the cafeteria and provide, in addition to revenue, an additional area for the meeting of generations. However, to meet the religious needs of the majority of the community, the kitchen is kosher and the type of food does not meet the tastes of a younger population. Therefore, the cafeteria incurs a considerable deficit and needs financing by United Help. However, it is considered a social service rather than a food service. It was necessitated by the need for meals of a small number of tenants who would not do their own cooking. It is very busy on Sundays when children and grandchildren come to visit.

Supporting social services are an essential part of this community and are operated by Selfhelp. A full-time social worker plus a student unit from Hunter College School of Social Work is available for counseling and other services, also considered inputs for the future in that the next generation is being prepared to treat the problems of the aging. The unit is financed by Selfhelp. All of Selfhelp's services, including summer vacations, are available to tenants. These include homemaker service and practical nurses for tenants who may need some temporary personal care and assistance in household management because of illness or other reasons. Referral to and assistance with other health facilities are also provided.

An important service, an information service for the aging, opened in 1969, is now in operation five days a week, staffed by one paid worker and trained volunteers. This service provides information, follows through on all relevant matters for the aged, and assists in making contacts with various resources in the larger community. It is available for all residents of the borough, not just the tenants.

The concept of being part of the total community is operationalized by setting up cooperative enterprises with community organizations such as the Red Cross and Arthritis Foundations. There are projects involving multiple sclerosis, arthritis for the community at large, Red Cross volunteers, and a Red Cross-sponsored training program for homemakers in which tenants as well as people in other adjacent communities volunteer their services. Thus, opportunities are given for the aging person to continue to contribute his services to others.

EVALUATION

There are no formal evaluatory procedures. However, it is assumed that the fact that there are fewer referrals to institutions than is customary among an exclusively older population speaks well for the health-inducing aspects of this service. It is felt that deaths have been less than is customary. Few people have moved. Vacancies occur primarily because of death, and to quote Dr. Hertz, "No one seems to hurry to die." The health of residents appears above average; the attitudes and the social bustle within the development all seem to indicate successful meeting of goals. Plans for the future envision establishment of a Midway House to provide health services on an outpatient basis and creation of a mental health center.

STRATEGY PROBLEMS

Some of the strategy problems have been mentioned. One of these is the cafeteria deficit, which has run approximately $18,000 a year. Prior to establishment of the project there was community opposition to housing exclusively for old people. One reason for this is the exemption given the project from the local real estate tax. It necessitated active work by United Help to obtain support from various citizen groups within the community. Of course, this has also helped to foster interest in the development once it began operating. The pride in the buildings and surrounding area that is frequently evidenced by tenants has at times been a detriment. Some have become overly involved with the physical property, so that at times they cherish it to the detriment of needed personal services. In Kissena II, particularly, the second building, there have been some problems because of acceptance of tenants with severe emotional problems and extreme age. In this building the selection process was quite lenient and did not screen out possibly troubled tenants.

On the whole, the diverse combination of strategies offered to the aged are believed to support the need of this group for a social role that sustains its members in their relationships with others. It is recognized that the Kissena Apartments project is unique because it represents a homogeneous group of similar background, life experience, and social values. It is felt that this type of living arrangement has potential for other groups since it aims to preserve the independence of the individual by building on his strength and by sensitively attending to his needs if and when they arise.

TABLE 4
Outline of Assumptions, Strategies, and Strategy Problems of Kissena Apartments: An Experience in Housing for Older People

Problem definition
- Decent housing for older people

Causation
- Changing neighborhoods
- Deterioration of housing
- Physical problems of aging and changing needs

Necessary inputs
- Housing project
- Senior center
- Supportive social services

Mandates and sanctions
- Agency mandate for client population
- Income, residence restriction from New York State law and mortgage

Strategies
- Target population
  - Aged victims of Nazi persecution—primarily a passive role in relation to receipt of agency services
- Service programs
  - Physically manageable, equipped apartments at reasonable rentals
  - Older adult center plus a community center—interagency cooperation
  - Cafeteria
  - Social services—counseling, homemaker services, and staffing information service—and staffing
  - Housing staff—managing agent, manager, and maintenance staff
- Monitoring and evaluation
  - No formal evaluation—some monitoring provided by elected tenant's council

Strategy problems
- Initial community opposition
- Cafeteria financial deficit
- Weakness in selection process—problem tenants

6. HELPING POLICE COPE WITH FAMILY VIOLENCE: A TRAINING MODEL IN COMMUNITY INTERVENTION*

As a person interested in the education of clinical psychologists, Dr. Morton Bard believed that traditional training was a losing proposition. Such programs would never produce enough professionals to cope with the mental health problem as he saw it. His new position as a member of the clinical faculty of City College included the directorship of a practicum facility, and his charge was the development of new modalities of training. The clinical faculty at the time agreed that the private fee-for-service model was inadequate to the needs of large segments of the population, and that traditional service delivery systems needed to be changed.

Bard saw his problem as creating a new practicum program for students that would be responsive to a community need and embody a new service delivery concept. His own prior experience included work with street gangs, cancer surgery patients, and narcotics addicts. Further, he had been a police officer for one year while in

* From an interview with Dr. Morton Bard, professor of psychology, The Graduate Center, City University of New York and his publications (Bard, 1970).

graduate school. He enjoyed the challenge of working with a system usually considered untouchable by social scientists and mental health professionals and felt studying that kind of system would reveal more useful information for the mental health professional than working within the usual service agencies and schools.

The law-enforcement system seemed to meet his criteria. It had potential for 24-hour-a-day service, instantaneous intervention, and early case finding, all of which is more than can be programmed by most agencies. He reasoned that if this system could be entered into by mental health professionals, it might be possible to exploit latent potential for service delivery. However, it would be necessary to first demonstrate to law-enforcement personnel that they faced problems with which clinical psychologists could be helpful.

Bard determined that in New York City close family relationships accounted for 35% of all homicides in 1965. In fewer than 20% of all homicides were the victim and perpetrator complete strangers. These statistics were close to the national average in both urban and rural areas. In addition to the family members who are victims of intrafamily fights, when police are called in to intervene, the police themselves frequently fall victim to the aggressive interaction. Of the policemen killed in the line of duty, 22% are slain while intervening in "disturbances" among people, most frequently in families. It is estimated that 40% of injuries sustained by police occur when they are intervening in family disputes.

The opportunity to develop a services program utilizing general police officers as psychological intervention agents offered the prospect of achieving the goals of both crime prevention and preventive mental health. In addition, such an approach held promise of revealing insights into aspects of human aggression and violence as it occurs in naturalistic settings and of providing doctoral students in clinical psychology with an unusual consultative training experience.

MANDATES AND SANCTIONS

Bard felt he had the backing of the clinical faculty since they verbally supported the idea that it was necessary for students to develop new skills. However, as it turned out later, many on the clinical faculty had a hidden agenda of which more shall be said below. There were no limitations placed on him, and all students were available to his program. Funds were made available for initial staffing and planning. The college as a whole also encouraged him since there was a need for more visible programs of service to the immediate community.

The administrators of the police department selected for the program were cooperative. Bard was able to convince them with carefully researched data that his program would improve the functioning of police and result in greater security, greater safety, and greater job satisfaction for them. They indicated that if he could obtain the financing for the program, they would fully cooperate with it.

Since the program, as conceived, involved a continuation of service to the community, the community itself was not approached for approval. This fit the perspective of the police whose view of the program was an intraorganizational reshuffling of priorities in performing normal duties. Bard felt community sanction would come after the fact, based on the value of the program. This was put to the test when militant students belonging to SDS attacked the program through demonstrations and the campus newspaper for not having obtained community participation and consent. Several members of the community spontaneously came forth to defend the program, and the SDS attack ceased.

There were several alternatives open for funding the project. Bard decided not to approach the NIMH because he felt they were jaded by the variety of innovative programs submitted to them. He also thought it would be worthwhile to attempt to educate other funding agencies—those that did not ordinarily fund psychologists—to the value of the services psychologists could provide. He chose the U.S. Justice Department and found them amenable to his notions, rather flexible, and able to give a speedy response. He submitted a proposal in January of 1967 and was funded in April. The Justice Department accepted his plan in its totality, stating that they liked best its action research element; they were relieved to find it was not just another study.

PREPARATORY PHASE

The program was designed for a West Harlem community of about 85,000 whose residents were mostly working class and black, with a sprinkling of Latin Americans (8%) and whites (2%)—a socially stable, residential community.

During the first month of the project 18 patrolmen were selected from among 45 volunteers. No effort was made to induce participation except by the offer of three college credits to be granted by the John Jay College of Criminal Justice of The City University. Selection was based on brief interviews to determine motivation, sensitivity, and stability. Applicants were required to have a minimum of 3 years' service and a maximum of 10. Nine white and nine black officers were selected for eventual biracial pairing.

For an entire month following selection the men were released from all duties to engage in an intensive training program that included lectures, "self-understanding" workshops, field trips, discussion groups, and a unique opportunity to "learn by doing" through real-life simulation. Three brief plays (Blake, 1971) depicting family crisis situations were specially written and performed by professional actors. Each play was performed three consecutive times, with interventions by a pair of policemen in each instance. Each pair of policemen was unaware of the events that preceded their entrance. The plays had no scripted conclusions, the actors having been instructed to improvise to the behavior of the officers when they entered the scene. The experience enabled the members of the unit to see how the same set of circumstances could have entirely different outcomes depending on the nature of their intervention. The technique proved particularly valuable to the officers. The practice interventions were subjected to extensive critique and review by all members of the unit. Particular stress was placed on values and attitudes about human behavior in general and about disrupted families in particular.

OPERATIONAL PHASE

At the conclusion of training the Family Crisis Unit began its operations. For the 22-month study period one precinct radio car was designated as the family car to be dispatched on all family disturbance complaints regardless of the sector of their occurrence in the precinct. In other words, departing from usual practice, the family car could leave its own patrol sector even if the disturbance was within the jurisdiction of another sector car. A special-duty chart permitted 24-hour-a-day coverage by members of the unit. A file of family disturbance reports was kept in the car for ready reference on the way to a dispute. The practice enabled the officers to know of previous interventions, if any, and of their outcomes.

An added feature of operations was the regularly scheduled consultation for each member of the unit. Once each week the 18 men appeared on campus in groups of six for individual consultation and debriefing with advanced graduate students in clinical psychology. In addition, each six-man group met with a professional group leader for the purpose of ongoing discussion of a broad range of issues relevant to family crisis intervention. Naturally, both experiences enhanced data collection, making possible additional, more in-depth information than could be provided by family disturbance reports alone.

EVALUATION

To facilitate evaluation, a neighboring police precinct with a population similar to that of the experimental precinct served as a basis of comparison. Comparisons were made based on changes in the total number of family disturbance complaints, differences in recurrence of complaints by the same families, and changes in the number of homicides and assaults involving both family members and policemen responding to family fight complaints.

The program was evaluated primarily in relation to aspects of police functioning as it affects certain categories of crime. Over the life of the project the demonstration precinct reported (*a*) a significantly greater number of interventions, (*b*) no homicides during the study period among any of the 962 families seen by the unit although there was an increase in total homicides, (*c*) a decrease in family assaults, and (*d*) no injuries to any unit members despite a high statistical probability of injury.

ASSUMPTIONS AND STRATEGIES

The basic assumption of the program seems to have been that police can be made an immediately available mental health source without compromising their basic responsibility for law enforcement. A program consisting of an intensive 9:00 A.M. to 5:00 P.M. training course and individual consultation for half a day a week was assumed to be sufficient for the purpose. Further, a mutual advantage was seen in that the consultation, research, and modeling experiences of the participating clinical psychology students would make a lasting impression on them. Local social agencies were expected to cooperate with the program and deliver the needed services upon referral by the police.

The cooperation of the police was solicited by emphasizing the benefits they would derive: for example, making their job easier, less dangerous, and more interesting.

Clinical psychology students were to be exposed to new possibilities for service, new techniques for helping, and new problems with which to work. They were to be given the opportunity to identify with an active, reaching out, collaborative model of functioning embodied in a public service delivery system. The program would benefit the community by immediate mental health intervention and referral at the earliest possible point of family conflict through crisis intervention by the natural care givers in that situation. Prevention was to be accomplished by early case finding for social agencies through immediate referral, and the population being served was to be educated to the availability of these services.

PROBLEMS

Although Bard was encouraged to pursue his program by the clinical faculty, their commitment to traditional clinical training and skills proved to be overriding. Toward the end of the project Bard felt that he had been exploited by faculty and students. Lip service was given to something in vogue but not really believed. In future programs he would ask the home system to make very explicit the exact nature of the commitment to whatever extent this is possible.

In general, the students who participated in the program did not appear later to pursue a community orientation. It was disappointing that although they apparently enjoyed their police experience and learned a good deal from it, their career patterns seemed not to have been influenced away from more traditional clinical psychology.

The police department was constrained in extending the program to other precincts. They did not have in-house capacity to do the kind of training the program called for, so that extending it would have required outside experts. Although these experts were available, the police department was uncomfortable with the notion of intimate relations with unpredictable mental health professionals. Even though Bard has passed the test of trust, there was uncertainty or unwillingness to risk involvement with so many others, each of whom would increase the possibility of detrimental outcome. To the police the issue was the best method of maximizing training, and to the outside experts the main issue was legitimizing a cooperative stance between mental health professionals and the police. In future projects Bard thinks this issue could be more easily negotiated if the program design included co-responsibility between the police department and the mental health professional, which could be accomplished by having a policy-maker from the police department as co-director of the project with equal accountability for outcome. The police would then have a stronger commitment to program continuation and expansion and would not be able to say, as they did in this instance, that it was an outside program with which they cooperated but toward which they had little responsibility.

Another problem was lack of follow-through by the local social services agencies. Although initial cooperation by these agencies was solicited and obtained, the agencies seemed unable to fulfill the referral needs efficiently and quickly. There were constant frustrations with regard to referrals.

TABLE 5
Outline of Assumptions, Strategies, and Strategy Problems of Helping Police Cope with Family Violence: A Training Model in Community Intervention

Problem definition
  To help police more effectively intervene in violent family crises
Causation
  Police are not trained in preventive mental health
  Mental health professionals do not reach families at the time of crisis
  Most families do not know how to reach mental health professionals
Necessary inputs

- Police training program
- Supportive social services
- Structural change in police procedures

Mandates and sanctions
- College and faculty support
- Police department cooperation
- Justice department funds

Strategies
- Target populations
  - Harlem families who have violent crises—prevention
- Service programs
  - Help police with more effective intervention
  - Expose clinical psychology students to community work
  - Develop special police family crises units
- Monitoring and evaluation
  - Formalized—built into program

Strategy problems
- Inability to extend program
- Isolation within sponsoring agency
- Lack of lasting impact on clinical psychology students
- Poor follow-through by local agencies

As the program progressed, it was learned that the basic training period for police participants need not have been so intensive or time-consuming. The training could have been accomplished in less time, thereby making it easier for precincts to assign patrolmen to the program.

7. A DEMONSTRATION PROJECT ON A MINIMUM BUDGET: THE GOALS FOR GIRLS PROJECT OF THE FOOTHILL FAMILY SERVICE OF PASADENA, CALIFORNIA*

When Mr. Patrick Riley became the executive director of the Foothill Family Service in 1961, he discovered that the agency had a fund of money, approximately $16,000, that had been provided by a foundation. The only restriction on its allocation was that it be used to supply small amounts of money to individual girls for a variety of reasons. Mr. Riley proposed to the board of directors that a substantial project be undertaken with the funds. He was supported in this plan and given free rein, with the stipulation that the project should be of value to the community as a whole. Organizations within the community were involved in discussions of possible programs.

TARGET POPULATION

The decision to focus on service for young women on probation was arrived at for several reasons. First, it appeared manageable within the limitations of money, staff resources, and the mandate of the foundation. Sec-

* From an interview with Patrick V. Riley, assistant general director of Family Service Association of America, who was executive director of the Foothill Family Service at the inception of this program (Webb & Riley, 1970).

ond, treatment agencies in the community tended to have a strong negative bias in accepting referrals for this group because of previous failures and the fact that this client group rarely followed through on referrals. Third, it was thought that the young woman offender was neglected within this particular community because this group did not constitute a community-wide problem since the number of girls involved was relatively small.

PROBLEM DEFINITION

The project was then conceived as a study of whether it is possible to involve young women probationers in a treatment program with an outside, voluntary casework agency, and if they were so engaged, would such an involvement significantly improve their life adjustments.

Defining the problem as lack of motivation for treatment of the target population called for an examination of what was involved in the concept of motivation. If the concept is defined operationally, it becomes reduced to how long applicants will wait before being seen; at how many doors they will knock; and how many forms they will fill out. In this sense the problem became the lack of motivation of the treatment agencies. Redefining the problem as difficulty in engaging in treatment girls on probation suggested that the etiology of this problem was the agencies' lack of motivation. It involved the assumption that a potential client group was deterred because of nonfunctional agency procedures such as long waiting lists, forms to fill out, and cost.

ASSUMPTIONS AS TO INPUTS

The decision to consider social work treatment as helpful for this population evolved from the belief that people on probation have problems in social functioning that lead to difficulty with the law. Since social work treatment aims to improve the social functioning of its clients, it should help such a group. However, the literature on casework treatment of adult offenders suggests that it does not occur and that individual treatment approaches tend to have less success with such a group than more innovative techniques.

With much of the responsibility placed on the service agency, changes in the strategies involving the delivery of the service needed to be considered. The first input was considered to be a commitment to make counseling available to girls on probation by making structural changes, but only those that could be used in everyday counseling. It suggested that a maximum effort to reach out to these young women needed to be made by the two agencies involved and that the project could demonstrate the effectiveness of close cooperation between the private family service agency and the public probation department. One of the changes in customary procedures involved the informal use of the authority of the latter agency. The probation office was in a directly authoritative position in relation to the subjects. In referring subjects to the project the probation officer was to primarily use persuasion, but if he met with resistance, he was to present participation in the project as a required part of the plan of probation. The effect was largely that of involuntary initiation. The strategy was deliberately chosen to test out the accepted belief that successful treatment depends on the initiation of treatment by the client.

It was recognized that this approach contained both philosophical and legal problems. Philosophically, could one see this as an infringement of individual autonomy? Does it raise questions about respect for the principle of self-determination? The legal aspect involves the fact that no judge ordered referral to the family agency, yet an important assumption involved using the authoritative aspect of the probation officer to convince the subject that she *had* to follow through on the referral as part of the conditions of probation. Dilemmas of this nature are not uncommon whenever an attempt is made to experiment, and they are experienced in all fields involving work with people.

RESEARCH STRATEGY

After the decision as to the nature of the project and its essential concerns had been reached, a series of meetings were held with staff people to develop formal procedures. This was followed by a beginning description of the project and the research design. The latter was considered an important aspect of the program since several commonly held assumptions were being examined.

The design of the program called for the establishment of two groups: (*a*) an experimental group to receive authoritorian pressure to enter casework treatment and (*b*) a control group that would not. When girls were placed on probation by the court, they were assigned to one of the groups on a random basis from the caseload of the Pasadena office of the Los Angeles County Probation Department. This was restricted to women between the ages of 18 and 25, excluding girls who received a jail sentence; those included had been given at least one year's probationary status by the court. Both groups showed no significant differences on the variables of race, religion, intelligence, socioeconomic or marital status, and criminal offense. The final total of 68 (34 subjects in each group) was whittled down to 26 in the experimental group and 32 in the control group. Among a variety of factors responsible for this attrition were some technical problems. For example, there were some unanticipated rearrests in the control group after the preliminary testing and in the experimental group after testing and referral, but before the first contact with the family agency, which automatically removed those involved from consideration for the project.

The first strategy that was different for the two groups began with the deputy probation officer's discussing a referral to the family service with the experimental subject. A variety of techniques, dependent on the attitudes encountered in the subject, was used in the actual referral process. For some, the probation officer simply explained the immediate availability of the service, provided the name of the liaison caseworker at the agency, and suggested the young woman call for an appointment.

When there was resistance, the probation officer tried to deal with the fears, explained what counseling meant and what could be expected, and when necessary insisted that the probationee participate on a trial basis. In a few cases the family service caseworker joined the probation officer in the discussion. If resistance continued, the probation officer made it clear that he wanted this participation and also expected it. Such procedures were not followed with the control group.

As part of the evaluatory process of the project two tests were given to all girls in the experimental and in the control group. For the first group this was before referral to the family agency and one year later. Girls in the control group were tested when they went on probation and again one year later. Testing was done at the probation department.

The probation department would notify the family service and forward both the test results and a court report for each experimental subject after each referral had been made. Where there was delay on the follow-through in calling for or keeping the first appointment at the family service, the deputy probation officer would be notified; he would then contact the girl involved. After the first interview the responsibility for continued follow-up remained primarily with the family service, but where necessary the probation officer was again asked to intervene.

ADMINISTRATIVE STRATEGIES AND PROBLEMS

Obviously, an important strategy that had to be developed involved a cooperative relationship between the two agencies. To develop this on a planned basis, conferences were held at the very beginning of the project. This involved the deputy probation officers, their supervisory personnel (who were scheduled to do the testing), their superiors, and the project director. The initial conferences concerned any potential areas of difficulty, but periodic conferences were called throughout the experiment. Regular meetings were scheduled to discuss progress and particular clients and to review and develop new approaches on combined knowledge.

Unfortunately, there were problems in the area of communication, primarily because of severe staff turnover. Within the life of the project, there were three different supervisors in the probation department and turnover in probation officers. This did not really effect the subjects since they did not experience the change. Very few project caseworkers left. In the long run these difficulties were primarily administrative.

Within the family service the initial interview was usually conducted by the family service liaison caseworker who either continued with the case or assigned it to the appropriate staff member. Though additional staff had been hired to compensate for the extra time needed for the project, cases were assigned to workers on a normal basis and within normal procedures. Thus, assignment was made to the staff member who might have time or the staff person to whom such a case might normally be assigned.

Problems arose within the family agency staff. Workers reflected the commonly held negative attitudes toward this population. They felt there would be problems about motivation, anticipated there would be many difficulties in working with the girls, and felt that a lot of time would have to be put into home visits. To combat this, it was necessary for the administration to establish that each worker would receive credit for extra work, that is, for the extra time entailed in home visits, etc. It was also necessary to open up more communication with staff and enable them to see themselves as effective parts of the research. Further, no worker was assigned more than two such cases at any time. In reflecting on this difficulty, Mr. Riley was very clear in stating that if he did it over, he would involve the caseworkers much earlier and more completely in the planning and development of the project. As it was developed, the project was somewhat inflicted on them, and they went along because of a sense of professional responsibility. In addition, reporting back needed to be more detailed; more staff meetings needed to be held in which objections could have been elicited at the onset. He felt that it needed to be made clear from the beginning that they would receive allowances for any inconveniences. Emphasis needed to be given to their potential contribution to the research, and their concern for people and their welfare needed to be related to the project.

One of the difficulties involved the lapse of time in the reporting back of test results to staff. It was the role of the research consultant to interpret these results and make them available to staff. However, because he had been hired on a part-time consultant basis for this project and was not on staff, he was somewhat removed from the project. There were also long delays in processing of the data. In retrospect, Mr. Riley believes that it would have been more efficient and would have facilitated communication, if the research person had been part of the staff.

RESULTS

At the conclusion of the project it was felt that the experiment had had an impact on the girls in the treated group. Not only was there a significant difference in their initial involvement in treatment, and continuation in treatment when compared with the control group, but they were also more successfully involved in a casework treatment program than regular agency clients. Using the number of interviews as the index of involvement, the experimental group had more interviews, 53% of them having at least six interviews as compared to 24% for the agency's regular caseload. In addition, this percentage was compared to the percentage of clients who have at least six interviews as reported by family agencies on a nationwide basis. The figure for this latter group was 27%. It was believed that the use of the implicit authority of the probation officer assisted in these results. To some extent each of the young women was taken "off the hook" in the sense that the responsibility for seeking counseling was not hers, and she did not "lose face." Such an assumption suggests the existence of some element within the sociocultural environment of these girls that mitigates against seeking psychological help.

The course of the casework treatment for these clients differed from usual procedures in the degree of outreach to resistant subjects. For example, the interviews were made more available because of the priority given to project participants. Where appointments were broken there was regular follow-up either by the caseworker or the parole officer. There were no fees, and scheduling was done as far as possible at the convenience of the client. Home visits were also made for a variety of reasons.

Thus, the more positive results may be attributed either to the use of authority or to procedural changes that were sensitive to the needs of the clients involved. Separately or in conjunction with each other, these changes and the results they achieved bring into question the whole concept of motivation for treatment as it is commonly used.

Thus, the project appeared to demonstrate that young probationers could be involved. But it intended to show that such involvement would make a difference; it would show an improvement in life adjustment. It was in this area that detailed evaluatory procedures had been programmed.

Two tests, the Minnesota Multiphasic Personality Inventory and a form of semantic differential, were administered to all subjects at the time they were identified for the project and then again one year later. The tests were administered by the probation department to both experimental and control group, with the expectation that no significant change would occur in the control group.

The concept of improvement in the life adjustment was operationized through noting if the before and after tests showed change on the following dimensions: (*a*) improved self-concept, (*b*) improved acceptance of female role, (*c*) increased ability to delay impulse gratification, (*d*) increased resourcefulness and adaptability, (*e*) reduction in anxiety, (*f*) greater acceptance of authority, (*g*) greater acceptance of the dictates of one's superego, and (*h*) greater acceptance of personal responsibility. In addition, the probation officer was asked to rate each subject on certain behavioral correlates at the time of the subject's entry into the project and again one year later. Such behaviors related to probation record, employment, school, family, social life, and emotional stability.

One finding was that during the project year the incidence of further trouble with the police was strikingly less for the girls who had seen caseworkers than for those who had not. The probation officers rated the former more cooperative, and their total performance improved. In addition, the employment status and pattern improved substantially for this group. Their test results also indicated an improved acceptance of female role, reduced anxiety, greater acceptance of authority, and greater acceptance of personal responsibility for the experimental group, whereas no such changes were indicated for the others.

It was concluded that such changes were more reflective of socialization and maturation than of basic personality change and might reflect progress in coming to terms with the demands and frustrations of life but that they reflected more progress than that manifested by the control group. If it is assumed that what was reflected was a reaction to demonstrated concern, to special attention, to being part of a project, the results suggest that this itself might be important and worth incorporation in future planning.

In addition to beginning an examination of some commonly held assumptions, the program offered some long-term gains to the family agency, the probation department, and the community involved in human services. The cooperation that was developed between the two agencies continued after the termination of the project. Referrals to the family agency continued to increase. In addition, general communication was opened and facilitated within the community.

Though the costs of the project appeared to be minimum, and primarily for research consultation and analysis as well as some staff time, there were expenditures of time in terms of the administrative staff responsible for planning and execution, for interagency communication,

TABLE 6
Outline of Assumptions, Strategies, and Strategy Problems of the Goals for Girls Project of the Foothill Family Service

Problem definition
- Lack of motivation for treatment of girls on probation

Causation
- Lack of motivation of treatment agencies

Necessary inputs
- Changes in availability of service
- Interagency cooperation

Mandates and sanctions
- Financial limitations
- Mandate of foundation
- Agency function

Strategies
- Target population
  - Girls on probation—a passive role as recipients of casework treatment
- Service programs
  - Casework treatment
  - Outreach
  - Interagency communication and cooperation
  - Testing and evaluatory procedures
  - Additional staff—research consultation
- Monitoring and evaluation
  - Formalized evaluation procedures
- Strategy problems
  - Case problems in terms of outreach
  - Loss of subjects because of rearrest
  - Staff turnover in probation department
  - Staff morale
  - Delays in processing data and making it available for use

etc. However, the extra work involved for both agencies was considered to be part of the normal activity and the process of change and development that are an integral part of the professional workload.

8. CONCLUSION

Most programs begin with considerable enthusiasm and a feeling of assured success. Both enthusiasm and expectations of success are important ingredients of any program.

What happens when programs end up not having met expectations? Funding sources are not likely to refund a program under such circumstances. Often services, jobs, and the status of the planners and administrators are at stake. Because of this, the deficiencies of the program may be denied or glossed over, the administration and staff stressing only what they see as the positive aspects of the program and spending considerable time in public relations to win support for the program. All that is needed, according to those who run the program, is more money to continue and expand the program.

What is needed more than money is identification and clarification of the concepts, processes, and assumptions under which the programs have operated. Until that is done, program discussion will be meaningless and subject to the senseless clamor of rival claims of success by competing programs. This monograph attempted to develop a conceptual framework around programs. It dealt with program assumptions, mandates and sanctions, strategies and strategy problems. Other conceptual frameworks could also be developed that might prove as or more useful than the one developed in this monograph. The authors feel that what is important at this point in time is that programs be thought through conceptually.

The interviews with program administrators took

place after the theoretical rationale had been developed, and we felt that when we spoke to program administrators about problem definition, mandates, and strategy problems, these concepts might be ambiguous and unclear and might have to be revised or changed. Our overall impression, after completing interviews with program administrators and reading their program literature, is that the concepts described in the monograph can be readily applied to programs. Administrators generally found discussions around mandates, sanctions, strategies, and strategy problems interesting and appropriate. The account of their programs in these terms is often surprisingly frank.

Feedback from administrators who were shown the outline of their program in terms of assumptions, mandates, and strategies indicated that it seemed helpful to them in giving them an overall view of the program process and putting in objective form the parameters of the program. Sometimes the outline helped to point out to them program ambiguities and dilemmas.

Besides administrators of programs, a conceptual schema for programs should be helpful to program planners, program reviewers, evaluators, funding sources, and social scientists. Often just the categorizing of programs is difficult. According to the conceptual schema developed in this monograph, programs might be categorized according to problem definition, their mandates, their strategies etc. Evaluators would find their jobs simplified if they had before them the program's definition of the problem, mandates and sanctions, target population, and service strategies. Investigators on a program level would have such interesting topics as why programs with similar problem definitions, mandates, sanctions, target populations, inputs, and service strategies often achieve different results. Or how some programs are able to develop service strategies that seem precluded by the program's mandates and sanctions.

An overview of the six programs described in the monograph stimulates considerable thought. Generalizations to other programs are not warranted since these programs are not representative; the particular programs chosen were picked because of the variety of problems involved, their different approaches, and their reputations for being outstanding programs of their kind. However, many features of these programs are striking, and they give leads as to the implications of program strategies.

All of the six programs dealt with problem areas that are troublesome to society: drug addiction, crime, poverty, poor academic skills of minority children, problems of the aging. Many of the programs defined the problem in terms of the individual and the symptoms or deficits he showed (PS Inner City, Phoenix House, Kissena Apartments). However, Bard's program for police defines the problem as creating a new training program in response to community need. The CSS defined the problem as the undesirable urban social situation and the large number of disadvantaged. The Foothill Family Services defined the problem as lack of motivation for treatment service. When the problem is defined in terms of the weaknesses of clients the tendency is to emphasize more conventional service strategies in mental health, social work, or education. Thus PS Inner City has a "saturation" educational program and a learning center; Kissena Apartments has supportive social services and a community center. However, this is not true for Phoenix House (perhaps because clients are assigned an unconventional, increasingly active role in the services themselves). When the services are not defined in terms of the weaknesses of clients, the service strategies tend not to be conventional services. Thus, Bard is involved with strategies to enlist the cooperation of police, the CSS with plans of opening the system to disadvantaged, and Foothill Family Services with improving communication between agencies.

Problem definition and problem causation must be considered hand in hand. These two will then determine the general nature of the program, including the target population. For example, Phoenix House, in dealing with the problem of drug addiction, focuses on the addict, believing the causation is the emotional immaturity of the individual due to faulty familial experiences, an assumption that has still not been adequately substantiated. Some say the problem of drug addiction is related to societal corruption that furthers the drug traffic because it is big business and vital to the economy of the producing nation, as well as very profitable to special interests. One has, with this argument, only to point to England's role in the problem in the opium addiction in China. The focus would not be on the individual. On the other hand, one might view causation as a deliberate attempt to emasculate certain sectors of the population, namely minority groups and youth generally, through drug addiction, thereby decreasing protest movements. Such an argument is espoused by certain activist minority youth as well as some radical movements. In this case politicalization of the youth would be seen as a logical strategy.

The causation of problems was believed to come from a multiplicity of factors for most program administrators. When the causation was seen as complex, the program strategies tended to be diverse. However, when one core causative factor was stressed, the services strategies tended to be more interrelated with each other and focused on the causative factor. Thus, the Foothill Family Services program that saw the causative factor as the lack of motivation by treatment agencies was able to concentrate its strategies around this one factor; the low cost of this program may be largely due to such a focused approach.

Even when there is agreement as to causation, assumptions around inputs might be seen from many viewpoints. Continuing with Phoenix House's view of causation, one might find agreement with faulty familial experiences but believe independence of the family is needed. A possible choice of inputs was considered by Kissena Apartments: A common belief is that integrated housing rather than a segregated housing project is more suitable as a strategy for older people. In the literature on Kissena Apartments and in the interview with Hertz, both integration and segregation are discussed. The final choice of strategy resulted from evidence of studies indicating that for the target population segregated housing was more appropriate.

It was the authors' impression that the concept "mandates and sanctions" was the least clear of the terminology used. Program administrators were clear about mandates that were spelled out by funding agencies as to the ways money was to be spent and what was prohibited. However, when the mandates and sanctions came from the agency of which the program was a part, administrators were often vague and uncertain as to what the mandates and sanctions were, which may be because agencies themselves are unclear on their policies regarding programs, do not strongly state their policies, or may change their policies during the course of the program. Bard indicates that an agency may even give double messages about a program, stating a public viewpoint but actually meaning something else.

Mandates and sanctions from the community were usually only stated by administrators when there was a confrontation about the program in the community. Kaufmann, in describing Phoenix House, indicated that confrontations occurred in middle-class neighborhoods, which would seem to contrast generally with the reports of confrontations about service programs occurring in poor neighborhoods.

If one reviews the description of CSS's proposed new program, one wonders about a program operating under the mandate of a board of trustees that represents power and advantage talking about helping the disadvantaged to get power and influence. What kind of power? What kind of influence? What will happen if the disadvantaged want the power of the board of trustees?

It was interesting to note that all of the programs in our small sample were, at least in part, supported by government or private grants, indicating the important role that these granting agencies play in mandating services and target populations for program support.

The target population in the six programs was either the clients, the staff (training), or both. What seems to be an important strategy concept about the target population is whether the clients play a passive or active role in the administration of services and the operation of the program. The two programs where clients play an active role are in Phoenix House and the planned program of the CSS. When clients are involved in this way, it cuts down on the need for scarce and expensive professional manpower (the ratio of professional manpower to clients is less at Phoenix House and probably will be less at the CSS than at other programs) as well as establishing different kinds of power relations between clients and staff and expectations of staff and clients, which in itself may have an important bearing on what happens to clients. The distance between the status and power of staff and clients is reduced, making for more equalitarian relations between them and enhancing the value and strength the client feels within himself.

Most of the six programs involved at least informal monitoring of the program as an evaluative strategy. In three of the programs, the Foothill Family Service, the CSS, and Bard's police program, sophisticated research designs were built into the program, usually in the form of an experimental and control group. Our impression is that the degree of research sophistication of these programs is highly unusual; most programs usually have no evaluative procedures. However, one should exercise caution in interpreting the results of the research procedures that show that the experimental group did better than the control group. It is uncertain as to what program elements, if any, were effective. A "Hawthorne effect" may be occurring. The study of program elements and effectiveness may have to await large-scale evaluation of programs in which program elements can be manipulated or multivariate types of statistical analysis can be applied.

Also needed is basic research to test the validity of the assumptions underlying programs.

As might be expected, these innovative programs had more than their fair share of strategy problems. Or it may be that the administrators of these creative programs are more aware of strategy problems than are most program administrators. Problems about implementation, probably the most common complaint of program administrators, occur among the six programs. The Foothill Family Service suffers greatly from staff turnover. PS Inner City never received most of the funds it had expected. Kissena Apartments has a financial deficit in an important part of its program.

In our small sample one commonly held assumption is shown to be commonly forgotten: No program is better than the people who do the work! The question of staff morale, cooperation, and inputs is invariably of importance. It would seem that involvement of staff in the planning process is a necessary prerequisite for successful manpower inputs and successful program output.

A troublesome area that is related to this point involves the direction from which the program begins. When it comes from the outside, as occurred in PS Inner City and to some extent in the Police Intervention Training Program, the program administrators are the outsiders, and the program appears an imposition, which may promote feelings of being controlled and being used. Under these circumstances resistance to the program from a variety of sources is almost inevitable.

Such a reaction is also induced by programs that develop primarily from the top echelons, as is demonstrated by the CSS and the Foothill Family Service projects. In both cases, the initial planning appeared to involve staff, but such involvement was minimal. Ideas were solicited, but in the long run these programs were also imposed. Earlier involvement in an active manner probably would have enabled some exchange of practical ideas, aired fears and resentments, and contributed to smoother program operation. Awareness of this potential area should be part of any planning process that can then build in the necessary planning strategies.

Other strategy problems occur in the six programs: Lack of motivation of clients, lack of knowledge of staff and administration, difficulties in sustaining an innovative program, and community opposition are mentioned as strategy problems. An interesting strategy problem around "therapeutic milieus" occurred in two programs. Phoenix House and PS Inner City developed special ideal temporary environments for their clients and then found that many of the clients did not want to leave the environment, which suggests that creating an ideal milieu on some temporary basis has built-in problems. Perhaps the strategy should be to take the favorable milieu elements and build them into the everyday environment of clients.

An attempt to conceptualize some of the processes that are inherent in programs has been made herein. Until the principles that underly programs are clarified and subject to examination, social scientists, planners, administrators, and funding sources have no meaningful way of communicating to each other except through hucksterism and advertising (often misleading advertising that makes fraudulent claims). With proper analysis we believe that goals will become more realistic, projects will be more concisely defined and limited to realizable dimensions, and communications will improve.

REFERENCES

Bard, M. *Training police as specialists in family crisis interview.* Washington, D.C.: Government Printing Office, 1970.

Blake, E. *Three scripts for family crisis intervention.* New York: Family Service Association, 1971.

Carp, F. *A future for the aged: Victoria Plaza and its residents.* Austin and London: The University of Texas Press, 1966.

Chambers, C. D. *An assessment of drug use in the general population. Special report no. 1. Drug use in New York State.* New York: New York State Narcotic Addiction Control Commission, 1971.

Coleman, J. S., Campbell, E. Q., Hobson, C. J., McPartland, J., Mood, A. M., Weinfeld, F. D., & York, R. L. *Equality of Educational Opportunity,* Washington: U.S. Government Printing Office, 1966.

Editorial. Prospectus for change at the CSS. *Social Service Review,* 1971, **45,** (2), 211.

Freeman, H. C. & Sherwood, C. C., *Social research and social policy:* Englewood Cliffs, N.J.: Prentice-Hall, 1970.

Hertz, K. G. Housing for the aged: Some observations on institutional or noninstitutional sponsorship. *Journal of Jewish Communal Service,* 1970, **XLVI** (3), 261-266.

Hertz, K. G. Community resources and services to help independent living. *The Gerontologist,* 1971, **II** (1), 59-66.

Kahn, A. J. *Theory and practice on social planning.* New York: Russell Sage Foundation, 1969.

Lubove, R. *The professional altruist.* Cambridge, Mass.: Harvard University Press, 1965.

Morris, P. & Rein, M. *Dilemmas of social reform.* New York: Atherton Press, 1967.

Phoenix House: A three year report. New York: Phoenix House Foundation, 1970.

Rosow, I. Retirement housing and social integration. In C. Tibbitts and W. Donohue (Eds.), *Social and psychological aspects of aging.* New York and London: Columbia University Press, 1962.

Rosow, I. Local concentrations of aged and intergenerational friendships. In P. F. Hansen (Ed.), *Age with a Future.* Copenhagen: Munksgaard, 1964.

Schorr, A. *Explorations in social policy.* New York: Basic Books, 1968.

Stimson, A. S., & Stimson, J. B. *New York City: A problem census and social report: Supplement I.* New York, Community Service Society of N.Y., 1970.

Webb, A. P., & Riley, P. V. Effectiveness of casework with young female probationers. *Social Casework,* 1970, **51** (9), 566-572.

Young, H. D. *Strategies for social intervention: Supplement II.* New York: Community Service Society of N.Y., 1970.

DEVELOPMENTS IN HUMAN SERVICES EDUCATION AND MANPOWER

by

Robert M. Vidaver, M.D.

(Part IV of Developments in Human Services,
Volume 1,
Edited by
Herbert C. Schulberg, Ph.D.,
Frank Baker, Ph.D., and
Sheldon R. Roen, Ph.D.

Library of Congress Catalog Card Number 73-6869
Standard Book Number 87705-079-1

BEHAVIORAL PUBLICATIONS, 2852 Broadway—Morningside Heights, New York, New York 10025

Printed in the United States of America

Library of Congress Cataloging in Publication Data

Vidaver, Robert M
Developments in human services education and manpo

Also issued in v. 1 of Developments in human servi
1. Social work education--United States. 2. Soc
service--United States. I. Title.
[HV11.V53] 361'.007'1173 73-68

CONTENTS

Preface v

1. **Expanding Parameters of Human Services Responsibility** 363
   The Widening Appeal of the Human Services 363
   The Escalation in Consumer Demand 369
   The Search for Identity 375

2. **The Changing Dimensions of Professional Intervention** 383
   The Myth of High Standards of Professional Manpower 383
   The Manpower Implications of Community Services 391

3. **Opening Up New Manpower Resources** 399
   Caveats from the Lincoln Hospital New Careers Experiment 399
   Human Services Education as a Developmental Process 409
   Defining the Professional 419
   New Careers Revisited 10 Years After 436

4. **Modular Education and the Development of Career Lattices** 448

Community Participation 448
The Community-College Mental
Health Worker Series 457
Training Goals, Service
Responsibilities, and the
Associate Degree Workers 468
Baccalaureate and Masters
Degree Modules 480

5. Academic Costs, Effectiveness, Evaluation, and the Associate Professional Process 508
The Associate Professional Process 508

PREFACE TO THE SEPARATES OF THE "DEVELOPMENTS IN HUMAN SERVICES" SERIES

Widespread inadequacies in the human condition, and concern for the difficulties and complexities of existing social arrangements, have created urgent pressures upon professionals to revise present care-giving mechanisms. Human service programs such as multi-service centers, which incorporate a wide variety of relevant services, are emerging as an alternative framework to the existing pattern of rigid, categorical services for meeting the bio-psycho-social needs of individuals and populations.

The editors of this new encyclopedic series have undertaken to develop materials which can serve as guide posts for those newly entering or already engaged in the field of human services. A flexible approach to the production and distribution of these materials has been devised.

The plan for the series is to publish annually indepth discussions and reviews on the following human service topics:

—Emerging Conceptions of human service such as systems and ecological frameworks

—Administrative and planning tools such as information systems, economic strategies, and legal mechanisms

—Innovative service programs within new organizational models and new communities

—Educational programs for changing professional roles and new manpower requirements

After several years, those who are standing order subscribers will possess an encylopedic library of human

services in either hardbound volumes or softcover separates.

The first volume contains an introductory overview by the editors, four substantitive sections on different human service topics as enumerated below, and a comprehensive index. Each of the substantitive sections, without introductory overview and index, are available as separates. These are:

Teaching Health and Human Services Administration by the Case Method
Linda G. Sprague, Alan Sheldon, M.D., and Curtis P. McLaughlin, D.B.A.

The Planning and Administration of Human Services
Harold W. Demone, Jr., Ph.D. and Dwight Harshbarger, Ph.D.

Strategies in Innovative Human Service Programs
Harry Gottesfeld, Ph.D., Florence Lieberman, D.S.W., Sheldon R. Roen, Ph.D., and Sol Gordon, Ph.D.

Developments in Human Services Education and Manpower
Robert M. Vidaver, M.D.

The Editors

1. EXPANDING PARAMETERS OF HUMAN SERVICES RESPONSIBILITY

THE WIDENING APPEAL OF THE HUMAN SERVICES

There was a time when human services were reserved for the lunatic, the beggar, and the orphaned child. Everybody else could shift for themselves. And if the concept of *service* was too narrowly construed, neither was there much visible agitation for its broadening. People seemed willing to die—at least insofar as their intent was interpreted for them by government and media—rather than depend on the charity of others. Keeping up appearances was valued for its own sake; helplessness or signs of weakness in intellect, emotion, or will were hidden lest public opprobrium further compound one's personal tribulations. Deviance was of the devil, and mental health services were the last resort of the vanquished spirit, perpetrated on those so far "gone" as to have "lost their minds."

Circumstances changed. Suffering became a thing not so much to be endured resignedly. The range of personal difficulties for which people could legitimately (in the community's eyes) seek help have gradually widened. The parameters of the services have correspondingly expanded. The asylums still exist, of course, but the trend to bring services to more and more people is unmistakable. Delineation of the nature of services—who is supposed to be helped for what ailments and through which techniques—expands inexorably to include services to persons less and less overtly deviant. Clients of the human services become more "normal" than sick, their ills more short-lived in duration. A person does not have to be insane or penniless to benefit from services as they have come to be. At an accelerating pace services would seem to be moving toward universal applicability, away from the pathology-based focus of the 1930s. Whereas once no more than a tiny fraction of the overall population was ill enough to warrant psychiatric intervention (i.e., state hospitalization), the elaboration of manifold mental *health* services means services relevant to a variety of life crises common to ordinary people. Soon enough an individual's decision to seek counsel will be taken as indication of mental health; the stigmata, if any, will come to rest on those who would go it alone, seemingly too proud to accept outside support.

Three major forces would seem at work, namely, (*a*) the geographic movement of services away from isolation into the closer proximity with the life space of the clients; (*b*) the ever-widening relevance of the services themselves to the less pathological (and more commonplace) afflictions, concomitant with society's new-found willingness to receive them; and (*c*) the gradual inclusion of the machinery for dispensing services within the ordinary neighborhood institutions common to American life.

The Changing Locus of Therapeutic Intervention

Since the last half century the locus of therapeutic intervention—the site or location of the helping facility—has gravitated out of the enforced isolation of the asylum in the boondocks, returning bit by bit into the bosom of community life. The effect of this trend can be illustrated geographically. The immediate descendant of the asylum was the specialized psychiatric hospital in the model of the Meninger Clinics, Chestnut Lodge, the

Yale Psychiatric Institute, or the Phipps Clinic. Concurrent with their development of active treatment programs specific to the psychological aberrations of their clientele, their physical plant gravitated toward the urban centers, the universities in particular. Bucolic approaches of the *retreat* became the insulin coma and ECT modalities of the medical school hospital, the mentally ill receiving care under the same roof as the medical patient.

From the specialized psychiatric hospitals also emerged the psychotherapies, essentially the adaptation of the analytic model to a broad spectrum of psychological conditions and less intensive, less structured clinician-client relationships. Outpatient clinics appeared, in part derivatives of the growing analytic movement of the late 1930s and the carry-over of the general hospital-outpatient clinic model into the human services. Private-practicing analysts, as also the new clinic structures and a beginning nucleus of private psychotherapists, made ambulatory care available on a widespread scale, at least to the middle classes of the big cities. Care became possible within the context of peoples' ordinary lives. The ambulatory approaches revolutionized clinical practice. Long-standing professional bias favoring treatment in isolation of one's job, family, community, and friends was shattered, permitting the rapid burgeoning of clinic facilities under manifold different auspices. Clinics sprung up sponsored by family agencies, state hospitals (as satellites in distant city locations), general hospitals, and children's institutions. Importantly, psychology and social work personnel came to assume clinical roles as practitioners, particularly vis-a-vis family and group modalities, at first considered secondary or supportive to the patient's psychotherapy, more lately emerging as primary modalities in their own rights.

More services available on a decentralized basis could not have happened without the development of new manpower types (which in turn made possible even greater dispersal of treatment facilities). Geographically operating in the community, the family agency outpatient clinic could for the first time move toward preventive interaction with indigenous social institutions. From the latter we are beginning to see now new conjoint modalities of services based on community-professional co-sponsorship. Convenient facilities meant persons not so afflicted as to require hospitalization could easily take advantage of the human services. Clinicians reciprocally produced new theoretical and clinical methods suited to the needs of their more "normal" clientele. Visibility of the community services dispelled much of the shame attached to the services, again fostering their wider use by more ordinary folks. Services took a turn toward crisis orientation inasmuch as many such persons were functioning acceptably until the point of crisis. As a secondary effect there developed crisis approaches within the larger frame of chronic, regressed, and organic patients.

The availability of psychopharmacologicals of an instant made possible the at-home community care of persons heretofore consigned to institutions entirely for reasons of social control. They could return to their families, and in the process new kinds of partial hospitalization programs came into being. Because the patient now lived in the community, the new partial hospitalization programs were placed there also, thus accommodating another population of not-so-ill persons who previously had no such facility available to them. The critical factor here was the development of specialized treatment facilities geared to definitive services specific to a narrow range of human difficulties. With the decentralization of the asylum via a panoply of community services there was a collateral change-over from nonspecific, custodial services to increasingly specialized but also more efficacious, clinical techniques.

The Gradual Absorption of Services Within the Ordinary Rubric of Neighborhood Life

Over and above the shift in whence services emanate

is the subtle integration of the services themselves within the neighborhood's ordinary social institutions: its schools, churches, and law-enforcement and recreation agencies. These indigenous-born services not only complement the espoused goals of community mental health—crisis intervention, continuity, accessibility, community participation in the design—but also, prophetically, make feasible development of services health focused rather than illness- or treatment-oriented services.

Conceptually, health-oriented services are concerned with building healthy social institutions and sanguine family relationships propitious to individual mental health. One by-product, of course, ought to be a reduced risk of overt illness, assuming the institutions were able to provide a higher quality of interpersonal life for a considerable number of area residents. Health-oriented services operate out of consultant and educational models; institutions and families can learn less stressful, more emotionally supportive ways of participating in the larger purposes of the institution. Healthier schools or recreational facilities ought in principle to lead to healthier children, in turn beneficial to family interaction.

In the improving of our societal institutions, enabling them to fulfill more effectively their natural functions, community life should improve. From this the coping mechanisms of individuals (and institutions) should stand strengthened, reinforcing people's natural propensity to establish emotionally sustaining interpersonal networks within them. In the building of these networks—person to person, person to institution, individual to group—the author assumes a great deal of flexible, responsive, intuitive skills will be readily available to persons in general, capable of periodically meeting the crisis needs of all the network's members. Professional skills of a consultative kind are needed first to formulate the basic principles of mental health services, then in effecting the liaison on a large scale. Such skills probably necessitate the utilization of persons from the neighborhood institutions, either professionals working within their programs or lay persons benefiting from its activities, senior citizens, for example, or mothers active in a community school's PTA.

Community Service Networks

The expertise does not yet exist, yet the passage of time will bring forth this kind of know-how, if not from the traditional professions, then out of the school system, learning theorists, corrections and parole, or similar experts in group dynamics. The need is there, and the public is ready. It behooves the behavioral sciences to direct the attention of their students to the inherent career possibilities of the education, law-enforcement, and recreation fields. Practicum opportunities organized around liaison roles in neighborhoods familiar to the student would allow for understanding of the three-way relationship of a community's leaders, its basic public institutions, and the human services professions.

In the larger sense experience gained from the community mental health center program suggests that a body of expertise can be developed pertinent to instructing the community in using itself as a therapeutic tool in its own behalf. Our heritage from the behavioral sciences is overly weighted in institutional care and professional skills. Perhaps we have projected too high a premium on the professional, acute treatment elements in the delivery of human services and too little recognized the importance of community skills in potentiating personality strengths, in building more positive individual and group identities. Quite apart from the utility of therapeutic groups in aiding troubled individuals, there is a societal void, particularly in suburbia, for meaningful group relationships, collections of "normals" organized around common leisure, and social or community goals. Societal conditions inhibit their development, yet there is the larger need, too, for the social consequences of group action. A whole new human services career awaits discovery.

THE ESCALATION IN CONSUMER DEMAND

The human services turn people on. Abetted by the news media, the general public and its elected officials call on the human services for answers to the people problems besetting modern urban society. Human behaviorists are asked to "do something" about the problems of alcoholism and drugs and suicide; the range of expertise expected of the human services extends from the unrest of blacks and adolescents to the anomie of the middle classes, pornography, highway safety, the deterioration of the elderly, and underachieving children.

Perhaps the one certainty attending tomorrow's human service training is the impossibility of including in-depth expertise across the full extent of the human services. Thus, this question. With each new addition to the profession's purview, will the ensuing body of knowledge merely coalesce as another subspecialty within the existing behavioral disciplines? Or will the new service programs and special missions stimulate the inception of bright new careers cocqual with the older professions? Early childhood education is a case in point. With the phasing in of hundreds of child-care centers, our understanding of children augurs to expand exponentially. As experts emerge in these new fields, will the inevitable training programs that follow emanate from our traditional graduate schools? Taught by the new experts? Or are the new professionals likely to stimulate training programs themselves for the generation of additional professionals? The same question could as well be asked concerning areas of human behavior as diverse as the application of behavioral science to highway safety or geriatrics or the rehabilitation of prison systems. If these manifold new areas of sophisticated behavioral knowledge come to be encompassed by the traditional professions, at what point in the curriculums will they be taught? Obviously, the sum total of expertise for any of the professions transcends the masters level. Will careers such as social work choose to utilize the undergraduate years to teach beginning *clinical* competence or extend the basic professional degree to the PhD?

The graduate curriculums are already overstuffed and overlong. Will educators choose to split off career-sized specialties built around a basic clinical and theoretical core? Or will the generalist design continue throughout, with specialization left for postgraduate internship or residency training?

New Manpower Types Attuned to People and Problems Heretofore Unserved

Until now the human services have mimed the medical professions in an exaggerated concern for the psycho*pathological.* Preoccupation with discreet nosological entities, the neuroses in particular, during the developmental years of ambulatory psychotherapy fostered continued ignorance toward the afflictions of large segments of our people. (Bluntly, sophisticated treatment approaches required the painstaking elaboration of numerous clinician-researchers. Their services were hired by those affluent enough to pay them.) Our first discoveries owe special pertinence to middle-class aberrations. Public-sector services had to wait upon the return of services to community environs via the professions thrust into, first, ambulatory services and later the community mental health centers. Until now, society has been disinclined to provide professional human services to its more superfluous members—poor folks, minorities, drunks, the retarded, immigrants, and convicted criminals, to name a few. Indifferent to their plight, services were little initiated; even less energy went into research scrutiny into the nature of their foibles, hurts, or strengths. That population now stands awakened and in search of relief. Their unmet needs, so much caught up in the larger social deprivation that engulfs low-status persons, will not disappear. Their clinical status is least understood professionally, and for good reason—a half century's professional indifference.

Momentum of the last ten years suggests emergence of a collective guilt. Services will be provided these underserved peoples. New Careers has demonstrated the feasibility of services derived out of the intuitive savvy of the residents themselves. Lack of career opportunities has slowed the full utilization of such a scheme. Career lattice inauguration will, in the next half-dozen years, bring a return to the heavy use of indigenous manpower, including their continuous upgrading into professional levels. Who will be the trainers? The training institutions? Into whose bailiwick will the nontraditional types fall? If they come to form their own professional society, it is likely that they will demand that the public colleges create an independent educational base for their sustained identity (and visibility). Curriculum needs for serving these marginal peoples—the alcoholics, recidivists, and broken Appalachian peoples—are much different from traditional models. How will this content become integrated within traditional educational structures?

With the advent of decentralized ambulatory services and the gradual formation of specialized programs or agencies, lack of knowledge by professionals led to the appearance of lay-organized and lay-staffed services, Alcoholics Anonymous (AA), for example. In recent years the emphasis on indigenous workers under the aegis of Establishment professionals has overshadowed the spontaneous eruption of community services from "Goodwill Industries" and the "sheltered workshops" to college tutoring programs for inner-city youngsters, ex-addict and former convict programs, and a myriad of young adult/teen-ager endeavors in the form of crash pads, quarter-way houses, and specialized communes, none of which have professional authorship. Responding to very real, unmet needs of the people around them, these spontaneous, often short-lived enterprises are evidence of a self-help capacity endemic to many natural communities related by geography or life style. The latter, such as the coming together of college students, housing development residents, welfare mothers, and antiwar protesters, are linked by common goals and a certain continuity of emotional experience. They evince a considerable degree of true egalitarian decision-making and the tendency toward multiple leadership that enhances the group's responsivity and flexibility in the face of change.

What will be the impact of these indigenous, powerfully relevant but professionally unsophisticated change agents on the traditional service agencies? Can the orthodox professions make themselves relevant? Have our graduate schools the know-how (and courage) to develop training packages useful to these unanointed workers. Equally important, many change agents arise in areas of human misery out of which they have themselves emerged unconquered. What they lack in behavioral skills they make up for in their expertise vis-a-vis the target affliction. Alcoholism, drugs, poverty, and even just being black or a Chicano represent bodies of professional knowledge equivalent in complexity to years of graduate study. Our graduate schools have been notoriously deficient in the pursuit of expertise in many of these fields. Is it likely that new worker-types will develop independent of the behavioral sciences or enter into the orbit of the medical or education professions?

New Services for Society's Marginal Individuals

They are a challenge to the human services—the skid-row drunks, pill poppers, the minimally brain-damaged, non-readers, the impulse-ridden and compulsive gamblers, the delinquents and the self-destructive "over-eaters." Theirs is an endless list. They are the accident-prone and the seriously deaf or blind, ill reconciled to their limitations; the socially inept, the loners, the lonely hearts, and the aged, unprepared for their fate. They are not sick in the traditional sense. They have not often been eligible for services before. They get into the system, but there is nothing for them, and they drop out or are rejected by personnel ignorant of how to help.

They are the ineffective ones, the disaffected persons committed to life styles ineffably self-defeating, if not outright destructive. Their adaptive failure extends far beyond any mental or physical liabilities. They form an elusive gray area between health and torment, characterized by a sad lack of personal alternatives, as if they are forever cut off psychologically or culturally from other happier ways of living. Society has justified its indifference by assigning their ills to the category of vices and the people to the devil. Professionals, to their chagrin, found these peoples ill suited to one-to-one psychotherapy (a truth usually concurred with by the marginal persons, too).

Many in number, their rehabilitation is an enormous task. The staffing required would equal all current service programs. Cost of an all-professional thrust would be greater than society's conscience and guilt, enlightenment notwithstanding. The answer is a function of training. It is a multidimensional approach: innovative group therapies, volunteers from the ranks, a continuum of nontraditional middle professionals, professional supervisors with special knowledge in the area, sophisticated applied research to elucidate superior treatment modalities.

The challenge to human services education includes the following: (*a*) flexible, unorthodox curricula designed to upgrade the indigenous workers in the behavioral sciences; (*b*) workshops and comparable continuing education offerings to the professionals of related disciplines having need of either clinical competence or specific background on the target clientele; (*c*) new curriculum flexibility that would permit earlier specialization, special sequences of electives devoted to the target problem, and the refinement of the traditional clinical modalities to meet the specific needs of the target population (i.e., group therapy as best deployed in alcoholism groups, behavior "mod" techniques in the training of retards, etc.)

New Strategies in the Care of the Chronically Afflicted and Aging

The infirm aged face a complex of dependency relationships based on the "professional" obligations of institutional staff where once there were kinship ties. Children are dependent, too, but theirs is a dependency founded in expectation of the youngsters eventual full participation in the adult world. For the aged there is the paradox of living in the real world while the concrete roles, objects, and relationships of that world are one by one cut away. They are simultaneously integral with and extraneous to the dominant culture; the only definable role left them is to be aged. Meanwhile, a brilliant medical technology reinforced by a panoply of life-support equipment maintains life where once death proceeded, only to abandon the aged to endless years of accumulating invalidism and helplessness. More and more the elderly and their younger, medically incapacitated counterparts, sustained through organ transplant and similar artificial organ devices, must relate to the nonhuman equipment on which they are totally dependent. We have not yet measured the emotional consequences of being alive day after day *ad infinitum* by courtesy of a machine.

Science's technology in maintaining life outstrips our social skills in providing meaningful identity to such people. Their immobility in a vehicular, mobile world sorely limits their group formation. If the logistic could be solved, then, via group interaction, the mutual support of one to another might offer viable identities based on a person's value as a human being vis-a-vis other humans. Meanwhile, the number of aged increases both absolutely and relative to the total population. Confrontation with the implications of interminable life (electronically), death, and the emptiness of available life space in the interim of 10, 20 or more years may provide the human services with its first experience with *future shock.* What actions might human services education take at this time? Is chronic disease and aging to be a subspecialty of the behavioral professions? In terms of clinical modalities should teaching emphasize individual, group, or liaison approaches, or work with society at large toward building more humane environments for the incapacitated? Or should expertise in aging become the jurisdiction of nursing, rehabilitation, or other of the allied health professions? Is there a place for the training of the "indigenous" elderly for services to the aged (or in child-care centers)?

THE SEARCH FOR IDENTITY

Just being a teen-ager, or a mother, or choosing a career is "harder" these days. The options seem infinite, and the ground rules of the past grow fuzzy. Doing one's own thing presumes, first, an awareness of what that thing is. Values have become existential, and conscience, freed of the public morality, answers to a personal world view. Whereas once there was pleasure in vicarious identification with the high and mighty, now all want a "piece of the action." We live in a continuous sense of becoming, if not for real then via the mind expanders. As human opportunities multiply—careers, spouse, life style, residence—as alternatives spring open without regard to caste or class, the stresses of decision bear heavy on the young. Indeed, any individual whose present identity is in natural transition from one phase in the human life cycle to the next finds that the guidelines are either ill-defined or have disappeared "underground."

In the transition process the generation gap widens; there are few models for identification; a constellation of roles must be entertained before the old can drop away. The very complexity of society, compounded by its increasing openness to social, career, and personal mobility, makes for inner conflict. It is a kind of technological-sociological/psychic gap natural to the "melting pot America" but now at an accelerating pace. It may well become endemic to the human condition in the centuries to come. At this point there are few societal institutions geared to helping the ostensibly normal individual grow up from one role, say young adulthood, to the next, marriage or child-rearing.

For want of a better name, we have termed services specific to the problems of identity transition in normals *developmental services*. Developmental services speak to the mother, her children, grown-up, seeking a second career, the retired "doctor" in need of his "own" identity, the middle-aged adult facing the death of a parent. While the traditional human services have always faced these kinds of problems, no formal structure has yet evolved. Instead, they have tended to emerge from the indigenous social system encompassing large numbers of the transitional persons. Examples run the life-cycle gamut from the Golden Age Club to Parents Without Partners, the Welcome Wagon, adolescent crash pads, and the several parent-teacher associations.

Like the "big" sister or brother of the entering junior high student, much of the manpower for developmental services emanates from peers, or other such persons a few years older who have already successfully negotiated passage. They own many auspices; some are built into their larger establishment institutions, college counseling centers, for instance. Among the most far-sighted was an Air Force PhD program to retrain Air Force officers as junior college administrators following the post-Korean War cutbacks. Women's Lib augurs to develop mutual-help programs of this sort; a variety of Chicano and "black caucus" groups have similarly developed them.

Training Implications of Developmental Services

Most of the manpower will flow into these indigenous programs out of the institutions themselves, for example, college seniors working with freshmen of that college or high school seniors elsewhere. Most are motivated, empathic individuals who drift in for six months or a year or two, moving on to their real careers or into higher education often with little thought about a human services career. They are a valuable potential manpower resource. College might seek to develop innovative workshops and service-oriented curricula suited to these quasi-professional volunteers. Admission on advanced standing to human service programs and vigorous recruitment efforts are in order.

Professionals of a unique kind are needed, too. The lion's share of the workers will be volunteers, untutored and unpaid; the professional's role is as consultant, plus undergirding the groups toward fulfillment of its helping potential. The professional's job will be to help the group of volunteers grow up as a "professional" organization even as the workers help their client-fellows to mature. By temper the professionals will have to enjoy serving *through* the volunteers rather than directly providing care, or even running the show. They will be responsive in accepting professional input, but the administration and decision-making will probably remain with the parent institution. Education of these consultant types is a delicate matter. They will need practicum experiences within ongoing developmental services and in comparable volunteer organizations. A stint in Vista, work as a labor union organizer or civil rights change agent, or participating in a citizen's environmental quality "clean-up campaign" would all be useful.

Consumer participation—students in student counseling, the aged in a senior-citizen center—offers another avenue for training. Programs growing out of a neighborhood base will in remaining stationary suffer a continuing inflow and exodus of volunteers. Any permanency must come from a few relatively permanent lay staff who ought to have professionally run continuing education or work-study opportunities.

University Operation of Developmental Service Programs

Because these cooperative ventures span institution-consumer-professional relations dissimilar to traditional hierarchical, authoritarian service structures, it would be useful for interested academic institutions to actually adopt one or more upstart programs, "cosigning" their activities, if invited. Graduate students would stand in for the consultant-adviser professionals as part of their practicum arrangements. (Colleges learn best by doing, too.) College and faculty should allow themselves the risk of participation in a program not under their control and emanating from the community to meet espoused community objectives. There is no way to galvanize a new generation of trainees to do what their teachers can not.

Program-Centered Services Targeted to Specific Population Needs

The widening parameters of contemporary human services call for experts, persons owning very specialized competencies that, in total, encompass a body of expertise beyond the limited purview of any one of the traditional disciplines. Thus, this paradox: (*a*) Sophisticated services require large numbers of well-trained specialists, yet (*b*) clients need personalized, inclusive (generalist) services predicated on longitudinal continuity of personnel and multicontact family and institutional relationships (multiplying the range of problems brought to the specialists).

Resolution to the generalist-specialist paradox demands a shift toward program-oriented services founded on team-delivered services to a broadly defined target population—children, for example, or the aged; or an entire slum, homogeneous by virtue of the common effects of the environs on people. By delivering services to a population homogeneous at least in its clinical requirements, the team can develop highly specialized expertise specific to the given population, while the natural heterogeneity of the large target group fosters generalist growth in the clinicians. Target programs are by definition interdisciplinary. Exactly because no single profession knows everything about children or aging, the services targeted to them must derive from all of the behavioral sciences. Second, there is the hypothesis that for a given target population an explicit body of expertise exists having special relevance to the target aspects of their human services needs: interdisciplinary teams, combining a spectrum of professional skills with long experience in dealing with that constellation of difficulties natural to the target group. The team carries general sophistication in the target problem: children's services, geriatric services, alcoholism services, emergency and crisis intervention, retardation; individual members of the team also possess those clinical skills unique to their human services discipline.

Target programs are not ultraspecialized services aimed at serving limited facets of the individual or the family. They are intended to provide a broad range of services to persons encompassed by the target problem or common denominator. They can be a function of phase in the life-cycle, geography, or diagnostic category. They offer primary care, but primary care within the larger context of the target problem as it might affect the overall individual or family constellation. Depression is ubiquitous. Yet the manifestations and causes of depression in children are different from those in the aged; different, too, when there is an underlying psychosis. The team serving children ought to own particular skills in handling depression as it appears in the child. Yet they are in no way restricted to depression, or children, for that matter.

Until now, specialization in the traditional disciplines has been intradisciplinary. In specializing, the professional kept within the circumscribed perspective of his discipline, adding to his knowledge in depth along ever-narrower confines of that discipline. Psychiatrists, for example, choosing to specialize in children, study from the perspective of psychiatric practice; psychologists seek to understand the child from their own, albeit overlapping psychologist's gestalt, educators and learning theorists from yet others. Impetus to further refinement of the target-program approaches to human services delivery is a likely consequence of federal and state efforts at cost containment. Ostensibly, the use of expert teams deployed around a specific target problem can provide superior care at lower costs out of their greater familiarity with the clinical idiosyncracies of the target population and/or their common afflictions. Because of the concentration on the larger theme, a number of clinicians along a continuum of experience and academic preparation might be deployed, each according to client responsibilities appropriate to their level of training. Everybody on the team need not be a consummate PhD professional; a variety of middle professionals will carry the more routine services safely and more economically.

Development of numbers of health maintenance organizations under the aegis of national health insurance and the federal "carrot" will accelerate conversion to health-team delivery systems in medicine. Inasmuch as mental health care will most likely be subsumed under the HMO rubric, it is critical that such services not regress but derive from a broad community mental health conceptual base. Were mental health care to become a mere one-shot psychiatric consultation in the face of acute psychosis or a suicide attempt, then the gains of the whole community mental health movement stand at risk. The team concept, however, permits continued pioneering in the preventative and developmental areas, and at a cost society can afford. Teams allow for continuity of care, day in and day out. Client, family, and community groups, in relating to a team rather than specific individuals, are guaranteed a team member knowledgeable about their family or personal situation. Similarly, the team spans a considerable expertise, bridging into the community on the one hand for jobs, foster care, and information and into the various agencies, governmental offices, and specialized professionals on the other. The implications for education are profound.

Education, which has always been organized around the historical profession rather than its academic or clinical content, per se, might move to a more interdisciplinary base. Thus, the graduate schools have in recent years tried to appease the demands for greater student specialization and to widen simultaneously the breadth of its horizons. Curricula, as a result, grow longer in duration and extend over an ever-wider range of services and techniques, in the meanwhile expecting in-depth expertise in certain of the specialties. Education above the entry professional level that emphasizes target programs would facilitate use of curriculum modules, units of which might well be taken across traditional institutional and discipline boundaries. Thus, a given professional already at the baccalaureate level might choose a graduate curriculum incorporating psychology, sociology, clinical care of children (taught by an interdisciplinary team), psychological testing, and psychopharmacology. Graduate education, particularly at the upper levels, would show a blurring of professional boundaries, with greater flexibility in the range of subjects pursued. In the process the traditional professions may themselves fragment, first accommodating to newer areas of service, then, as these mature, splitting apart to reform as several entirely new professions. Another alternative is the Michigan State University model. Michigan rejected the usual dichotomy of graduate and undergraduate structures, likewise any division of the social sciences into isolated clinical and so-called basic science departments, and created an omnibus college of social sciences. The single social science structure housed the several undergraduate and graduate programs in sociology, anthropology, psychology, and also, notably, the school of social work and the clinical psychology program. Students are free to build their curricula across departmental lines so long as the whole makes pedagogic sense. This kind of multidepartmental, individuated education promises to become more common with students, their faculty adviser literally selecting a portfolio of courses fitted to the individual interests and needs of students. The old identity of the orthodox professions may be lost in the melting pot. Separate schools of social work, and psychology, vocational rehabilitation, school counseling, and early childhood development will merge within the administration of a single university faculty of the human services and behavioral sciences.

2. THE CHANGING DIMENSIONS OF PROFESSIONAL INTERVENTION

THE MYTH OF HIGH STANDARDS OF PROFESSIONAL MANPOWER

There was a time when a handful of human services professionals, together with their legions of nonprofessional helpmates, could staff the asylums and welfare apparatus of the day, but no longer. The promise of community mental health cannot be realized by any such motley constellation of manpower. Active treatment, far-ranging services, prevention, these are synonymous with large numbers of sophisticated practitioners. Definitive services, in contrast to custodial care, are time consuming of professional skills, demanding longitudinal continuity and multiple contacts within a problem family or institution. If the human services are to be manned by all-professional teams as we have traditionally defined them, then there is not money enough in the nation to pay for them. We could not recruit so large a reservoir of professionals, nor have we a fraction of the graduate educational machinery with which to train them.

Either we develop alternative manpower resources commensurate with new patterns of utilization, or we write off hope of services to major segments of the American population for this century. It is no charity to the poor that we "protect" them from any but the most orthodox professionally delivered services when in so doing we deprive them of services entirely. The grave danger here is not that unschooled and unqualified clinicians will be loosed upon a helpless public but that by holding to antiquated or unreachable goals we thwart the invention and training of nontraditional manpower that might do the job.

The Myth of Equal Care

Equality of services for all is nonsense. Equality of care is a patent fiction enjoyed by nobody. Professionals are not equal, less so as regards a given clinical situation. Professionals differ in competence. And when differences of training or extent of clinical practice (or the specificity of that practice to the problem at hand) are considered, arguments for "equality" turn specious. Equality of care means merely equal access to minimal standards of professional competence. It is a pragmatic thing, valuable, but tied to the nitty-gritty realities of regional norms, social conventions, and the state of the art. At best, equality requires that certain minimum qualifications be met in keeping with the clinical role assumed at a given place and time. Reasonable qualifications, of course, depend on the nature of the service, the potential complications, and the proximity of consultation. Standards are a function of the service to be rendered not the larger identity of the practitioner. (While doctors draw blood—it is part of their identity—there is no reason why other qualified persons should not as well, and that without harm to high standards. That the poor man's arm is punctured by the nurse-wielded needle and the rich man's by the physician's is not unequal care so long as the nurse is equally proficient.) Standards are task-specific. They presume training, experience, and talent equal to the immediate clinical task; there is no need for universal excellence across the field.

Standards change. If society is changing, then standards must adapt, too. As the health maintenance organization appears on the neighborhood scene, manpower standards must relate to the new delivery styles.

Manpower utilization standards must reflect the needs of the community as a whole from the vantage of actual resources. They are not supposed to afford any special protection to the middle classes or prestigious clinician. Standards are for everybody. Above all, standards should be written so as to encourage prudent, controlled experiment in new modes of manpower use.

Excessively high manpower standards are counterproductive. They are harmful to minorities, adding to the maldistribution problem. Standards that seem unattainable or too expensive to the body politic are soon ignored, or else they are subverted into "paper" standards, the public lulled into false confidence by meaningless rhetoric. Initial hard-hitting federal Medicare staffing standards, for example, were boldfacedly disobeyed by public institutions everywhere. An instance of paper standards might be many of the state hospital residency programs. Under the guise of their being psychiatrists-in-training, vast numbers of foreign-trained, non-English-speaking, often unlicensed physicians are used in lieu of more expensive human service professionals. (In the process educational accrediting bodies are blackmailed. Inasmuch as the foreign-trained MDs are literally the entire treatment staff, albeit trainees in "paper" curricula, their loss would leave no one to tend the patients. If the institution's accreditation were suspended, all residents would leave as a body in search of an approved program.)

Would not lesser standards, standards less hung up on the physician, lead to higher levels of patient care? Were institutions free to choose the most talented clinician regardless of their professional pedigree, service could improve without increases in costs. For whose protection are they rigidly maintained?

Who is to judge the "rightness" of standards? Who is to set them? Is this the sole prerogative of the professional societies? Government agencies? Elected officials? Failure to apply private-sector standards to the realities of public mental health has now brought the courts into the standard setting business. In *Wyatt* v. *Stickney* U.S.

District Judge F. M. Johnson ordered the Alabama commissioner to guarantee "appropriate and adequate treatment" to all persons confined to his care. Staffing patterns and qualifications are now purview of the court. Interestingly, the judiciary may be less constrained than the human services in "legitimizing" utilization of newer, nontraditional manpower. If the human services do not hurry with career lattices by the mid-1970s the courts may well do it for us.

Standards that define the academic prerequisites appropriate to a given human services role are no better than their appreciation of the community's total services needs as judged by the unnecessary wastage of the people's innate potential. People's needs, when obvious and long unmet, are as much violations of manpower standards as any direct affront in the hiring of unqualified personnel. The certification of PhD psychologists and psychiatrists in a region, for example, devoid of children's services is hypocrisy. False values take priority. Take psychoanalysis; it is not illogical to require a decade's professional study pursuant to its practive. Yet to then demand training of similar depth for everybody in the behavioral sciences is absurdity. The practice of outreach mental health from neighborhood centers must be according to very different training criteria, validated within the practice of community services, not psychoanalysis, institutional psychiatry, or any other subspecialty.

Perhaps qualifying standards should derive specifically from the clinical activities to be practiced, not because of the generic discipline customarily assigned to them. The job, not the history of the profession, should determine standards. Roles are shuffled with each new service approach. Certification needs to be broken into smaller units. A given cluster of service tasks should delineate a parallel constellation of qualifying prerequisites. Dissection of the traditional professional identities into role segments would allow the analogus restructuring of curricula into matching career lattices. With the further growth of the human services into wider realms it is imperative that these new clusters of expertise own their own separate manpower qualifications. The generalist's "bag" is already overstuffed. Ever stretching the beginning worker's scope of supposed competence merely adds to the duration of training without concomitant improvement in the quality of services. Since persons can practice in only one broad field at a time, there is no point to universal mastery even before initial employment. Training might well be more diversified at all training levels. Why cannot students approach a common core of human services expertise by way of many different practicum concentrations? Their training completed, persons might elect for certification in selected, limited portions of the total profession, their practice circumscribed accordingly. A rough example exists in the psychiatry and neurology boards. Individuals choose certification, depending on their specific training sequence, in psychiatry, neurology, or both. Graduate students, no longer obligated to "know everything," could, in actuality, pursue a more free-spirited generalism. Thus, the physician aiming at an analytic career could pursue intensive psychotherapy skills as a resident along with elements of, say, community mental health or liaison psychiatry in sufficient depth to be useful clinically.

What if we continue as in the past? With consumer demands escalating in numbers, seeking services and over a wider range of expertise, current manpower deficits will worsen. As it is, the rural and urban poor and a considerable number of the middle class are without access to sustained treatment. Academicians, in their concern for the students' educational completeness, are wont to forget this basic manpower rule: the greater the expertise required of entry-level students before employment (the longer the duration of schooling), the less the number recruited into the program, or graduated. More strenuous programs require greater admissions' selectivity; less students apply. And the more arduous, the longer a given curriculum, the higher the attrition rate.

Where this greater complexity is necessary for adequate performance, then a burdensome, lengthy course of studies is worth the price. And therein lies the rub. Exactly how much of the contemporary doctorate level programs are truly required prior to beginning professional roles, assuming assignment of lesser-trained persons to roles narrower in scope? Disastrous as it might be to throw away standards merely for the sake of numbers, so, too, is it folly to exclude many of journeyman stature out of a compulsive need for educational completion. Equally wrong, in the author's mind, would be the unnecessary elimination of potentially adroit clinicians because of overlengthy, uneconomic curricula that, in their content, are divorced from the real needs of public-sector clients and the evolving network of community centers.

Recruitment into the human services, as into any other occupation, is not by chance. Recruitment is a variable very much tied to mundane factors like the career's visibility, its pay range, the prerequisite educational requirements, and the likely return to the student for his educational and experiential investment. The human services manpower pool is obedient to the operation of the overall manpower market. What the human service worker is worth, reciprocally, is tied to the manner of his utilization, the efficiency with which his academic and intuitive skills can be mobilized in service to clients for which they, or somebody, will pay. That level of remuneration, measured against the worker's own investment in his training, must stand comparable to other like occupations, or the flow of persons into human services careers will inevitably decline. Academic relevance, then, is the turnkey to adequacy in the manpower reservoir.

A Multiplicity of Human Services Models

Community mental health is its own thing. It is not intensive psychoanalytically oriented psychotherapy. The latter, however, is the prestige role, and its practice bears the highest per-hour level of remuneration of any of the human service activities. Psychoanalysis, along with its psychotherapy derivatives, has long been not only the model par excellence to psychiatrists but also has acted to mold the practice of psychology, social work, and the other human services professions. Secondary to the special place of analysis has been primacy of private practice as the structural model for services delivery. Despite the fact that the vast majority of human services dispensed—this year, or any year—stems from multiprofessional organizations, the ideal of private practice, particularly on a solo practitioner basis, remains "top dog." Family agencies, state hospitals, social welfare departments, and school counseling notwithstanding, clinical education in the human services thinks one-to-one analytic psychotherapy from a private-practice perspective. Sad consequence has been the relative downplaying of therapeutic modalities (and their research counterparts) more amenable to institutional, agency, and community mental health services (and their team-delivered service mechanisms).

For the last 25 years the National Institute of Mental Health (NIMH) has poured nearly two billion dollars into human services training. The behavioral science manpower pool has expanded severalfold in that quarter century. Judged by numbers graduated, the NIMH efforts have been rip-snorting successes. Quite apart from the additional psychiatrists generated, large numbers of social work, psychology, and psychiatric nursing personnel owe their university-sponsored education to NIMH funding. Within the university centers one model predominated: analytic psychotherapy. In fact, the only "brand" of human services that could pay its own way was private practice; hence, psychotherapy oriented and geared to the psychological and sociological convenience of the middle classes. Whereas public institutions were always overcrowded, understaffed, and the staff underpaid, the middle-class psychotherapy clientele paid in hard cash. Opposite fiscal mechanisms for public and private sectors has had a profound (and little-recognized) impact on the nature of the science itself, its theoretical base and seeming indifference to group and institutional modalities.

Thus, though the manpower goals of the NIMH initiated in the mid-1960s have been achieved, no renaissance in public manpower has ensued. Public-sector agencies remain short on professionals, particularly psychiatrists, but loss of superior persons to private practice, research, and university teaching identities is found in all of the disciplines. To no little degree the very visibility that NIMH monies gave to the behavioral sciences through its research and teaching and trainee stipend programs contributed also to the paucity of public-sector manpower, thus enfeebling the selfsame community mental health movement that their service division takes as the NIMH's chief purpose.

That this has happened is no fault of psychoanalysis, per se, nor does it negate the needs and rights of those it has served to profit from its benefits. Merely, it is time we wake up to this truth: No amount of increase in the numbers of traditional professional manpower will much alter the maldistribution problem with its attendant crisis in services to the poor, minorities, rural folk, children, or the aged. Other manpower, drawn from other societal tracks, trained initially by our undergraduate colleges, and attuned to new services models, is needed. Traditional manpower types are needed, too, and always have been. It is fruitless to wait for augmented training programs to generate an excess of professionals in hopes that the overflow will trickle down to the public sector. The drought never ends. The private sector will conceivably develop surplus professionals in the 1970s, yet the inner-city and rural public programs will not benefit. New graduates will merely take less prestigious, lower-paying peripheral positions in high-status areas, waiting for their chance.

Nor would it be a good thing. It makes no more sense to generate community mental health manpower as a by-product of intensive psychotherapy training than to make instant analysts of new careerists.

THE MANPOWER IMPLICATIONS OF COMMUNITY SERVICES

The pressure for additional human services professionals (and the academic centers to train them) is predicated upon the unceasing transition from custodial and welfare approaches to active, definitive treatment programs and, concurrently, community education and preventative programs.

Staff serving in the nation's mental health facilities, hospitals, clinics, and day centers total some 333,000 persons; of these 12,800 are psychiatrists, and 7,000 are psychologists (masters and above). Taken altogether, they average one psychiatrist to 26 clients; the psychologist/client ratio is 1 to 48. That is a far cry from public custodial institutions. Unfortunately, all but the tiniest fraction of Americans who receive mental health care are recipients of public (state) services. Many operate "efficiently" on one-tenth of that *average* professional/client ratio. In some there are as few as one psychiatrist per 1,000 clients. But no matter, there is not much for the highly polished psychotherapist to do in the typical "total" institution. The gamut of custodial care encompasses: (*a*) hostelry services and grounds keeping, (*b*) management of the inmates social controls, (*c*) provision by the staff for the patients' social, leisure, vocational, and religious needs *en masse, (d)* mediating between the inmate and the institution, and (*e*) between the inmate and the "outside" world vis-a-vis matters otherwise prerogative of the individual—deciding on a job, seeing family, or voting, and (*f*) administration and record-keeping.

Not a very sanguine environment for years of education and specialized interpersonal skills. The monolithic asylums may have a thousand staff members yet charge none of them with tackling the mental, physical, or societal factors that necessitated the clients' hospitalization in the first place or impede their return home. Custodial institutions are for nurturing; staff of a loving disposition are sufficient. (If society wanted better conditions for its castoffs, there would be no custodial-type institutions.) Definitive intervention in the life of a person or a group demands specialized interpersonal skills, multiple skills appropriate to the many faces of human behavior. *Sine qua non* of the custodial institution is its utter sameness of approaches, its mass application of uniform solutions to the varied needs of diverse populations. With the asylum's professional staff tied to administration and the enforcement of social policies (sometimes, too, research and teaching), the human services themselves are little considered.

Cause is not the manpower shortage. With institutional energies and budget absorbed by the costs of food and clothing, buildings, housekeeping, bureacucracy, and the surveillance of inmates, there are no monies remaining for definitive services even if the professionals were available for hire.

Conversely, active community-based ambulatory and home-care services reduce the dependency on custodial institutions by forestalling chronicity and by augmenting self-help and family-care capabilities. Alternatives to hospitalization—foster care, halfway houses, "crash pads"—protect hospital treatment programs by inhibiting the indiscriminate "dumping" of people on overcrowded institutions. Strong community programs multiply therapeutic options, thereby making feasible services individuated to client and family needs. They reduce the flow of admissions into custodial institutions, particularly admissions unwarranted by the clinical picture, stemming from a dearth of alternatives. The presence of community resources fosters earlier discharge of patients; higher discharge rates and shorter hospital stays result. Total per-patient hospitalization costs decrease (albeit per-diem costs rise). State hospital populations decline. Regional nurturing costs decline proportionately. Budget and staff are freed, becoming available for redeployment in active treatment and rehabilitation programs within the institution or outside in new community ventures. A self-regenerating spiral develops in which improved community resources are translated into a reduced custodial census, heightened hospital programs, and further census declines. Savings in turn facilitate amplified neighborhood services. At this point further improvement hinges on a massive injection of new manpower sufficient to actuate the neighborhood facilities on a region-wide basis. (A few scattered model community programs do not make a dent in the typical asylum's huge catchment base.)

Emptying the state hospitals merely to lower their census is not being suggested, however. Without viable community resources, discharge, per se, solves nothing. What have been the institution's hostelry and nurturing functions are well within the ken of ordinary community folks and the commonplace neighborhood organizations. Feeding, bathing, watching over the marginal or regressed person, and introducing a modicum of family and social interaction are better accomplished, for less money, via a family context. Where kin are unavailable, foster families, community volunteers, group homes, and church homes in the client's own neighborhood are much preferable to the asylum.

Sustaining clients (and their care-taking families) in their own world at an optimal—for them—level of function is contingent upon quality outreach and ambulatory services—psychological, social, pharmacological, and medical. Traditional psychiatric OPDs do not suffice. Most require a healthier patient. They do not have the flexibility of approach to cut themselves loose from the center's apron strings to range into the community relying on these indigenous resources to maintain clients. The OPDs' range of services is usually too strictured to serve persons more needful of reading skills than intensive psychotherapy. If the general public is to assume new, quasi-professional roles in the care of the elderly, the retarded, and the chronically afflicted, then back-up professional help is imperative. Crisis intervention and home consultation, family education, volunteer homemaker teams, and jitney-type transportation must be readily available, certainly on a same-day emergency-call basis, plus evenings and weekends to a limited degree. Patients and their families must be known to the center staff; hence, nothing occurs until the facility is built and the staff hired to man it. (Even then people take time to understand proper use of an outreach facility.)

Ordinary families are not geared to handle major medical or psychiatric crises. In a few days they go to pieces. While families can well serve the crotchety or disoriented invalid so long as his condition is stabilized, this tolerance crumbles under stress. Within a week the patient has been abandoned to the state hospital. Once admitted, regression sets in, and the family's guilt mounts; hard-won community ties must again be established over months, while few return to the same home. Time is of the essence. If, within a brief period, scattered moments of acute disruption can be ameliorated, then families are prone to carry on for years. Staving off hospitalization can be life-saving to the client and tax-saving to the citizens of thousands of dollars. The principle of community-based nurturing is fine. Its actuation in fact presumes prior existence of a system of diversified, accessible, and "likable" ambulatory-care facilities offering, additionally, home care, rehabilitation, physical therapy, adult education, and leisure and social services—no mean task indeed.

A greater challenge is manpower. Considerable expertise of a professional kind is required, yet the round-the-clock schedules plus the need for a sizable cadre right from the start precludes constituting all-professional outreach teams, neither are these roles suited to the state hospital's psychiatric aides or LPNs.

Transition to Active Treatment Modalities: The Multiplier Effect on Manpower Needs

Decentralization, along with the translation of previously custodial goals into definitive, often-specialized intervention in the client's life, creates a manifold increase in manpower requirements. Journeymen practitioners, not nonprofessionals, who are competent over a wide spectrum of behavioral skills, are required. A heterogeneity of ethnic, racial, and educational backgrounds is important, their roots roughly paralleling the demography of the region served. Yet the very size of the manpower pool and the time urgency to their readiness concurrent with the NIMH centers' phase in, precludes their education by traditional graduate school means.

Because the new services are targeted as much to prevent chronicity as restore community life to those afflicted, its service goals entail much that is remedial—educationally, socially, and vocationally. Community organization work and liaison responsibilities with the back-up institution and related medical affiliates, not to mention the more orthodox therapies, in sum spell an enormous range of behavioral expertise. Obviously, no single training program could generate manpower so all-knowledgeable, certainly not at a middle professional level of education. The answer lies in the development of many overlapping manpower types encompassing, as a group, the total services spectrum. Their expertise, in the field, would not emanate from any single staff person but would derive instead from their corporate capabilities. Similarly, their deployment would be as teams having complementary skills.

Admittedly, any system of ambulatory mental health care ought to own wide mastery of the behavioral arts. But it is not at all necessary that maximum expertise reside at the clinician-client interface. Primary care requires the generalist's people-centered concern and continuity over time. Ultrasophistication, so long as it can be freely tapped by the staff as a whole, may judiciously be centralized or flow from outside consultants. It is enough that personnel in the immediate services arena as a team coordinate their activities with the same family and collectively know where to find the answers (or help in emergencies). The need today is for bridge personnel, individuals in primary care able to bridge the gap separating the amassed clinical expertise of the behavioral sciences and the difficulties of application in the given clinical instance. The latter, so much contingent on the ethnic, racial, and socioeconomic commonality of worker and client, and the nuances of their communications, may well proceed more efficiently mediated through the bridge person rather than specialist to client. Knowledge to be usable clinically must translate into forms meaningful to clients, thence disseminated by persons and in words acceptable to the client's sense of himself—a role for the bridge person. Reciprocally, the conjoint nature of the services, incorporating neighborhood and center activities, ensures the flow of information back through the bridge person from a variety of neighborhood inputs. Translated by the bridge worker, this time into the professional's lexicon, this feedback, perhaps community vision is vital to the professional's understanding of the human services process. Without it, relevance of the programs is inherently abridged.

Vigorous community programs hold promise of reducing the nation's custodial population of 500,000 by half or more, provided that the new middle professional manpower is ready; concurrently, the return of some 150,000 incapacitated individuals to the community will free between 75,000 to 100,000 nonprofessionals working in the custodial institutions. Their training for, and utilization in, our forthcoming community programs is a major challenge to both our educational and services planners. Meanwhile, the public, potential clients, nonprofessional workers, and the labor unions, public officials, and personnel offices all must be educated to accept the larger societal role, accommodating to the unfamiliar presence of chronicity in their midst and also learning how to use the unfolding system of outreach services soon upon us.

Community Mental Health as a Network of Complementary, Interdigitating Services

Community services would seem destined to proliferate in number over the 1970s while simultaneously differentiating in function. Form, structure, staffing, and purposes of future community services will, chameleonlike, vary much, depending on the clientele served. They will also interdigitate to form functional networks. Despite decentralization and heterogeneity of design and administration they will coordinate along a continuum of operational levels from one worker to another, as through, equally, a system-wide, unified program for in-service education. Gravitation of the centers toward target program operations will likely lead to a division of labor within a region's centers. Consequently, the quality of services at any one center will reflect the integrity of the network as a whole. Adequate numbers of operational centers, their geographic balance and availability of subsidiary back-up hospitals, relative to the total community needs, are the turnkey to the success of any one center. Efficient operation of any one center is a function of at least the following components: (*a*) a system for community dialogue and the education of persons and institutions in the basics of sound family mental health practices; *(b)* a related complex of neighborhood-accessible ambulatory and outreach services tied to (*c*) neighborhood, relevant, preventative, school, law-enforcement, and probation programs, *(d)* back-up partial hospital and general hospital psychiatric services, and (*e*) regional specialty, diagnostic, and long-term support facilities; and *(f)* the sum of these need articulate with neighborhood health maintenance or comparable family health care centers.

3. OPENING UP NEW MANPOWER RESOURCES

CAVEATS FROM THE LINCOLN HOSPITAL NEW CAREERS EXPERIMENT

Thus far we have examined manpower from the perspective of services needs. The intent of Chapters 1 and 2 was to derive manpower and training recommendations out of the nature of future services facilities and their programs. Necessity for augmented manpower resources was tied to predicted expansion of services, facilities, their decentralization and growing proximity to the community, the coalescence of services networks, and widening parameters of services to be offered. Criteria were clinical. Compared with the present, how many persons having what kinds of skills (and training) will be needed, based on anticipated patterns of services delivery? The evidence suggested the need not only for additional professionals but more importantly the elaboration of new manpower types, persons with training, background, and experience fitted along a continuum of competence levels and possessing diversified clinical skills appropriate to new, perhaps unorthodox neighborhood services modalities.

Manpower needs, as seen by the services facilities and their planners, is one thing; actually recruiting people, then training them is another. Manpower needs, no matter how desperate, cannot by themselves generate the personnel to fill those needs. This can be exasperating. Jobs going begging, horrendous vacancy rates, yet nobody is interested. Crippling shortages of personnel, per se, attract no new recruits, entice no new academic programs, afford little luster to the career's public and professional image. If anything, severe shortages drive people from the field; less young persons are willing to consider its career prospects for themselves. Manpower entering a given occupation hinges on many factors: regional attitudes, pay, competing opportunities, prestige of the job, chances for advancement. Is the job worth having? Where does it lead to? Would you recommend the career to your own son of daughter?

The Myth of "Enough" Professionals in the Human Services

If there is to be manpower at all in the human services of the 1970s, then educators, clinicians, and government officials must be brutally frank with themselves and the public. Dishonesty here comes in several forms. Ignorance is one of them. So long as the facts of recruitment, manpower maldistribution, and the clear signs of unmet human needs are conveniently ignored, then "wrong" solutions can in good conscience be recommended, reality be damned. Neither is it honest to project into the future the manpower realities of a generation ago. It is a brand-new ball game. Planning must take account of the societal and professional future as it affects people's career choices.

First, despite the major manpower gains of the two decades past, the production of professionals has fallen short of actual needs, measured by growth in the amount of human services distributed annually. Transition to active, community-based programs, plus the burgeoning of preventative, developmental, child care and the behavioral science-related fields, augurs a decade of manpower crisis, its beginning currently masked by the 1969-71 economic downturn and the Viet Nam war.

Following quickly upon any resurgence of business

prosperity and even minimal reordering of national priorities will come an avalanche of consumer demands for new human services. Of a sudden, then, manpower requirements will jump, services in effect striving to catch up for the sluggish early 1970s. Interestingly, as the nation shifts away from manufacturing jobs toward the delivery of services, recruitment into the human service professions relatively declines. That is, as a plethora of competing service careers burst on the employment scene, the human services lost its pre-eminence. Moreover, the predictable increase in facilities' staff promises parallel increases in operating costs. Rising personnel costs act negatively on salary levels, inhibiting the use of remuneration as a recruitment lever.

Second, the nature of the human services professional, his sophisticated research skills, specialization, and erudition, and nearly a decade's pursuit of higher education preclude his deployment in journeymen outreach roles. PhDs and MD psychiatrists will, in the future, continue to be no less valuable in supervisory, teaching, research, and consultant roles, but their use as front-line primary-care personnel is wasteful economically and inefficient clinically. The price of the PhD's training is too dear, their number too few, and their training too long to justify primary mental health care roles for them. The penalty for overtraining is premature obsolescence of hard-won skills. For many, graduate school becomes a poor personal investment.

How then are sufficient professionals to be mobilized? Answer: It connot be done! Like it or not, it is time we face up to the reality of our educational and recruitment limitations. To push on doggedly in the attempt to generate enough professionals to meet the needs of all Americans is only to invite disaster. Viable alternatives exist. If traditional academic mechanisms—college, graduate schools, clinical internships, and residencies—and traditional sources of recruitment are unequal to the nation's needs, whence is the manpower and human services expertise to come?

Expanding the Recuritment Base into Human Service Careers

Any significant growth in the supply of human services professionals is contingent upon attracting categories of persons heretofore disinterested in, or *de facto* excluded from, human services careers or their academic procursors. In view of the public relations campaigns of the past 20 years, the NIMH trainee stipends, and the whole thrust of the "New Society" and its media reverberations, there is little expansion possible out of our customary sources of graduate school candidates. Fortunately, graduate schools represent only a portion of the young adult population owning the potential for success in the human service professions.

Six major population categories offer promise for the future:

1. Non-professional workers—persons currently working as hospital aides via work-study programs and selective, stepwise advancement of those *qualified.*
2. Indigenous community workers—recruitment of persons indigenous to rural and inner-city areas with provisions for remedial and behavioral science education appropriate to their life style, intuitive strengths, and academic deficits.
3. "Second-careerists"—persons such as housewives, retired military, "late-bloomers," and others who have "outgrown" their first careers and are in search of another role more suited to their then-mature interests and background.
4. Related professionals—professionals employed in any of the health, teaching, corrections, law-enforcement, and recreation fields inclined to add behavioral expertise to their own professional know-how as means to the more effective practice of their primary profession.
5. Human services professionals—retraining of existing professionals, particularly those employed outside the behavioral fields or long inactive, affording instruction and practicum in the newer community modalities of their profession.

6. Associate degree (AD) and baccalaureate college students—that large body of "middle America" young persons who, though interested in two or four years of college and jobs of a professional nature, simply do not aspire to graduate school or those careers customarily requiring graduate education for beginning practice. (In numbers, this group represent the majority of today's young adults.)

Before examining these categories in more detail, it might be well to look at what happens when innovative, nontraditional education enters the existing human services training and patient-care scene. The Lincoln Hospital Mental Health Service's experiment in the training of new careerists is an example from which to learn. The Lincoln experiment offers in microcosm many of the inevitable incongruities that follow the attempt to integrate side by side the traditional and nontraditional training programs (and the graduates that flow from them). The challenge, of course, is not merely to generate a new breed of manpower but the larger task of developing an overall service-training system within which the several categories can productively, creatively work together toward common goals, the special skills of one group complementing voids in another.

The Lincoln Hospital Mental Health Services' New Careers Training Program

In the years 1964-67 the Lincoln Hospital's neighborhood service center operations to some 25,000 South Bronx (NYC) poor included a pioneering New Careers training program for the recruitment and utilization of indigenous community workers drawn from the population served. Applicants were "home-grown." Area residents were among the poorest, least-educated, least-employed, and underserved peoples living in the slum enclaves of the city. In selecting their 1967 class of 20 candidates from 200 applicants, the Lincoln trainers wisely eschewed the usual academic selections criteria. The large number of applicants, however, allowed the elimination of all but the most superior candidates.

Superior by which criteria? The area's racial, language, and ethnic diversity—as much black as Puerto Rican as white—the transiency of its population, and the high levels of school transfers, dropouts, and family disorganization rendered meaningless school records or standard intelligence tests. Nonetheless, the Lincoln trainers knew that certain individuals living in the neighborhood were held in high esteem for their ability to help persons in difficulty. What common characteristics identified the "helpers"?

Not pretending to know the nature of this special gift in some, the Lincoln staff sought to devise admission's approaches that might offer clues. Candidates were interviewed in groups of 10 to 12, including two staff persons. Sessions were informal. Candidates were moved to discuss neighborhood problems and the ways of its various peoples, individual problems, and group differences. Selection was made by the faculty as a whole, including new careerists from previous years, listening together to audiotapes of the candidate's sessions. Performance was evaluated in terms of an applicant's style of relating to others—neighbors, staff, persons of the same or opposite sex, or of another race. Willingness of the applicant to get involved within the group, constructive interaction, and the responsiveness of group members to the applicant scored high. Equally important was the applicant's manner of formulating personal or neighborhood troubles and the conceptual processes used in offered solutions.

Education of the Lincoln mental health aides was an apprenticeship. Instructional format was tutorial, albeit as a preceptor-group dyad. Authority was played down. Behavioral science content was presented informally, typically as an exchange of ideas between colleagues. Clinical approaches that seemed to gain group consensus were reinforced by role-playing and rap sessions on the individual's performance in the role. Most clinical supervision flowed from peers. Practicum work in the Lincoln Service Center was introduced early, the trainees working under supervision in twos and threes. Faculty and supervisors were of the highest caliber, a byproduct of the center's medical school parentage and national reputation. The center's director Harris Peck noted:

> We tried in training them to make some contribution to the competence and skills they already possessed. . . . In addition, the aides themselves, in the course of their work, are becoming increasingly knowledgeable about and competent in dealing with the community's needs and problems, as well as with those institutions associated with them. Thus, although the core of the aides' training has been preparing them to provide specific services, it is becoming evident that some aides will become competent leaders in community action as part of their job, as well as in their lives as private citizens.

Education of the aides was conspicuously "nonacademic" in the graduate school sense. In addition, their baptism in clinical studies was without benefit of undergraduate college preparation. Their education was open-ended, continuing after the training cycle much as before via clinical supervision, staff conferences, peer interaction, and, importantly, from the services situation itself. Not at all like college (and without college credits or credentials) the aides' education was qualitatively comparable to traditional internships and residencies of psychologists, MSWs, and MDs. Preprofessional preparation, so to speak, was the amassed wisdom of the ghetto built into the candidates' previous life experience, in particular skills learned through participation in the mutual-help infrastructure endemic to the neighborhood. As with undergraduate preprofessional programs, the effect of the indigenous helping system was not only to teach certain behavioral basics but also to screen and sift out the most gifted clinicians. (Lincoln candidates were atypical in that their interpersonal competence, measured admittedly by traditional criteria, *quantitatively* exceeded neighborhood norms.) Another of their mentors, Frank Reissman, wrote of them:

> In response to the deficiencies of the service system, the poor have developed their own informal systems and traditions (and manpower) in order to cope and survive. Storefront churches, cellar clubs, hometown clubs, the extended family, the use of the street as a playground, the block party, the mutual assistance of siblings, music constructed from pots and pans, the informal know-how and self-help system of the neighborhood, the use of peer learning, street language, the rent strike and other forms of direct social action and protest.

To this substrate was added the orthodox theoretical and clinical stuff of the behavioral sciences. That this information was by design reformulated to fit the language and life experiences of the trainees while holding to original concepts in no way negates the fact of their gradual clinical excellence—by professional standards. Periodic re-evaluation of the trainees as outreach workers acknowledged their continued growth and undiminished capacity to further advance in expertise. Over the years most of the aides carried increasingly complex individual and group-therapy responsibilities, growing professionally in the process. Tape recordings of aide-client interaction audited by the author literally sparkled with natural sentience to client needs and adroit intervention in their behalf.

It is no surprise, then, that three or four years after completing training the aides were journeymen professionals by our standards, well able to articulate the nuances of clinical practice, to teach as well as do, and to theorize. Much respected for their interpersonal prowess by the Lincoln professional staff, they were still seen as aides by the professionals, perhaps a special kind of aide but a "nonprofessional" nonetheless. Indeed, their pay, status in the general hospital, and chances for promotion either within or outside of the Lincoln system were patently "nonprofessional." As a city hospital, even Lincoln could not bypass the civil services system that ruled the new careerists ineligible for more responsible clinical or administrative positions since they were neither nurses nor college graduates. Lincoln administrators were not unaware of the situation. They worked hard to do something about it, though concentrating their attack on extending the aide series. While senior-aide positions entailed pay increases, it left the new careerists still non-professionals within the human service and city personnel hierarchies. They could train other "non-professionals," supervise them, but not run a service. Disdainfully, they called themselves *"Superaides"!*

What happened? As everybody knows, the Lincoln experiment worked, worked so well that by the fourth year these "born-again" new professionals liberated themselves from their Establishment superiors and re-opened the clinic and service centers under their own authority. Because they had gained the respect of their own community, the city was forced to capitulate in the showdown that followed, the medical school likewise.

What precipitated the upheaval? For several years close rapport existed between Lincoln staff and the new careerists; both groups ultimately felt themselves betrayed by the other. Of the many factors responsible, perhaps none was as important as the long-standing failure of the parent university to deliver on its promise of college credits and work-study programs for the workers' continued academic advancement. Back in the middle 1960s the urgency to the continued collegiate upgrading of talented nonprofessionals was little perceived. Ironically, though the workers' learning was under the auspices of an accredited university, the faculty all holding university appointments and the curriculum documented and substantial, the university held that it lacked authority to award college credits upon the program's successful completion.

Perhaps it was a matter of being ahead of its time. While pedagogy proceeded admirably, the visible, material proofs of it, acceptable to government and the professions, were not forthcoming. Clinical roles, in themselves stimulating and for which the new workers were well suited, turned sour in the absence of growth potential. In a mobile society unfairness rests hard. The greater the clinical expertness of the careerists, the larger the unspoken discrepancy between the workers' competence and that of the beginning professionals promoted past them to positions of leadership. Excluded from the regular channels of administrative and clinical advancement, they also found themselves locked out of the training programs prerequisite to such roles. They were ineligible not because of any personal failing but because their Lincoln education was deemed by the same establishment disqualifying. Even the public colleges would not have them without credentials or college-type credits.

Pay, by itself, was a minor issue. It was the identity of the new careerists that hung in the balance. Initially, they had identified with their professional teachers; their theories and techniques, too. There seemed no conflict between outreach and psychotherapy concepts. Their roles and expertise lay in the neighborhood activities warmly praised by the professionals but little rewarded by the "system." Conversely, the professionals, notwithstanding lip service to community mental health, devoted their energies to the orthodox research, teaching, and individual psychotherapy roles that meant dollars and advancement, same as always. Eventually, to further identify with the professions entailed denegrating their own skills and, secondarily, alienation from their neighborhood constituency. To disavow traditional psychotherapeutics as well as their teachers left them doubly vulnerable, cut off from any personal or intellectual linkage with the human services professions. All that remained to fill the void was a headlong flight into identification with the most radical elements of their South Bronx. Denied credentials, lacking any other options, the only professional role available to them was: *"Power to the people now, man, now!"*

In sum, consider this paradigm: Were the new careerists after four years of supervised, increasingly complex clinical responsibilities capable of continuing uncomplicated professional activities as assigned by the professional in charge? Were they ready for independent, judgmental roles, albeit circumscribed and under the professional's eye? If the answer is "no," then their long-standing performance of such duties was a serious ethical breach, dangerous to client safety. If "yes," if they were in fact qualified, then their arbitrary exclusion from upward mobility into the professionals ranks (and graduate education) was unwarranted, a covert prejudice of the professions against persons owning a different life style, culture, language, or schooling.

HUMAN SERVICES EDUCATION AS A DEVELOPMENTAL PROCESS

Education for the human services, the underlying theoretical basis of practice, and the sum of cultural values and historical precedents dear to the commonweal form a single contiguous line, interconnected manifestations of the same larger society of men. The behavioral sciences are no less scientific because they derive from changeable and human origins. Objectivity becomes more difficult, but then the very relativity of human behavior that obscures absolutes offers powerful clues to its causal mechanisms. In the human services both training and practice derive from a common first premise. Clinical practice starts with the *a priori* faith that the potential for behavioral change exists in all persons, however buried may be this potential and despite the individual's unwillingness to exercise the option. The professions operate on the principle that learning is at least possible in everybody and, as corollary, that people—individuals, families, or institutions—can build on inner resources to achieve more satisfying, more successful behavioral patterns. (This is not to deny the prevalence of contrary forces inhibiting change; the constraints of age, physical limitations, and impediments of a psychic, familial, or societal nature.) Merely, it is postulated that human beings, families, and social structures are capable of productive change that, once accomplished, can be independently sustained. Taken one step farther, it can be postulated that:

Inherent in the human condition is the unceasing capacity to grow, to adapt, to acquire new patterns of behavior, to profit from past and current experiences in forming new modes of coping, more sanquine interpersonal communications, and deeper awareness of one's own motivations, greater sentience to the feelings and needs of others.

The signal objective of the human services is the potentiation of such a process. It is also, interestingly, descriptive of the educational process preparatory to the services roles themselves. And there are societal reflections as well.

The Implications of Neo-Utopianism

Congruent with our professional position toward the adaptability of man stands the larger Western certitude in the inevitability of progress. Twentieth-century neo-utopianism permeates American thinking; as a people we expect progress. The American believes things exist in order to improve, or potentiate improvement. The purpose of our political, social, and economic institutions, in the public's mind, is to secure the betterment of people's lives; any slowing down of the rate of progress calls forth angry cries of "sabotage." Just as we Americans expect social change, the human services professions entertain hope that the goals espoused by their clients should be realized. Fundamental to the clinician-client encounter are expectations on both sides. Each clinical program—child care, alcoholism services, public education—are founded on a panoply of professional expectations. Unrealistic as it may be, it is part of the American dream. Its effects are many.

The state hospital psychiatrist expects that the severely regressed psychotic patient will accommodate to the open-ward milieu, will adjust to the intrapsychic consequences secondary to chlorpromazine. Expectations need not be tied to pathology. The human services professional may expect that his client's arduous practice at the violin or tennis or ballet will develop the desired psychomotor coordination, that his performance will thereby improve. The new careerists might expect that a well-organized attack on their community's deep-rooted sense of inadequacy will galvanize volunteers into collective action. In turn, their expectation would be the formation of more permanent "block councils" that in time could coordinate major neighborhood improvement. The latter could be expected to sustain community self-development projects long after the new careerists or their second-phase volunteers had left the scene.

The Professionals' Expectation of Continued Growth

Human services practitioners, in addition to their hopes for clients, expect growth for themselves—personally, professionally, economically—consequent to their clinical practice. Professionals anticipate that as a result of a job well done there will follow promotions (or higher fees), academic appointments and awards, greater clinical responsibility, greater clinical wisdom and prestige, veritably an endless series of expectations. Expensive as these may be, they are worth the price.

Our "Puritan ethic" remnants would reject the appurtenances of rank and material wealth. Service ought to flow from the heart. Perhaps, but the author believes that services gain in effectiveness within the context of such mutual expectations. It is difficult to encourage, year after year, the self-realization of one's clients while trapped meanwhile in a dead-end job devoid of advancement potential. In an era long ago lacking in social or vocational mobility, this may have been easier to tolerate. Hard, unchanging social stratification allows one to rationalize permanent subordination, the failure to advance thus ascribed to deficiencies in blood or the social register. But no more. Clients and practitioners alike seek answers to conflictual and situational discomforts, whereas once they wanted merely to live with them less disagreeably.

An Equal and Opposite Reaction

Much has been written on the ways in which the clinician's expectations toward the client's goals impinge on the "therapeutic contract." What impact does the practitioner's expectations vis-a-vis his own professional and personal future have on the effectiveness of the services themselves? Without denying the complexity of the clinical situation, the author suggests that the practitioner's ability to help his clients, families, and communities to achieve positive change in themselves is a relative function of the clinician's own expectation of growth—individually and within the context of the service structure. Without the real probability of periodic advancement (relative to the community of professionals) and the accompanying sense of personal validation, the practitioner's capacity to help clients initiate and sustain new and more satisfying identities is significantly compromised.

Time and custom have led to such a structure in psychiatry. The assistant resident moves up to resident, then chief resident; the instructor to assistant professor; there are "boards" in psychiatry and advanced boards in administrative psychiatry. The ward chief is promoted to division chief, striving in turn to achieve superintendent. The analytic candidate moves up stepwise, class by class, through personal analysis, becoming analyst himself, eventually training analyst. Annual society meetings allow for the presentation of professional papers; the acknowledgement by peers of the professional's progress is solemnized by honorariums, awards, testimonials, and elected offices; the "member" is elevated to "fellow," perhaps trustee.

All so much vanity and self-indulgence? Certainly, but also the very essence of our social "beingness." Practitioners are human, too! Behavioral science clinicians are no less susceptible to the titillation of status and the accolades of colleagues as anybody. And no less needful of this social input, either!

The delivery of human services is a people-centered operation the science of which lies in touching the irrational nuclei of those served as rationally as our equally human communications apparatus permits. Our tools, if not our precepts, are human bound; practitioner and person are inseparable. Because we are human we care, but we are therefore subject to the anxieties, fears, emptiness, and narcissistic runaway fantasies that infect humanity everywhere. Such is the price of involvement, without which there is no leverage for helping. For good or ill we are bondsmen to Western society's complex system of values, prejudices, imperatives, and dreams. Inasmuch as we cannot extract ourselves from the value system surrounding us, the better it is to confront the consequences directly. Therapists are human. The tangible, crassly materialistic, aggrandizing concerns of status, the trappings of eminence—fat paychecks, applause, the sure step of command, and the deference of brilliant subordinates—are all appealing. Meaningless they may be, but pleasurable nonetheless.

New Careerists and Associate Professionals

In facing up to the clinical implications of the professionals' expectation of continued growth, it is well to remember the increasingly clinical role played by the nontraditional workers. What's in it for them?

"Who?" The coming legions of associate professionals and upward-bound new careerists we hope will man our future outreach and community services. "But they're not professionals!" "Surely the associates will be key team members, but what's that to do with the vicissitudes of professional growth?"

We are wont to ascribe professional competence to the mere acquisition of a certain body of knowledge, at most, the added perfection of pertinent interpersonal techniques. We equate professional stature with so much practicum, general education, and a bit of ethical integrity for good measure. Much of what it is to become the human services professional derives from the step-by-step assumption of the helping role, itself a function of concomitant endorsement by faculty, peers, and clients. Not the least of these signs are the accoutrements of professional office, the agreed-on status symbols of the helping professions. Endorsement, of course, from colleagues and teachers assumes a minimum knowledge of the field and a rhythm of personal bearing that speaks maturity and "right" ethical values. Historically, these latter attributes of a subjective kind rarely surface in the nonprofessional categories. Why? Perhaps they are not acceptable behaviors in persons who are neither professionals nor students becoming professionals? Certainly, as the Lincoln experiment illustrates, knowledgeability of a professional sort is not acceptable evidence of professional qualifications. As will be described more fully later on under the "college effect," traditional programs for the training of human services professionals subtly but invariably instill the demeanor of the professional during the course of training.

Unauthorized persons, beware! William Caudill, sociologist and noted "biographer" of the mental hospital scene, documents the inhibitory effect of low status on the activities of hospital personnel at the Yale Psychiatric Institute (YPI) in *The Psychiatric Hospital as a Small Society*. To be a professional is to be important, that is, to hold opinions worth listening to. Others should not obsfucate the air waves in deference, of course, to the patients' needs. Month after month Caudill painstakingly recorded the frequency and intent of contributions made by all staff during the daily patient-staff conferences that, in principle, involved the entire YPI family, staff, trainees, buildings people, patients, and their family, if available. Patient-staff conferences were a YPI institution; as in town meetings everybody was free to speak his piece. The obligation to contribute was overtly everybody's, laggards supposedly called to task for their unwillingness to contribute.

In actuality, participation was part of a tightly controlled ritual organized according to a clear pecking order based both on the ranking of one's professional category and one's individual standing within that discipline. Caudill writes:

> Just as it was noted that the head of the hospital talked more than the chief resident, so it can also be seen from Table 10-7 that the supervisor of nurses consistently talked more than the average charge nurse. The main point in showing the breakdown by subcategories of senior (faculty) and nurses is to underscore the fact that the status hierarchy was not only related to which group talked most among the several role groups, but was also related to the subcategories of status within the role group.

Staff nurses were least likely participants, ranking behind social workers, then psychologists, and finally psychiatrists, starting, of course, with residents, then junior staff, etc. In fact, many of the duty nurses neglected to come at all, as if the menial tasks still to be done on the wards were more important than anything they could possibly contribute to the "family" interaction. One could ask if the student nurses, attending the patient staff conferences along with trainees from all the other disciplines, were not learning a powerful lesson on the nonprofessional role of the RN in psychiatry. Obviously, the "professional" psychiatric nurse, while she could demonstrate her place in the nursing lattice, proved her "professional" stature by not saying anything about patient behavior, thereby avoiding competition with the social work and psychology personnel. And since the nursing staff was in constant proximity to the patients seven days a week, 16, 18, or more hours a day, what message, spoken or unspoken, did they bring to the clients? What kind of model for personal integrity, for the right of the individual to be, were the RNs in that milieu? As for the aide staff, one notch lower down on the totem pole, what vicarious strengths did their image give to the clients?

Becoming a professional in the human services is a growth process further complicated by the limitations on who is eligible to grow. Without permission to take the next step toward professional status, personnel are unable to enter either the training or experiential on-the-job roles necessary to gain professional expertise. Analogus to the Hindu "untouchables," the system demands that personnel constantly emit signals not only of their present status but also their claim on future advancement. Nonprofessionals are thus required to signal their allegiance to the system by the very flow of their bodies, by uniforms, by silence, by the deference of posture, and, fearfully, by their "nonthinking" of professional thoughts, the nonlearning of its jargon! (Remarkable, is it not? Nonprofessionals, so many of whom by life style daily assimilate the latest fluctuations in street slang or counterculture usage, never seem to break through into the lexicon of the professional. Why?)

Elmer and Mary Lynch Gardner, searching for the causes underlying the deterioration of their Temple University Community Mental Health Center's services and training programs, similarly noted the invidious effects of caste:

> Team members (sophisticated indigenous workers) either found it difficult or simply resisted following their patients in the hospital and being "on call" for the crisis center. Although the team were serving as the "private practitioners" for their patients and were (supposed) to participate in decisions for hospital admission and discharge, they lacked such status and were usually ignored by other centers staff and staff of the Department of Psychiatry.

Their aversion to the hospital milieu may represent a reaction to the foreign turf, unfamiliarity engendering discomfort, though they seemed to effect a credible job representing their clients in other Establishment settings. More likely their reluctance represented their sensitivity to the nonverbal messages of the Temple professional staff. They "listened," they "heard," they obeyed and accepted the importunings of the director as customary Establishment "don't believe a word of it" double talk meant to be overlooked. (It is a safe bet that none of the indigenous were ever penalized for failing to follow the hospital protocol, though you could get fired for other violations.)

> In addition the mental health assistants could and did participate in any general staff training series, e.g., religion and psychiatry, urban issues, family and group therapy. Professional staff were reluctant to invest themselves in conducting an advanced training series for mental health assistants, and funding could not be obtained to provide leave and financial support to allow them to pursue formal education, e.g. courses towards a B.S. In addition, the latter did not appear relevant to the assistants' functions in the Center.

Relevance of the baccalaureate curriculum to the human services professions is of equal import, yet no one suggests a moratorium on graduate admissions until colleges achieve greater relevance. Interdiction of work study, however, kept the new careerists locked out of the "growth" system. Dr. Gardner's confidence in their clinical skills—"the team serving as the private practitioners"—pales at the point of further education. Why their second-class status? Why should these practitioners, apart from their professional counterparts, be permanently affixed to that one mental health center? Why constrain them to a single service role like serfs bound to the land by oath of fealty? The stultifying effects on the development of the new careerists, long accepted by the human services, raises ugly questions regarding the basic philosophy of the field toward human dignity. Failure to utilize the human potential represented by their vast years of people-care experience is an unaffordable luxury.

And what are the effects on clients and services? The

human services pay homage to the self-realization of those they serve. What is the real message perceived by clients, particularly those of lower-class or minority origins, in observing the professionals' "lording it over" their non-professional colleagues? The thrust of the community mental health movement is the development of manpower out of the constituency served. Relegation of the indigenous workers to an endless series of subordinate roles cannot but reinforce the suspicion of poor peoples that mental health is just another cleverly disguised Establishment machine designed to "put them down" via their own people. Could the Lincoln new careerists have perceived the credentials' bind choking off their future as anything but a manifestation of the same societal forces that, having formed the ghetto, incarcerated them and their peoples within its boundaries?

Aspirations as a Function of Predictable, Known Options

The psychological literature offers ample proof of the changeable nature of human aspirations, varying in resonance with the range of alternatives seemingly available at any given time for a given individual. Diminished career opportunities yield shrunk-down ambitions; with the influx of opportunity, hopes spring up likewise. Reality has a way of fitting all but the most unique individuals into graspable ambitions.

Gist and Bennett a decade ago, among others, and James Coleman more recently have documented the similarity of young peoples' ambitions, for example. Within the protected nest of high school, black and white high schoolers, measured nationally, show little differences in their expectations for the future. Ten years later, closed-off opportunities for many radically reduces their expectations for themselves. Dreams of a decade are relinguished silently, well in advance of actual disappointment. The likelihood of gaining entree into a certain job considerably colors a person's subjective desire to choose such a role. Roles deemed by the youngster as unobtainable turn off learning in areas related to the "forbidden" occupation. Let a glimmer of a chance open up, the competition fall away, and abruptly motivation and learning rates skyrocket. Beyond accessibility, the hoped-for role must also be relatively consonant with a person's ego ideal if learning is to proceed optimally.

Most people are adept at sensing the views of others toward their own capabilities. All too often young people of minority origins do see themselves as others see them. Brody, Derbyshire, and others, Coles most eloquently, have demonstrated this time and again. Unfortunately, the distortions of teachers, peers, and parents reflect back to the student or trainee so as to deflate ego and ambition simultaneously. Suitability of an individual for a given role—in this case the human services professions—as judged by others is notoriously subject to distortion, skewed by personal and cultural prejudices. To what degree have the public media worked to fire the ambition of many heretofore settled with mediocrity? And to what extent have we in the human services professions reacted to these new-found hopes with dead-end, demeaning jobs emblazoned with New Society poetics to camouflage their melancholy future?

Thus far it would seem that anything worth having in the human service careers, is also the perogative of the professionals. But what defines "professional"? Their options include advancement, education, status, private practice, and control over the future of the system. What then are the ingredients that define "professional"?

DEFINING THE PROFESSIONAL

Fashions come and go in human services manpower. Disciplines seem to grow in public or professional favor for a time, then plateau or decline in popularity. Recruitment follows suit. Agency and institutional programs, and the assignment of clinical responsibilities, tend to reflect the changing status relationships of the several human services disciplines. Individual clinicians, like ambassadors at a state function, each have their special place in the professional hierarchy. By and large a person's position in the overall pecking order is a product of his discipline's prestige, number of academic degrees, and place of training. Professional writings and research modify but do not determine ranking. Actual work activities, as a matter of good taste, are not considered in the ranking process. (Indifference to performance as a criterion of professional quality carries over, naturally, to the academic sphere, curriculum design becoming a function of the ideal professional regardless of current modalities of practice or the exigencies of the service scene.)

The Dichotomy of Professional Vs. Nonprofessional

Despite the noisy rivalry of the several human services disciplines, or perhaps because of it, the professions as a group form a closed, complete circle. Almost nobody breaks into the circle. The big losers have been the nonprofessionals (and, of course, the patients). Thus, no matter which of the professions might currently be in vogue, there is no room for the so-called nonprofessionals in the clinical practice of the human services. Nonprofessionals may function in subordinate roles only. In the human services you are either a professional or a nonprofessional; there are no in-betweens. Professional and ideological distinctions are insignificant. The primary identification is across the professional/nonprofessional axis.

The chief criterion in the allocation of clinical duties, the chance for a promotion, or advanced training is belonging to one of the "professions." Once a professional, always a professional; but equally, identification as a nonprofessional is a permanent label notwithstanding an individual's talents, performance, or seniority. Like apartheid, two inviolable classes, separate and unequal. Passage upward into the professional ranks is not permitted within the system. (Admittedly, the nonprofessional is free to quit work and return to school as a high schooler or college freshman, but he receives no advantage for his experience or in-service education. Yet within his work institution or agency there is no route upward.)

Interestingly, this is not industry's way. Take big steel. The mill hand must belong to the union because he is a worker. A foreman's job opens up. The union rules call for in-house promotion. Once promoted to straw boss, he is out of the union. He is a management type now; it is a matter of conflict of interests since management and labor are supposed to be at cross-purposes. Bethlehem Steel, for instance, derives its shop leadership and many of its front-office and sales personnel from its blue-collar pool by way of college work-study and tuition reimbursement programs.

Conversely, the human services draw their "elite" exclusively from outside via the graduate professional schools. In principle professional and nonprofessional are teammates; what is advantageous to one, ostensibly, benefits the other as well.

Nonprofessional is a pejorative. Nonprofessional means what it says, namely, that you are not an associate professional or assistant, or preprofessional kind of person. Ever hear of a nonprofessional athlete? Compare the human services with the military in this regard. Army regulations provide clear channels for the enlisted man to qualify for officers' candidate school, hence an officer's commission. Why the link between NCO and the commissioned officer pool? Could its purpose lie in the message back to all the other NCOs who do not apply? Something about their identity?

Common usage has lent to the appelation "professional" connotations of excellence. *Professional services* means you are in good hands, professional hands. Nonprofessional, by implication, is a negative term, like "antiprofessional." How did this all begin?

Is the Nonprofessional Capable of Learning Anything Professional?

From the 1930s through World War II and on toward the 1950s the overwhelming majority of mental health personnel worked in state hospitals. Over those years America was barely a literate nation. In 1950 less than one-third of Americans 25 years and older had completed high school. A decade later, 1960, and there were but one in five nonwhites with a high school degree or its equivalent. Nonprofessionals typically functioned at an eighth-grade level. Between unskilled aide and professional nurse, nothing. The LPN is a phenomenon of the 1960s. Just 20 years ago the educational gap separating nonprofessional and professional was immense, seemingly unassailable. At that time, however, the aides low levels of academic preparation past unnoticed. Americans, generally, in the post depression years were ill educated, particularly the working classes.

Moreover, recipients of the human services, the asylum inmates, the welfare mothers, and the convicts, were disproportionately undereducated. Clients and their custodians flowed from a common demographic pool. Low pay and abominable working conditions meant that a well-educated corps of nonprofessionals was neither feasible nor much desirable in view of the purely custodial nature of services. Within the asylum milieu distinctions between inmates and their caretakers were not so important. The aides lived on the grounds; conversely, the veteran inmates worked in the kitchens, tended hospital boilers, drove the farm tractors, scrubbed floors, painted walls, repaired shoes, and in many ways supported the nursing staff.

Before chlorpromazine, definitive mental health services within an asylum setting were limited; and if the social welfare armamentarium had wider range, preoccupation with the "man in the house" stifled its use. Prerogatives of the professionals were few and jealously guarded. Psychiatrists, wardens, and welfare chiefs, charged by society with defending the commonweal against the insane, the drunks, the psychopaths, paupers, and profligate, stood firm—certifying, committing, disallowing, locking up, paroling, lobotomizing, and electroshocking "good" health into their reluctant wards. If clients and nonprofessionals lived side by side, the professionals remained aloof, estranged by their education, middle-class life style, and need to defend their authority.

The nonprofessionals gradually came to be seen, popularly, as aligned with the keepers in the harsh control of their own peoples. As a consequence, they drew the universal approbation of clients, public, and professionals, as if they had betrayed those incarcerated. Meanwhile periodic revelations of "snake pits" in the public press, reinforced by grand-jury inquests, challenged effectiveness of the professionals. Taxpayers challenged the utility of the institutions themselves. "Why have welfare?" The professionals, in an attempt to justify their historical rights to preside over the system, fell back on legalistic and authoritarian proofs. Of many, it was the academic credentials that proved acceptable, convincing the public of their knowledgeability. Graduate education thus became the wellspring of the professionals' legitimacy to office, quite apart from the technical skills required for performance. Small wonder, then, that out of the primeval asylum slime should emerge the professional/nonprofessional apartheid.

Contemporary apologists subscribe to the dichotomy on educational grounds, citing the nonprofessionals' lack of basic social and behavioral sciences background while alluding also to a certain dullness, even ethical deficiency, that they see as haunting the noncollege-educated. Old prejudices die hard, facts to the contrary. A sensitive psychiatric technician, knowledgeable in the use of behavior modification techniques, for example, establishes under his own authority a token economy regimen for his back-ward, severely regressed charges. Professionals are outraged at the temerity of the nonprofessional dealing in "professional" techniques. The Marine Corps drill instructor, however, wields absolute authority over 500 trainees, "modifying" their behavior greatly. Not an eyebrow is raised. Aides passing out prescribed medication? Heaven forbid, except that the same patients are given three days' supply when they are out on weekend leave.

Society's Preference for "Unskilled" Personnel

Nonprofessionals in the human services, no matter how experienced, are unskilled according to most state personnel policies. Lacking formal education in the field, they are considered unskilled and classified as nonprofessionals along with the other noncollege types. Obviously, there are numbers of psychiatric technicians and teacher aides and indigenous workers owning superior competence in interpersonal relations, along with not a little behavior theory and years of work under reputable professional supervisors. Nonetheless, the system has permanently defined them as nonprofessionals. Nonprofessionals are always nonprofessionals not because they cannot or will not learn but because those human service skills that are open to their mastery within a given institution are equally defined as nonprofessional (or they would not be open to the nonprofessionals in the first place), completing the tautology. As we will see, this sets the stage for a second myth, namely; that truly professional skills are the automatic result of formal education, or at least the consequence of clinical experience built on a graduate school foundation. Who gains by this? The professionals? Higher education? Surprisingly, neither the professionals nor the schools are the prime movers or beneficiaries. The colleges lose a vast number of potential students, from continuing education, upgrading, and work-study students. Professionals may be the most vocal, but for them territoriality is more an intraprofessional jurisdictional dispute. And no doubt, professionals, being human like plumbers or salesmen or dope pushers, would react were nonprofessionals to move upward in competition with them for the better jobs. Strictly speaking, however, the nonprofessionals are not "put down" by the professionals.

Neither should the professionals' high salaries camouflage the real issue, vis-à-vis the nonprofessionals: credentials. (If all of the professional salaries were divided among the nonprofessionals in the average state hospital, the net gain would not be much. There are too few professionals relative to the legions of nonprofessionals to make a difference. But the opposite, the opening up of salary scales for the nonprofessionals to collective bargaining would cost a fortune. If a mere third of its most recommended nonprofessionals were paid the lowest professional salary grade, the system would go broke. In a typical state hospital an increase of $1,000 in the nonprofessionals' salaries would increase its annual budget by 15%. If the aides, psychiatric technicians, and the LPNs were paid at a rate equivalent to the actual state pay schedules for the responsibilities inherent in their routine duties, the hospital's budget would need to be 30% higher. In Maryland, with a roughly $60 million institutional budget that would equal out to a mere $20 million additional *just to fairly pay nonprofessionals for the actual job they are doing and without adding a single new activity.*

The Myth of the Manpower Shortage

For 25 years we have had a manpower crisis in the human services. Professionals have been too few; budgeted vacancies have reached horrendous numbers. Let no one be fooled! Most of what we euphemistically term budgeted vacancies are not vacant at all. They are jobs permanently filled by nonprofessionals. Ostensibly, they are just filling in until the emergency is over. After 25 years it is clear that "emergency" is the state's way of utilizing uncredentialed personnel in roles calling for full professional preparation. Thus, the same civil service policy that "protects" clients by forbidding the in-service training and upgrading of superior but uncredentialed personnel is used to deny those personnel their rightful compensation when they are used in positions of responsibility, anyway.

There is nothing hypothetical about this. It is not an allusion to what nonprofessionals might be doing but in fact records their routine deployment in jobs demanding of "professional" expertise by law. The experienced LPN or senior psychiatric technician who fills a permanently vacant professional slot may or may not be qualified. No matter, in our public institutions he will be paid thousands of dollars less annually than the duly-authorized wages for a professional carrying his slot. Example: The LPN II assigned to RN duties gains a few hundred dollars increment under cover of a promotion to LPN III. But that is still some $2,000 under the lowest beginning RN wage were she hired to carry the selfsame duties. Why can she not be found?

It is an old story: low wages. Keep public-sector professional wage schedules just a shade below the going regional rates in the private sector. Result? Everybody flocks to the higher-paying, more prestigious institutions. So long as the demand for professionals, regionwide, minimally exceeds the supply, then public institutions and agencies need pay just a wee bit less, and *voilà,* large numbers of professional vacancies filled for the patients' sake by nonprofessionals. Keep up the pretense of recruiting, and no one—not accrediting committees, professional societies, or licensure boards, the "Feds," no, not even the public and its nosy media—will hold the officials culpable for standards of care unacceptable by any criteria.

Matched Pairs of Work Experience and College Study Units Carrying College Credits

The sports fan judges the "pro" on his performance. Can he make the hard ones look easy? The civil service bureaucracy customarily defines "professional" as that person who has completed a recognized graduate course of study in any of the traditional human services professions. A goodly number of educators believe there is more to being a professional than classroom mastery of didactic material. Some go farther, suggesting that well-supervised work experience be equated with its academic counterpart, with both accepted for credential credits (assuming the experiential candidate can demonstrate clinical competence by challenge exam even as the academic candidate must take final exams). It is a lovely dream. There has been a lot of hullabaloo concerning experiential equivalents, waivers for ex-medics, and military mental health specialists. Honest men would have it so. Unfortunately, they are impotent to bring the dream to fruition.

While it is easy to facilitate the entry of "noncredentialed" workers onto the lowest rung of the human services occupations, perhaps a notch or two higher, beyond that is a dead end. To do that requires only a waiver of civil service educational requirements that, in effect, gives preferential treatment to one group of nonprofessionals over another. The status quo remains unchallenged. To allow for challenge equivalents equal to beginning professional status puts the challenge group in direct competition with the current crop of graduate school seniors about to enter the job market. What happens next? The best of the challenge professionals are slated for promotion to a senior social work position ahead of traditionally trained applicants. All hell breaks loose. Nobody minds the noncredentialed individual moving up to the job one notch below. Jumping over the professional is another thing. Like anybody else, the professional will defend his territory, in this case by casting allegations of inferior preparation at the uncredentialed. And the public will believe the professional; after all, they believe in the myth of academic superiority themselves. Look at the double bind facing associate degree RNs. They are professionals; they are licensed. Nonetheless, they are locked out of further advancement in their own profession for want of baccaulaureate credentials.

Definition of a Professional

There is a little bit of autobiography in the professional's vision of the professional. Definitions tend toward two broad categories:

1. Educational completeness—a static, once-and-for-all definition based on successful completion of a standard syllabus and/or authorized period of study. Professional becomes defined as passage through an authorized course of study encompassing minimum expertise required in the proper practice of the profession.
2. As a developmental process—a more functional definition; professional is conceptualized as a dynamic, unending process of becoming, which for practical purposes, like employment, certifies the individual as "professional." The certification point may be located anywhere along the continuum toward professional competence, though usually several years following completion of formal study.

The first definition assumes a specific identifiable body of professional knowledge that can and ought to be mastered during graduate school. Future advances in the profession, differences between schools, and the evolutionary changes in society are paid little account. Exceeding breadth of the professions is ignored, as if all could be packaged in a tight little basic curriculum. Neither definition attempts to measure the would-be professional in terms of performance at the real-life clinician-client interface. Educational obsolescence and lateral mobility into subspecialties are ignored. We lack precedents or models through which clinical competence could be monitored and, if necessary, upgraded periodically over the course of an entire professional career.

We live a double standard. We choose as a society to ignore the sorry ineptitude of the beginning professional, at least for legal, bureaucratic, and ethical considerations. The psychology intern or psychiatric resident are evaluated in terms of their long-range potential not their immediate competence. Meanwhile, older colleagues, variously termed supervisors, chiefs-of-service, and department chairman oversee their initial performance. Senior personnel intervene subtly, teach a fine point over coffee, or stir through the medical records, but always discreetly so as to preserve the image of professional independence and infallibility. Why not the same for nonprofessionals? Licensing of the young professional is a gamble on human nature. Society bets on the nature of an individual's behavior some 20, 30 years hence. We are betting on orthodoxy, that the professional once licensed will continue to show the same drive and fixity of purpose during the length of his career as evidenced in his previous decades of academic perseverance. We assume anybody who has made it through graduate school will keep on pushing themselves toward whatever other stigmata come to be part of the "complete" professional. The *non sequitur* that makes it all seem reasonable is the unproved (and unlikely) equation of scholastic prowess with clinical competence.

The Making of the Professional

The American professional is a social phenomena. The identity of the professional is born in people via the corporate expectations of family, friends, colleagues, clients, and subordinates. Motivation, intelligence, and the rest have their place, but their crystallization into the professional is incumbent upon the reflected expectations of a person's human environment. The professional derives from an ambiance far-sighted enough to see professional where as yet stands none but a student.

But there is nothing exclusive about the phenomena; its genesis is not confined to the academic environs. The deep desire to draw knowledge out of the rhythm of one's daily client activities—to entertain curiosity, to question, to read, to seek out and profit from counsel, to act independently—these derive from many causes. It is not solely born of graduate schools but stems from a deeper, more elementary stuff. Many workers demonstrate these attributes, professionals and nonprofessionals.

What are the impediments to the further evolution of such qualities in nonprofessional manpower? What thwarts the gradual synthesis of basic behavioral science and clinical wisdom with these personal characteristics under the aegis of sound professional models? The chief obstacle in a literal sense is the absence of any administrative or academic structure through which the nonprofessional might ascend. And nobody can much feel like a professional, nor assume his functions, without the chance to practice as a professional under supervision either in school or on the job as apprentice.

That there are no access routes is no accident. The argument is raised that the nonprofessionals are unsuited by mind or temper to upgrading. And maybe the psychiatric aide, *circa* 1950, burdened by severe reading and educational deficiencies, had too far to go. Nonprofessionals today are very different. Many of them, such as the LPNs, not only have a high school degree but also a full year's college-level nurses training and a fair amount of continuing education on an in-service basis. More importantly, so long as nonprofessional careers are a dead end, the very talent needed to effect upgrading take jobs elsewhere. Open up the route to higher education for the employed nonprofessionals and the composition of recruits will alter radically for the better.

Building a way up through the lattice is only part of the story. Any bridge between nonprofessional and professional categories must also contend with the tradition that the human services be taught at the graduate school, not undergraduate, level. Ostensibly, the four undergraduate, general education years are a necessary ingredient to the nonprofessional's understanding of anything taught him of a professional nature. It is supposed to be akin to the traveler in a foreign land who knows nothing of the language. Unable to speak or comprehend the language, much of the experience is lost as the guide's words fly "over his head." Poppycock! What about Erik Erikson, he never finished college? Or Anna Freud, a nonprofessional? Perhaps there are larger cultural reasons for society's failure to build ladders for the nonprofessional.

College = Professional = Clinical Competence

College sets a man apart. Americans see the "college man" as an authority in things intellectual, a leader. Society has put the college graduate high on a pedestal. Why? On the surface it is because he is different. He acts differently from noncollege persons. College graduates, as individuals, have their own ways and values, sure, but also there is a collegiate interpersonal style. Collegians have their own variants of speech, syntax, dialect, and importantly, their own manner of kinesthetic communications—the silent language of posture, gestures, and body attitudes. College people think they are better. Noncollegians choose to let them think that way. While the collegiate minority gleans status from its self-imposed "collegiate style" of communications, they are able to maintain this visibility only because the noncollege majority willingly assumes reciprocal, subsurvient attitudes of posture and voice. The college/noncollege distinction is sustained by the culture as a whole. Why?

In a complex society institutions are multipurposed. Higher education as a social institution serves not only as a vehicle of education and a place for young people to mature in the company of like peers, but it is used less overtly as a cultural *deus ex machina* for designating which individuals of the coming generation are to assume roles of leadership. That is, under the seeming guise of democratic fairness, entrée to the best jobs—in industry, government, the professions, and education—becomes the responsibility of the colleges and graduate schools. Naturally, the division between leaders and followers, the first cutoff, hinges on college attendance. Gradations in leadership follow from one's higher-education track record. (There are numerous cultural ways for assigning roles and apportioning among specific individuals the collective sum of a society's wealth and power. Some cultures allocate these on the basis of family pedigree, caste, or the clan's totem; some on the basis of individual bravery in tribal warfare. Wealth and power have been important in this regard for Western cultures, and certainly the offspring of the rich and powerful obtain, in general, the "best" education. One-third of all medical students come from families whose income is in the highest 3 percentile; one-fourth of the executives in *Fortune*'s "500 largest" firms were undergraduates in one of the eight ivy-league schools. But reality sits poorly with the American dream; our egalitarianism is belied by the facts. Hence, we conjure up a society-wide myth of equal opportunity through the "open" competition of the college process. In fact, this is something of a compromise since admission to college is not closed but merely skewed in favor of certain groups. Unfortunately, existence of the "myth" acts as a powerful inhibitor to rational discussion of the nonprofessional's competence or educability.

Why Is Entry-Level Education to the Human Services at the Masters' Level and Above?

Why should the introductory professional curricula for human service careers not be pegged at the baccalaureate or associate degree levels? There was a time when the bachelor's degree was a terminal degree, qualifying the graduate for employment. Persons interested in the professions might then choose, on completion of secondary school, between the law school, the medical college, the engineering, technological, or agricultural institute, or the military academy. These were undergraduate curricula. Even the BA degree was complete in itself, preparing the undergraduate in the liberal arts appropriate to a young gentleman of means. How, then, did the human services come to be taught in the graduate schools? Primarily, reasons of prestige, a distant by-product of the reformation in medical education following the Flexner Report in 1916.

More importantly, why should they remain limited to graduate education? A case could be made on the grounds that the increasing body of clinical information required in the practice of the professions can no longer be packed into two, three, or five graduate years (themselves obligated heavily to independent research, the theses, and specialization). But this is not the argument of educators. Instead, they are likely to call for more general education, arts, humanities, and the natural sciences, not any undergraduate pursuit of the social and behavioral sciences. They would argue that without the undergraduate liberal arts the "professional" character of their profession would be tarnished. They say that professionals would be no more than technicians. It is not that there is a fear of any decline in clinical standards consequent to undergraduate study of the professions. Rather, it is that the training of these "uncultured" individuals would undermine the profession's image vis-à-vis the others.

But wherein lies the real danger? In maintaining the undergraduate prerequisite to professional study we *de facto* exclude a vast number of mature candidates—the woman of 40, her children grown, the retiring cop, 20 years on the beat, the hospital experienced LPN, now ready to use herself more professionally, the 30-plus ex-addict who has beat the habit and "cares." Can we in the human services afford to lose their contributions to the art of practice? Undergraduates not infrequently fill their elective time with courses dealing with the facts and consequences of poverty, minority status, urban problems, and the welfare system—which is good and the award of course credits appropriate. But are not many of the nonprofessionals born and reared in the vortex of this milieu, many of them experts in social problems? They have lived the textbooks; many, too, are well versed in the underlying theory and its application to the specifics of urban life. Should not these indigenous experts be a valuable adjunct to any growth in the theoretical and practical basis of the human services professions? Can the professions, as they are presently constituted, survive without these experts? And if there is any lesson to be learned from the catastrophe of the cities relative to our growing suburban sprawl and the anomie of its people, who better to decipher the warning? (This is not to bypass professional education, it is merely a plea to cut away those superficialities of class and caste that impede the recruitment of talented persons into human services careers by way of whatever academic input is required for full professional competence.)

So long as the prerequisite to professional study of the human services is closed to all save persons showing four years, any four years of college, content be damned and without exceptions, then we can expect to face charges of racist exclusion. Historically, the "American Way" to exclude certain ethnic, racial, or religious groups from high-status jobs was to make education for those jobs inaccessible. Composition of our graduate schools in the human services is remarkably homogeneous. First of all, everybody is a "college" type. If he did not exemplify the college ideal he would not have been admitted to graduate school; he was chosen by an admission's committee notably collegiate in its public character. His undergraduate recommendations afforded evidence not only of classroom prowess (good grades) but adaptibility to a classroom, didactic learning milieu. Moreover, without personally accommodating to the college demeanor, recommendations and interview would have turned off the admitting group. Out of this relatively pure culture of middle-class, intellectual, college types come the next generation of faculty. The nature of the student body and its strengths and foibles tend to control the nature of the instruction, the syllabus, the instructional modalities, and the nature of examinations. Orthodoxy is perpetuated one generation to the next, such that those selected do best not because they are better clinicians but because they are better suited to the pedagogy of graduate education. Without greater heterogeneity of the student body, can we say anything at all about the characteristics of good clinicians, teachers, and researchers in the human services? Would a more demographically balanced student body prove much if the faculty were not similarly representative? And, too, would not instructional approaches also have to speak to the strengths and weaknesses natural to each of several student populations, each strong in its own way?

Until the 1960s, to be a professional had been, literally, to be just like us! (And since we are all pretty much the same, that proves it.) Then came New Careers.

New Careers has given blunt comeuppance to some of our most cherished notions about the roots of professional competence and the way human services ought to be dispensed. Long-ignored human resources, rich in the savvy of survival, were mobilized into service careers that in turn were radicalized by the new expertise of indigenous origins. Indigenous workers brought forth, and justified, a whole new dimension in people services. Neighborhood storefronts moved services out of the Establishment into their clientele; eventually, services were afforded by their number. The era of consumer participation in the design and delivery of human service was begun.

New Careers gave visible affirmation to the unspoken truth that everybody knew, namely; that within the ranks of the poor can be found a cadre of sentient, clinically intuitive persons inclined by temper and the exigencies of poverty toward careers in the health care and human services industries.

NEW CAREERS REVISITED 10 YEARS AFTER!

New Careers began as a social strategy in the war on poverty. New Careers promised resolution to the paradox of the slums: that poor people are left without adequate human services while burdened by unemployment and the perennial underutilization of what services are available. New Careers sought to parlay the one commodity in surplus—idle manpower, underused talent—into a cornucopia of decisive action. For the New Careerists themselves New Careers has been the best and the worst, simultaneously. For the New Careerists it has been a "cop-out" in the grand manner and a lifeline into the real world of economic solvency and upward mobility. For taxpayers and the middle classes in general it has been equally a mixed bag of blessings and nuisances. The best of its advantages are also the most dangerous of traps to the new workers. For example, here are some of the seeming objectives that, if achieved, would be an immediate blessing to the New Careerists, yet over time a dangerous obstacle to continued growth of the movement.

1. Is New Careers a vehicle for mobilizing the undereducated and unemployed off welfare rolls and into gainful employment? Is it a means for transforming nonproductive idleness into socially beneficial productivity—services to the poor without increasing the cost to society above what they are already paying for welfare?

2. Is New Careers a way to reach untapped manpower resources for work in nonprofessional roles otherwise going begging? Should New Careers be expected to ameliorate the personnel problems of public-sector services: high turnover, absenteeism, alcoholism, etc.?

3. Is New Careers to serve as a mechanism for multiplying the effectiveness of scarce professional manpower through their crystallization as a cadre of professionals' assistants? New Careerists could, for example, serve as a cadre of assistant social workers, relieving the MSWs of

routine, often tedious, unrewarding but clinically necessary duties.

4. Is its mission to be breakthrough of organization, at last bringing adequate services to the poor? Because of the efficiency of its neighborhood location and low-cost manpower trained on the job, can New Careers succeed in delivering adequate services cheaply, without added tax burden for the care of the indigent?

5. Should a major goal be the retraining of semiliterate segments of the poor in order that they possess the necessary reading and work-oriented habits for employment in the health and human services industries? (In a technologically ultrasophisticated world the unskilled laborer or domestic is a heavy liability of society.)

6. Should New Careers push its own special brand of genius? As one careerist postulates, New Careerists everywhere possess a unique set of skills born of their common legacy of poverty and, often, the added burdens of minority status. Ought, therefore, the New Careerists eschew the professionals' techniques lest these bastardize their one special gift? Ought New Careerists to avoid entanglements with other nonprofessionals, like the "1199" union or AFSC&ME union or the psychiatric technicians?

Each of the six, taken by themselves and apart from the larger societal context of the coming dozen years, offers tempting advantage to the poor—for the immediate present! Each, if divorced from its eventual consequences, would be beneficial to the New Careerists. But these goals, admittedly the first steps of a potential "total program," could well become sore poison to the initial dream of New Careers. How? New Careers, carried part of the way, creates a new breed of nonprofessionals, this time ever the more expert but still locked out of any bonafide route upward beyond their hospital or center training certificate. Young persons, mostly, they would be trapped into second-class jobs over the next generation, low pay, low status, dead-end jobs without transferability between institutions, let alone advanced standing in public colleges.

Bluntly, if the six objectives are all there is to New Careers, then young people would be well advised to seek occupations other than the health and human services. Back in the early 1900s, when the nation was an agrarian society of small towns, it was good for a young man to "have a trade." Being a skilled mechanic was a defense against unemployment. A trade meant a good living. No more. Apprenticeship to the human services would not be so bad if the promised career lattices were constructed along with it. Without clear channels for open-ended upward mobility, lateral transferability, and accessible work-study, tuition-refund arrangements "on line" with new career's training, there is little hope of it coming later. New careers, without a master plan for its reintegration within the fundamental rubric of the human services system, is a "loser."

The Dream of the Intrepid Assistant

New Careers is another of the endless string of hoped-for assistants to the hard-working professional. Over the years professionals everywhere have conjured up the fantasy of a sophisticated, sentient, motivated, utterly reliable (and low-salaried) assistant who would carry all those unrewarding tasks unbecoming our professional status. (We have dreamed of our own Dr. Watson, aide to the brilliant Sherlock Holmes, happy on a $6,000 to $9,000 salary.) And maybe this was possible once, in a bygone era when folks plain "knew their place and were content not having to run around all over the place looking after big salaries and big titles!" No doubt over the years New Careerists could be trained to carry uncomplicated professional tasks, but would they stay forever at those wages in view of the responsibilities?

Psychiatric technicians have had the same problem. In the late 1950s several states sought to upgrade the quality of their aides and instituted increasingly sophisticated training programs in the Ohio design. Maryland's lasted a full year, the program was intensive, and the aide carried no duties but supervised practicum during the year (a full 12 months). In California, psychiatric technician training was the minimum academic level for aides, an amazing degree of expertise for a state hospital system. What has been the result? Since 1965 salaries for registered nurses, prodded by intermittent threats of strike, have jumped some 60 to 80%. The aides and psychiatric technicians have barely met inflation. Nurses, backed by their national organization, have moved to practitioner roles. RNs, however, are few in number in public-sector programs, their duties for the most part carried by LPNs and nurse's aides. Which is the problem for the psychiatric technicians and inevitably the New Careerists. Society is unwilling to pay the price of adequate wages and career development. Society does not believe they or their clients are worth it. Nonprofessionals in general and New Careerists in particular have no clout in the employment marketplace. Employers lump them all together, wiping out critical differences of individual talent and past experience. But that is the way it is with the unskilled. By definition they are expendable, their replacement always available from the unskilled, transient labor pool intrinsic to any urban metropolis. As the number of New Careerists swells during the 1970s, their job chances diminish, especially vis-à-vis senior or supervisory jobs. Competition for them augurs to be fierce. The older, more experienced nonprofessionals of every description will be "shooting" for the very few senior positions for which they are eligible (lacking college credentials). To make matters worse, the proliferation of numerous small autonomous community centers (and HMOs), each with its own tiny training program, will make a farce of the New Careerists hard-won certificates. How will the typical personnel officer differentiate between them? Annual modifications within the same center will obfuscate the quality of a single program, while in-service education at some will add to the chaos. (As things are going, the New Careerists will be clamoring for, surprise, credentials before the late 1970s.)

As New Careers is presently constructed, there are no viable common denominators across divers centers to permit transferability without a loss in job classification. Factionalism is sure to breed contempt among the New Careerists for each other, an eventuality fueled by the Establishment. One group pitted against the others helps keep wages low, institutional loyalties high, and the antiquated human services system unchanged. If there are but two or three senior jobs for a hundred New Careerists, then who gets the jobs is going to be a matter of favoritism. And then begins the sad travesty of soul brother hating soul brother, the clients be damned.

Preserving the Nonservice Status Quo

Whatever may be said for community mental health, it still serves but a small fragment of the nation. The vast majority of people live in cities unserved by any program; what exists is likely the OPD leftover from the distant state hospital. Given this milieu, there will be innumerable independent, community-sponsored, agency, and public-sector storefront centers heavily dependent on their own New Careerists. Each storefront will be staffed by the very best of their several years' training crop. The others, who knows? New Careerists, despite their pragmatic importance to the services programs, will have little career leverage. Lacking mobility and with new trainees graduating once, twice a year, they are expendable. What have the veterans got to show for 5, 10 years of good work, good supervision, and not a little formal continuing education? Good people working for little pay, dispersed and lacking organization. A perfect substrate for a new kind of custodial care. Instead of the virile preventative and developmental programs discussed earlier, the community is offered the tempting alternative of maintaining the status quo. Not that the asylums would remain; there would be a replication of the custodial modalities within the skid-row flophouses, charity old folks homes, rooming houses, and highrise monoliths of our great cities.

If we do not sell "program," but instead emphasize New Careers' poverty clientele, off-the-welfare-roles manpower, and discontinuity with middle-class life, the centers will get short shrift from the public exchequer. The poor have always come last. That is not likely to change. The availability of low-cost yet proficient community workers would lend fiscal credibility to the false economy of custodial approaches in lieu of costlier but more productive prevention and public education. While the New Careerists might make excellent assistants to the professionals, what ought to be the proper ratio of professionals to assistants? Unlike a career lattice founded on a continuum of increasingly expert persons, the professional-assistant split invites the gradual accumulation of assistant types. Under the guise of New Careers there would be over use of inexperienced personnel in public-sector programs. Matching skills and education to services assignments requires a stepwise assortment of personnel categories. As of now, New Careers has not demonstrated any better luck in breaking the "college barrier"; New Careerists have not been promoted to professional levels, measured by civil service classifications or salary schedules. At best, work-study programs through the community colleges have facilitated advancement through the academic system, but nobody has made an "end run" based on their New Career's expertise.

Moreover, as the years pass, the very success of the New Careerists in mobilizing the youth of their neighborhoods into higher education will act to damn their own nonacademic qualifications. Again, candidly, lack of minority professionals has fostered employment of blacks and Chicanos in the care of their own on a different credentials standard than in suburban facilities. This is good, except that it lulls the New Careerist into a false sense of security. Not that the Establishment much cares who treats the poor, so long as it is cheap, but the people themselves will want staff whose credentials exactly mimic the middle classes'. Meanwhile, a sufficient number of black professionals will graduate during the 1970s to rapidly supplant their New Careerist brothers, the new academically trained workers holding to their special prerogatives even as their white, middle-class colleagues have before them. White professionals will back them up, siding against the New Careerists. At best the New Careerists have a chance to enter the services and a moratorium of half a dozen years in which to catch up on college and the credentials bag. Beyond that, they will be missing out on the professionals' continuing education and upgrading arrangements and seniority, too (which will start over, beginning with one's initial professional classification, not on the day of first employment).

Table 1 presents some of the criteria against which to measure a given New Careers program's success in establishing the foundation for long-range effectiveness, not the least of which is the open-ended career development of the New Careerists themselves. Professionals have questions to ask themselves, too.

New Careers Is For Whom?

New Careers did not just happen! New Careers is "manmade." It was begat by the system, not the dis-Established. Early New Careerist programs at Howard University or New York's HARYOU were no populist uprising, no spontaneous implosion from out of the ghetto's bowels. New Careers was not born of the poor nor the blacks, nor was it a consumer revolt against execrable services. Neither was it a coming together of the nonprofessionals in the style of the nineteenth-century trade union movement. Genesis of New Careers was the Establishment through its more creative professionals, but Establishment professionals nonetheless.

TABLE 1
Guidelines for the Assessment of Individual New Careers Programs

Evidence of continued community interest, particularly recruitment rates, character of applicants; recruitment activity progressively undertaken by indigenous community institutions. Evidence of spillover of higher recruitment rates into other of the health and human services.

Evidence of higher utilization rates by target population of New Careers-related health and human services facilities (vis-à-vis pre-New Careers or comparable demographic control). Similarly, signs of improved utilization of other societal services, such as vocational rehabilitation, social services, legal aid, Man Alive, AA, family planning, etc.—thus over five years New Careers *should* effect higher welfare caseloads and lead to seeming increases in addiction and alcoholism rates through additional requests for services.

Evidence of diffusion—by fifth year a trend toward ready employment of the program's graduates in services outside the administrative parameters of the parent institution. (Careerists working in "outside" agencies should be utilized in appropriate ways compatible with their center training or in supervisory/teaching roles commensurate with their professional maturation.)

Salaries of New Careerist grads should compare favorably after 3, 5, 10 years in the field with similar career opportunities, both within the health and human services industries and elsewhere. Attrition from the human services and termination rates for grads should show significant differences versus proximal "nonprofessionals."

Evidence of continued career advancement of graduates, promotion rates, and proportion returning to school for advanced education; comparison with control "nonprofessionals." Are New Careerist graduates competing favorably with traditionally educated personnel, particularly community-college grads, for services positions of responsibility? (Educational costs per grad should be stabilized, comparable to state colleges.)

Demonstrable evidence of progressively increasing community participation in the programs real decision-making process (i.e., administrative board membership, control over program director, program objectives, etc.).

Gradual phasing into orthodox ("hard money") state or municipal funding sources; evidence of program growth outside of grant-money expansion. Equally critical, evidence of proliferation of similar models under Establishment auspices, especially in situations where outside grant monies are *not* available. (Good programs after five years are replicated readily; people want more of them, the political "wheels" churn.)

And professionals are still in the catbird's seat. There are many reasons for this, some a reflection of government grant policies, civil service regulations, or the overall program leadership of the neighborhood centers. Still, there are few programs, or divisions of programs, under the helm of bona-fide New Careerists. Nor have we given the poor much real authority over their programs or New Careerist workers. Advisory boards are commonplace, but rare, if any, is the board of directors formed with a majority of residents presiding. The effects of continued professional dominance on the indigenous worker movement are as subtle as they are destructive. The danger is not overt sabotage. Rather it is the insertion of professional ideas, ideals, and models in a void that is better used as a creative vehicle for the people and their New Careerists. They have a different world view, and services to the poor are in sore need of innovation and the unorthodox. Worse, so long as the professionals do it, endemic leadership and know-how is stifled.

There is nothing very equitable about life. If the purpose of New Careers was to help mediate between the have-nots and the sources of power and resources, then the loyalties of the ombudsman is always subject to question. Ostensibly, New Careers is to develop acceptable bridges between the poor and the powerless and those possessing same. Fine, but no one can simultaneously serve two masters honestly. The feelings, prejudices, present status, and future attainments of the professional are inextricably connected with the existing social structure, the Establishment's universities, bureaucracy, church, and chamber of commerce. So long as New Careers and its service programs are under "professional" direction, its actions, no matter their intent or result, are subject to the charge of "cop-out" by the dissidents of either side.

In addition, there are all the nitty-gritty realities of service and training to be performed, no mean tasks in themselves in the most tranquil locations. New Careers is not for free; salaries must be paid, rent and other operating costs assumed. New Careers programs, much as the mental health centers, must convince the political and public Establishment of their validity professionally and effectiveness clinically. The "good" program gets continued funding. But "good" as perceived by the suburban white majority is not necessarily "good" in the eyes of poor folks. Conversely, inadequate programs by the people's standards are not worth refunding. The turnkey is the ability to present multidimensional programs in the best possible public relations light in hopes of pleasing the poor, the professionals, and the system. Failure is of no import to the system; personnel, New Careerists included, look for other employment, and the people have again no services. For them the damage is irreparable.

Some suggestions to New Careerists on ways to ensure viability of their program are contained in Table 2.

TABLE 2
A New Careers Guide to the Establishment

Organize: New Careerists themselves must organize across agency and institutional boundaries on a regional or, preferably, state-wide basis (even as the MDs, RNs, and school teachers before them). Careerists must develop a relevant professional association; membership ought to be inclusive in design, spelling out procedures for involving human services workers over the widest range of work and training backgrounds. If desired, concurrently organize union! (If possible, consolidate disparate union groups—1199, AFSC&MEs, etc.—under a single representative "council" or "committee" authorized to speak as one voice state-wide and act in liaison with the professional association.)

Build bridges: Political/professional impact of the New Careerists' organization can be amplified via federation or *working* liaison with related workers' groups, in particular (a) psychiatric technicians (b) LPNs *and* (c) evolving community-college mental health worker associations.

Develop standards: Under aegis of the newborn professional body, develop broad standards of education and experience and include a comprehensive system of "equivalents" or "trade-offs" through which individual differences can be formally equated, or, if necessary, deficiencies remedied. (New Careerists must work fast and collaboratively on this or the local Establishment will do it for you, and not so advantageously.)

Establish hierarchical categories: Heretical as this may seem to the ideals of New Careers, it is again a case of New Careerists doing it their way or having some far-away personnel clerk in civil service arbitrarily assign classifications. Develop step-by-step articulated categories within the New Careers series but also lateral branching—lattices—and vertical steps at the so-called "middle professional" level right on through to full professional grades. Make it all one package; include guarantees that individuals meeting the stated criteria will not be blocked anywhere on the ladder. The Establishment will buy it now. For help look to federal grants, foundations, the unions; they have money and expertise available to design the lattice.

Civil service: New Careers job categories should be integrated wholly within the regular employment/classification system of the hiring agency. (Discrepancies should be resolved by upgrading titles or modifying existing nomenclature without cutting back pay or maintaining any "special case" visibility; teacher's pet fares poorly after school. Basic rule #1: Wherever possible, use the Establishment's traditional channels; there are more of "them" than New Careerists. Make the bureaucracy work for New Careers. Cumbersome, illogical, hidebound, perhaps, but personal relationships can expedite things, and the machinery, from grievance proceedings to salary review boards, adds an aura of legitimacy and compliance to people and programs whose very successes provoke resentment in others by nature squelched and afraid to "try."

Professional separatism: Basic rule #2: Join the System but avoid inclusion under any of the existing health disciplines (i.e., classified as part of the nursing, social work, psychology series, etc.) Wherever this occurs, New Careerists are identified as "little" social workers, etc., and with the traditional disciplines top-heavy with MDs and PhDs, advancement is impossible except via orthodox graduate school credentials. As profession unto itself, New Careers can set ground rules of its own choosing garner expertise on an interdisciplinary basis, particularly out of its own ranks.

Training under collegiate auspices: Basic rule #3: All training—in-service, workshops, etc.—should accrue orthodox "credentials," college credits. Colleges, community colleges in particular, are not unwilling to radically restructure curricula to make them relevant and accessible to New Careerists. Collegiate credits are relatively transferable, certainly within a given curriculum; on-the-job programs by service centers count for naught. Professionals learn on "company" time (and expense). Released time, tuition-refund, full-stipend work study should be available to New Careerists; conversely, colleges are better able to carry training costs than the service centers.

New careers via college: Viability of any career hinges on the continuing influx of young people. Societal pressures toward higher education and the growing proportion of the poor following collegiate routes to the health careers must inexorably undermine New Careers' recruiting. Alternate and equivalent routes of entry are in order, experiment, too. (Collegiate, yes; tedious and irrelevant, no.)

Modular educational units: To ensure career-long advancement, in Maryland we have developed the associate professional process, college education organized into *modules* of one to two years duration, which lead to regular degrees, add professional expertise, parallel continuing education, and can be taken part-time. Spanning 10th-grade high school through the masters, the modular units are fully articulated—generalist to multiple specialties—with all credits transferable upward and the completion of one module automatically meeting admission prerequisites for the next. More importantly, students are encouraged to take employment, full-time between modules, employees to continue their schooling.

Matching job categories: Parallel job categories should be delineated within civil service, matching the educational modules, thus ensuring stepwise career advancement in step with increasing expertise. Agency roles require clarification and rearrangement to permit increasing responsibility based on smaller increments of education and work experience (salary scales following suit).

Competence criteria for promotion: Basic rule #4: Promotion up to and including full professional levels should be according to individual competence apart from staffing pattern tables. While a variety of qualifying mechanisms are possible—academic degrees, licensure, challenge exam, work experience, seniority—once passed, individuals should automatically receive promotion (which cannot be made dependent on the opening up of corresponding job slot). (The beginning school teacher progresses toward "maximum" independent of any requirement for department chairman or principals; Baltimore police, regardless of rank, receive an extra $2,000/year upon completing college.)

New careerists as faculty: Who is doing the teaching can be as important as what is being taught. The long-haul vitality of New Careers requires development of superior faculty from out of the ranks of the New Careerists, both for clinical supervision and as these appear, the collegiate programs. Faculty teams, including New Careerists and "credentialed" professionals, should be organized; they will be a more effective educational "organism," and the presence of the MAs and PhDs sidesteps the accreditation bugaboo.

Community-financed programs: Employment by the Establishment should not inhibit continued evolution of New Careers-community collaboration. New Careerists should work conjointly with their communities to advance the cause of community-instigated, administered, and community-financed service programs. Use of service teams and a continuum of skilled New Careerists will help reduce costs. Turnkey will be the use of basic community institutions—schools, PTAs, churches, social clubs—as partners in the delivery of prevention-education-rehabilitation services.

Cost-effectiveness data: New Careers must eventually prove itself to the Establishment in hard economic terms. Survival of New Careers will then be a function of having solid data capable of demonstrating the dollar efficiency of New Careers in recruitment, manpower development, the conservation of human resources in the ghetto, the economic, accessible delivery of quality services to a satisfied community. Collecting, analyzing, disseminating such data is up to the New Careerists; nobody else cares that much.

4. MODULAR EDUCATION AND THE DEVELOPMENT OF CAREER LATTICES

COMMUNITY PARTICIPATION

The societal resources available for the human services is not unlimited. Nor will any rearrangement of national priorities alone make resources equal to the need. Given those resources as are available, the good results that they obtain in mental health for the people are a function of *(a)* the expertise of the manpower employed, which, in turn is *(b)* a derivative of the quality and relevance of their training, multiplied by *(c)* the manner of their utilization in the field of institution. None of these variables, it is premised, may operate free of the composition of the human services personnel. That is, efficiency in the system is dependent on a steady flow of manpower from all walks of life, all races and ethnic minorities.

Optimal cost effectiveness derives from the deployment of personnel that, at every level and category, stands roughly comparable to the demographic composition of the region. Efficiency and quality of services diminishes whenever there is not the upward flow of manpower emanating from and educated within all population segments of the region.

Career Lattice: for the Many or the Few?

New careers was a way for unused manpower to break into the health and human services occupations. Many came, but few were accepted into the programs, and an even smaller number received permanent jobs. As for the colleges, it was no problem of theirs. Nonetheless, it is the educator's obligation that the first rung of every career ladder should extend well below entry-level curricula and, stretching into the farthest corners of the community, seek to capture the imagination of persons who had never before dreamed of "making-it" in a responsible human service career.

We are our brother's keeper. That racial prejudice, or poverty, or a broken home, or an emasculated secondary school system have early frustrated, and embittered, and scared off so many minority youngsters is no excuse for professionals to continue "business as usual." Higher education is not immutable; educators have answers to the failures of the past. Contemporary remedial education techniques—audio-visual aids and closed-circuit TV, along with a variety of behavior "mod", programmed instruction, and machine instruction devices—offer the chance to "save" the present generation vis-à-vis human service's professional careers. We have a growing armamentarium of counseling, tutorial, and work-study approaches with which to reach a larger audience and the teaching modalities to ensure the success of a considerable proportion of people otherwise lost to the professional categories. As will be discussed more fully in the ensuing sections, any real renaissance in the broad utilization of people in the human services hinges on their moving through the higher-educational system for the learning of clinical skills. It is not that the higher-educational system is the best teacher or the only reservoir of clinical expertise. Quite the contrary, innumerable other formulae can and are proving effective mechanisms for teaching entry-level human services skills. But that is the point; in the anarchy that results it is the nontraditional workers who pay the piper. The "American Way" is via college; and the undergraduate institutions have the wherewithal to do the job. All that they need is the professional input toward the curriculum design and the facilities' willingness to utilize the graduates.

Recruitment into our college human services curricula must be by many paths. Colleges must reach out to all population segments, utilizing a multitude of communications tactics, not just the circumscribed guidance counselor approaches of the past. "Good" secondary schools (i.e., high-budget suburban) have the guidance personnel; inner-city schools do not. Other means of alerting people to the possibility of human services careers must be used, particularly the media and community centers of choice to the minorities we have need for. Entry-level college curricula must be designed to directly articulate with the community and secondary schools on the one hand and with the next academic steps upward. Practicum facilities are always potential employers; the professional societies, sources of faculty, supervisors, consultation, and sanction for new college curricula and manpower types; government agencies, a reservoir for funding and financial support to students. They form a single system. Educators can bring them into common meeting and in their new curricula afford them bond of common purpose.

The Disagreeable "Realities" of Today's Manpower Scene

Before proceeding with a discussion of the role of the undergraduate colleges in the recruitment and training of entry-level professionals for the human services, a number of enigmatic paradoxes, tending to undermine the best intentions, are worth our examination:

1. The need for larger numbers of personnel qualitatively professional in competence yet recruited from segments of our society historically little represented in our graduate programs. Apparently unqualified for admission to graduate school, they are the untapped manpower needed for bold community programs.

2. The need to employ large numbers of sophisticated clinical personnel in the face of inflexible budgetary limitations and increasing demands by consumers for additional human services.

3. The urgency of client needs for generalist practitioners—persons who will stay with them and their families over time in a variety of circumstances—in contrast with the facilities' need for sophisticated specialists conversant in the human services specialties.

4. Similarly, the need for specialized expertise, traditionally purview of graduate education, within the context of rapidly changing service modalities; thus, the resultant dangers of oversupply at the PhD levels, overspecialization, and premature obsolescence of narrow-focused experts.

5. The seeming contradiction between pressures for the centralization of professional education within a few university programs and the contrary necessity for the disbursement of training close by the "living space" of all population centers and, in particular, proximal to service facilities for the continuing education and upgrading of existing personnel.

6. The exceedingly high costs of new graduate schools—construction, program initiation, and operation—in an era of unprecedented expansion in public undergraduate institutions, especially the community colleges.

7. The tendency for expert faculty to congregate within the university, attracted by the university's higher pay, prestige, and flux of innovative ideas, while most vigorous growth in services takes place peripherally, often under auspices of comprehensive neighborhood health centers and possibly health maintenance organizations in the near future.

8. The need for a more heterogeneous student composition as regards their life experiences, intellectual styles, immediate aspirations, and natural manner of learning, while mediating with a contrary-disposed system of graduate education, particularly in terms of the clinical arts.

College-Bound Young Americans, Circa 1975

Compared with their parents' world, the sky is the limit for most middle-class youngsters today. In search of education and preparation for a vocation they enjoy ever-widening horizons. Many of the shackling restrictions—economic, cultural, familial—that bound down their fathers and grandfathers have melted away. The most striking change differentiating the young people of the 1970s from their parents of the 1950s is their pell-mell rush into higher education. In 1910 less than 1 person in 12 finished high school. By 1930 this figure jumped to 1 out of 3; by 1940, nearly half of the 18-year-old population completed high school. In the course of one generation, 30 years, high school moved from a cultural rarity to the dominant mode, in effect becoming a part of growing up in middle-class America. Educational importance of high school took second place to its cultural imperatives. Much the same process overtakes higher education. In 1940 perhaps one-sixth of high school graduates completed college (less than 10% of the 18 to 22-year-old population). By 1960 the college-graduate ratio had soared to 25%. Presently, the Carnegie Commission on Higher Education estimates that some 35% of America's young people attend college, nearly 45% in much of the more affluent urbanized Eastern megalopolis. By the year 2000 Carnegie expects predict more than one-half of all Americans will be completing college, roughly two thirds of all high school graduates. (Their estimates may well be too low, forgetting that the poor, minorities, and other low college attenders are likely to catch up with prevailing American norms; that is, growth curves for these groups should roughly mimic the middle-class pattern, but on an accelerated schedule.) Moreover, when all forms of post-secondary-school education are included, the technical schools, for example, or diploma (hospital) nursing, the 1975 projections already suggest a two-thirds figure.

A formidable manpower pool! Nor should the college explosion necessarily precipitate comparable increases in graduate education enrollment. Recent statistics, corrected for the effects of students avoiding the Vietnam draft, imply a leveling trend. The total number of doctoral candidates continues to soar, but this growth is concentrated in new, emerging fields of study or fields not previously entertaining graduate curricula, for example, nursing, per se, or the several business specialties. Older, traditional courses of doctorate study, like psychology, are not so affected.

In sum, we bear witness to the democratizing of American higher education. College, once reserved for the few, becomes a natural ingredient to vocational readiness. From a college/noncollege dichotomy there is now a three-tiered system of doctorate types, college graduates, and finally, noncollegians. Exponential growth in the middle group has come primarily at the expense of the noncollegians. These college but not graduate-school types, once represented by the normal school and hospital nurse graduates, has swelled to include average Americans everywhere, from military officers to "home ec" majors and civil service bureaucrats. Much of the training preparatory for entry-level quasi-management roles in business and industry comes from our colleges. Once persons entered business after high school and rose up through the ranks, managers learning via on-the-job apprenticeship.

Middle Manpower for the Nation's Service-Based Economy

Metamorphosis in higher education is exactly paralleled by American business and industrial manpower patterns. Nineteenth-century manpower usage, typically a tiny executive or professional elite surrounded by a mammoth, functionally illiterate working class—unskilled factory workers, farm hands, domestics—is long gone. The increasing technological complexity of modern production and distribution leaves no room for the unskilled. Automation and the shift of American employment out of production jobs into service roles intensify this elimination of the untrained in favor of the new "technocrats"—the considerable collection of quasi managers, intermediate between skilled workers and the decision-making management team. The middle group is characterized by its considerable responsibilities exercised within a most limited frame of alternatives. Examples include an ever-increasing pool of new technical specialists, from highly skilled electronics equipment servicemen to draftsmen and programers, sales representatives (collegians because they must know the product's technology in order to sell it), and a vast array of "unit" directors, consequent to the burgeoning of innumerable branch offices, subassembly plants, product diversification, and national franchise distributorships.

In much of American business and industry the middle groups serve also as a screening mechanism for the identification and development of upper-echelon managers. Where advanced education is necessary, this may well be added on a work-study or strict fellowship basis. That individuals return for advanced graduate studies on company time at full pay is a not unusual practice in the electronics and aerospace fields. More commonly, however, good management prospects are rotated through a planned series of job responsibilities cutting across broad areas of the company's overall activities. In the process the pre-executive assumes increasing decision-making prerogatives, along with greater breadth and the intermittent opportunity to move laterally into one of the company's "clinical" specialties on a permanent basis, accounting, for instance, or the comptroller's office. Obviously, not everybody continues to move up; few reach the executive suite, let alone some assistant vice-president's job. Which hopeful, out of a given crop of new management trainees just hired out of college, is likely to be that 1 of 20? Who could tell? Industry, in order to ensure its pick from the best, as evidenced by performance in their company's milieu, allows the maturation process to proceed. Selection comes later. In this sense industry is inhuman, demanding proof after proof of competence, using people so long as they might blossom and selecting for its purposes those whose attributes conform most to company needs, rewarding them well to reinforce such behavior, no matter its effect on the individual. Nonetheless, a person's growth is potentiated not stultified, not categorized on the first day of employment forever after.

Soon enough perhaps, one-third to one-half of all American jobs will fit into this middle quasi-management group. Because these jobs tend to arise in infant industries, expanding industries, both capital-rich and showing immediate economic growth, they typically pay well. Many, too, as in computer programming, hotel management, or the mass media, bask in the reflected glamor of the field, which helps attract workers. (Waitresses who fly, called stewardesses, are looked up to despite the evening and weekend hours, tedious work, and lack of advancement. Why?) The pay is excellent, and the young people have been caught up in the spirit of mobility. The manpower implications to the human services are profound.

For good or ill these are the industries competing for the best of America's young men and women. Our youth seem most susceptible to the blandishments of hoped-for excitement, unlimited career advancement, relatively high initial starting pay, and the chance, however small, to hit it big. Pie in the sky? Maybe, but it is from this same pool of young adults that the human service careers must attract the majority of its future manpower. What would they do? That is exactly one of the impediments to their recruitment; nonetheless, the services have no alternative but to develop appropriate roles, advancement channels, sound pay schedules, and continuing educational opportunities for their efficient utilization. We have not ever used them, yet already they are crucial to the continuation of adequate public-sector services? How could that be? The answer lies in our rapidly changing service modalities and their exponential demand for judgmental-type personnel. The role of the non-professional aide ceases with the demise of the great asylums. California, for instance, has in less than five years reduced its state hospital population from some 42,000 to a mere 12,000. The kind of care these persons are currently receiving in their communities may be good, or less so, but the role of persons working with them is very different. Good community programs for the sustaining of even the more chronic individuals require staff capable of going out to the homes, small nursing facilities, and foster-care residence, rooming houses, and intervening directly in the patient's management. Consultant, therapist, activity leader, call them what you will; they necessarily must take responsibility and be rightly trained for it.

Use professionals? (And here we human services professionals need be brutally honest with ourselves and the public.) The numbers of professionals available through the 1980s could supply only a fraction of the practitioners required to implement outreach and preventative and child-care programs on a true community-wide basis. There are other caveats. Though underpaid, professionals cost too much for the public purse. This, too, is real and should be faced up to, and that without leaving the poor out in the cold. They are overtrained, particularly in areas as research methodology and one-to-one analytic psychotherapy, and therefore ill-suited to routine journeyman roles—predictably, the majority manpower category in tomorrow's human services.

Interestingly, there is little leverage for attracting large numbers of additional candidates to our graduate professional schools. The bottleneck would be the lack of liberal arts undergraduates willing to forego vocational preparation until the graduate years, thereby losing the chance for employment options. Thus, initiation of undergraduate educational programs in the human services will siphon off potential graduate school applicants even as they pull into the field many otherwise lost for want of undergraduate entry points.

Any notable increase in the utilization of professionals in subordinate roles consequent to some "crash" program toward community services would lead to the parallel reduction in entry-level salaries. Historically, municipalities that peremptorily moved to all "professional" social welfare staffs did not choose to offer salaries commensurate with attracting sufficient MSWs to fill subordinate positions. Characteristically, these vacancies gravitated into the temporary or unclassified category to be filled with any college graduate, or less, most of them without practicum work of any kind. True, they were only temporary, with high turnover and none of the civil service benefits such as continuing education or tuition refund that might have facilitated their professional growth. Net result? Although ostensibly these unqualified temporaries could have been replaced whenever professionals applied, in fact the low—purposely low—starting salaries ensured the opposite. Except for brief periods of recession when jobs are tight, attempts to utilize fully trained professionals in journeyman, routine, client services' roles have backfired, through the covert insertion of untrained, low-salaried personnel, the professionals restored to managerial duties.

This fact of public-sector-service life is mentioned to underscore the urgency to inaugurate new undergraduate curricula in the human services, the best that can be fashioned. Only insofar as the professional societies and the graduate school professors join with the undergraduate faculty and administrators in building professionally sound undergraduate programs can the standards of the traditional professions stand protected.

THE COMMUNITY-COLLEGE MENTAL HEALTH WORKER SERIES

The Maryland Department of Mental Hygiene, in search of solutions to the then-growing crisis in skilled manpower for the public care of the mentally ill, moved to instigate development of community-college curricula in the human services. The aim at that time (1966) was to generate a new kind of mental health worker designedly an associate professional by training and future potential. Although initial emphasis was placed on the associate of arts worker, the department's planners conceived of a unified process of manpower development, a continuing flow of persons into and up a latticework of human services careers and matched educational modules. Clear articulations both below, with Baltimore's secondary schools, and vertically, with regional state colleges, was envisaged and will be described more fully.

Antecedents date back to the department's initial tooling up for comprehensive community mental health (1964-65). Student enrollment in the human services professional schools, as projected against the implicit manpower requirements of a forthcoming state-wide system of neighborhood service centers, pointed up the sharp discrepancy between our graduate-training capabilities and oncoming manpower needs. Moreover, any abrupt thrust into federally subsidized community mental health would likely act to push up salaries. Competition for scarce professionals would, by a process of supply and demand, raise wages to the detriment of public-sector facilities. Major losers augured to be our already understaffed state institutions, whose prestige, pay, and geographic liabilities made them least attractive professionally. Community programs built at the price of decimated state hospitals seemed to us purposeless.

Enactment of Maryland's Community Mental Health legislation (1966) ushered in the step-by-step inauguration of 100 % state-supported but locally planned and administered services facilities. Under the law's plan for decentralization of services, challenges of a state-wide dimension—as manpower development—rested with the department. Educational planners, in their approach to graduate and potential undergraduate resources, were faced with these four imperatives:

1. Decentralization: small, autonomous, often community-operated "storefront" centers are little able to recruit professionals, yet are also too small to develop their

own high-powered training programs. Conversely, although numbers of indigenous residents are interested in pursuing human services careers, they are locked out of traditional academic routes of entry; university programs, meanwhile, lacked for minority applicants, others being rejected for lack of general education skills.

2. Innovative service modalities: Neighborhood outreach services called for new manpower types, persons trained in the unfolding modalities of team care, community consultation, family health care, and prevention. We needed workers gifted in the group therapies, and family therapy who could speak the language of the poor.

3. Educational Relevancy: programs and curricula attuned to public-sector services as they really are or ought to be; theoretical models, practicum assignments, tuition support, and faculty types consonant with community practice (the development of training programs not so much "anti-private practice" as offering a viable alternative for those interested, particularly undergraduate opportunities).

4. Staff development: Programs explicitly designed to utilize more efficiently the vast reservoir of human experience contained in the existing professional and nonprofessional workers in the public sector. Programs able to both capitalize on the nonprofessionals' strengths and build in needed remedial ("3 Rs") and work-study components; ready accessibility to all parts of the state.

Fortuitously, reports of unorthodox approaches by Rioch, True, Fishman, Peck, and Reissman and the momentum of New Careers encouraged the department to think innovatively. Wellner had earlier demonstrated receptivity among Maryland agencies toward new manpower types. Because of the department's success in developing one-year certificate training for psychiatric technicians (based on LPN models), many argued for development of a comparable community model, perhaps incorporating New Careers monies. Controversy ensued, especially vis-à-vis the relative career opportunities of the nonprofessional versus collegiate training sites.

Abetted by the Southern Regional Education Board's NIMH-supported Community College Mental Health Workers Project, the department threw its full weight behind the collegiate model.

To this end, a two-year undergraduate curriculum leading to the associate of arts degree was elaborated by the author and introduced at the Catonsville Community College in the fall of 1967, aided by a modest departmental grant in support of the program's director, Dr. Shabse Kurland. Concurrently, a parallel curriculum was offered by the Community College of Baltimore under Dr. Eveline Schulman. State civil service and personnel offices were moved to authorize a new job series in advance of the college's first classes, an important ingredient to success about which more will be said later. A year later, 1968, Essex Community College phased into operation as the third cooperating college.

Delineating the New Workers' Education

We began on a simple thesis: We believed that the Maryland community colleges were capable of training *beginning* professionals for a variety of generalist roles in the human services. We believed that while the traditional liberal arts background is an impressive adornment, valuable for its own sake, it is not mandatory for professional competence, given superior social sciences and practicum instruction. Moreover, we believed the human services could be taught at the community-college level without compromise to either academic quality, our students' future employment, or educational or personal maturation, acknowledging that two years is two years, not four or six.

Thus, no attempt was made to develop finished professionals in the two years. This would have led to too task-oriented, too narrow-focused a curriculum more in line with technical education than beginning professional preparation. We used the term "beginning" advisedly. It presumed the initial utilization of the young graduates

TABLE 3
Mental Health Associate Composite Curriculum for Associate of Arts Degree

Anne Arundel Community College, Catonsville Community College, Community College of Baltimore, Essex Community College, and Montgomery Community College

First year

First semester	*Credits*	*Second semester*	*Credits*
English composition	3	Expository writing	3
Public speaking	3	Psychology of personality	3
Introductory psychology		Contemporary social problems	3
Introductory sociology	3	Group dynamics (MHT 103)[a]	3
Humanities	3	Field work in mental health (MHT 101)[a]	4
Physical education	1	Physical education	1
	16		17

Summer employment in a mental health, welfare, antipoverty or similar human services occupation.

Second year

First semester	*Credits*	*Second semester*	*Credits*
Biology	4		
Psychology of exceptionality/child and adolescent development	3	Anatomy and physiology	4
Activity therapies (MHT 104)[a]	3	Abnormal psychology	3
Field work in mental health (institutional)[a]	4	Art, music, or humanities elective	3
Advanced social science elective	3	Field work in mental health (community) (MHT 201)[a]	6
	17		16

a Indicates clinically oriented mental health course, taught primarily in small group subsections within a community mental health or institutional setting by college faculty.

Brief course descriptions for the specialized mental health courses:

MHT 101-102: Field work in mental health (4 credits each). Two hours of lectures, six hours field work each semester.

First semester: cross-cultural studies on human adaptation; historical perspectives; techniques of observation, recording, summarizing, and communicating human interaction; interviewing, ethical considerations; mental health roles; patient roles. Second semester:

psychosexual development in children; testing techniques; group process in various settings; dynamics of total institutions. Field assignments: students rotate through three five-week assignments, first semester; two nine-week assignments, second semester.

MHT 103: Group dynamics (3 credits). Two hours lecture, two hours small group labs: factors involved in group cohesion and conflict; communication systems; role functions within groups; individual sensitivity and self-awareness; affective interrelationships; role-playing; psychodrama and sociodrama. The small group studies itself; communication and sensitivity skills are practiced.

MHT 104: Activity therapies (3 credits). Three hours lecture, one and one-half hours laboratory. Within a context of milieu therapy and group social interaction, elementary techniques of the several activity therapies are taught. Activity therapy programs of the participating agencies serve as demonstration models and practice sites.

MHT 201: Field work in mental health (6 credits). Two hours lecture, 12-15 hours field work per week: community organization; deviant behavior as a function of culture; availability of social mechanisms in support of psychic equilibrium; alienation; community agencies in theory and practice; delinquency; alcoholism and narcotics; retardation; social class structure, education, vocational skills, family relationships, stress, somatic disease, and self-image as factors in the emergence of overt symptomatology; principles of transference, over identification, denial, and projection. Field assignment: 18 weeks, two days each week to a single community mental health facility; beginning clinical work under close supervision; work as responsible member of mental health team with individuals, families, and in consultation to larger groups.

under supervision, in facilities able to afford them good orientation to the specifics of their new roles. We expected that assignments and clinical responsibilities would at first be routine and undemanding, yet graduated on a progressively more taxing scale, additional responsibilities accruing in proportion to the workers growing expertise. The guiding rhythm to the whole program was the unshakable faith of students, faculty, and department personnel in the new workers' eventual assumption of full professional skills and concomitant services responsibilities.

Curriculum included standard first-year English, public speaking, humanities, physical education, and a year of biological or physical science; the lion's share of the program, first year included, was background social and behavioral sciences—anthropology, child development, political science, psychology, sociology, and urban studies. Practicum assignments, along with an ongoing group experience termed "group dynamics," were instituted during the freshman year; major emphasis of the second year was individuated clinical clerkships under faculty supervision. All students rotated through at least one inpatient, outpatient, childrens and community agency practicum, though not the same ones necessarily. Continuity of didactic faculty and practicum supervisors ensured the functional synthesis of campus and service learning.

Reading assignments and lectures were tied to the small group seminars keyed to clinical topics, introducing students to psychodynamic issues, communication theory, and group process, as well as the dynamic interplay of social, familial, genetic, and developmental factors in the genesis of human behavior and the crystallization of personality. [See Table 3]

The students themselves contributed much to their own education not only via the numerous nonprofessionals attending under departmental work-study policies but also in the sharing of their life experiences with each other. Feedback toward the curriculums was intermittently elicited (and sometimes volunteered heatedly). Programs evolved under repeated modifications over the first years. Since it was nobody's intent to produce "instant professionals" by way of carbon-copy miniatures of the traditional human services professionals, the curricula reflected no single perspective. Faculty helped the students in their inevitable search for self-awareness. Instructional vehicles included much role-playing and some on-tape, psychodrama, activity therapies (one college utilizing dance therapy in the model of Chestnut Lodge). Most valuable was the students' simple expression of themselves before their peers and faculty and their learning that it is okay to be oneself, to have feelings, to be wrong, to listen, and to be heard. Considerable group solidarity developed, contributing to the individual's own sense of identity. That they were pioneering a new kind of training reinforced their strong intragroup bonds and, as well, a "chip on the shoulder" attitude.

The students' last semester was structured to include an elective full-semester practicum in an agency and area of focus approximating the student's major professional interests. Concentration or not, their final practicum added to their overall generalist skills. Where possible, the semester practicum included roles on service teams, their activities inherently demanding multilateral cooperation. Because no one student rotated through more than a fraction of the total practicum possibilities, there was considerable exchange of experiences and, too, gripes between students. (We had hoped the ensuing flux of descriptive and evaluative comments would press the students to define terms, programs objectives, and their own communications skills.)

Summer employment and, where possible, part-time employment in any human services-type role was strongly encouraged and facilitated by departmental aide jobs for all who desired them. No practicum ever duplicates the inexplicable realities of a real job for pay. Employment in a clinical role, too, allowed students a time for assessment midway through the programs, a chance to ask, "Is this my 'thing'; is this the career I want for a life's vocation?" For some, work proved invigorating, allowing them a more realistic vantage point from which to pursue further study; for others, a useful sobering. Because of the collegiate context of the curricula the latter could switch into other occupational fields with most of their credits transferable.

The First Years After the Associates' Graduation

Developing appropriate services roles for the first (1969) graduates was no mean task. Models were scarce, being either derived from New Careers or basically four- to six-year professional stereotypes. The Purdue graduate workers had been working but a few months, none of them yet employed in a mental health setting. Among some of the jobs carved out by students, departmental representatives, and the indefatigueable program directors are the following: Consultant to a city junior high school; family therapist (in association with a private practicing psychiatrist); "caseworker" on a crisis intervention team; group therapist on a locked adolescent drug ward; family counselor in a Maryland county psychiatric OPD.

By 1970, graduates, numbering some 75 individuals, moved farther afield. Three associates working as a team developed primary mental health care for a rural county, continuing as inpatient liaison for those hospitalized in the regional state hospital. Another associate is a full-time faculty member in a community-college program. Associates were employed to set up a prototype "behavior mod" token economy in a state hospital ward, and a larger group was hired to establish a 24-hour telephone suicide prevention and follow-up service in Baltimore.

The most conspicuous development has been the assembly of small associate teams by local practicing psychiatrists for the serving of Medicaid patients under Maryland's Title XIX program. Under the aegis of the psychiatrist's supervision and intermittent consultation the associates are carrying an increasing services load, and to a population heretofore unserved and considered unservable. (Is this unheralded phenomena portent to a services revolution a decade hence?)

To no little degree the selling of the new associates was accomplished by the students themselves; their performance on practicums proved an unbeatable medium for convincing prospective employers of the associates' capabilities in that milieu. Success of the Maryland programs in gaining employment for their graduates meant a lot of hard-sell public relations targeted state-wide by the department. No single college could effectively radiate across the several neighboring counties required for the students' placement. In addition, the presence of some 6,000 department jobs time and time again allowed for judicious transfer or temporary employment of associates. This kind of state-level intervention is a powerful stimulant in the early phases of any new program. Such becomes eloquent testimonial of the commissioner's support, a silent backing no official edict could ever reproduce.

A Network of College Programs and Employment Facilities

Graduates have been well received. None, to the author's knowledge, has yet lacked for employment in the several human services fields. As of January 1971, a job registry operated by the associates themselves showed some nine jobs going begging. (A state association of community-college workers ties together the more active local groups, for the most part aligned with the parent colleges but also serving as an important bridge between students and the real world of jobs and careers.)

Employer support justified expansion. Thus, three additional community colleges—Montgomery, Anne Arundel, and Prince Georges—were phased in during 1968-71. College program directors and department educators have intermittently met over the four years since inception, collaborating on curriculum minimums and moving as a group in dealing with problems of budget, accreditation, faculty salaries, and the like. (Since January 1971 a coordinator of associate manpower has catalyzed intraprogram communication between employers, students, the associates, and college faculty.)

Not everybody knows about the college programs, of course. Unfortunately, it is just those rural poor and ghetto youngsters most in need of access into viable careers who, along with their parents and high school guidance people, are least informed. While the Maryland Mental Health Association is vigorously attacking the problem of visibility, resolution hinges on the sustained proselytizing of minority peoples by the associates themselves. They can give the career credibility, impossible from on high. Nonetheless, applicants are plentiful. By the third operational year the colleges average freshman classes of 40 to 50 (out of perhaps some 60-odd applicants per college). As community college programs go, this is fast growth, the more impressive in view of the career's newness. At present the nearly 300 students enrolled in all constitute a body of future manpower larger than the combined enrollment of all Maryland's graduate human services curriculums, public and private, across the spectrum of the traditional disciplines—psychiatry, psychology, social work, and psychiatric nursing.

Current projections suggest that by the years 1972-75, numbers of Maryland associate degree graduates will plateau at about 120 to 160 annually, of whom we anticipate two-thirds (i.e., 80 to 120) will seek full-time employment immediately upon graduation. Of the remaining one-third, (approximately 40-60) perhaps from 25 to 40 will transfer uninterruptedly to senior colleges for their junior-senior years. Another 20 to 30 will leave the field, at least temporarily, for a variety of reasons, from military service to pregnancy. Given universal work-study opportunities in all community-operated services facilities and agencies, we believe an additional 15% of each annual crop of graduates would eventually, two, five, or more years later, return for their baccalaureate. Moreover, the ready availability of upper-division bachelor's courses on a part-time continuing education basis would enable a final 30% (40 to 50) to progressively advance academically while on the job. That is a wealth of manpower on its way up! Included, too, are a goodly number of department employees, part of the over 100 hospital aides currently attending community-college RN, dietary, and mental health associate programs on a full-time, full-pay arrangement.

In recent years the department has attempted to temper college enrollments in keeping with departmental and community-wide manpower needs as projected five years hence. The six operational programs afford accessibility throughout that four-fifths of Maryland's population residing in the Washington-Baltimore-Central Maryland corridor and the growing cities of Annapolis and Columbia (student driving time: 30 minutes or less.) By 1975 it is hoped that three more peripheral programs will directly support the Chesapeake Bay, rural Eastern Shore, and westward, Appalachia regions. Consummation of the latter will afford state-wide coverage.

TRAINING GOALS, SERVICE RESPONSIBILITIES, AND THE ASSOCIATE DEGREE WORKERS

It has only been over the past decade that from the evolving associate degree programs has crystallized a discrete, coherent body of ideas that, in Maryland, has been termed the associate professional process. Pragmatically, associate professional curricula, as recognizable pedagogic entities, derive from the *terminal* curricula of American community colleges, circa 1960-65. Initially ignored as merely a part of two-year technical education, the associate professional concept in fact transcends issues of academic site or the limits of the two-year associate degree design. The term is best known as applied to the "AD" nursing curricula, through which the once ubiquitous hospital (diploma) nursing programs came to be abbreviated in duration and incorporated within the community-college structure, faculty, credits, sciences, general education, and all.

Associate professional curricula aim at the creative integration of traditional lower-division undergraduate general education courses with both the theoretical and applied curriculum elements fundamental to beginning professional roles in any of the health and human services fields. Educators should not be turned off by the vocational reputation of the old junior colleges. The clinical heart of the human services can, and is, taught on a truly professional, albeit introductory, plane. The faculty are clinicians, fully qualified professionals. Underlying the associate professional approach is the premise that behavioral science theory, background social sciences, and the techniques of practice are inherently synergistic. Taught concurrently within a larger curriculum design, they act to reinforce learning, one complementing the others to maximize their educational impact. Far from subverting the liberal arts and social sciences, the presence of practicum and other clinical input enriches them, giving substance to the didactic speculations that otherwise tend to pass unperceived in the naïveté of middle-class youngsters little experienced in the world. The seeming unreality of campus-bound professional studies in the minds of certain students oftentimes disappears following the assumption of practicum responsibilities. Some students need the stimulation of real, concrete events to learn.

Associate professional curricula attach importance to early, heavy doses of practicum experiences. Much as laboratory work is deemed an essential component to mastery of the physical and biological sciences, the supervised clinical scene makes real the behavioral sciences. Judged professionally, associate professional programs are not weak sisters; community colleges, no less than any public institution of higher learning, are capable of building academically strong curricula. Certainly, there are exceptions, but these are failings of an individual institution or program. (Associate professional implies preparation for entry-level professional duties, a start in the field, but based on sound professional training for roles inherently maturing into full professional responsibility. The term stands quite apart from the usage of "associate" in associate degree.)

Graduates of the Maryland mental health associate programs are well practiced in the limits of their own clinical competence, cognizant of the kinds of situations that augur difficulties and habituated to the seeking of help from more experienced colleagues. Bringing in the "right" consultant is very much part of their role as they see it; there is neither loss of prestige nor any pressure to do it all themselves. And since nobody is professionally competent in all aspects of any profession, the associates by their very limitations are less likely to go beyond their clinical depth than many a professional whose ego concedes bounds of no kind. Short on clinical depth, the associates do possess the academic tools through which to grow professionally. They know how to use the professional literature and are equally at home with supervision, regardless of the supervisor's professional affiliation.

Clinical Training Objectives

Frequently, the question is asked: "But what can the associates actually do?" Initially, after graduation, they require orientation and the time to accommodate to the specific routines of the employing facility. Their training has been generalist's training. Unless they have had a practicum in the facility during training, they will be unfamiliar with the overall role assigned them. Initially, specific tasks must be assigned and follow-up supervision accorded to ensure their utilization of college-taught skills to the client needs of the moment.

Curriculum of the several college programs, while not standardized, follow a roughly uniform pattern, particularly in their overall clinical objectives. Students should achieve at least rudimentary professional skill in the following:

1. Interviewing techniques—In observing behavior and in interviewing, the associate is able to *(a)* harmoniously talk with others toward a clinical purpose and expeditiously elicit information without doing harm; *(b)* collate and synthesize substance of the interview; *(c)* effectively communicate selected portions to colleagues in form meaningful to them; *(d)* maintain awareness of the impact of feelings, institutional/neighborhood forces, and cultural values on the transactional process.

2. Consultation techniques—The associate can help people—clients, families, and organized groups—find solutions to an immediate dilemma drawn from, and in

the language of, the societal system served. They are taught to mobilize endemic strengths and to push for approaches likely to generalize, becoming useful other times in other circumstances. Client solutions must be "workable" in their worlds; problems must be defined in the widest parameters possible.

3. Community action—Utilizing available community structures and value systems in concert with intrinsic leadership, the associates are expected to seek conjoint tactics effective in awakening a community's dormant resources in the cooperative amelioration of common afflictions. In roles akin to so-called change agents, indigenous associates might work in environmental quality control.

4. Care of the chronically ill—Through routine confrontation with the many chronic conditions—old age, retardation, the degenerative diseases, regressive schizophrenia, unremitting poverty—the associates are expected to be knowledgeable in instigating bridges for them back to their communities and in establishing close-by resources through which the chronically invalided might maintain themselves in the community. Their aim is not cure but the optimization of the client's and his family's residual strengths, more on an educational model than medical.

5. Teaching—Curriculum of the associates includes practice in the art of teaching. Throughout their careers they, like the orthodox professionals, will be called on to instruct others in the nuances of living together—volunteers, colleagues, client groups, students, and most important, via participation on teaching teams in the community colleges, the next generation of associates-to-be.

6. Behavioral modification—Availability of ongoing pilot projects within the department's institutions and the special expertise of several of the college faculty in behavior modification has led to general familiarity of the student associates to this new modality. As graduates we assume a number will continue on in research and treatment programs utilizing primarily behavior "mod" tech-

niques; some may, hopefully in time, initiate investigative programs of their own.

7. Group dynamics—Understanding the theory and practical leadership involved in diverse group work, associates might, for example, lead an ongoing group for mothers of disturbed children, or alcoholics, or apply the principles of group process to the umpiring of a ball game among correctional inmates.

8. Liaison techniques—A still-unfolding area of expertise that combines aspects of communications, group process, intuitive interpersonal sensitivity, management skills, and the systems analysis-operations research bailiwick. Because of the thrust into decentralization and the reintegration of human services within the larger context of comprehensive health care or the HMOs, associates might advantageously serve in administrative capacities, their behavioral skills enabling them to bridge the interface between divers units. Ombudsman roles might similarly evolve out of the predictable rivalries and red tape within the bureaucracies.

At the point of graduation the associates should be neither finished professionals nor perennial subordinates. Without grooming them for any narrow specialty role or single cluster of tasks, we anticipate their growth on the job according to services needs and their own professional interests and personal predilections. The latter implies the prior development of both the bureaucratic structure and services roles conducive to stepwise career advancement and, therefore, a complementary series of educational modules.

The author believes no arbitrary constellation of activities can be prescribed in detail, *a priori,* for all institutions and outreach facilities, now and forever. The joy of the new manpower lies in its flexibility and freedom from outdated, parochial traditions. Given the appropriate educational and supervisory input, they are free to grow in ways as innovative as the farthest dreams of tomorrow's services. There is room for joint discovery by the associates and their professional colleagues. While they are ready for uncomplicated professional duties delegated to them under professional supervision, they naturally own unique skills of temper and past experience that ought to be used. But such begs the real question inasmuch as the beginning worker is not a stagnant, unchanging statue but a living, expanding, learning being different tomorrow from today. The real question then is: What are to be the skills and breadth of clinical judgment of these selfsame associate professionals after 5, 10, 20 years of human services experience, along with a congruent inflow of professional ideas, advanced education, and progressive assumption of greater responsibilities?

Job Categories and Pay Scales

The community-college associates were keyed into the Maryland civil service scheme parallel to the beginning registered nurse. Since most RNs are entering now by way of comparable community-college programs and are considered professional nurses, this seemed a logical niche for them, too. As will be noted in Figure 1, pay scales for the associates overlap the upper range for the senior psychiatric technicians and LPNs. But these persons are also eligible for the department's work-study programs—full-time community college study on full pay, with an obligation of half-time services, (Technicians are also free to take the released-time, tuition-refund road to community college, allowing them up to eight hours weekly off to attend classes.) There is thus continuity of both pay and career advancement between lower-echelon nonprofessionals and the new associates. Their coming into existence does not thereby thwart mobility of any below them, a crucial point.

Similarly, the associates may both move up within their own mental health associate job category, or via operational upper-division human services modules at the Morgan State College, jump vertically into the higher mental health "specialist" category. The latter, paying in the range of $9,217 to $13,321, is a not "unprofession-

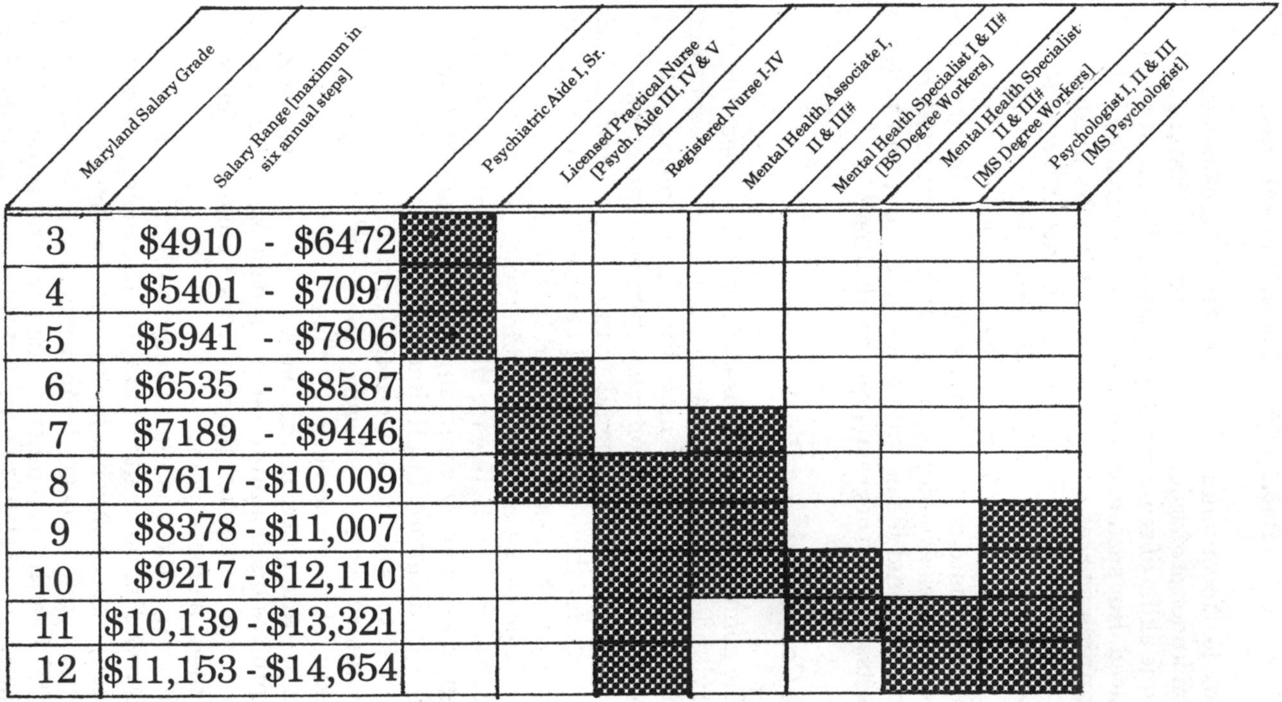

Maryland Salary Grade	Salary Range [maximum in six annual steps]	Psychiatric Aide I, Sr.	Licensed Practical Nurse [Psych. Aide III, IV & V	Registered Nurse I-IV	Mental Health Associate I, II & III#	Mental Health Specialist I & II# [BS Degree Workers]	Mental Health Specialist II & III# [MS Degree Workers]	Psychologist I, II & III [MS Psychologist]
3	$4910 - $6472	■						
4	$5401 - $7097	■						
5	$5941 - $7806	■						
6	$6535 - $8587		■					
7	$7189 - $9446		■		■			
8	$7617 - $10,009		■	■	■			
9	$8378 - $11,007			■	■			■
10	$9217 - $12,110			■	■	■		■
11	$10,139 - $13,321			■		■	■	■
12	$11,153 - $14,654			■			■	■

Figure 1. CAREER LATTICE SALARY RANGES: interrelationship of traditional and non-traditional workers
*salary range based on authorized schedule beginning 1 January 1972
#as proposed

al" level of remuneration. At the baccalaureate level the associates are similarly entitled to attend college part-time on the same eight-hour released-time, tuition-refund policy. (Classes are offered at times convenient to working applicants.)

Departmental planning anticipates eventual availability of graduate-level curricula, organized by human services program—child care, services to the elderly, acute psychiatric admissions, social welfare services, etc. Because of the overlap inherent in the two "specialist" curricula, plans call for a combined upper-division bachelors/masters program of three years' duration as an option. The interrelationship of the several nontraditional career categories within themselves and with the other professional/nonprofessional groups is pictured in Figure 2. One warning, the job categories, while basic to all departmental facilities do not necessarily obtain in the autonomous community mental health centers. Decentralization requires each political subdivision to develop its own categories and pay scales, though the existence of state-level classifications helps influence the local county decisions. Educating 23 separate county health officers, their mental health units and advisory boards, is a major public relations undertaking, yet without which positions for the new manpower cannot be budgeted.

Bringing the Associates on Board

In the department's facilities the associates have not been assigned to any of the professional departments, per se (i.e., nursing, social work, psychology, etc.). Instead, the associates are assigned to programs or to area units such as buildings or geographic catchment areas. Administratively, they "belong" to the area chief in charge of the services on which they are actually working. The chief may be a psychologist, social worker, nurse, or psychiatrist. He gives them their day-by-day work assignments much as any other professionals on

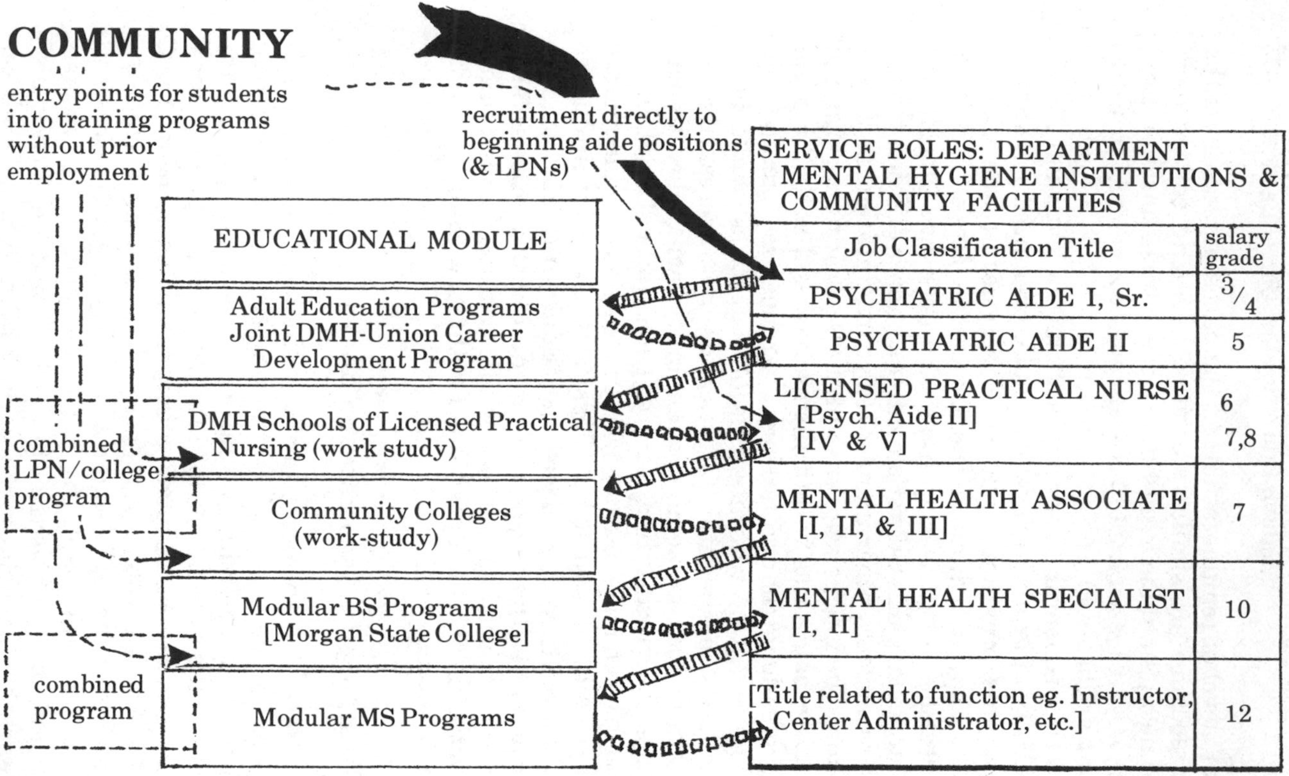

COMMUNITY

entry points for students into training programs without prior employment

recruitment directly to beginning aide positions (& LPNs)

EDUCATIONAL MODULE
Adult Education Programs Joint DMH-Union Career Development Program
DMH Schools of Licensed Practical Nursing (work study)
Community Colleges (work-study)
Modular BS Programs [Morgan State College]
Modular MS Programs

combined LPN/college program

combined program

SERVICE ROLES: DEPARTMENT MENTAL HYGIENE INSTITUTIONS & COMMUNITY FACILITIES

Job Classification Title	salary grade
PSYCHIATRIC AIDE I, Sr.	3/4
PSYCHIATRIC AIDE II	5
LICENSED PRACTICAL NURSE [Psych. Aide II] [IV & V]	6 7,8
MENTAL HEALTH ASSOCIATE [I, II, & III]	7
MENTAL HEALTH SPECIALIST [I, II]	10
[Title related to function eg. Instructor, Center Administrator, etc.]	12

Figure 2.

his staff, supervising them either himself or via another member of this treatment team. The unit chief knows what he wants done, knows the capabilities of his staff as a whole, and is best able to assign priorities for staff activities in relation to the unit's overall services mission.

We believe this fosters the associates' ready identification with the system and its system-wide objectives on the broadest most human basis, not merely from the limited horizons of a single professional discipline. Their roles are still evolving. Their charge is to complement the professions not replicate them. We hope to avoid the kinds of identity diffusion that follow subordination of a small, unorthodox minority under an older, larger, traditional group (membership in which is not possible to the lower-status group). For these reasons the author takes strong exception to any apprenticing of the new associates as "assistant psychologists," "assistant social workers," etc. No doubt many of them will and ought to, work in close support of their senior professional colleagues. Indeed, many of their activities at first could fairly be termed beginning social work or beginning activity therapy. But the activities should not obstruct the progressive identity formation of the associates. Lodged in an administrative "cubbyhole" as a perennial assistant would thwart the full unfolding of the new professionals, obstructing their flexibility to mold their role in accord with future services needs. Our position is that so long as there is not any direct route upward into the next higher career category via in-service or work-study education, then any subordinate group is *de facto* second-class. And there is no use to generate another dead-end manpower category in the health or human services.

Candidate Selection

Admission to the mental health associate programs presumes that the student first be admitted to the parent community college, though the college's requirements are minimal. The Community College of Baltimore, for instance, accepts students lacking either a high school diploma or QED on a reduced-credit-load basis. Students requesting entry into the mental health curriculum are counseled by the clinical faculty before matriculation, which affords the students a chance to learn about the career firsthand and the faculty to appraise the potential students. Some choose not to enter; others, grossly unsuited to an interpersonal career, are helped by the faculty to find another occupational choice. Most students, as many as four-fifths, do matriculate. This is planned. We believe selection should derive only from performance in the clinical field not by way of prior success on exams, arbitrary personality screening, or anything except the well-studied evaluation of their person-to-person effectiveness in the clinical scene.

Life experience, we believe, and one's habitual ways of coping may be as valid a criteria for predicting good performance in the human services careers as academic scholarship measured in activities far removed from the nitty-gritty of real people work. What is the predictive utility of psychological testing or faculty recommendations? It is our prejudice that interested applicants at least have the chance to try to find out for themselves in the real-life situation. (After all, they are already college students, and there is nothing to guarantee passing the curriculum except that the student prove himself qualified in the judgment of the clinical supervisor's mind.) Students grow at different rates before college as well as during college years. We feel that much of human services training is allied with identity building. Well-designed practicums under good professional "models" may well allow the "laggards" to catch up, to become sentient clinicians in the process. Those who cannot, despite added input of counseling and remedial education, are dropped from the program.

In actuality this rarely happens. While the attrition rate is comparable to "AD" nursing, between 15 to 25%, most students who fail to complete drop out on their own initiative. We have been struck by the large proportion of students who perceive, themselves, their unsuitability for interpersonal work. That clinical practicum work begins in the first college year makes it possible for students to realistically feel themselves in the human services; those who do not like the feel are fortunately not bound down by the graduate student's four or six year's investment in a behavioral career. The author is reluctant to substitute his prejudices for the free "market" decisions of prospective students and the reality of the practicum encounter. Judgment of most professionals may have statistical validity in predicting risk of failure or success, but for the student rejected as having only a 30% likelihood of making it, this is little solace. We feel he deserves the right to make this decision himself, preferably with some awareness of the staff's doubts during the initial counseling session. And for those who do not make it, there are the college's portfolio of other careers for which a considerable amount of his human services credits are applicable in transfer.

Selection at the baccalaureate level is another kettle of fish. Inasmuch as entry into the upper-division modules at the Morgan State College requires completion of the associate degree curriculum, there is sound evidence of performance in the field on which to accept or reject a given applicant. But even here there is no finality to rejection. Since most are already working, they are simply asked to continue a while longer at their employment, leaving open the possibility of admission in the future following demonstrable improvement in their clinical performance. If one applies a year or two later, we expect he can be judged on his supervisor's evaluation. There is always motivation to succeed; second, third, perhaps "seventh" tries are available without stigma.

In-Service Orientation

The community-college students are exposed to a varied lot of institutional and community practicum experiences. Nonetheless, at graduation they are an unfinished product, measured by professional standards. Like professionals, they require on-the-job orientation to the nitty-gritty routines and paperwork of their specific activities. This has been the department's weakest link in the program. In the monolithic institutions it is easy for a couple of new associates to be lost from sight. Conversely, in the smaller neighborhood centers there is a sparcity of supervisory staff and too few "indians" to spare the associate for prolonged "breaking in." We would recommend a year's formalized in-service program, say, three to five hours per week, in order to strengthen the new associates' sense of professional identity and their clinical expertise as well. Supervisors should be available readily. If the associates are to grow and also take on judgmental duties, good supervision must be accessible. But the more formal in-service should not be a haphazard thing. A single professional should be assigned responsibility for its coordination, though the instruction itself ought to be interdisciplinary. Where feasible, older, experienced associates should be used as teachers alongside the professionals. Unless the in-service is multidisciplinary there is the risk of somebody modeling them into junior psychiatrists, junior MSWs, RNs, etc.

BACCALAUREATE AND MASTERS DEGREE MODULES

In retrospect, the department's choice of a collegiate training vehicle for its new, nontraditional community manpower came about by default. Alternatives seemed doomed beforehand. As we saw it in 1965-66, the enormity of Maryland's public sector manpower needs, the sheer numbers to be first recruited, then trained, precluded the department's reliance on its own hospital training capabilities or the single university-based community mental health center to be built. Hospitals were little attuned to community mental health, programwise. They had no remedial education or general education-social sciences components. Not only were the community mental health facilities as yet embryonic but also the chief impediment to their early implementation would inevitably be their lack of trained manpower. Because of the time lag between instigation of a new training program and the outpouring of its graduates in any numbers, training must be planned and started up well in advance of the construction of the new facilities themselves.

Failure to act, however, raised the specter of several dozen autonomous neighborhood centers independently spinning off their own on-the-job, do-it-yourself training endeavors, none of them owning academic or interinstitutional transferability. Graduates of the programs would not only be in competition with the more traditional disciplines—professionals—but with themselves, too, at least for wages and promotions across institutional boundaries.

The Public Undergraduate Colleges as Turnkey Educational Resource

The single medium for the advancement of human services manpower is the public undergraduate college system, the community and four-year state and municipal colleges. Why is this so? Why should human services education necessarily be enchained within a collegiate framework? Why not greater emphasis on new careers, in-service education, challenge-type examinations as criteria for promotion, even the use of apprentice-type programs on the order of the physician assistants?

While many alternatives to the collegiate model may exist in theory, none are acceptable in practice. America espouses the credo that a man's worth is indelibly inscribed on the seal of his academic diploma. If ridiculous, it is reality! Body and soul, the nation is committed to the use of collegiate mechanisms for the vocational preparation of its youth. Maybe it is all one grand hoax, but that is the way we are going, and the devil take the hindmost.

The momentum of engineering, hard sciences, education, and business-industry-sales, and communications media careers is toward college training for entry-level "professional" or associate professional jobs. The human services cannot long move counter to the nation's educational and employment patterns. While a limited success of sorts over the next decade might be possible, where would that leave the new manpower come 1980, or 1990?

Today, most practitioners in the human services, like the health industry, are bona-fide college/graduate school-trained professionals. Nonprofessionals do not count. In the future, an increasing proportion of young Americans will pass through college on their way to regular employment; if professional competence and higher education are deemed synonymous in the human services today, how much more so in the 1980s when nearly everybody will have at least some posthigh school training and perhaps half of all Americans will be college graduates. While today's human services are composed of a majority of nonprofessionals, their presence in the outreach picture of the 1980s is dubious. The proportion of professionals vis-à-vis the total of human services workers, professional and nonprofessional, will steadily increase. By 1980 the majority of all persons working in the behavioral sciences will be college graduates and up. Young adults entering training for the human services during the years 1972-76 ought to be entering their most productive clinical years in the 1990s, by then in their late thirties to midforties. What will be their claim to full professional responsibilities? And on what basis will those lacking college backgrounds prove themselves in a milieu whose manpower is predominantly academically trained? (Equally, there are implications toward those whose truncated college studies become short-circuited by lack of re-entry points back into the higher-education mainstream.)

Will people not wake up by then, will the human services not divorce themselves from such provincial attitudes? People have a way of justifying their own special place in any hierarchy; the human services is no exception. Thus, professionals in their thirties and forties now will be entering their fifties or sixties in the 1990s; in addition, a whole flock of younger graduate schooled professionals will keep pouring in. As evidence of their competence they will necessarily point to their academic preparation. Those in charge now will, as humans, tend to perpetuate the system in their own image, selecting subordinates to key positions because of their graduate education, all other things being equal. Only the most gullible idealists will expect that any monolithic system made up of human beings is going to generously, graciously yield up a century of precedents in its favor for the sake of a minority of "uncredentialed" youngsters simply because they are talented.

Moreover, society will side with the credentials. Society has built the college buildings, for decades paid the faculty, supported the students, tolerated the tuition costs, and most of all, believed! That is a tremendous investment, a mammoth agglomeration of taxes, cultural values, aspirations, and, as well, the ongoing lobbying of the academic organism, all aiming at the sustained dominance of the college way and the products of that way, the young graduates. Students of the next 20 years, having invested 4, 6 or 10 years of their lives in expectation of commensurate gain during their professional years, are not likely to devalue their credentials and invite the nonprofessionals or noncollege trained to *jump over* them to positions of greater responsibility, status, or remuneration. To repeat: Nobody's going to fix things so as to ensure continued advancement of in-service or community college-trained manpower into jobs they themselves aspire to. (Help the New Careerists up into the system and past the veteran nonprofessionals, surely, but when it gets to my job, or my supervisor's, that is different.)

But maybe there is no basis for conflict. Suppose the human services gave over to the higher-education system responsibility for training everybody, from lowest to highest, with only the proviso that education at all levels articulate with curricula above, below, and laterally. At risk is only the relevance of curricula to service modalities, the accessibility of programs, and the provision of continuing education. In other words, devise an egalitarian manpower development program by making it one system—the lower echelons joining with the collegians not fighting them. Persons otherwise trained outside of the collegiate structure today can just as easily be sent off to the colleges, the facilities later mediating to their advancement by arranging for their periodic return for advanced professional education.

While the momentum to higher education is an irreversible American phenomena, the nature of the educational input is very much open to change. Content, instructional methods, and goals are literally in search of direction. The author takes the position that if it is worth teaching then it is worth college credits (the realities of which dictate thinking through the substance of informal and in-service curricula so as to build workshops and continuing education programs under college auspices out of these now-scattered bits and pieces of professional expertise). With few exceptions the community colleges and a considerable number of four-year public colleges are only too willing to radically modify existing curricula or add new ones in favor of career-oriented, clinically focused programs in the human services. What they require is only the professional expertise in how to do it. Public colleges are responsive to the services manpower needs and the career opportunities of their graduates. They will accommodate their policies to the needs of minority recruitment and the exigencies of the local service scene.

Undergraduate colleges, by their cultural pre-eminence, can do for the nontraditional human services workers what no other societal institution or legislative licensure act could hope to accomplish. That is, by reorganizing their curricula to suit entry-level professional roles and their intermittent stepwise advancement via continuing education, equality of job opportunity becomes a feasible goal.

In reaching out across a given state or region, the community and state colleges offer the basic social science and general education faculty, physical plant, community relationships, hard money financing, and above all, the natural flow of students needed to recruit and train large numbers of beginning human services professionals. The BS degree and lately, too, the AA degree are the universal credential. Bachelors and associate degrees from accredited colleges, like Bank Americard, are recognized nationally, and to a considerable degree transferable nationally. Federal health manpower legislation will hasten this process; provisional studies point to the federalization of accredation proceedings in the years 1972-75. (Introduction of a national system of licensure and examinations should not obscure the underlying fact that entrance into the examination will routinely follow completion of the appropriate college curriculum. In the same way that the high school equivalency exam has not superceded the traditional high school degree, challenge exams will, if anything, legitimize the college credentialing system by defining a limited number of alternatives, with college the most feasible.)

Campus is where the young people are—and the housewives, the part-time student/workers, the retired military, and others seeking a second career. Tax supported and legislature controlled, the public undergraduate colleges are sentient to societal needs. What they lack in practicum sites and clinical faculty and services traditions are economically and conveniently available through affiliation with proximal mental health and social welfare facilities, interested practitioners, and the several professional societies. These all are genuinely interested in helping the college define and operate viable clinical programs; if there is any impediment at all, it is the lack of communication channels between traditionally separate service and higher educational institutions.

Baccalaureate Options at the Morgan State College

The Morgan State College in September 1970 opened to transfer students the second phase of Maryland's three-stage career lattice in the human services. Completion of phase II at Morgan—eventually a panoply of parallel two-year curricula leads to the BS degree in mental health. Structured at the upper-division baccalaureate level (i.e., junior-senior years), the Morgan *modules* are open to graduates of any of the community college mental health associate programs (and by 1973 to mental health associate programs (and by 1973 to Morgan juniors currently enrolled in the lower-division counterpart of the associate degree curriculum). The initial curriculum is in community mental health, with child care/educateur and neighborhood health center administrator scheduled for mid year 1972-73, drug abuse/alcoholism counselor, behavior modification technologist, and mental health nusing to follow. Curriculum content and objectives for each module are free standing, although there is much in common at the third year and common electives the fourth. Graduates of all the modules are subsumed under the bachelor of science in mental health degree, by design an umbrella classification intended to protect the future mobility of the graduates. We believe the graduates to be generalists whose upper-division differences of professional interest are less conspicuous than their commonality of skills and human services expertise (see Table 3). Likewise, a single umbrella job category is anticipated by the department of mental hygience (mental health specialist). The interrelationship of the Morgan College upper-division baccalaureate programs to each other and to the community-college offerings is diagramatically pictured in Figure 3.

Enrollment for 1971-72 is expected to run from approximately 35 to 40 students, many of whom are mental health associates employed by the department and at-

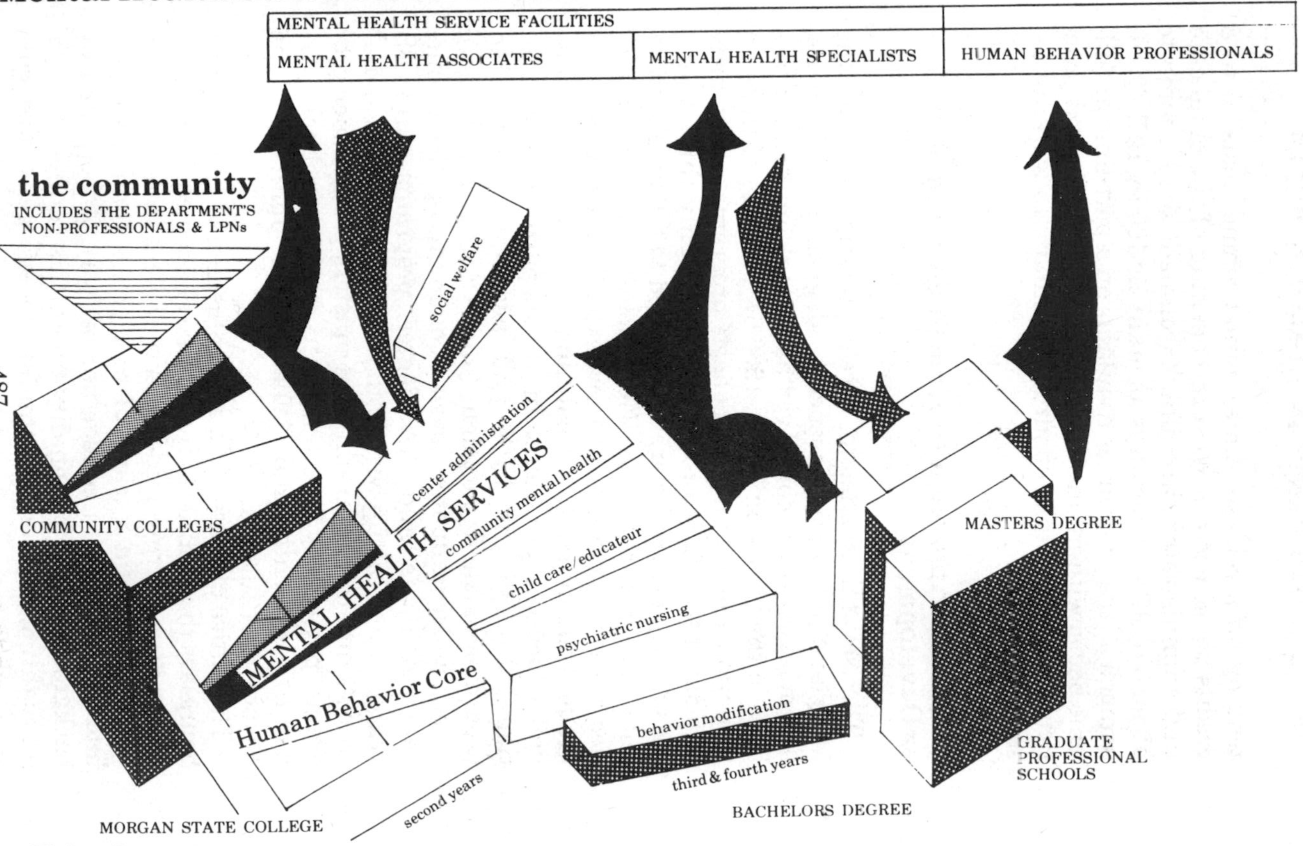
Mental Health Series Career Lattice
MENTAL HEALTH SERVICE FACILITIES
MENTAL HEALTH ASSOCIATES
MENTAL HEALTH SPECIALISTS
HUMAN BEHAVIOR PROFESSIONALS
the community
INCLUDES THE DEPARTMENT'S
NON-PROFESSIONALS & LPNs
social welfare
center administration
MENTAL HEALTH SERVICES
community mental health
child care/educateur
psychiatric nursing
behavior modification
third & fourth years
COMMUNITY COLLEGES
Human Behavior Core
second years
MORGAN STATE COLLEGE
BACHELORS DEGREE
MASTERS DEGREE
GRADUATE
PROFESSIONAL
SCHOOLS

Figure 3.

tending on a released-time, tuition-refund basis (6 to 8 credits per semester). With the opening of the child-care and administrator curricula, enrollment should jump to about 60 (1972-73), perhaps as many as 100 by 1973-74 inasmuch as the program is available on a part-time or full-time basis, with multiple sections and individuated practicum assignments to ensure accessibility to working associates.

A Systems Approach to Human Services Manpower Development

The several academic levels encompassed by the Maryland programs—associate degree, baccalaureate, and masters—were conceived as a single unified process back in the planning years, 1966-67. Because of their articulation the community-college programs necessarily antedated the Morgan modules by roughly three years; the masters programs are anticipated to follow a similar lag of two to three years. Nonetheless, they form a unified system of manpower flow, extending from eleventh grade (Dunbar High School) and adult education-remedial education programs in the department's institutions, through the LPN and psychiatric technician programs of the department (and AFSC & ME Union), three undergraduate levels—community-college one-year certificate and AA degree programs, and BS degree—then link up with both the graduate professional schools and the nontraditional masters practitioner programs, potentially in the Morgan graduate schools, Urban Affairs Center, and elements of the Johns Hopkins Medical Institutions.

The lattice operates like an old-fashioned egg timer or hourglass that connects two funnel-shaped containers together at a narrow middle section. The inverted lower funnel attracts a variety of non professional types up into the community college narrow way. A potpourri of backgrounds and personality types thus funnel through a roughly consistent community-college generalist curriculum, whence the funnel expands laterally as it extends upward. The baccalaureate and masters programs growing out of the AA degree curriculum allow for increasing concentration of professional focus, eventually admission to the discrete professional graduate schools.

While the community-college programs are not identical, they are geared to a single agreed-upon constellation of training objectives, modified by the variations of practicum, supervisor, and student. The next module, the upper-division baccalaureate unit, is viewed as one route to continued professional maturation for the AA generalists in the area of service most useful to their clinical work (or future aspirations). It is one step up vertically; yet it is also one step laterally on the road to specialization. They form a family of human services career options at the bachelor's level that provides not only special skills in one area but also continued general familiarity with the human services *in toto*.

The Community College Mental Health Workers and College

Before continuing with the lattice's design, it is well to ask why, if the associates are doing well in their various jobs and are "programmed" to grow professionally in the process of their daily service routine, send them back for more formal education? What can another two years of campus and practicum accomplish not just as available to the associates on their jobs? Nothing!, that is, provided that exactly those skills the young associates individually might want to learn are natural to his daily work routine. If the working associate wants to learn more about family therapy, he can, provided that there is a family therapy program operating in his community center under the direction of a knowledgeable professional not only skilled in the medium but also adept at teaching and supervising others as well. (Even if there were, it would be necessary for the center to free the associate from other duties in order to concentrate in the area of family group work.)

In an era of decentralization neither teacher nor ongoing program is likely available in the right place and right time for a given associate's needs. The staffs of small neighborhood facilities are too limited, while community institutions using the associates as consultants and in liaison roles are without expert faculty entirely (e.g., the courts or elementary schools). And the logistics of state hospitals precludes any multidimensional in-service education, particularly to suit the student's needs while still an employee. After all, impetus to the generation of the new nontraditional workers was the shortage of mental health professionals in public-sector institutions. There is hardly sufficient staff in our beleaguered facilities for them to double as educators, nor can they freely branch out into whatever area of focus to which a student might be interested in moving.

Thus, the first reason for inaugurating the baccalaureate programs is the improbability of the typical community-college mental health worker attaining additional professional education on his own. The baccalaureate institutions function as a kind of curriculum clearinghouse, making visible and available a heterogeneous mix of professional skills, then delivering them on a schedule and annual repetition that ensures accessibility (and that quite apart from the young clinician's employment obligations). The second reason for the BS modules relates to the associates' expectation of growth.

The Concept of Manpower Flow

A decade ago community-college vocational curricula were perceived as terminal education; that is, preparation for jobs demanding of two years' training and not a jot more, ever. Terminal curricula produced technicians not professionals. Albee, and others, long ago urged development of middle-level persons, motivated and not unintelligent, suited to the tedious, unrewarding aspects of the professionals' routine. (Someone to do the things the professional did not want to do but had to be done.) In theory a splendid idea. Professionals, once relieved of the mundane, could concentrate on activities more suited to their academic preparation, and institutional costs would drop through the more efficient use of expensive professional time.

Unfortunately, no one wants to be a perennial assistant anymore. Measures aiming at generating middle professionals floundered not because such personnel were not needed—they were—but because the approaches used in the early 1960s were incompatible with the realities of the labor market.

Most people competent enough for beginning professional duties and bright enough to assume the professional's routine chores responsibly simply had better offers in other fields. Through the magic of community colleges very average persons could, in a matter of two years, acquire entry-level training for open-ended careers without the perennial assistant "hangup." In the health occupations lab technology, inhalation therapy, radiological technology, dietary technology, and professional nursing appeared among the dozens of careers suddenly available in competition with anything the human services had to offer.

Manpower flow, the process of career-long job mobility, was postulated as a remedy to the dilemma. Maryland's career lattice structure was designed to bridge the static, hierarchical nature of human services manpower via clear channels for upward and lateral mobility. The role of the assistant or middle professional could be elaborated and successfully recruited so long as the role was not permanent. The key was to provide a route upward. Lower-echelon jobs instead of being dead ends became steppingstones toward professional roles. Everybody has to start somewhere. Beginning at the bottom rung is not demeaning provided you are going someplace. How long it takes and the nature of the immediate duties are not so important if in the meanwhile the individual's work identity acknowledges the future potential (and the chance for advancement is real). The physician accepts the internship and residency roles despite their long hours and "scutwork," exactly because they are transient things associated in the public's mind's eye with progress toward later importance.

Nor is the middle person's advancement any setback to the professionals. Some have argued that it is silly to emphasize the passage of middle persons up to professional status since what we most urgently need is the middle or assistant person. Need alone draws no one. Without an "escape up," nobody at all can be hired for the job. Yet with careful attention to the advancement elements numerous persons will seek the job, their eyes looking to the future. In turn, once there is a flow of middle-level persons upward and into higher education, then new recruits flock to fill their places, attracted by the appeal of open-ended employment. It is a quick way "in," with a future. Community colleges, too, are able to tap new, and perhaps better, manpower for the same reason; namely: The two-year semiprofessional programs provide an easy entry into professional careers without sacrifice to later educational options. The second goal of the Morgan baccalaureate programs, then, is to make available the advanced academic-professional options necessary to give credibility to the associate degree programs.

The Morgan Programs Are Complementary to Professional Training, Not Competitive

Activation of the Morgan upper-division modules augurs no threat to the traditional human services disciplines. The Maryland lattice presupposes continued development of the graduate professions while concurrently offering alternative routes to comparable skills. So saying, it behooves the nontraditional system to avoid placing the new workers at a disadvantage in the employment market. Availability of the advanced educational components ensures the associates a rational mechanism for their own continued professional growth and career progress parallel to, but outside of, the promotional opportunities built into their employing agencies. It would be nice if human services facilities everywhere incorporated a system of in-service education, work study, and stepwise on-the-job promotions. It would be nice if those who do institute internal advancement procedures coordinate their approaches into a single formula. Transfer between institutions or geographic locations depends on universally agreed-upon educational and experiential minimums.

The realities of human nature dictate the impossibility of any common promotional system accepted and promulgated by a majority of human services employers in the near future. (And the nontraditional nature of the associates makes it all the less likely, and more imperative, that alternative pathways exist.) Not only is it all important to the individual community-college workers, but also, in terms of the sum of their individual career successes, so stands, or falls, the entire community-college thrust. Without the influx of superior persons into the programs, no viable manpower system is feasible. And the entry of solid, effective young candidates hinges on the appeal of the overall career.

As guidelines to others, the author suggests the following objectives as pertinent "obligations," as it were, for baccalaureate curricula vis-à-vis the community colleges and the nontraditional movement as a whole:

1. College programs offer, in their highly structured system of hours and credits, the rational system of promotional criteria described above. Equally important, the presence of a concrete human services upper-division curriculum permits designation of experiential equivalents or challenge exams for those trained outside of either the orthodox professional or newer collegiate modes.

2. Similarly, colleges can be readily accredited, their curricula approved. Mechanisms for federal, state, and

professional society certification of the college or its program are readily implemented. This, too, stands as a guarantee of upward mobility for the associates; civil service commissions and public-sector personnel are amenable to academically based job categories even while unaccepting of new classes within their own facilities. Again, once collegiate standards are established, on-the-job equivalents can be matched against them.

3. College programs planned with due concern for overall region-wide educational resources—faculty, practicum sites, long-range funding, proximity to untapped recruits—effectively conserve those resources. Inasmuch as there is neither enough to go around nor any way for smaller, decentralized neighborhood facilities to break the maldistribution barrier, the assembling of training resources within the public colleges multiplies their utility (as compared with their helter-skelter disbursement in facilities across the state).

4. Colleges offering a broad spectrum of advanced courses act as a clearinghouse for the upward-bound associate. College catalogs are visible; in an instant, anybody can ascertain where and how his academic needs might be satisfied. Curriculums span a definite time and they are repeated yearly. Workers need not leave work or change jobs necessarily to get a piece, part-time, of the upgrading action.

5. Because of their innovative, often vocationally oriented, approach, the community colleges stand at some disadvantage in gaining the university's approval for the transfer of nonstandard course credits. Historically, university graduate schools do not accommodate the community-college student enrolled in the so-called terminal curriculum. Even when the university offers similar courses, if they are given in the lower division (100 or 200 courses) at the community college, it is "no go." Fortunately, state colleges are more flexible, more attuned to the two-year institutions, and more responsive to the services agency manpower needs. Note, without the missing upper-division module, there is no route into the orthodox

graduate professional schools for the AA degree workers. This is important. Any bright, new educational scheme that purports to be an alternative to traditional human services education ought to link up with it at certain interchange points. The BS degree is one natural point of both academic closure and interchange with the several graduate disciplines, a must for associates aspiring to them. (Achieving full integration of the community-college curricula within the Morgan baccalaureate program was no mean task. Many months of conferences and committee meetings were required, along with plenty of good will and faith by all; trade-offs were common, for example, the elimination of the foreign-language requirement by Morgan in exchange for a tightening up of the community college's biological science sequence.)

6. College programs that open their upper-division courses to persons from the other health and corrections and teacher training professions permit the dissemination of human services expertise into other kinds of "people programs." Hybrid professionals, their education combining the basic professional elements of two or more traditional disciplines, are another possibility, to be explored more fully. (eg., community college RN plus upper-division child care).

7. Because the new baccalaureate curricula need not slavishly follow any single traditional discipline, there is freedom to explore innovations in content and methodology. One such unorthodox approach is the reorganization of human services content so as to concentrate on a given target population or target cluster of common services. The broadening of consumer demands so as to include services to marginal persons and the disabilities of the life cycle tend to further fractionate the existing professions whose expertise is organized by "profession" and not by people needs. As delivery mechanisms and staffing patterns modify to meet the specifics of target services—such as services to the aged, drug abusers, and the minimally retarded—appropriate majors programs can be introduced at the upper-division bacca-

laureate level for rising community-college workers.

8. The bachelor's modules as a group encompass a wide range of continuing education components. Both traditional and nontraditional workers interested in pursuing any given aspect of the behavioral fields ought to be able to take one, two, or several courses from one or more of the modules without enrolling in the full program. The quality of the continuing education would be monitored, thereby, with the students picking up additional credits toward the bachelors or masters degree. Key curriculum components could also be taught on an extension basis, brought to the students working far afield (or attending a distant college lacking the desired courses).

The Morgan State College Curricula in Brief

Details of the Morgan State community mental health curriculum are presented in Table 4, neighborhood health center administrator and child care/educateur in Table 5. A breakdown of the 60 to 66 credit upper-division modules reveals: *(a)* 32 to 36 credit hours allocated to professionally supervised clinical work with agencies and community groups; *(b)* 12 to 16 credit hours in advanced social and behavioral sciences; and *(c)* 12 to 16 credit hours of upper-division general education and humanities. The practicum hours, as with any laboratory course, involve considerably larger blocks of time than the number of credits might first suggest. Students are expected to devote roughly three hours in the field for each credit hour received in the clinical courses.

Something of the spirit of the programs may be gleaned from a more detailed accounting of the major third-year practicum course (Table 6). Graduates of any of the five community-college mental health associate programs receive, as a package, full transferability for their entire associate degree programs. No problem here since the lower division of the Morgan State curriculum is identical with the community colleges'. In fact, a number of the clinical faculty from the community colleges assist in the comparable Morgan offerings as part-time faculty. Since both curricula derive from a single six-year design, there is no duplication or redundancy between modules, no voids, either. Community-college graduates in transferring enter as "rising" juniors. In contrast with the associate degree RN, for example, who still must take a "major" of 24 to 30 credits in achieving the BS Degree, the mental health associates move right on through the Morgan upper-division 60 credits in the usual two academic years.

The Controversy of Specialist Versus Generalist

Despite their relative narrowing of focus during the senior year we believe the Morgan graduates are nonetheless generalists by contemporary academic and clinical standards. Take community mental health: The students' clinical experiences run the gamut of human existence, from asylums and jails to traditional psychiatric OPDs and the nominally "healthy" societal institutions endemic to community life (i.e., public schools, senior-citizen centers, child care). Within their target neighborhood or services dimension, they serve everybody, hence a broad cross-section of traditional diagnostic classifications and socioeconomic categories. Whether it is as educateurs, administrators, or community workers, they are the human services analogue of the primary-care physician.

A typical business administration major attending the famed Wharton School of Business is likely to cover subjects like accounting, personnel management, and collective bargaining during his freshman-sophomore lower-division years, which frees his junior-senior upper-division years for specialist (i.e., professional) courses. Here are a few examples: systems analysis by simulation techniques or case studies in business management. Though specialized, the Wharton student's 30 to 40 credits of upper-division business courses are, in fact, merely

TABLE 4
Community Mental Health Curriculum:
Upper Division Baccalaureate Masters Program

Third year			*Fourth year* / *First graduate year*			*Second graduate year*		
HS 301 Community determinants of individual behavior		4	HS 401-2 Advanced seminars & field assignments	4	4	HS 503-4 Community subspecialty clerkships; 12 credits from graduate electives 5A	6	6
HS 302 Consultation & group therapies		4	Humanities elective		3	HS 443-4 The community as a self-care system	3	3
Humanities Elective	3		Great issues 54.402		2	HS 423 Elementary Neurobiology	3	
Speech 84.202		2	Political science/economics elective	3		HS 424 Intro. Psychopharmacology		3
American history 40.201-2	3	3	Clinical electives 6-9 credits [see electives 4A]	4	4	Public health elective 6 credits [see electives 5B.]	3	3
Physical education		1	Applied social science elective 6 credits [see electives 4B]	3	3			
Psychology exceptional child 70.306	3		Adolescent/drug abuse elective		3			
Sociology of the family 80.304		3						
Mental health electives 6-9 credits [see electives 3A, below]	4	4	1st year graduate students take an additional 8-12 credits from Electives 5A in lieu Humanities, etc.					
	17	17 = 34 Credits		17	16 = 33 Credits		15	15 = 30 Credits

Electives 3A:
HS 341-2-3 Dynamics of health services organization (4, 4, 2)
HS 313 Urban health problems (3) 38.202 Public & community health (3)
38.418 School hygiene & health prob-

Clinical Electives 4A
HS 533-4 Behavior analysis & environment design (4&4)
HS 411-2 Group dynamics: special treatment groups (4&4)
HS 476-7 The culture of drug abuse; re-

Graduate electives 5A
HS 503.1 Aging & chronic care (6)
HS 504.1 Community-institutional articulation problems (6)
HS 503.4-504.4 Comprehensive family health care (6&6)

lems—group solutions (3) 60.315 Community recreation (3)

80.305 Juvenile delinquency (3)

80.308 Criminology (3)

HS 381-2 Activity therapies: vocational rehabilitation (4); recreational rehabilitation (4).

habilitating the young offender (3&3)

HS 351-2 Children, the Family & the community (3&3)

HS 455-6 Community, family, & self-care approaches in retardation (4-4)

Applied social science electives 4B

80.404 Collective behavior (3)

68.420 Government & social welfare

HS 345 Formal institutional structure

HS 346 Planned change in bureaucratic systems (3&3)

80.303 Public opinion & propaganda

80.309 Welfare as a social institution (3&3)

34.309 Urban geography (3)

HS 515-6 Mobilizing community resources; protest leadership (6&6)

HS 503.6-504.6 Alcoholism & suicide prevention (6&6)

HS 503.7-504.7 Corrections & parole; indigenous adolescent gangs (6&6)

HS 503.8-504.8 Drug abuse: ambulatory care; public & community approaches (6&6)

Public health electives 5B

HS 445.1 Principles of health administration: Intro. operations research (3&3)

HS 445.2 Levels of care and manpower utilization (3&3)

Principles of epidemiology (3&3)

HS 445.3-446.3 Electronic data processing & records retrieval (3&3)

TABLE 5
Neighborhood Health Center Administration: Upper Division Baccalaureate Masters Program

Third year			*Fourth year* / *First graduate year*			*Second graduate year*		
HS 341-2-3 Dynamics of health services organization (4, 4 & 2)			HS 441-2 Neighborhood health center administration	6	6	HS 541-2 Field clerkship in neighborhood center administration	6	6
HS 341: Structure & organization	4		HS 443-4 The community as a self-care system	3	3	Administration electives 5R 8-12 credits	4	4
HS 342: Prevention, the community & chronicity		4	Humanities elective		3	Public health electives 5PH 12 credits	6	6
HS 343: Community liaison practicum		2	Great issues 54.402	2				
Humanities elective	3		Political science/economics elective	3				
Speech 84.202		2						
American history 40.201-2	3	3	Administration electives 4R 6-9 credits	3	3			
Physical education		1						
Administration electives 3R 6-8 credits	3	3	[a] First-year graduate students take an additional 8-12 credits from administrative electives 5R in lieu of humanities, etc.					
Psychology exceptional child 70.306	3							
Sociology of the family 80.304		3						
	16	18 = 34 credits		17	15-18 = 32 - 35 credits		16	16 = 32 credits

Electives 3R
Principles of accounting (3&3)
Principles & methods in statistics (3&3)
Formal institutional structure (3)

Electives 4R
Institutional and government accounting (3)
Cost-accounting principles (3)

Electives 5R
HS 543.1 Aging & chronicity (4)
HS 543.3-544.3 Advanced PPB procedures (4&4)

Planned change in bureaucratic systems (3)
Urban geography (3)
Welfare as a social institution (3)
Personnel management (3)
Labor economics (3)

Business law (elementary) (3)
Principles of health administration: Intro. operations research
Levels of care and manpower utilization (3&3)
Electronic data processing and Records retrieval (3&3)

[b] Morgan State graduates seeking advanced standing in the graduate program must take 8-12 credits from administrative electives 5R, to be offered summers as well as during the regular year.

HS 543.9-544.9 Comprehensive health planning; New patterns of manpower utilization (4&4)
HS 503.4-504.4 Comprehensive family health care (6&6)

Electives 5PH
HS 545.1-546.1 Alternatives to hospitalization; Home care services (3&3)
HS 545.2-546.2 Economics of services & prevention; Health law & licensure (3&3)
HS 545.4-546.4 Applied operations research (3&3)
HS 515-6 Mobilizing community resources; Protest leadership (6&6)

TABLE 6
Major Third-Year Practicum Course, Morgan State College

Human Services 301/302: The first semester aims for broad exposure to those societal and familial mechanisms through which an urban community (*a*) corporately sustains the personal identity and emotional integrity of its many and divers citizens, and (*b*) mediates to the clinical and custodial needs of its overtly maladapted (and discomfited) members.

Students are invited to study and help implement in the field those socioeconomic, cultural, political, educative, and familial processes that might be expected to potentiate mutually productive interplay between individuals and families with their multiple environments. The *society* of children and adolescents, as a self-contained subculture, will be examined, as also its relationship to the larger community. Issues of individual identity and the natural flow of the family life cycle, as these are affected by an inner-city milieu and concomitant peer values, are explored within the immediacy of supervised clinical work in community facilities.

The second semester concentrates on the modalities of (*a*) group leadership and (*b*) institutional consultation. Students will carry a variety of community groups, from those primarily of a recreational or educational nature to others more therapeutic in character, such as work with senior citizens, alcoholics, school underachievers. Under supervision, students will serve as mental health consultants to a variety of indigenous nonmedical community institutions. Examples: halfway houses, public schools, neighborhood action groups, public housing, etc.

Students will be asked to evaluate the effectiveness of their practicum institutions (and their own roles within those agencies) vis-à-vis the espoused institutional goals, the expectations of those served, and the costs to society for services rendered *and the costs consequent to any observed service omissions.* In addition, HS 301/302 students will be urged to discover innovation in themselves and in the population served; senior faculty, in turn, will offer structure and community entree propitious to the self-discovery process.

the kinds of focal depth that amplify not diminish the generalists scope. To function as a generalist in a complex, intricate profession, persons must know enough and own sufficient depth of expertise in key areas so as to be able to tackle problems on graduation that demand in-depth knowledge. It means less general education and less humanities for the Wharton graduates, but it also equals out to greater employability. It takes them far enough into the field so that they are ready for beginning professional roles from which further growth is possible and expected. It does not at all block their entry into graduate school; on the contrary, without this generalist's portfolio of specialty courses they are not eligible for the Wharton graduate programs. (Neither does it rule out later sophistication in the humanities or the historical precedents of one's profession. Education for life is lifelong, just as professional training extends over an entire career's length.)

That an undergraduate curriculum is inherently "clinical" is not evidence of its generating "specialists" in terms of narrow-minded technicians not comprehending the theories and goals of their profession. Neither does a plethora of liberal arts and civilization survey courses produce generalist practitioners in the human services. Admittedly, the human services need practitioners whose vision reaches beyond the psychopathological, persons whose experience and learning makes them cognizant of man's many variegated roots in history, the arts, the East, the metaphysical. The Renaissance man of today is neither generalist nor specialist, merely well informed. Both kinds of undergraduate curricula in the human services are available today. Differences between the liberal arts and practitioner curricula are illustrated in Table 8.

In comparison with the generic psychology and social work baccalaureate curricula currently in vogue, the Morgan State modules are conspicuously clinical in orientation. Before the student is admitted he has spent two years in the pointedly clinical community-college mental health associate program—not everybody's meat. It is neither better nor worse than the traditional route through graduate school; to the extent that it skips over the usual liberal arts subject matter it is a "better" program for those persons in search of early employment. Others, with the time, and family resources, and temperament would be well advised to follow the liberal arts pathway. Thus, by the time students graduate from Morgan College they have had at least four years of profession-

TABLE 7

Field instruction sites & the trainees practicum roles

HS 301: Community factors in mental health and illness

First semester practicum: six to eight hours in the field/week, (including one hour supervision, one hour conference

Areas of professional content *Typical practicum locations* *Community mental health centers:*	**An outline of trainee practicum responsibilities**
Preadmission evaluation, alternatives to hospitalization and precipitating influences. *Department of Mental Hygiene Baltimore City Receiving U.* *Johns Hopkins Psychiatric Emergency & Neighborhood S.*	Trainee, under supervision expedites entry and evaluation process; explores referring sources, acts as liaison with same; coordinates follow through with appropriate health and mental health professionals; may interview patient, family, and other involved persons; makes home visits, individually and in conjunction with public health nurse; touches base with indigenous helping resources; synthesizes total situation and presents findings to professional-in-charge and, if directed, may intervene therapeutically, maintaining records and close contact with supervisors; responsibility for follow-up after the crisis subsides and intermittently thereafter to assess overall family/neighborhood disequilibrium; examines individual problem situations for evidence of family or neighborhood patterns and their causation; on request surveys the professional literature, prepare reports; establishes liaison with referral sources so as to gain entree before crisis develops.
Crisis intervention/suicidology/homicide and similar psychologically determined violence *North Charles Crisis Intervention Center* *Baltimore City Hospitals E.R.*	Takes rotation on 24-hour *"phone watch,"* calls for appropriate assistance when necessary—*follows through on referral to ensure contact;* serves as coordination center for communications during individual and family crises; may act to initiate client interaction with needed family, law-enforcement, community, and medical services. Acts as liaison person with, and may accompany, police and medical emergency teams on mental health problems

	(e.g., emergency commitment); in target areas, work with indigenous groups to resolve etiologic issues.
Routine ambulatory, home care and indigenous, informal helping agents *Provident Hospital-OEO Neighborhood Health Center* *The Johns Hopkins East Baltimore Comprehensive Care Center* *The Baltimore Community Action Agency (selected neighborhood centers)*	As directed, assumes simple clinic administrative duties; selected individuals will progress from "intake" and history-taking to counseling; takes planning role in deployment of indigenous health aides; participates in intramural therapy and activity groups; affords counseling to "healthy" school, community, and family organizations; assumes simple teaching and supervisory tasks; takes role in determining consumers' impression of services; aids in bringing community into decision-making process; works on trainee teams; makes home visits; and, part-time, works with chronic disease and geriatric services. Learns ombudsman's role; has coordinating responsibility for a small number of patient/family clients, ensuring continuity of care over time and multiple agencies.
Partial hospitalization *Sheppard Pratt Day Hospital* *Baltimore City Day Hospital* *"Man Alive" Program for Drug Abusers* *"Echo House" (alcoholism rehabilitation)*	Acts as group leader in activity, social, work-therapy senior citizen, or recreational group; learns counseling techniques within framework of group activities, e.g., hospital volunteers; initiates behavior modification programs; participates in neighborhood posthospitalization endeavors, e.g., AA, homemaking service paid employment, *sheltered workshops*, etc.
Satellite and neighborhood *Outreach programs* *"Cherryhill Neighborhood Association* *Inner City CMHC, University of Maryland-DMH* *Dunbar High School KAPS Program*	Under supervision takes limited administrative responsibilities, for example, scheduling employees, ironing out disputes; discover, and work with indigenous community leadership and if possible serves in consultant capacity to them; facilitates community-Establishment dialogue toward improved human services; acts as liaison *from* neighborhood groups *to* satellite facility and upward to the central complex; attempts to discern effective from ineffective outreach, and why, with which peoples. Facilitates community use of governmental services in ways profitable to residents—*schools, libraries, courts.*
State/chronic hospital communication with community institutions and interested people	

TABLE 8
A Comparison of Curriculum Categories

General education	*Pre-Profes-sional [i.e., social and biological sciences]*	*Profes-sional (clinical) subjects*	*elementary pro-fessional*	*advanced profes-sional*	
Generic baccalaureate curricula					
Social work curriculum [Bowie (Md.) State College]	58	63	8	8	*none*
Social work curriculum [Morgan State College]	62	60	16	*11*	*5*
Modular human services curricula (BS degree)					
Community mental health [Morgan State College]	37	35	63	*30*	*33*
Business administration curricula					
BS in business, accounting major [Morgan State College]	47	63	34	*18*	*16*

ally supervised practicum work with clients and community, plus considerable work experience summers or during intervening periods of full-time human services employment. They are journeymen practitioners, by training the equivalent of most masters social work or psychology persons and second-year resident psychiatrists, too. Like engineers, they are neither uneducated nor unprofessional.

The generic psychology or social work programs, however, are of a very different intent. Essentially, they are orthodox four-year liberal arts programs to which has been added a valuable taste of clinical life via a senior-year block of seminars and field observation trips. The sum of these courses amount to from 6 to 16 credits, perhaps half a day in the field for one or two semesters at most. Their thrust is to afford otherwise cloistered, typically middle-class youngsters a much-needed window into the human services prior to their application to graduate school. The generic curricula make it possible for undergraduates to decide more realistically on a future career from a basis in personal experience rather than fantasy.

As is manifest in Table 8 the purpose of the generic curricula is not to prepare practitioners for direct employment in the human services. They are not professional curricula and were never meant to serve in lieu of sound graduate education. Endorsement by the NASW and the APA, respectively, should not be construed as an appeal to bypass the professional schools. The author cautions educators against the misapplication of such curriculum titles as social welfare generalist, as if the term generalist implied real clinical sophistication. Their "generalism" relates to general education and derives from the strength of foreign language, the fine arts, music, the ancients, which is valuable to the individual. But care should be taken to avoid the implication that any clinical competence is inferred by the generalist or generic appellations.

5. ACADEMIC COSTS, EFFECTIVENESS, EVALUATION, AND THE ASSOCIATE PROFESSIONAL PROCESS

THE ASSOCIATE PROFESSIONAL PROCESS

The crux of any career lattice is its use. How much traffic is generated across lattice bridges to higher categories and laterally into new fields? Most lattices in the health and human services do not work. Paper lattices! They fail because the paper linkages across significant differences of job classes fail. The Social Worker I who rises to Social Worker V tells us nothing about job lattices. Only when the Social Worker "X" assumes the responsibilities of, for example, mental health center director, has there been any "lattice action."

Modular education is a new kind of bridge across categories. In principle it is all old hat. After all, how does anybody get from a "nobody" to center director? By going to school and getting a PhD or MD. Right?

Unfortunately, the jump from high school to PhD transcends the reach of most Americans. The concept of modular education is merely to reduce the size of the steps necessary in moving across career boundary lines. How big should the modules be? Answer: as many sizes as is economically feasible. Our Maryland lattice is built primarily on a two-track module system: (*a*) full-time study, with the modules arranged mostly in two-year "units" and (*b*) part-time study, with the minimodules arranged by 8 semester hours "units" (compatible with the state's tuition-refund, released-time arrangement of 8 hours/semester times up to $38.50/credit hour).

Skeleton of the Modular System: the 2+2+2 sequence

Figure 4 illustrates the Maryland community college-Morgan State system of modular education. Each of the two-year modules—associate degree, upper-division BS, and masters—is self-contained, pedagogically viable in its own right. Each leads to advanced clinical roles commensurate with the workers' greater acumen; each leads to award of the next higher academic degree. While the curricula may be unorthodox, the credentials are not.

Taken in 2+2 sequence, we believe the two modules are synergetic, the specialist concentration of the upper division complementing and completing the generalist overview of the first two years. But you do not have to go directly from module I to module II. Good jobs follow completion of the community-college programs, and we feel it is wiser to work awhile, grooming skills and growing some. Following each curricula there are four options: (*a*) work (full-time), (*b*) school (the next module, full-time), (*c*) work-school (part-time work and school), and (*d*) lateral shifts into the orthodox human services curricula, undergraduate or graduate.

Not everyone follows the same stereotyped pattern, which is as it should be. People are differently motivated, possess different and changeable gifts; they will move at different rates upward and laterally, and some not at all. In the expectation that everyone, however idiosyncratically, is growing, we have termed the developmental process the associate professional process (or concept). The associate professional process postulates that so long as individual associate professionals have access to advanced professional education relevant to their clinical duties (or future aspirations), then they will take advantage of it whenever they are ready. Meanwhile, associate professionals would level off for varying periods in satisfying professional roles—and that without stigma.

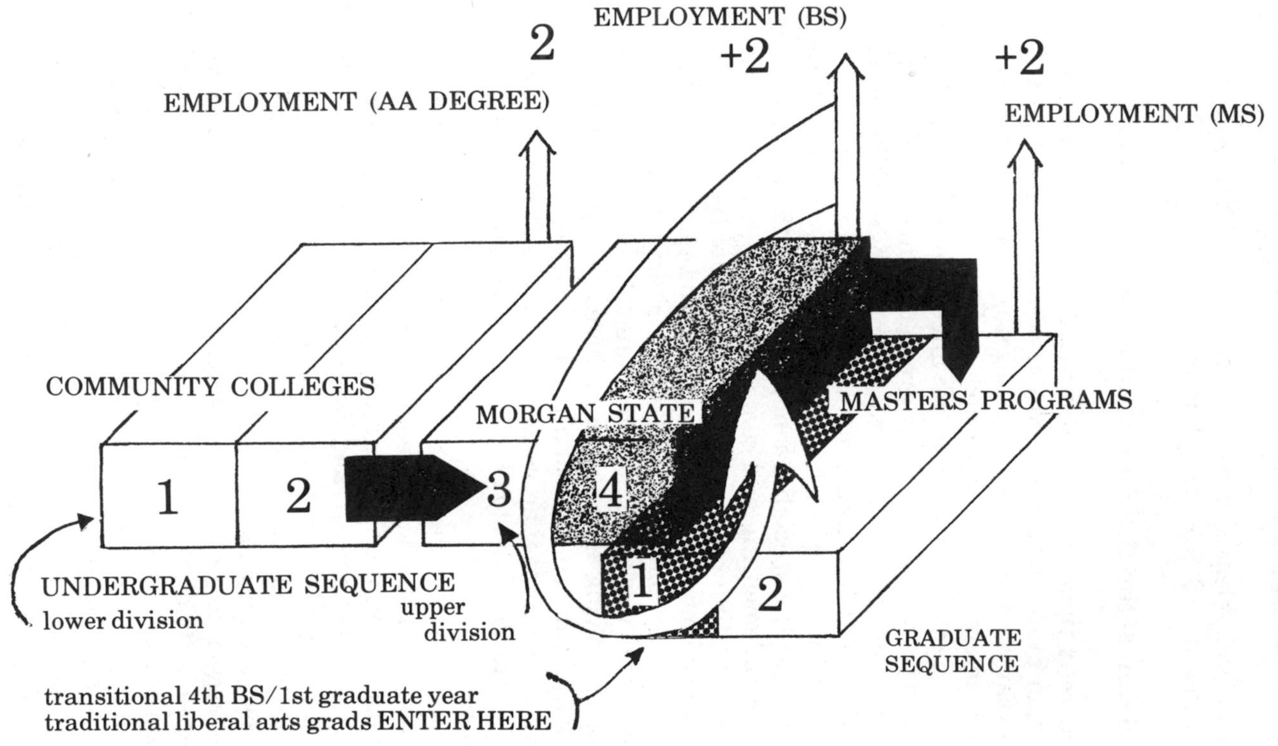

Figure 4.

MODULAR EDUCATION: SCHEMATIC OUTLINE OF AA/BS/MS CURRICULA [2+2+2]

(The schoolteacher who eschews administration in favor of working with kids is not thought the less for it; nor is the principal unrewarded for his choice of administration.)

Personnel would, via the associate professional process, invest in the next educational step (for them) only when they felt it personally advantageous. There would be time to gain acquaintance with the breadth of the human services and time for them to come to know themselves and their place in the profession. Stopping off in a service role ceases to lock the associate professional out of further advancement. He is always free to return to the next academic module. Likewise, in moving to the next employment step from school, it is at the convenience of the worker, when it makes sense to him in the context of his personal life, family commitments, and career opportunities.

Separating the modules is often the institutional boundaries of community college vis-a-vis state college, certification, licensure and the degree, and the intervening work experience. Less concretely, graduation from each of the modules *de facto* serves as the lattice's juncture points. These act much as the terminals in a railway or air transport system. They allow for a change in direction, for getting on or off. They are way stations for shifting career interests laterally or updating one's professional skills; adding to them, too. Academically, the presence of juncture points facilitates the building of common core curricula, core courses, conjoint electives, and interdisciplinary faculty. That is, the closer together the terminals, the more acceptable it is for two or more curriculums to briefly merge in the form of shared courses, faculty, or practicums. Juncture points facilitate the student's lateral transfer, reducing the risk of being forced up an educational "blind alley" simply because there is no way to go but forward (or out). Because of the modules' relatively shorter duration, it is easier for institutions and agencies to send their personnel off to work-study without losing them following graduation.

Interdigitation with the Health Care Professions

Education for the human services ought not to stand in isolation—one of the major advantages of a modular system of education. By utilizing the public community and state colleges as the training mechanism there is the potential for student movement and the cross-pollination of ideas, the fashioning of student teams within college-affiliated ambulatory care centers. But cooperation just does not happen. Structure must be built into the system so as to make possible the smooth operations of the many participating programs. Just gaining agreement on a single academic calendar can be a major undertaking. Yet if semester dates, finals, and holidays do not coincide, there can be no conjoint programming. Developing a common modular framework in Maryland has been a challenge to the Maryland Consortium for the Health Sciences since 1969. Table 9 illustrates the projected six-year modular sequences in administration, human services, and nursing arts (much currently operational).

Each of the three six-year sequences begins from a unitary community-college curriculum, namely, professional nursing, human services (mental health associate or occupational therapy associate), and business administration (which includes computer programming and data processing). What is unique here is not the associate degree programs but that these should be the nucleus of a series of interdigitating upper-division curricula leading to the BS degree. It has meant the continued conjoint planning of Community College of Baltimore educators with their Morgan State, Coppin State, and Towson State counterparts. The diverging options of the second-phase modules are counterbalanced by the umbrella nature of the job titles and degree credentials. And while people enter from a variety of levels and institutions, they are brought together within the larger lattice mainstream. Dead ends and second-class careers are eliminated. How far up or across the lattice should a person move? And at what speed? These now are personal deci-

Modular Curricula in the Health Care and Human Services: An Overview of Ongoing and Projected Curricula in Maryland's Public Undergraduate College

Phase 1 module *Community-college AA degree programs*	*Phase 2 module* *Upper-division baccalaureate program [BS degree]*	*Phase 3 module* *Masters programs [MMH degree-master in mental health]*
AA curriculum in computer programming	Health systems data processing Hospital communications and control systems	Health systems design and analysis information retrieval, processing and distribution Communications and logistical networks Control systems and computer simulation
AA curriculum in business	Nursing home administration Public health administration	Hospital and nursing home administration Comprehensive health planning Health programs organization and evaluation
Mental health/human services	Behavior modification Corrections, probation and parole Child care/educateur Community mental health General hospital emergency and liaison services	Rehabilitation neurologically disabled child Child care/educateur Community mental health
Mental health associates	Neighborhood health center administration	Gerontology Neighborhood center administration
	Retardation	*JHU mental health counselors*[a] *RETARDATION*
Occupational therapy (Asst.)	Occupational therapy	
AA professional nurse curriculum	Public health nursing zgeriatric/chronic disease nursing Maternal and child nursing Nursing services administration Psychiatric nursing Intensive care nursing	Community health practitioner Chronic care practitioner Midwifery Pediatric practitioner Respiratory/cardiac intensive-care nursing Nursing education

[a] *Ongoing two-year Hopkins program in psychotherapy for mature women.*

sions instantly renegotiable throughout one's career! Nobody need remain stuck in a career rut. The remedy is to shift from work to school (or vice versa). No need to start all over again in order to switch human services fields. To move laterally, say, from child care to administration, the individual merely picks up those pieces of the administration curriculum lacking in his own background. Credits are fully transferable; to the extent that subjects are common to both fields, there is no reason to repeat them. (Other elements might have been mastered through work experience. Hopefully, challenge exams will be developed to allow for formal certification of experiential equivalents, making it all the easier to change fields without abrogating the standards inherent to the bachelors' curricula.)

It should be emphasized that the Maryland modular system differs from the traditional separation of health careers into upper and lower divisions. In the past this partition has been used to separate general education from so-called professional subjects. Thus, the baccalaureate RN student might spend her first two college years on the liberal arts campus studying liberal arts, then switch over to the university hospital for the junior-senior nursing education years. Our phase I modules are entry-level preparation for beginning professional roles (comparable to the old upper-division professional components in baccalaureate nursing or OT, PT). Thus we have done away with the anachronistic hodge podge of survey courses previously crammed into the university freshman and sophomore years under the aphorism preprofessional—such as prenursing and predentistry. Not only does this permit the work option after two years (AA degree), it frees the junior-senior curriculum for not only additional professional studies but sophisticated general education courses, too. Thus, as with philosophy, history, or the hard sciences the older upper-division student, already knowledgeable in the fundamentals of his profession, is in a better position to individuate his curriculum, selecting those general-education courses most appropriate to his interests. We feel this may both add to the appeal of the liberal arts and maintain the academic interest of others whose need for concrete action is betrayed by the campus-bound approach of conventional preprofessional designs. The author realizes the importance of background basic sciences, yet if these are memorized abstractions for want of clinical realities through which to understand the total phenomena, for lack of real-life people matching developmental theories, is anything gained?

Modular Education: Education à la Carte

Interchangeability of the Maryland modules and their inherent completeness within themselves permits the individuation of curricula by merely arranging the two-year modules like children's blocks. Four signal advantages accrue:

1. Flexibility of human services education in responding to changing service modalities; changing manpower requirements—new techniques, funding, consumer demands—can be accommodated;
2. Adaptibility of human services education to the needs of other professions—health care, as nursing; teachers; law enforcement; corrections; recreation.
3. Interdisciplinary professional education becomes feasible; individuals whose professional pursuits extend across the interface traditionally separating the professions—psychiatric nurse from social worker, teacher from child-care worker—can, by linking modules, build hybrid education packages for themselves.
4. Continuing education under the modular system is substantially upgraded through becoming part of the public higher-education system; consistent region-wide standards and minimums can be conjointly instigated.

So long as all students entering a given human services discipline are obliged to follow roughly identical studies in order to master the essentials of that profession in whose name they would practice, then bold innovation in curricula cannot happen. Experimentation, whether to meet a new kind of service need or in response to augmented demand and expanding roles, must involve only a small segment of manpower in training. Pilot studies cannot include everybody. If human services education is to be free itself to change flexibly, economically, and without grave penalty for error, then its pioneering ventures must be of limited scope. Pilot studies, of course, are common enough, but most stand isolated from the ordinary behavioral programs, their graduates for good or ill clearly differentiated for their pioneering. In the building of a new module (or radical reconstitution of an older one) experiment becomes possible within the bosom of the status quo. Only when it has proved itself will it much affect the other modules; meanwhile, it benefits from the natural flow of students and the prestige of the umbrella baccalaureate degree and human services namesake. Permanent hard-money funding is also present. Because it is just a fraction of the overall human services modules program, the demise of any one of them causes no great waves; faculty and students are absorbed into other ongoing, related curricula.

Modular education is a potential breakthrough in the "recycling" of antiquated academic resources. Old curricula never die, no matter how little needed—or attended; and new programs remain unborn for want of the same public monies. Modules can be started up cheaply and expediently. Easily opened, and closed, perhaps faculty might strive to intermittently divorce themselves of their old ones in order to instigate newer, more relevant varieties.

In the face of so multidimensional a constellation of academic options as the Maryland upper-division lattice, orthodoxy does not have a chance. We hope this sets the climate for experiment. The modules are not from Uranus. They are nestled neatly on pages of the several state college catalogs. Students at one college are entitled to register for any course at any of the others. (The three are a mere 15 minutes apart by car or the college bus that travels the circuit.) While some of the sophisticated practitioner courses may have certain prerequisites, most of the modules are an open invitation to all students interested in the behavioral sciences to enter and browse. Teachers-to-be and future nurses and prospective personnel people should profit from the chance to learn about behavior and also learn and practice the rudiments of clinical work. There is no reason why supervisors cannot select practicum sites and supervisors specific to the kinds of environments the nurse or teacher might later enter, thus learning the mental health aspects in, for them, a real-life situation. Some might choose to pursue an entire module, in effect achieving beginning professional certification in two professions, likely related by common target program or population served.

Professional Education Across Traditional Categories

Professionals with training in two disciplines until now have been relatively rare. (Persons, in adding to their education, habitually move within the confines of their own profession; few social workers pursue a doctorate in psychology.) And as long as clinical role depended on professional pedigree, this was natural. Merging of service roles, and their differentiation by target population or geography, creates the need for multiprofession personnel. Separate curricula and separate institutions, mostly without transferability of credits, have blocked emergence of dual-trained professionals. It has been like learning two professions, each from scratch.

Modular education permits it to happen. Examples of the kinds of curriculum combinations feasible under the Morgan College lattice modules are shown in Figure 5. A 2+2 or 2+2+2 system offers allied health personnel the unique opportunity to learn and assimilate mental health skills within the rubric of their "native" profession. Take the example of the associate degree RN interested in working with children, especially in the context

Figure 5

a] Example of 2+2+2 non-traditional modular education AA thru masters degree;

b] Augmentation of other helping professions via human service expertise;

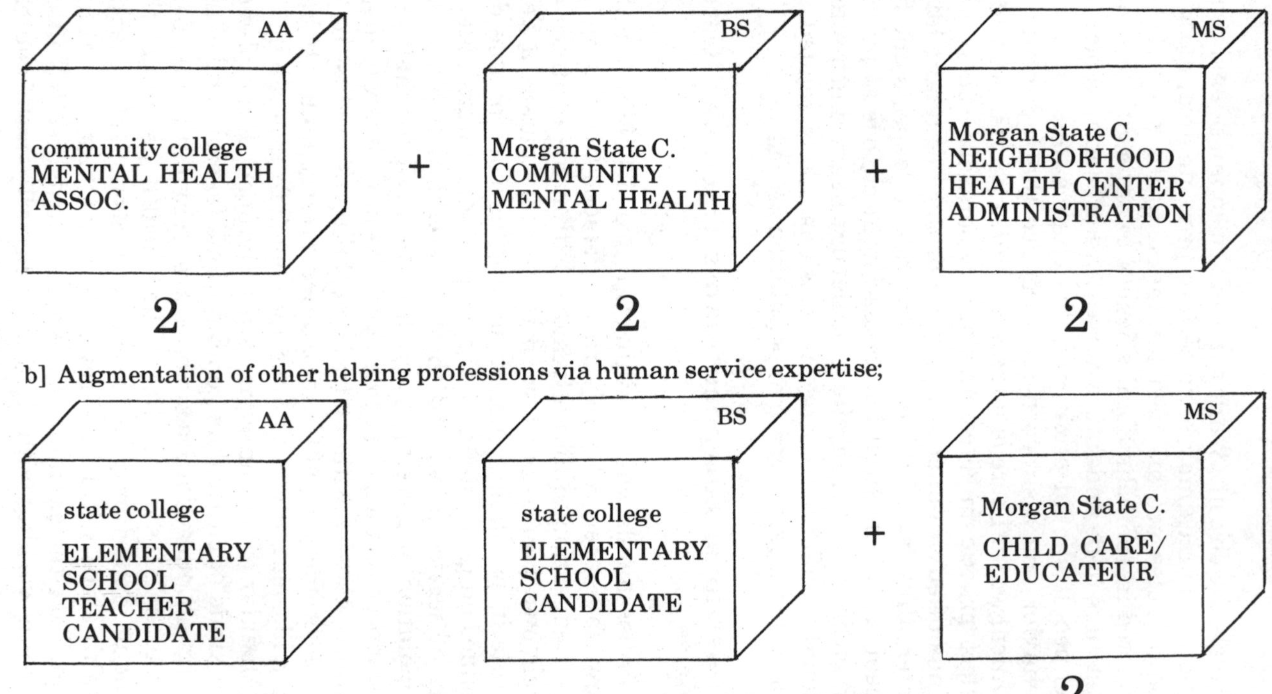

c] Interdisciplinary or "hybrid professional" education via second phase module;

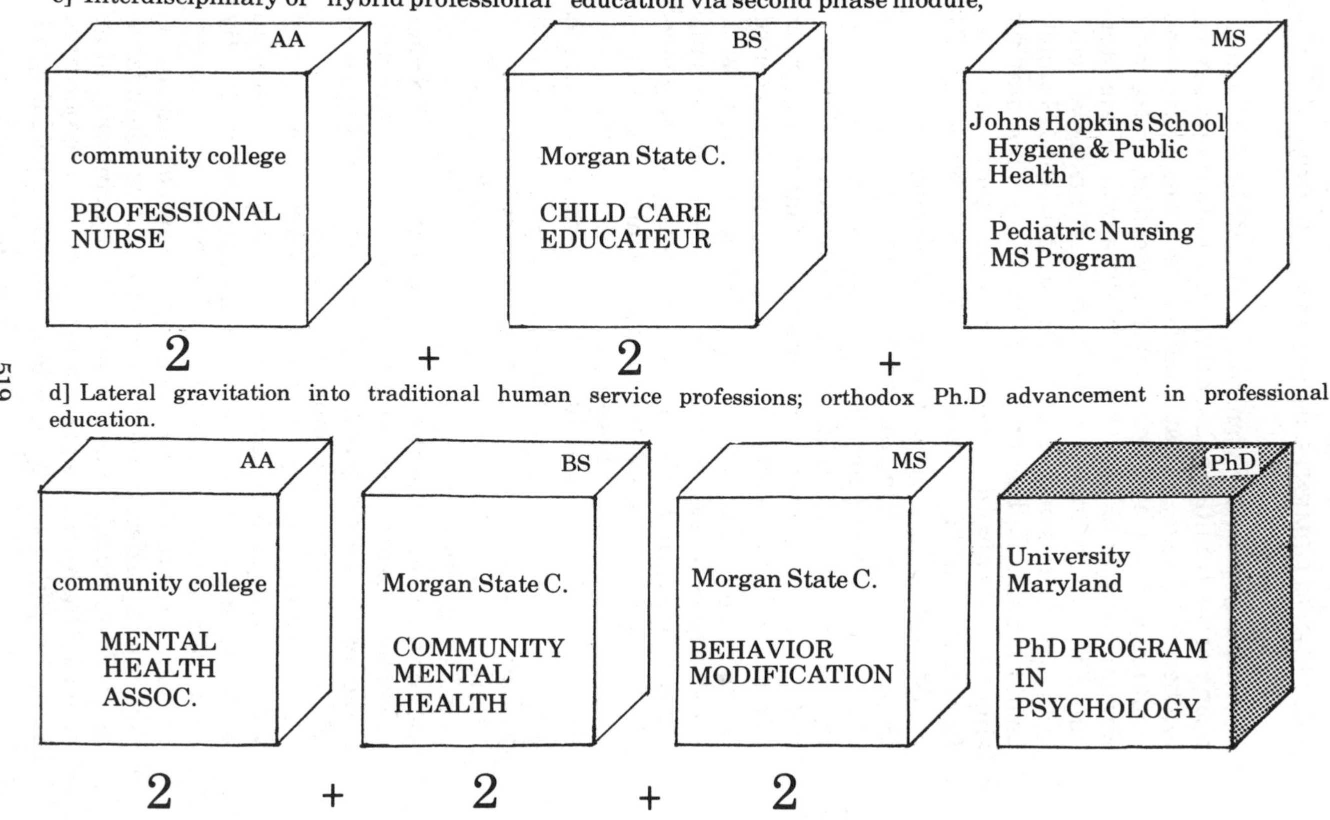

d] Lateral gravitation into traditional human service professions; orthodox Ph.D advancement in professional education.

of inner-city minority youngsters. The RN might return to any of the traditional baccalaureate nursing programs for her BS Degree. That would take three years. She would repeat much of her community-college entry-level nursing in the process. Or she might enroll in the Morgan child care/educateur module, graduating in two years with a bachelor's degree, also. (In this case the BS would be in the umbrella human services category, not nursing since she was already a registered professional nurse before matriculation.) Within the child-care module, the RN would likely take some of the community mental health electives, familiarizing herself with the local community scene and its indigenous leaders. Hopefully, in then taking employment in an outreach children's health program, she has learned something about mediating good nursing within an inner-city milieu; she also has earned the right kind of credentials, the BS degree along with the expertise. Thus, she meets civil service requirements for advancement. Had she merely returned for the general-education BS degree she not only would have lost one year but also learned nothing about either pediatrics or the inner-city health picture. Of the two routes, which leaves the RN the better prepared professionally? Which path is the least hypocritical in academic terms?

Certainly the child care/educateur nurse is no less prepared for graduate work in pediatric nursing or any of the related fields than the general education BS/RN; her community experience as well as behavioral expertise make her the better generalist; the years of employment add to her maturity and clinical breadth.

Another community-college RN might, after several years of ambulatory-care nursing, choose to return to school in search of additional administrative skills. By temper and personality she would make a good center administrator, a role steeped in group process, needful of behavioral expertise. For her the health center administrator module is ideal. The module is multidisciplinary in its outlook. Others in the class might include a majority of mental health associates, a fair number of business administration majors, and a scattering of human services professionals as part of their agencies' continuing education programs. As will be described shortly, the Morgan upper-division modules are dual-purposed, combining the fourth undergraduate year clinical components with the first graduate year of study. The 2+2 sequence would in reality be three years for the person passing directly through them. Most persons, of course, would take but one of the modules, either entering at the graduate level for years two and three (see Figure 6), or following the associate degree for years one and two, culminating in the bachelor's degree. As a result, we expect each of the curriculum sequences to be shared by both associate degree personnel and their more traditional BS and masters-trained colleagues. Thus, while the associates might take the first and second years of the upper-division BS module in, say, behavior modification, others, professionals—psychologists, psychiatrists, social workers—would likely pursue a more sophisticated course commensurate with a second masters degree upon completion.

Why should the professional choose to enter one of the modules rather than an advanced course of study in his own discipline? Why a second masters instead of the doctorate? The answer lies in the lack of specialty programs concentrating on administration, geriatrics, community work, or child care within the orthodox human services graduate programs. The PhD ought not to be watered down in an effort to train large numbers of journeymen practitioners. No doubt the years to come will see the increased technological sophistication of clinical practice demand commensurate expansion of education, but not necessarily education in the singularly rigorous mode of the PhD degree program. The author suggests a division of graduate education into investigative and clinical branches. The former, comparable with existing PhD programs, would continue; in addition, a more service-oriented, less creative sequence would allow for professional maturation without the requirements of thesis or original research. (Such a practice has long been the rule

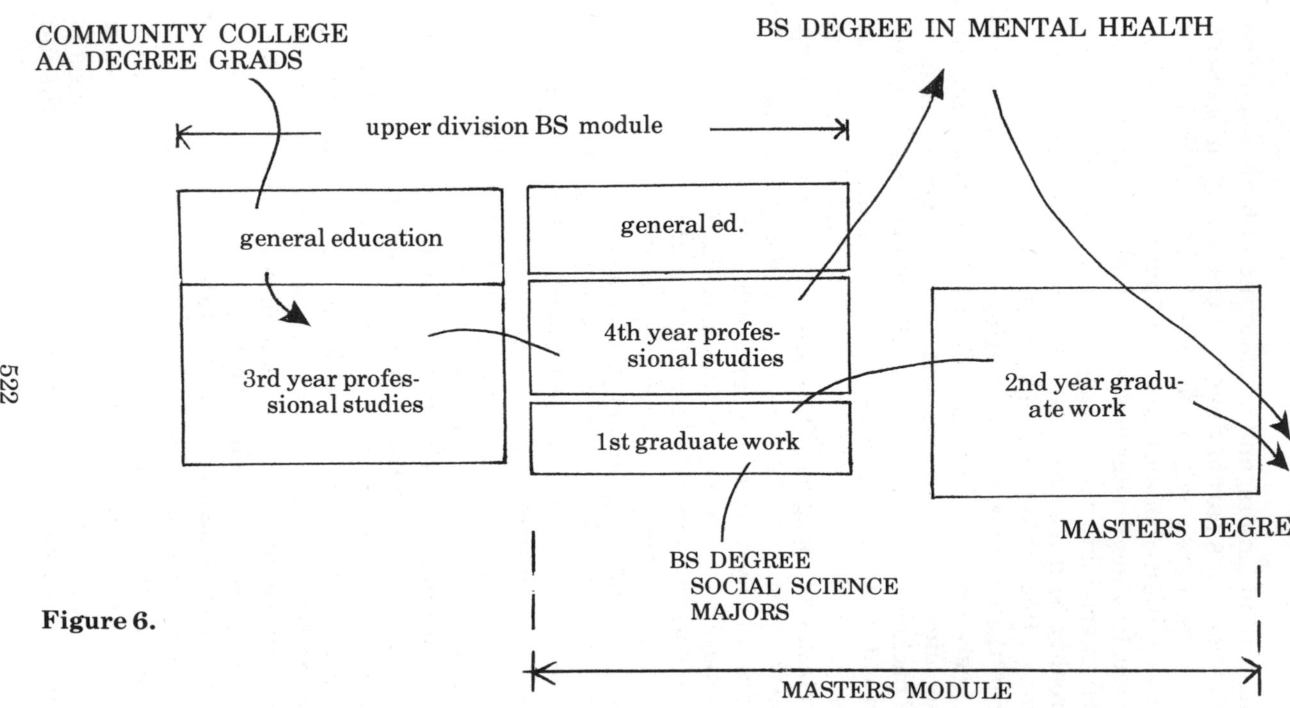
COMMUNITY COLLEGE
AA DEGREE GRADS
upper division BS module
BS DEGREE IN MENTAL HEALTH
general education
3rd year profes-
sional studies
general ed.
4th year profes-
sional studies
1st graduate work
2nd year gradu-
ate work
MASTERS DEGREE
BS DEGREE
SOCIAL SCIENCE
MAJORS
MASTERS MODULE

Figure 6.

in theological education. Following their graduate studies, divinity students receive, in effect, a second bachelors degree, the BD.)

While the modules are inherently interdisciplinary, they do require that students have made up their minds toward their professional goals. The individual who does not know what aspects of the behavioral fields interest him most would be well advised to follow the more orthodox graduate programs. Professionals certain of their next career steps will learn more under the modular system. Thus, the psychologist devoted to the care of the elderly, the sociologist whose research into the microcosm of the aged lacks clinical astuteness, the would-be nursing home administrator, and the occupational therapist hired by the nursing home, all would profit from the geriatrics module in ways not possible within their own discipline's curricula. That the module was first instituted in order to facilitate advancement of the associate degree workers in no ways lessens its appropriateness for other professionals. Electives and stepwise, increasing complexity of the courses permits curriculum individuation to suit a panorama of entrance backgrounds and levels of expertise.

Reciprocally, mental health associates ought to be able to study entry-level nursing as an optional upper-division choice. Taking the basic "AD" community college nursing program plus behavioral electives, such individuals would have a special utility in institutional facilities that tend to combine behavioral with nursing care duties. Care of the severely retarded might be one example, severely regressed psychotic persons another. Both involve considerable nursing-type responsibilities, particularly medications and custodial nurturing. Yet both also involve the interrelationship of family and other community persons with institution, patient, and staff. Leadership of a group of mothers of retarded children, or kin to the chronically invalided, or the sentient alteration of ward morale are examples of needed behavioral expertise. (Towson State College, Towson,

Maryland, conjointly with the Sheppard and Enoch Pratt Hospital, is instituting (1972-73) a baccalaureate human services worker curriculum with special emphasis on inpatient skills, milieu therapy, and ward management from a program-activity perspective in particular.)

The potential for mix-and-match combination curricula is infinite. The tendency toward individuation not only adds relevance to the programs, but the large number of feasible permutations acts to inhibit formation of new career splinter groups. Whereas one or two bright new curricula are sure to spawn a new health or human services occupation, the hybridization and multiple overlap of people's education under a modular system fosters coalescence of individuals into larger groups, something that umbrella titles and job classes helps along, too. Moreover, having studied together and having shared parts of courses and electives together, it is hoped that in their later working years the various module "specialists" and their multidisciplinary professional colleagues will draw together into services teams. Having worked in practicum teams during their Morgan State tenure, perhaps this can be maintained out in the neighborhood centers, too.

INDEX

Addiction specialist, 309
Administration, 33, 34, 37-39, 41, 44, 45, 233-245
functions of, 234
health and human services, 41-49
personnel, 242
strategies of, 238
Advocacy, 221-223, 273
African American Teachers' Union, 293
Albee, G., 22-23
Alinsky, S., 217, 218, 221
American Assembly, The, 220
American Indian, 272
American Public Health Association, 204
Ardell, D. B., 210
Aronson, J. B., 202
Associate Professional Concept, 468-469
Associate Professional Process, 508
Assumptions, 269, 270, 271 308, 337, 338
Auditing, 175
Baccalaureate and Masters Moduces, 480
Baker, F., 28, 155, 161, 169, 206
Banfield, E., 226, 228
Bard, M., 26, 327, 352, 354
Barker, R., 27
Barnard, C., 234
Bauer, R., 195
Beck, B. M., 216
Bedford-Stuyvesant, 294
Bell, D., 249
Benne, K., 168
Bennis, W. J., 168, 237, 239, 253, 254
Biddle, F. J., 147
Black Power, 294
Blacks, 272
Blake, E., 330, 354
Blake, R. R., 168
Blau, P. M., 165
Board of Directors, 150-151, 174-175, 214, 217
Bouton, Jim, 238
Brager, G. A., 221
Braybrooke, D., 156
Broskowski, A., 25
Budgeting, 174, 175, 255
Bulletin of the Foundation Library Center, 178
Bundy, M., 258
Bureaucracy, 165, 166, 213, 253-254
Bureaucratization, 165, 166
California, 159, 164
Campbell, E. Q., 273, 354
Caplan, G., 221

Career Aspirations—
Limiting Factors, 418
Caregiving Networks, 3, 8
Importance of Environmental Influence, 5, 6
and Capital Planning, 9-10
and Systems Concepts, 8-9
Caro, F., 28
Carp, F., 319, 354
Carter, L. F., 220
Case
definition of, 36
discussion of, 95-96, 101-107
material available for health and human services administration, 115-139
materials, development of, 109-113
preparation for teaching, 91-95
sample, 51-85
teaching note for, 85-88
writing, 110-113
Case Method, 33-39
bibliography (selected), 114
teaching style, 98-101
teaching techniques, 96-98
Categorical programs, 15, 17, 18
see also: Federal funding
Catonsville Community College, 460
Caudill, William, 414-415
Causation, 272, 273, 350
Chambers, C. D., 307, 354
Change
models of, 168, 218, 220
organizational, 152, 164, 166, 167-169, 176, 202, 237, 238, 241, 250
social, 152, 157, 165, 218-221, 227, 241, 218-221
strategies for, 152, 218-221, 228
Child guidance clinics, 8
change in caregiving orientation, 6
Chin, R., 168
Cities: see "urban problems"
City College, 327
Civil Service, 151, 157, 175
Clients, 161, 162, 215, 216, 258
Clinical psychology, 292, 327
Clinician
role of, 4, 5
Coalitions, 191
Colbourne, R., 188
Coleman, J. S., 273, 354
Columbia University School of Social Work, 284
Committee on Environment of the American Public Health Association, 205
Community, 4, 12, 13, 273, 274, 276, 282
action, 205, 207
action programs, 270, 276
control, 216-217, 252
organization, 184
participation: *see* Participation, commu-

nity
role of in caregiving decision-making, 4-5
Community College Mental Health Workers, 457-480
Community College of Baltimore, 460
Community Mental Health, 3, 4, 7, 164, 205-208, 226-227
centers, 13-14, 15
during 1960s, 3
programs, 272, 276-277
Community Mental Health Centers Act, 205
Community Service Society, 283-291, 349, 351, 352, 353
Community Services Society (CSS) of New York, 11
Compensatory educational programs, 272, 273, 278
Comprehensive health planning, 155, 201, 210
Comprehensive Health Planning and Public Health Service Amendments of 1966, 210
Comprehensive human services, 17
Computers, 188, 195, 256, 258
Conflictual strategies, 10
Confrontation, 227, 230, 239
Consensus, 229-230
Consultation programs, 276
Consumers, see Clients
Cook, S., 5
Cooperation, 153-154
Coordination, 276, 279
Cost
cost-benefit analysis, 150, 240-241, 258
effectiveness, 277
Cost of human services, 146, 147, 153, 158, 197, 214, 231-232
estimating costs, 193
Counseling, 273, 338
Crime, 278
Curran, W. J., 221
Dalton, G. W., 243-244
Daniels, A. H., 165
Data collection and use, see Evaluation
Davis, S. M., 48
Decentralization, 164-166
Decision-making, 148, 154, 158, 159-160, 161, 164, 166-167, 184-185, 213, 235-236, 238-240, 250, 258
see also Policy
Definitions, 269, 271, 273 308, 337
Demone, H. W., Jr., 166, 187, 189, 191, 206, 209, 220, 225, 227, 258
Demone, H., 9, 10, 12, 14, 17, 24, 28
Denver Research Institute, 188
Department of Justice, U.S., 13
Deteriorated housing, 278
Diagnostic Center, 5
Discrimination, 177
Dixon, J. D., 250, 251-252

Dixon, R., 8
Domains of agencies, 228
Downs, A., 221
Drug addiction, 271, 281, 282, 307, 350
Dunbar, A., 220
Ecological model, 27
Education, 145, 148-149, 159, 160, 166, 167, 186-187, 257
  low minority-group achievement, 11
  schools, 209-210
Educational skills, 273
Effectiveness of human services, 147-148, 150, 154
Efficiency, 150
Elderly, 317-326
Eldredge, H. W., 257
Emery, F. E., 151-152, 162, 214
Encounter groups, 313-314
Environment
  environmental health, 251
  environmental health planning, 203-205
  Environmental Protection Agency, 205
  of human service organizations, 157-159, 160-161, 162, 164, 214
  role of in human services delivery, 4, 9
Etzioni, A., 216
Evaluation, 147-149, 150, 151, 152, 154, 155, 157, 218, 230, 231, 242-243, 277, 280, 315, 324, 332, 342-345
  data collection, 152, 154, 209, 234
  relationship to planning, 155-156
Evan, W. M., 161
Facilities, 198-199, 208-209, 210, 211
  planning, 208-209, 210
    Family, 145-146
Family Service Agencies, 187
Federal Environmental Protection Agency, 205
Federal funding, 13
  categorical, 15, 18
  relation between and law enforcement of multi-service centers, 15
Fee-for-service contracts, 12
Feedback, 148, 151, 236-237
Feingold, E., 184
Feld, S., 205
Fogelson, F., 189, 191, 206
Foothill Family Service, 336-346, 349, 350, 352, 353
Ford Foundation, 178, 295
Ford, R. M., 244
Foundation Library Center, 178
Foundations, 178-179
France, 257
Freed, H. M., 206
Freeman, H. C., 270, 355
Friedmann, J., 218
Fund-raising, 175
Funds, *see* Resources
Futurism, 194-195, 247
  definition of, 247
Gardner, Elmer, 416

Gardner, J. W., 163
General system(s)
concepts and human services organizations, 8-9
and planning, 9-10
See also Human services networks
See also human services programs
Generalist vs. Specialist, 503-504
Gilbert, N., 216
Gilmore, J. S., 188
Gluck, M., 24
Goals, 158, 159, 160, 161, 165, 184, 226, 228
formulation of, 184
Goffman, E., 149, 166
Gomberg, W., 238, 239
Gordon, S., 17
Gottesfeld, H., 4, 5, 10, 12, 14, 28
Gould, W. S., 188
Government, 171, 175, 254, 255, 258, 259
See also Politics
county, 172, 204
federal, 145, 172-174, 186, 198-199, 205, 215, 227
funding, 273, 295, 351, 352
local, 145, 172-174, 186, 198, 199, 204, 215, 227
state, 145, 172-174, 186, 198, 199, 201, 215, 227
Gragg, C. I., 35
Grants, 173-174, 254
Gross, B. M., 161, 195
Guaranteed annual income, 254
Guidance counselor, 300
Gurin, G., 205
Harrington, M., 194, 256
Harris, T. G., 168
Harshberger, D., 9, 10, 12, 14, 17, 28, 149, 166, 235
Harvard Business School, 33, 34, 41, 110
Hawthorne effect, 352
Hayden, T., 194
Health and welfare councils, 159, 186-187, 198-199, 219, 253
Health care, 273
Health services, 143, 145, 146, 153, 159, 160, 161, 176, 198-203, 231-232, 250-251
health care planning, 198-203
Hertz, K. G., 317, 318, 324 355
Hill-Burton Act, 199
Hilleboe, H. E., 250
Hirschowitz, R. G., 166
History of human services, 147, 189, 193, 198-200, 201, 209-210, 225
Hobson, C. J., 273, 354
Hochbaum, G. W., 191, 229
Hofstadter, R., 222
Holder, H., 8
Hoover Commission Report, 240
Hopkins, Harry, 176
Hosmer, L. T., 37
Howard, D. S., 171
Hull, R., 233

Human Services
  concept of, 7-8
  definition, 144
  development of 60s, 4-7
  history of, 147
  origins, 146, 148
  personnel, 19-26
  planning for, 9-10
Human Services Networks, 16-18
  definition, 16
  factors affecting strategies to implement, 17-18
  role of professionals, 4-5
Human Services Programs, 12-28
  and education, 13
  examples of, 13-14
  implications of, 18-28
  manpower patterns, 19-25
  practice, 25-26
  research, 26-28
  Types of, 13-36
    Diagnostic Center, 15
    Information and Referral Center, 14-15
    Multiservice Center, 15-16
  See also Human services; Human services networks, Human services systems
Human Services Systems, 4ff
  Cooperation and coordination in, 6
  Differences between 60s and 70s, 4ff
    Conceptual rationales, 4-5
    Treatment modes, 4
  Environmental influences, 4
  Professional orientations toward, 4-5
  See also Human services networks; human services programs
  Program operation in 70s, 12-18
Hylton, L. F., 161
Ideology, 250-251
Illegitimacy, 271
Illiteracy, 271
Infant mortality, 278
Information and Referral Service, 14-15
Interorganizational issues, 161-163
Intervention, 14, 15
Intraorganizational issues, 163-167
Involvement, 190
Iscoe, I., 21
I.S. 201 demonstration program, 297
Jacob, T., 21
Jain, S. C., 36, 48
Jobs, 273, 275, 278, 311
Jones, D., 223
Jorrin, V., 221
Juvenile delinquency, 278
Kahn, A. J., 270, 271, 355
Kaplan, S., 14
Kaufman, P., 307, 351
Kelly, J., 27

Kiesler, F., 14
King, M. L., 294, 305
Kissena Apartments
(Queens, N.Y.), 317-326, 349, 351, 353
as example of comprehensive human services network, 16
Korten, F., 5
Kristol, I., 166
Kopkind, A., 194
Kornhauser, W., 165
Kurland, Dr. Shabse, 460
Lacey, J., 5
Lawrence, 147
Leadership, 191-2, 253-254
Learning Theory
principles of, 4
Lecture method
of teaching, 34, 91
Lehman, S., 27
Levine, S., 161, 162, 228
Likert, R., 234
Lindbloom, C., 156
Little, J. D. C., 33
Litwak, E., 161
Logue, E. J., 210
Lorsch, J. W., 147
MacKenzie, R. A., 233
Management practice, 276, 277
Mandates and sanctions, 269, 270, 273, 281, 308, 321, 322, 329, 330, 351
Mann, F. C., 221
Manpower Flow
concept of, 490
Manpower training, 275, 278, 279
Maryland Career Lattice
salary, scales and job categories, 474
Mattison, B., 180, 181
McGrath, M., 206
McGraw-Hill, 304
McLaughlin, C. P., 21, 169
McPartland, J., 273, 354
March, M., 7
Medicare, 20
Mental health, 143, 144, 148, 159, 164, 167, 198-199, 205-208, 226-227, 272
planning, 198-199, 205-208, 226-227
Mental Health Associates, 457-480
Mental institutions, 144, 159, 164, 166, 206, 226-227
Merton, R. K., 165
Mexican American, 272
Michael, D. N., 194, 248, 257
Middle Manpower, 453-454
Militancy, 221-222
Miller, L., 206
Miller, S. M., 218
Minimum budget project, 336-346
Minnesota, 164
Mobility, 185
Model Cities, 220, 280
Models
of administration, 238-240
of change, 168-169, 218-219, 220-221
of employees evaluation, 243-244
of health services, 202-203,

252
organizational, 157-161, 166-167, 251-252
of planning, 202-203, 226-227
Modular Education, 509-519
Mood, A. M., 273, 354
Morgan State College, 486
Morris, P., 270, 355
Mott, B. J. F., 184, 193, 229, 231
Mouton, J. S., 168
Moynihan, D. P., 194, 218
Mullen, E., 285, 289, 291
Multiorganizations, 252-253
Multiservice Centers, 15-16, 161
Multiservice programs, 276
Murphy, C. G., 220
Myrdal, G., 247
Nader, R., 221
National Commission on Community Mental Health Services, 176
National health insurance, 145, 146, 159, 201-202, 254
National Information Bureau, 174
Needs, 154, 160, 162, 163, 176, 202, 214, 216
Neighborhood service center, 167
Neighborhood store front, 161
Nerry, R. W., 91
Neurotic symptoms, 272, 274
"New Careers", 10, 435-447
assessment of individual programs, 443
New Careerists
organizational guidelines, 445
New Left, 292
Newman, E., 187, 193, 220, 225, 227, 258
New York City, 166
Noble, J. H., Jr., 155
Nonprofessionals, 12, 166, 233
North Dakota, 159
Ocean Hill demonstration program, 297
O'Donnell, E., 166
Office of Economic Opportunity, 216
Operational planning, chap. 5
Operational research, 155
"Organic populism", 168
Organizational independence, 177
Organizational self-maintenance, 151, 153-154, 158, 163, 225
Organizational stability, 157-158
Paraprofessionals, 250
medical, 159
Participation
citizen, 175, 176, 228-229, 258
community, 205-207, 216-217
consumer, 190-191, 229
Partnership for Health Act, 199
Patronage, 151

Peattie, L., 221, 223
Peck, H., 14
Penchansky, R., 51, 88
Perlman, R., 223
Peter, L., 233
"Peter Principle", 233-234
Philanthropists, 178-179
Phoenix House, 307-335, 349, 350, 352, 354
Planners, 9
  See also Human services networks, planning
Planning, 155-156, 174, 183-195, 197-211, 248-249, 258
  constraints, (Chap. 7)
  definition of, 183-184
  of human services, 12
  operational planning, (Chap. 5)
  relationship to research, 55-156, 203
Planning, programming, budgeting systems (PPBS), 194, 240-241
Platt, J., 248
Police and family violence, 327-334
Policy, 148, 178, 214-217, 228, 250, 258
  See also "decision-making"
Politics, 145-147, 148, 149, 157, 163, 178-181, 192-193, 198, 202, 204, 207, 217, 220, 231
Pollution, see Environmental health
Poverty, 270, 272, 275, 278
  program, 275, 279
Power, 147, 150, 192-193
Pray, K. L. M., 184
Private enterprise, 171
Professional Motivation, 418
Professionalism, 149, 151, 157, 165, 166, 231, 243, 250
Professionalization
  of personnel field, 149-150, 213, 242
Professionals, 177, 225, 227, 229, 233, 250, 255
  mental health, 205-206, 207-208
  social work, 184
Professionals, Human services, 3, 4-7, 9, 12
  of planner, 9-10
Profit in human services, 147, 148, 149-150, 213, 255-256
Program input, 273
Project Beacon, 294, 295
Psychiatric Hospital as a Small Society, The, 414-415
Psychotic symptoms, 272, 274, 275
Public health, 13, 182, 186, 204
Puerto Rican, 272
Purchase of services, 177
Racial prejudice, 278
Racism, 143
Rand, G., 211
Recovery, 275
Regional human services, 159, 200-201, 227-228,

257
Regional medical program, 199, 200
Rehabilitation services, 164, 177, 251
Rein, M., 218, 270, 355
Religious organizations, 171
Reporting systems, 274
Research, 151, 203
See also Evaluation
Resources, 146, 147, 148, 152-154, 162, 163, 167, 168, 174-175, 210-211, 213, 231-232
amounts, see Costs
acquisition of, 152-156
allocation of, 154, 156, 158, 160, 173-182, 197, 203, 214, 216, 217, 240
and planning, 155, 247
sources of, 160, 171-173, 177, 178-81, 199, 205
Revenue sharing, 173
Rice, A. K., 147
Riley, P. V., 336, 341, 342, 355
Roethlisberger, F. V., 234
Roles, 147, 150, 157, 167, 181-182
Roman, M., 14
Rosow, I., 319, 355
Ross, M. G., 184
Rothman, J., 184, 220
Ryan, J. D., 188
Safe Streets Act, 210
Sanders, I. T., 220
Sarrinen, Erro, 203
Saskatchewan, Canada, 164
Schaeffer, M., 182
Scheff, T. J., 221
School dropouts, 278
School of Public Health
University of Michigan, 51, 88
University of North Carolina, 45
Schorr, A., 270, 355
Schorr, D., 201
Schroder, D., 206
Schulberg, H., 24, 28, 155, 161
Schulman, Dr. Eveline, 460
Selfhelp, 317-318
Self-maintenance
organizational, see Organizational self-maintenance
Sheldon, A., 21, 28, 169
Sherwood, C. C., 270, 355
Shick, A., 254, 255
Simon, H., 225
Slater, P. E., 168, 185, 238
Sloan School of Management, Massachusetts Institute of Technology, 33, 34
Smithberg, D. W., 225
Social action, 10
Social change, 152, 157, 164, 167-169, 213, 218-221, 237, 247
models of, 168, 218
strategies for, 218, 221
Social competency, 272
Social disruption, 274
Social pathology indices, 277
Social planning, 270

Social stability, 249
Social work, 184-185, 283, 337
schools of, 184, 185
Sonthoff, H., 244
Specialization, 227
Spielberger, G., 21
Spivak, M., 206, 209
Sprague, L., 21, 22
Stability
social, 249
Staff attitudes, 289
Stahl, O. G., 242
Stimson, A. S., 285, 286, 355
Stimson, J. B., 285, 286, 355
Strategies
strategy problems, 269-282, 285-291, 303-305, 308-315, 318-326, 329-335, 336-346, 353, 354
Sullivan, M., 166
Sussman, M. B., 221
System maintenance, 217-219, 227
Systems analysis, 160, 188-189, 194, 204, 256, 277
Systems theory, 161, 169
Systems transformation, 218-219, 221
Tactics, 269
Target population, 148, 160, 201, 206, 274, 275, 309, 336, 352
Taubenhaus, L. J., 240
Tax Reform Act of 1969, 179
Taylor, F. W., 234
Teaching
administration, 33-34
Teams
as personnel tool, 25-26
Temple University Community Mental Health Center, 416-417
Tenure, 150
Terreberry, S., 162, 164
T-group model, 168
Therapeutic milieu, 354
Thomas, E. J., 147
Thompson, J. D., 252
Thompson, P. H., 243
Thompson, V. A., 225
Toffler, A., 248
Torrens, P. R., 220
Townsend, R., 47, 245
Towson State College, 523
Training of personnel, 11
Treatment concepts
psychoanalytic, 4
social psychiatric, 4
Trist, E., 151, 162, 214
Two Bridges demonstration program, 297
Unemployment, 278
United Federation of Teachers, 293, 295, 297
United Fund, 172, 181, 213
United Help, Inc., 318, 319, 321, 322
Urban planning, 209-211, 227-228
Urban problems, 143, 173-174, 217, 255
Values, 148, 149, 192-193, 218-219, 241, 271
Veroff, J., 205
Vidaver, R., 12, 19, 20, 25
Voluntary organizations,

145, 149, 172, 174-177, 185-186, 228
Von Bertalanffy, L., 169
Walsh, J., 179
War on Poverty, 3
Warren, R., 161, 207-208, 219-220
Washington Post, 299
Webb, A. P., 355
Weinfield, F. D., 273, 354
Welfare, 143, 145, 146-147, 148, 153, 159-160, 164, 241, 252, 254, 278
  reform, 159
Welfare councils, see Health and welfare councils
White, P. E., 161, 162
Williams, W., 26
Wood, R. C., 240
Work Skills, 273
World Health Organization, 183
Yale Psychiatric Institute, 414-415
Yeshiva University, 294
York, R. L., 273, 354
Young, H. D., 285, 355
Youth, 275, 278